Praise for *A Radical Faith*

"I've always believed that responsibility, honesty, and faith are the three pillars of a strong character. Sister Maura Clarke, who recognized the humanity in everyone she met—from schoolchildren in the Bronx to farmers in Nicaragua—lived a life that served as a testament to that strength. Eileen Markey's beautifully told narrative reminds us of Maura's courage in the face of brutal dictators and shocking suffering. It's an important story that has been forgotten for too long, and Markey's book returns Maura to her deserved place in history."

—MARTIN SHEEN

"Eileen Markey's *A Radical Faith* is a beautifully rendered account of a true radical hero, who was born in Queens, New York, and was murdered, along with three other Christian comrades, in El Salvador. Markey's important book is a loving testament to their life and work."

—GREG GRANDIN, AUTHOR OF *THE EMPIRE OF NECESSITY*

"Eileen Markey has given us a spiritual and political thriller that is meanwhile a tender chronicle of one woman's journey into history. Maura Clarke's death helped define a generation of faithful opposition to US-backed brutality abroad, and now a new generation can rise up under the inspiration of Clarke's life. This extraordinary book is a must-read for aspiring saints and rebels of all persuasions."

—NATHAN SCHNEIDER, AUTHOR OF *GOD IN PROOF* AND *THANK YOU, ANARCHY*

"In death, Maryknoll Sister Maura Clarke became known as a symbol of the brutality of El Salvador's pitiless conflict in the 1980s. In this rare and beautiful book, Eileen Markey brings Maura to life. From her childhood in a tightly knit Irish Catholic neighborhood to her departure for Nicaragua in 1959 and subsequent murder in El Salvador, Maura's life became interwoven with the tumultuous history of Cold War Central America. Drawing on personal correspondence and extensive interviews, Markey skillfully evokes the transformation of the Catholic Church during those turbulent decades, crafting a searing testament to the meaning of faith amidst the hard choices imposed by desperate circumstances."

—CYNTHIA ARNSON, DIRECTOR, LATIN AMERICAN PROGRAM,
WOODROW WILSON INTERNATIONAL CENTER FOR SCHOLARS

"*A Radical Faith* is a vivid and richly detailed book about a rebel and a martyr. It is also the epic story of an ordinary woman swept into the maelstrom of Central American terror who becomes a committed shepherd to her flock in the pursuit of justice."

—JUNE CAROLYN ERLICK, AUTHOR OF *DISAPPEARED:
A JOURNALIST SILENCED, THE IRMA FLAQUER STORY*

"I am grateful for Eileen Markey's beautiful and moving biography of Maura Clarke, the Maryknoll nun from Queens murdered by the Salvadoran army for embracing the full meaning of God's love for the poor. The book shows how radical it was for Maura to live the implications of her faith as a missionary in humble Nicaraguan and Salvadoran communities. The story of her life, and of her murder together with fellow missionaries Ita Ford, Dorothy Kazel, and Jean Donovan, sheds light on the true nature of the Central American conflicts of the 1970s and '80s."

—HÉCTOR LINDO-FUENTES, PROFESSOR OF HISTORY, FORDHAM UNIVERSITY

A RADICAL
FAITH

THE ASSASSINATION
OF SISTER MAURA

EILEEN MARKEY

NATION
BOOKS
New York

Published in the United States by Nation Books, an imprint of Perseus Books, a division of PBG Publishing, LLC, a subsidiary of Hachette Book Group, Inc.
116 East 16th Street, 8th Floor
New York, NY 10003

Nation Books is a co-publishing venture of the Nation Institute and Perseus Books.

Cover photo courtesy of Maryknoll Mission Archives, Maryknoll, New York.

Books published by Nation Books are available at special discounts for bulk purchases in the United States by corporations, institutions, and other organizations. For more information, please contact the Special Markets Department at the Perseus Books Group, 2300 Chestnut Street, Suite 200, Philadelphia, PA 19103, or call (800) 810-4145, ext. 5000, or e-mail special.markets@perseusbooks.com.

Designed by Jack Lenzo

Library of Congress Cataloging-in-Publication Data
Names: Markey, Eileen, author.
Title: A radical faith : the assassination of Sister Maura / Eileen Markey.
Description: First [edition]. | New York, New York : Nation Books, 2016. |
    Includes bibliographical references and index.
Identifiers: LCCN 2016027763| ISBN 9781568585734 (hardcover) | ISBN
    9781568585741 (ebook)
Subjects: LCSH: Clarke, Maura, -1980 | Missionaries--Latin
    America--Biography. | Maryknoll Sisters--Latin America--Biography. |
    Missionaries--United States--Biography. | Maryknoll Sisters--United
    States--Biography.
Classification: LCC BV2832.2.C53 M37 2016 | DDC 266/.2092 [B] --dc23 LC
record available at https://lccn.loc.gov/2016027763

10 9 8 7 6 5 4 3 2

Contents

For Martin and Sally Markey, who gave me this faith; for Owen Markey Murphy and Hugh Kozlowski Markey Murphy, who inherit it; and for Jarrett Murphy, who lives it.

■ ■

Our sisters were killed because they lived as the Gospel of Jesus directed them to live. That Gospel illuminates and touches all aspects of human life and is never separated from it. It proclaims total freedom for all persons and societies from the slavery of selfishness, hatred and fear. This Gospel judges the proud and powerful who put their trust in the idols of money, power and status. It lifts up the needy and the poor who put their trust in God and His love.

To those who are blind to the message of that Gospel, our sisters and countless others who daily witness to it by their lives are dangerous! They threaten political structures which promote false idols and destroy the image of God in the human person. Ita and Maura were committed to the Gospel and thus gave their lives in love with and for the poor. That and that alone is why they died.

—From the joint statement of the Maryknoll Sisters and Maryknoll Fathers and Brothers, December 1980

Four Dead in El Salvador

The grave was fresh. The soil yielded easily to the shovels. It was no trouble, really, to uncover the bodies. They were piled one on top of the other, buried quickly the day before by orders from the local military commander. In minutes they were hoisted from the narrow ground and laid beside each other in the cow pasture. Their clothes were askew and their faces dirty, their hair matted with blood. Two of the women appeared to have been raped. A tigüilote tree, its limbs reaching over the place where they lay, cast a little shade. The women had been missing a long day and a half. Now they were found.[1]

An onlooker stumbled to the ground, fell on her knees. A veteran nun who had been working in El Salvador for four years, Maddie Dorsey had seen dozens of bodies like these: bloodied, discarded, floating in a lake or tossed helter-skelter on the roadside. They were often left in places where people could easily discover them; the bodies became a message of fear and warning for all who saw them. *See what happened to her? This is what troublemakers get.*

A son didn't come home at night. A daughter didn't arrive where she said she'd be. Then began the waiting. Finally, a day or a month later—but sometimes never—someone would find a body in a ditch and word would spread and the mother or husband or sister would go and try to claim the body, would hope to be able to recognize it. Maddie often went with them. Sometimes she simply visited the family when the grieving mother tried to have a funeral, but friends were too frightened to show their faces at the church, lest they be marked for execution as well. Now Maddie was kneeling for women she called sisters. Just days earlier she'd been at a retreat with two of them in Nicaragua. She and two other Catholic nuns, Terry Alexander and Elizabeth Kochik, prayed quietly as the bodies were lifted out.[2]

The American ambassador, Robert White, had been called to the scene. He blanched and muttered the words "I am sorry" when he saw the dead women's faces. They were four US citizens: Jean Donovan, a church volunteer who had grown up on the gold coast of Connecticut and gotten involved in missionary work when she moved to Cleveland, Ohio, after business school; Dorothy Kazel, OSU, a Catholic nun of the Ursuline order who was also from Cleveland; Ita Ford, MM, a Catholic nun of the Maryknoll order, who had worked in the 1970s in poor neighborhoods of Santiago, Chile, under the dictatorship of Augusto Pinochet; and Maura Clarke, MM. At nearly fifty Maura was the oldest of the group; she had been a nun for thirty years. Effervescent and gracious, with emotive brown eyes and a knack for paying intense attention to people others might prefer to ignore, she'd grown up in New York City, the eldest of three children. The green skirt her mother had made her clung to her legs now as her body lay on the ground, one arm extended above her head, her pretty face turned to the right. After living and working for seventeen years with the poor of Nicaragua, she had arrived in El Salvador at the beginning of August, hoping to share the troubles of the people. Four months later, here she was.[3]

More than 8,000 people were killed in such a way in El Salvador in 1980 alone, the first year of a twelve-year civil war that left over 75,000 people dead.*

The killings weren't random. They were carried out by the country's army, by the National Guard, by the National Police, by squads of citizens organized and trained by those military entities, and by groups of off-duty military men operating in clandestine brigades named for Maximiliano Hernández Martínez, the right-wing dictator of their fathers' generation. The people killed were members of farmworker unions and cooperatives, students, nurses and doctors who

---

* "At that time the population of El Salvador was about five million, one-fiftieth of the United States. So, in proportion to the U.S., El Salvador was experiencing the equivalent of fifty thousand deaths a month—nearly the total of American casualties in a decade of warfare in Southeast Asia."[4]

gave public health training to poor people, teachers, people involved with their parish youth groups, catechism instructors, Bible study group members—indeed, anyone who questioned the economic and political system in El Salvador. Ambassador White had been reporting all this to Washington and struggling to maintain a space for US diplomacy between a military government and a left-wing insurgency bolstered by the ranks of people who found the bodies of their loved ones in places like this cow pasture in Santiago Nonualco. A few days before this latest killing, the political leaders of a newly united opposition group, the Democratic Revolutionary Front, were kidnapped from a meeting at the Jesuit high school in San Salvador. A day later, their bodies were found, mutilated. With the loss of these men, the American ambassador lost his best negotiating partners on the left. Now, looking at the broken bodies of these four church workers, he committed to bringing to justice the military that killed them. "They won't get away with it this time," he said. Within a few months his diplomatic career was over.[5]

The people who lived in the area or worked on the hacienda next door covered the bodies with the palmlike branches of the tigüilote tree. At midafternoon the Salvadoran sun was hot and close, even in December, and there would soon be flies. The branches helped a little. The soldiers, clutching their guns, stood around the way soldiers do. The ambassador and his staff filed into their vehicles, bringing with them Juan Santos Cerón, the local justice of the peace who had authorized the opening of the grave, and sped down the dirt road, back toward San Salvador to confront the Salvadoran military and send a cable to Washington.[6]

Two days earlier, on the morning of Tuesday, December 2, a member of his staff handed Fr. Ephraím López a letter that had been left at the church office in Chalatenango, an old colonial town of narrow streets and stucco buildings built hard against the road, in the mountains of northern El Salvador. The Spanish-style church rose high and gleaming white in the sun. Taller than any other building in the provincial capital, it dominated the central plaza. Or maybe more accurately it split influence over the central plaza with the town's other great institution: the army barracks. Military Detachment No. 1 was housed in this building.[7]

In the past year, a military intelligence unit had moved in as well. In addition to housing the soldiers and the administrative offices, the facility served as a prison for people arrested on suspicion of subversion. Many, many times Fr. López, a deliberate man whose face barely moved when he spoke, the son of local landowners, had walked into the army barracks to speak to the commander and request the release of this prisoner or that, the husband of a woman in the village of San José Las Flores, the son of a family in the town of San Antonio Los Ranchos. The commander of the base, Colonel Ricardo Augusto Peña Arbaiza, did not like priests and nuns. He kept a bible, a gun, and Norman Vincent Peale's *The Power of Positive Thinking* on his desk and quizzed visitors on scriptural passages. He liked to lecture on the dangers of Catholicism and communism. Catholics are subversive, he'd told one of the now-dead women a month earlier, because they side with the poor.[8]

Fr. López looked at the paper he'd been handed. On it were his name and those of everyone who worked in the parish: the seminarians, the Salvadoran nuns, and the two American nuns—Ita Ford and Maura Clarke—who had been working in the parish the past few months. "All these people are subversives. They will be killed. It starts today," the missive read.

Shaken, Fr. López decided to bring the message to the head of the Catholic Church in El Salvador that very day. Bishop Arturo Rivera y Damas had only held the position for nine months; he was named to the role after the previous archbishop, Óscar Romero, was murdered while saying Mass in March 1980. Fr. López drove through the steep streets of Chalatenango, where he had been appointed pastor just two years earlier, past land his brother owned and where he had grown up to San Salvador. He brought the letter to the bishop at the archdiocese headquarters at San José de la Montaña, an imposing church and seminary in downtown San Salvador. Its once elegant grounds had become a makeshift refugee center for the hundreds of people fleeing repression in the countryside. The priest stayed overnight in a house his family owned in San Salvador. He knew Maura and Ita were in Nicaragua and planning to stay in another part of El Salvador the night they returned. He drove back to Chalatenango the next morning, only to learn that they were missing. By the end of December he would flee to Washington, DC.[9]

Hours after Fr. Ephraím López read his own name on the death list, Maura walked from house to house in Ciudad Sandino, Nicaragua, visiting old friends. She had been in Nicaragua for close to a week, at a conference with other sisters from the Maryknoll religious order who worked in the Central American countries of Panama, Nicaragua, and El Salvador. The group of nuns in the region got together a few times a year to check in with each other, buoy one another's spirits, compare notes, and assess their work. It was a good meeting and a lot of attention was focused on the sisters working in El Salvador. How were they holding up? Were they traumatized by so much death? Did they think there was still room for them to work, or was it too dangerous? Maria Rieckelman, a Maryknoll sister who was a psychiatrist, came to the meeting to talk about trauma and help the sisters assess themselves. The four from El Salvador told their fellow nuns how frightening it was in the country, but insisted that they didn't want to leave. They pressed the regional leadership to find a way to send more nuns. There was a lot of work to do with so many people suffering, they explained, and they needed more than four Maryknoll sisters to do it all.[10]

On the last night of the Nicaragua retreat, the nuns held a prayer service. They sat together in the informal chapel, read from the book of Ezekiel, and thought about the parable of the Good Shepherd: "It is not easy Lord, for us to lay down our lives for one another. We fear the challenge of shepherding," Maura prayed with her Maryknoll sisters. They sang. And they sat in silence. The final prayer asked for courage, "Give us a power of concentration and a gift of energy to make our love unobtrusive, almost casual, but strong as death."[11]

A crowd of sisters accompanied Maura and Ita to the airport the next afternoon. Maddie and Terry had left a few hours earlier. When the 5:15 flight to San Salvador was delayed, the sisters had coffee together, talking and joking. They hugged their friends good-bye, waved and smiled as they walked through the departures gate. Takeoff was at 6:15. They were met at the airport in San Salvador by Dorthy and Jean, who planned to drive them to La Libertad in their van. They'd ridden in this van dozens of times, often with bulging sacks of rice or terrified Salvadoran peasants fleeing the violence of Chalatenango. They drove out the dark airport road.[12]

Three hours later, farmworkers in Santiago Nonualco heard the guns. They thought maybe it was guerrillas in an exchange of fire with the National Guard. Then came the sound of the van racing on the dirt road, its interior lights on and music blasting from the radio, a surreal apparition cutting through the thick night.

The next morning, December 3, a farmer driving his milking cow spotted the four bodies in a ditch along the lonely dirt road. He told the local justice of the peace, Juan Santos Cerón, who went to the pasture and found an officer of the National Guard and several soldiers and peasants digging a grave. Cerón took a ring from the finger of one of the women, possible help in identifying her if anyone came looking. Some people who lived nearby saw the burial and told their parish priest.[13]

By now, people were beginning to wonder what had happened to Dorothy, Jean, Ita, and Maura. In La Libertad, Paul Schindler was waiting. Dorothy and Jean didn't show up at their weekly staff meeting. The night before he'd seen the bags from the duty-free shop in the La Libertad convent. The women must have come in and left them. Good, he thought. They made it home from the airport. Every journey was a little risky, especially with Jean and Dorothy doing these food runs up to Chalatenango now with the Maryknollers. Schindler, a solid, round-faced man with a broad midwestern accent, wide shoulders, and a frank all-American manner, was a priest from Ohio. He'd been in El Salvador since 1972, running parishes in La Libertad, saying Mass and celebrating First Communions in an overwhelmingly Catholic country that had always had too few priests. But increasingly his time was spent visiting army barracks to ask that parishioners be released and burying church members who showed up dead. Sometimes the bodies were dumped at the bottom of a precipice outside the port town, left for the buzzards. Schindler rigged ropes and rappelled down to the water's edge. He immolated the bodies he couldn't carry back up, saying the funeral prayers and letting the ashes wash into the embrace of the sea.

By noon on this day Schindler and the other team members were deeply worried. A year earlier when the bishop from Cleveland had been down to check on the mission, he asked a frank question: What happens when one of you gets kidnapped or killed? Schindler and Jean and Dorothy and Christine Rody, a Vincentian sister from Cincinnati had laughed. "They don't kill gringos," they assured the American bishop. But even so, they put in place a protocol. A list of who to call first, second, and third. A system for signing in and out. A phone log. Now, like a grim dance he wished he didn't know, it went into effect.

Schindler called the American ambassador. Just two nights before, on December 1, he and Jean and Dorothy had had dinner with White and his wife at the ambassador's residence. Conversation ran long and the ambassador invited them all to stay over; they shouldn't be on the roads at one in the morning. Now Schindler told the ambassador that Jean and Dorothy were missing. He didn't know whether Ita and Maura had arrived from Nicaragua or not. At four p.m. on December 3, while driving to the airport in hopes of finding some clue about their friends, Christine Rody and Elizabeth Kochik saw a burned-out van on the road. Although much of the van was now unrecognizable, they noticed familiar dents on the fender.[14]

By the next morning, December 4, the news was all over the United States and Latin America. Headlines in dozens of papers screamed: "U.S. Nuns Missing near San Salvador."

Paul Schindler got the phone call around noon. The bodies of four North American women had been found by the side of the road in Santiago Nonualco. The priest in San Vincente whose parishioners had told him about the bodies the day before had called the bishop. When Maddie, Elizabeth, and Terry heard the news, they went straight to the office of the judge in San Juan Nonualco, the nearest proper town to Santiago. They found the judge's assistant in a hot little office. He pulled open a drawer in a battered wooden desk and removed a simple silver ring with a symbol carved into its face: *chi* and *rho,* the first letters of the Greek word for "Christ," encircled in a line that represents the Earth. The symbol has been used in Christian iconography since the third century and its shape evokes the death of Jesus by crucifixion. The ring is worn by every Maryknoll nun as a sign of her commitment. This one had been given to Maura Clarke the day she knelt in the convent chapel in the spring damp Hudson River Valley in May 1953 and professed her vows as a Maryknoll sister. Maddie called the rest of the group in La Libertad.

"They're our dear girls," she said.[15]

Who was this woman in the dirt? What forces in her life, in herself led her to this vicious death so far from home? What did that ring, slipped on the slender finger of a twenty-two-year-old, have to do with farm laborers and death squads, clandestine meetings and military orders?

In the thirty-five years since their murder, Maura and her companions have become symbols. Many forces—personal, religious, and political—combined to deliver Maura to that hastily dug grave at the edge of the cold war. This book seeks to put her back in her context, to understand her death by examining her life, to make her whole again.

In doing so we can see in this one woman a history of the mid-twentieth century: the cohesion and power of an immigrant New York neighborhood, and the romantic inheritance of the Old Country. Maura was raised on stories of the Irish Revolution, her worldview shaped as much by her parents' experience of subjugation as by the New Deal and World War II. The circumscribed roles for working class women combined with a sincere desire to do good led thousands of women in her generation into convents. For Maura, being a nun was never about locking herself away; it was a means to lead a bigger life, to be part of the wide world. Her life tells the story of the dramatic shifts that swept through the Catholic Church in the 1960s, which reordered nuns' role and reimagined the dictates of faithfulness in the corporeal world. Maura's life as a missionary in Central America maps the reach of US power and delineates the Faustian calculus Washington, DC, adopted: supporting any regime that resisted Cuba or the Soviet Union. The parish priest in Maura's first mission had blessed the planes that deployed to the Bay of Pigs. Nicaragua's dictator came to cut the ribbon on the school she ran, built by President Kennedy's anticommunist Alliance for Progress. The man who directed her murder was trained by the US military.

The deaths of the churchwomen, as Maura, Ita, Dorothy, and Jean came to be called, were met with shock and confusion in the United States and kept Central American policy in the headlines for a decade. That the four were clergy became a rallying cry: surely the United States was backing the wrong side if it was arming and training nun killers, the sisters' advocates argued. The image of Maddie, Terry, and Elizabeth kneeling in that cow pasture as the bodies were exhumed was seared into the public consciousness.

But as much as the churchwomen's murder elicited outrage and inspired opposition to continual support for the government that killed them, it also provoked suspicion. What were those nuns doing down there? The question floated behind any discussion of the crime or its repercussions. Jean Kirkpatrick, foreign policy adviser to incoming President Reagan, argued that the churchwomen were something other than nuns: that they were social activists operating on behalf of the leftist guerrillas of the Farabundo Martí National Liberation Front (FMLN) and that someone opposed to the FMLN killed them. Secretary of State Alexander Haig went several steps further in January 1981, suggesting in a congressional hearing—and in contradiction of ballistics evidence collected by the FBI—that the women may have been killed in an exchange of gunfire. It wasn't true, but it muddied the waters and gave oxygen to a suspicion: what were those sisters doing down there?

Our cultural memory is filled with narratives of nuns' dedicating their lives to God. These images usually involve high walls and fences, angelic voices, restrictions, penance, purity, and innocence—a renunciation of the world. But what if God, or if that word hangs you up with all its baggage, what if the sacred exists not somewhere else in rarified unattainable form, what if it's here? What if commitment means a dedication to God in others, a seeking of the holy in the messiness and in the complexity of a real life? What if following God means not so much attempting to order one's life into fidelity to rules, but working to change the circumstances of a world that insults the sacredness of most men and women?

Sometimes it seems we demand that our victims be powerless, that innocence—pristine separation from the world—is a prerequisite for being wronged. But Maura had agency. She wasn't a hapless innocent. She was an actor in a fraught and shocking place, struggling to hear God's direction in the cacophony of fear and violence, grief and terror. The repression of Salvadoran farmworkers and church members drew outrage and condemnation from human rights organizations because it was directed at noncombatants, people innocent of armed rebellion. And undoubtedly, Maura's murder carried extra currency because she was a nun. The military regime conducted its anti-insurgency operations as though there were no innocents, anyone criticizing the regime was de facto a guerrilla sympathizer. At the same time, the military chiefs pleaded innocence, claiming to know nothing about the death squads, pledging over and over again to rout out the perpetrators of atrocities that they themselves were directing. The US diplomats wore that most infuriating trait of American innocence amid world affairs: the inability to see.

But Maura could see. She rejected the innocence of blindness, and she chose to act. Her death and life raise profound questions about the intersection of religious conviction and political action. What does belief compel in the real world? If the holy is not only in the sanctuary but also in the street, what are the obligations of the faithful? Maura was killed because of the work she was doing. That work was an expression of her religious practice. We like our martyrs at a distance, uncomplicated by political context. But Maura, assassinated in a war so recent its architects and coaches are still alive, was killed for her belief—because her belief drove her to act. Her death had power. It could be used as an indictment of US foreign policy. Her murder alerted people in the United States to the carnage in El Salvador. She died just like the Salvadorans she went to help, just like the campesinos who were disappeared and tortured by their government, the tens of thousands of women who were raped, the unending toll of bodies torn from their homes by death squads and discarded on the roadside. In Maura and the other churchwomen we began to see the mass of Salvadorans cut down for the crime of asking for something better and we learned something about state violence, about the viciousness of power, the willingness of those in control to commit atrocities so as to preserve absolute privilege. Maura changed sides. She stood not with the prerogatives of the most powerful nation or its allies, but with the people getting their teeth kicked in. She died just like seventy-five thousand Salvadorans during their civil war.

Her death was also used as an example, a model. In schools and parishes throughout the country, the churchwomen story has been taught for a generation as an example of committed Christianity. It is not difficult to read the churchwomen as Christ figures. They gave their lives, offered themselves as a sacrifice, were willing to risk every-thing to share the suffering of others. The very physicality of Maura's death links her to the Christ story: The divine is not remote. It's here in a broken body. Those nuns kneeling at the grave become Mary and St. John at the foot of the cross, witnesses to horror and great love.

But before she was any of these things, indictment, martyr, or Christ figure, she was an individual woman. As much as Maura's story is the story of the implications of belief or a window into the ugliness of the Salvadoran civil war or an outgrowth of the changing Catholic Church, or as much as it reveals about the applications of cold war policy and the power of her father's stories of the Irish Revo-lution, it is at heart the story of a woman trying to be true.

I set out to understand how a beloved daughter from Rocka-way, Queens, could end up in that grave. In the course of trying to answer that question, I met a singular woman. Maura believed in love and she believed everyone was important. A profound belief in the value of every person undergirded everything in Maura's life. But she often felt she wasn't measuring up. She merged that insecurity, her need to feel loved and worthwhile, with a preternatural ability to connect with others. That ability drew her into their suffering and inspired her to struggle for something different. She noticed every-one, believed and acted as though everyone—customers she waited on at a gift shop as a teenager, to desperate farmworkers in a remote village—mattered. Maura's convictions began in the personal and flowed, eventually, outward.

In Maura we watch a timid and rule-bound woman find strength. We see a woman come into her own, even as she devoted herself to others. She threw in her lot with disregarded people, and in so doing grew bold. In the end her story is about connecting the interior with the outside, the spiritual with the physical. Maura's is a political story, but it's a personal story.

Chapter 1

Between City and Sea

The bells at St. Francis de Sales Catholic church tolled in the evening of August 15, 1945, in Belle Harbor, Queens, on the edge of New York City. Their commanding clang reached the beach and the crashing Atlantic Ocean a few blocks away and sounded along Harbor Boulevard and into the tidy yards and through the screen doors of the brick houses planted on what a generation before had been sand dunes of the narrow Rockaway peninsula. The bells were ringing not for the daily Mass or for the duty of evening Angelus at six p.m. as husbands and fathers streamed out of the Long Island Railroad station at Beach 116th Street. They were ringing in celebration. War was over.[1]

The streets filled with noise as neighbors banged pots and pans together, cheered and honked their car horns. A few miles away amid crowds jammed into Times Square, a sailor and nurse gave that iconic kiss. But here in the Irish Catholic working-class Rockaways, people streamed into church. The pastor, Monsignor J. Jerome Reddy, knew his parishioners well from his strolls along the Rockaway boardwalk and beach. He had led Catholic Charities in the diocese of Brooklyn for thirty years, overseeing its network of orphanages, soup kitchens, and old-age homes, and introduced a labor rights study group into the parish. He was the man parishioners called when they needed a lawyer, help with the rent, or wanted to quit drinking. On that warm August evening, he offered a Benediction of the Blessed Sacrament service, a group prayer in which the Eucharist—the wafer that Catholics believe is the body of Christ—is venerated. It is a grand and stylized ritual that celebrates a very earth-bound belief: God dwells in the midst of the people.[2]

The congregation of deliverymen and grocery clerks and mechanics, mothers and children sunburned and with sandy feet just off the beach, immigrants and first-generation Americans recited the prayers they knew from their weekly observance of this ritual, one of dozens of prayers that united them with Catholics the world over. Surely many of them wondered when the 450 men and women of the parish who had served in the war would return from the South Pacific or bases in Europe. Others mourned the twelve men who had been killed on faraway battlefields. Under stained-glass images of sixteenth-century English martyr Saint Thomas More and mystic St. Terisa of Avila, in the cool, dark church they knelt as Monsignor Reddy burned incense, its sticky, sweet smoke surrounding the tabernacle where the Eucharist is stored. He placed the silver dollar–size wafer in a monstrance, an elaborate silver and crystal case, and carried it to the marble altar. The people sang the Latin hymn "O Salutaris Hostia": "Oh saving victim opening wide the gate of heaven to man below. . . . " The priest knelt and the worshippers prayed in silence, concentrating on the Eucharist in front of them, a reminder of God's personal presence in the world, in the neighborhood, on the block.[3]

Monsignor Reddy lifted the monstrance and made the sign of the cross, blessing the people in the pews. An altar boy rang a small bell three times and the pastor placed the monstrance back on the altar. He then knelt and began the Divine Praises, the congregation repeating his every line in one voice.

> *Blessed be God.*
> *Blessed be his Holy Name.*
> *Blessed be Jesus Christ, true God and true man.*

With great ceremony, he carried the monstrance across the sanctuary and placed the wafer back in the tabernacle.

Then they all sang "God Bless America" and "The Star-Spangled Banner."

This was the world where Maura Clarke was raised, a world swept by the wild Atlantic Ocean and ordered by a staunch and confident

Catholic church. Here on a spit of land in the sea, on the ragged edge of New York City, the children of Irish immigrants were becoming Americans. The patriotism and the Catholicism were assertive, unapologetic, and intermixed.[4]

For the small number of year-round residents when Maura was growing up, Rockaway Park felt more like a village than a neighborhood of New York City. A narrow stretch of earth dangling off the landmass of Long Island, separated from the mainland by the wide Jamaica Bay and pointing back toward lower Manhattan, the Rockaways had been home to just a tiny year-round settlement since the early nineteenth century.[5]

Even as the neighborhoods of Lower Manhattan and Brooklyn—crowded with tenements and teeming with street vendors, crisscrossed by trolley cars and awash in noise—came to define the American urban experience, the Rockaway peninsula remained barely inhabited. A bridge didn't unite the western end of the Rockaways to Brooklyn until 1937. The subway didn't arrive until 1956. Even then midtown Manhattan was an hour by train and a world away.[6]

Growing up in the Rockaways carried with it a certain expansive sense of freedom. The neighborhoods were empty in winter and felt like a place apart, an outpost where Maura and her siblings could bike and roller skate in the street with little fear of cars or wander on the windy beach, experiencing the air and sea in a way most New York children do but once or twice a year. Just sixty thousand people lived on the 11-mile peninsula year-round and when Maura was growing up, residents in the individual neighborhoods of Rockaway Park, Rockaway Beach, and Belle Harbor left their doors unlocked and parents knew their neighbors well enough to correct their children. Shops offered credit and made deliveries. When Maura ran down Beach 116th Street to buy the late edition of the *Journal American* for her father or when she and classmate Patricia Thorp stopped into Rogoff's Fountain Shop for milk shakes, the proprietors knew her name. Maura's brother, Buddy, and his friends dug a network of tunnels in the sandy ground beneath empty summer bungalows and played for hours in grassy open lots.[7]

But summers were a different story. Each June the peninsula was transformed from an outpost to the center of the party. Some boy would jump in the ocean in April or May and then it would begin. Summer visitors poured in from the rest of New York City from June to September, filling the narrow peninsula with music and crowds and stories loquaciously told. In 1947, when Maura was sixteen, the summer population of the Rockaways was 225,000, more than five times that in winter. These summer people were subway workers and firefighters, cooks and cleaning ladies in grand Fifth Avenue homes, plumbers, sanitation department men, and elevator operators as well as nurses, teachers, bank clerks, and shop owners: Irish immigrants and their children. Entire families from the Bronx, Manhattan, Brooklyn, and Queens relocated for the summer, squeezing into accommodations with shared bathrooms and outdoor showers. Restaurants that were shuttered in winter flung open their doors and Irish bands made up of fiddler, accordionist, and crooner took up residence in such places as Curley's, Hugh McNulty's, and Allen's Dancehall. The Rockaways, sometimes called the Irish Riviera, were a place the rest of Irish New York came to stroll on the boardwalk, drink at the bars of Irishtown, gawk at the amusements of Rockaway Playland, and pile into bursting guest houses and bungalows. On weekends, traffic on Cross Bay Boulevard from Howard Beach was backed up for miles. The Long Island Railroad disgorged bathing-suited day-trippers carrying their dinner in metal pots.[8]

The summer people and the year-rounders represented the tail end of a giant wave of Irish immigration that began with the Irish potato famine in 1845. It would taper off by the Great Depression, having utterly transformed New York City and the country, established norms of urban experience, and all but created and then dominated the American Catholic Church.[9]

Maura was shaped by this world as much as by her parents and their histories. Born Mary Elizabeth Clarke, she was the eldest child of John and Mary Clarke, Irish Catholic immigrants who built a life in New York City.

Mary Clarke née McCloskey was the oldest of eight children of Catholic dairy farmers Lizzie and Charles McCloskey. As a child she was sent to live with her grandmother and uncles, an arrangement that instilled a certain steady confidence in her. She was doted on. But, growing up in Antrim, a county of Ireland where the British had relocated and awarded land to Scottish Protestants three centuries earlier, so as to shift the political and ethnic balance of the island, Mary knew the discrimination of being a minority in one's own country. Catholics in County Antrim learned to choose their words carefully. A person never knew who to trust and a loose detail could scuttle a job or bring the neighbors' ire. When family members wanted to buy land, they might send a friend or relative from somewhere else to the land auction. The price would jump if a Catholic were known to be trying to buy it. Discretion became a habit. If you were in Ballymena, the nearest market town to her parent's farm, and someone asked where you were from, you named the Protestant town nearest to where you lived. No need to invite trouble by revealing you were Catholic by naming your own village. Mary developed the habit of keeping her thoughts to herself. Doing so didn't change *what* she thought, but it meant she learned from her elders not to broadcast her ideas.[10]

On the hilltop at Armoy, about an hour away where Mary was raised by her grandparents, the vistas were expansive, soft green hills rolling into fields of flax and wheat. The sky was wide and close, mist turned the hills to impressionistic smudges, and the dark soil was fragrant. There was room for beauty. An oblique Irish sun found its way into the whitewashed stucco cottage, its central room catching the morning light. Her grandmother found money to buy little Mary colored pencils and paints. Once when Mary and other farm children resumed school after a long absence for the harvest, a teacher derided them as winter birds—students that come only for a season. But Mary's grandmother kept her in school beyond the age many children quit to work on the farms. Beloved and at ease at the grandparents' house, Mary was shy at her own parents' home, unsure why she didn't live there. It was common for parents to send one or more children to their grandparents or other relatives, to lessen the burden on a mother with a string of young children and a family with little money. Mary had been sent to her grandmother's when her mother was busy with a baby. When her parents came to retrieve her some years later, Mary ran up the round hills and hid behind a tree until she could no longer hear them calling for her. As an adult, though, Mary forged a close relationship with her younger siblings and their families, exchanging weekly letters and visiting Ireland nearly every summer as she grew older. Perhaps because she missed her mother, she was especially close to her own children, cheering them on, holding them close, and praising them.[11]

Mary McCloskey had a remarkably unconventional young adulthood for a Catholic farm girl in 1910s Ireland: When World War I created a shortage of male laborers, she went to Scotland to work as a gardener on an estate. Ever after, she planted seeds in egg cartons and coaxed beauty out of windowsills and backyards wherever she lived. Returning from Scotland, she enrolled in art school in Belfast, then went to Dublin to study nursing, the tuition paid by one of the uncles who helped raise her. She didn't marry until 1930, when she was thirty-five. She didn't look for validation or approval from other people, cultivating instead her own confidence and an ability to manage difficulty without making a dramatic display of it. She was the only one in her family to immigrate to America and built reliable and abiding friendships in her new country. In the face of discrimination and social exclusion she, like many Catholics in Antrim and nearby counties, cultivated a sense of personal pride that defied and resisted the stereotypes about rough and ignorant Irish. Mary presented herself carefully, always with a touch of glamour in an impeccably tailored dress and stylishly arranged hair, and carried herself gracefully, almost regally.[12]

Ireland had been an English colony for eight hundred years, a testing ground for British ideas of empire-building, a site of proxy wars between European powers, and a source of land and raw materials for its master. An English and later an Anglo Irish aristocracy established feudal manor houses throughout the country, confiscating land and then charging rent to the people who had been living on it. In the mid-1600s, after the English Civil War and the Reformation, Oliver Cromwell imposed a regime of cultural annihilation on the native Irish. The people were forbidden to speak their native Irish language. Dancing was outlawed. Priests were imprisoned for celebrating the Catholic Mass. The Penal Code, a network of Jim Crow–like rules circumscribing every aspect of life for Catholics, became the law of the land. The codes were lifted over the ages, but they were remembered; Cromwell's name became a curse. In the region that would eventually become Northern Ireland, Catholics were an occupied people, barred from many professions, denied admission to certain schools, their rights severely limited until the late twentieth century. Mary McCloskey's experience of discrimination shaped her attitudes in her new country. She didn't truck with racism: she knew what it was like to be the despised. A quarter century after she left Ireland, the family took a road trip to Canada and were driving through upstate New York late at night, in need of a motel. A sign emerged on the road: THE CROMWELL INN. Mary wouldn't consider stopping.[13]

Maura's father, John Clarke, was born in Dromard, County Sligo, the tenth of twelve children in a family that had seen its fortunes ebb over the course of a few generations. His father and grandfather were schoolmasters and the family lived in a house beside the school, at the crossroads of their village. Cousins worked farms throughout the neighborhood, one field running into another dotted with sheep and fragrant with turf fires, a Clarke or a Kearns in every direction. The family ran a simple shop out the back door of the house, selling staples brought in from Sligotown, the county seat. The Clarke house was always full, the broad-shouldered, garrulous Clarke men and neighbors stopping in for gossip, a hand of cards, and impromptu music. But drink ran through the savings and despite being a bright pupil, John had to leave school at eighth grade. He worked the family's farm, a short walk away where a series of low stone houses rambled across the green fields. In 1914, when he was eighteen, he sailed to America to join his sister Julia Kate who had come to New York years earlier and married a wealthy Irish American hotel owner. John worked in his brother-in-law's hotel in Manhattan and lived in a tenement filled with Irish on the East Side of Manhattan. New York was not the placid countryside of Sligo where half of the neighbors were other Clarkes. Coming back to East Seventy-fourth Street one day shortly after arriving in New York, he could not remember which of the buildings he lived in. They all looked the same. After leaving the hotel job, he worked as a clerk in a grocery store and on the Third Avenue El, one of the elevated train lines that was carving up the farmland of the Bronx and making it city. There were tens of thousands of Irish immigrants in New York City in the 1910s, most of whom had arrived as single, unattached adults.[14]

John's brothers, still at home in County Sligo, were active in the fomenting rebellion against the British. The house at the crossroads beside the schoolhouse where John's father and grandfather taught became a place of meetings and whispers, planning sessions, arguments and plots. Fellow revolutionaries, men and women who'd plowed fields together all their lives, walked across the dark nights to meet at the Clarke home. John's brother Michael was a member of the Irish Republican Brotherhood, an oath-bound secret society pledged to achieving independence for Ireland. Merging with other armed groups, it later became the Irish Republican Army (IRA). Michael, called Mick, was a local commander, organizing hijackings, kidnappings, and attacks on British bases. Mick and his men evaded patrols by the Black and Tans—dreaded British counterinsurgency regiments that operated on terror, burning farmhouses of suspected guerrilla members and sympathizers. They barreled through narrow hedge-framed dirt lanes and pounded on the doors of simple cottages with bayonetted guns slung across their shoulders. Their attacks on and assassinations of civilians drew the condemnation of a significant portion of the British populace, who rightly feared their brutal tactics were driving previously ambivalent Irish into the arms of the rebels.[15]

The Irish Republican Brotherhood operated on both sides of the Atlantic and called for recruits among the Irish immigrants in the United States. John Clarke, likely at the urging of his older brothers, took up the call. He traveled to Boston to take the secret oath, pledging:

> *In the presence of God, I, John Clarke, do solemnly swear that I will do my utmost to establish the independence of Ireland, and that I will bear true allegiance to the Supreme Council of the Irish Republican Brotherhood and the Government of the Irish Republic and*

*implicitly obey the constitution of the Irish Republican Brotherhood
and all my superior officers and that I will preserve inviolable the
secrets of the organization.*

In 1921, after seven years in New York, John joined a remarkable operation—the return of hundreds of Irish immigrants and their children back across the sea to fight for their homeland's liberation. When the war began, it had seemed impossible. The British were a powerful empire bestriding the world, but in Ireland the Republican guerrillas were fighting on their own turf. John knew that if a man pressed himself to the damp brick under the Cloona road where Lacey's stream ran through the back field, he could avoid detection. He knew his uncle Paul Clarke, a cattle trader with a big, two-story house in Lismacbryan that faced toward the fog-shrouded Benbulben Mountain, would open a back door and let him hide on the second floor. There were cousins and second cousins at every corner. John was involved in the takeover of a British barracks and was imprisoned more than once.[16]

But, by 1922, the glory of the revolution was a heartbreak. A compromise treaty was signed with the British to grant incremental independence to two thirds of the country and leave the six northern counties in British hands. Former brothers at arms squared off as the Irish Army and antitreaty militias battled each other in a sad and bitter Irish Civil War. John Clarke fought with the antitreaty forces, engaging in ambushes, lying in the same ditches he'd fetched footballs from as a child and had lain in wait in during the past year, but this time he was ambushing fellow Irishmen.[17]

In the midst of street fighting in Dublin, John Clarke brought a wounded comrade to the door of a private convalescence home. Mary McCloskey opened the door and allowed them in. John came every day to visit the wounded soldier and fell in love with the nurse. Years later, whenever she was annoyed with her husband, she would tease him, "I never should have let you in. I never should have saved your life." After the war ended, John returned to New York, heartbroken that the liberation he'd fought for was incomplete, disgusted with the political deal-making and compromises that ushered in the modern

Ireland and wondering whether the sacrifice and violence had been worth it. He reestablished a life in New York and Mary followed him in 1929.[18]

They married in 1930 and moved to the Bronx, part of a migration of tens of thousands of working- and middle-class New Yorkers following the newly planted subway lines up the Grand Concourse, a broad boulevard modeled on Paris's Champs-Élysées. The Depression had hit and work was scarce, so the Clarkes shared an apartment with another couple and their son. Soon, the apartment became even more crowded: Maura was born at Fordham Hospital in the dead of the winter of 1931: January 13. She was christened Mary Elizabeth at Christ the King Church on the Grand Concourse, but at home she was always called Maura. The baby had deep-set, soft brown eyes and an alert, expressive face. Mary brought her to a photography studio and paid extra postage to send the stiff photo frame home with her next letter; her mother and grandmother would know this New York baby.[19]

Life in the crowded apartment was close. When company was in the house, John pulled out his accordion and stoked up a party. He charmed friends; he was the kind of man the Irish said had the gift of the gab. But John Clarke also had a streak of melancholy, a tendency to see the glass half empty and to succumb to dark moods. When he was low, he'd stretch on the couch and his mood could suck the air out of a room. When he drank, he was sometimes gone for days, sleeping in the apartment of an old friend, showing up eventually at home, sick and contrite. He might be sober for months or even years, and then find another excuse. He ran through jobs and frequently Mary's paycheck was the only source of income. After the birth of their second child, James, two years after Maura, the family moved to Rockaway. Mary had worked at a hospital there when she first arrived in New York and the wide, wild sea felt closer to home—more like the open fields of Antrim and Sligo—than the cramped streets of the Bronx. Two-year-old Maura couldn't say the word *brother*, calling James "Buddy" instead. The nickname stayed with him for the rest of his life. In 1935, another daughter was born, Julia, five years younger than Maura. The family called her Judy.

In Ireland, John had walked along the ridge in Dromard, the hulking giant of Benbulben Mountain rising beyond the sweep of green, a stretch of the cold Atlantic just visible at its base. In Rockaway he strolled the wooden boardwalk beside the same ocean, his little daughter on his shoulders. Maura learned the alphabet before she started kindergarten, eagerly identifying the letters her father pointed out on signs along the boardwalk.[20]

The Irish Rockaways were served by two Catholic parishes: St. Camillus in blue-collar Rockaway Park and St. Francis de Sales in the more middle-class Belle Harbor, each a nexus of communal life. On summer Sundays St. Camillus, a small wooden church on Beach 100th Street, was as tightly packed as the bars were the nights before. The revelers of Saturday night filled the pews and spilled out the doors and onto the sidewalks. In 1930, St. Camillus built an auditorium that sat 1,200, to accommodate the summer faithful.[21]

The Catholic Church in New York was growing, building new schools and new parishes every year, expanding hospitals, and seeding an army of nuns. The thirty years beginning in 1920 that Archbishop Thomas Molloy led the diocese of Brooklyn and Queens, saw the creation of eighty-eight new parishes and one hundred new schools, a new teacher training school, and a seminary. There were now so many priests that Brooklyn clergy were sent to staff parishes overseas and in the sparsely Catholic southern United States. By 1953, 1,180 parish priests in the diocese of Brooklyn were serving 1.4 million Catholics. The nuns were welcoming young women into their convents in even larger numbers. When Maura was born, there were 135,000 nuns in three hundred American orders. By the time she was twenty, that number had swelled to 150,000. Entering the convent was so common in certain heavily Catholic neighborhoods in Brooklyn and Queens that department stores carried the distinctive dark dresses of postulants, or first-year recruits, and girls would go to Finnegan's or Doherty's to buy the garb of the Josephites, Dominicans, Maryknoll Sisters, or Sisters of Charity before they presented themselves at the convent. Three of Maura's close high school friends became nuns.[22]

During Maura's childhood, 75 percent of the people in the parish boundaries were Catholic and the goings-on at the parish dominated life. It's a measure of the role the church played in people's lives
that fifty and sixty years later, Catholic New Yorkers—long having
moved up and out to the suburbs—define the city's geography by
parish. People didn't live in Bedford Park or University Heights. They
lived in St. Philip Neri or St. Nicholas of Tolentine. "What parish?"
became the new version of the Irish immigrants' question "What
county?" Far from a place reserved for Sunday mornings, the parish
was a locus of daily life, a center of social as well as spiritual activity.[23]

Maura's house was frequently filled with visitors, John trying to
re-create his home in Sligo by welcoming old comrades and holding
forth. In the summer her mother took in the children of friends from
the Bronx, insisting it was no trouble to have a few extra youngsters
about, that it would be fun for them to be on the beach. Mary kept
an open door. She didn't rush about making everything perfect for
guests, but when she came home from her job as a head nurse at
Kings County Hospital in Brooklyn, she was armed with funny stories and ready to relax. She'd walk to the beach, carrying mugs, a jar
of milk, and a teapot wrapped in a towel, to warm up the children.
They'd have been waiting for her to get off a day shift at the hospital;
permitted to play on the sands, they couldn't go in the water until
she came and so they strained to see her tall, straight figure walking
hurriedly across the empty lots of late spring.[24]

Mary Clarke made going the extra mile in generosity look like
the most obvious thing in the world. She had a patient once, dying of
cancer, who loved Irish ballads. So, Mary called her nephew James, the
son of one of John's brothers who was then living with the family from
time to time, and told him to sing "Galway Bay" to the dying man.[25]

Maura inherited the same instinct, but not always her mother's good sense. During World War II, soldiers from nearby Fort Til-
den were stationed on the beach, camping in tents, alert for German
U-boats. Maura and a friend, then twelve or thirteen years old, once
brought cookies over and stayed to talk for a little while with the
young men. The girls felt sorry for them, far from their homes and
alone on the beach. But in the strictly regulated mores of Catholic

Rockaway, that was not done. The word went out in the parish: there would be no fraternizing with the soldiers on the beach. The same compassionate instinct got Maura in trouble a few years later when she was helping a neighborhood family care for its many children. A toddler had soiled his diaper. The father was angry and rough with the child, hosing him down with cold water from the backyard hose. Maura grabbed the boy and ran to her parents' house, his body still dripping.

Often Maura's family was evicted from its home in late spring, told to find another place because the landlord could make as much from a few families in July and August as in several off-season months. The Clarkes moved frequently, hopscotching across the Rockaways from Seaside to Rockaway Park, to Belle Harbor and back. They lived a somewhat peripatetic existence, buffeted by rents, unstable work, and changing fortunes. Maura's transcript at St. Francis de Sales school bears a litany of addresses, each crossed out and replaced by another: 70 Beach 92nd, 330 Beach 86th, 248 Beach 127th, 517 Beach 132nd, 515 Beach 127th Street. In high school it was the same: 160 Beach 99th, 145 Beach 92nd, 162 Beach 115th Street. Maura and her mother squared their shoulders and arranged the furniture in each new place, spread the blankets on the beds, and made a home. Mary found something to make the new place pretty and the family kept on. There was no point submitting to complaint or pity.[26]

When Maura was in seventh or eighth grade, the family moved to Belle Harbor for a few years. The kids in that neighborhood were less scrappy and had more substantial homes; the houses were still modest but the lawns were bigger than in Rockaway Park or Seaside and not sandy. They couldn't hear their neighbors' parents when they fought. And while it felt as if everyone was Irish (that is, everyone who wasn't Jewish), the children were also very explicitly assimilating, embracing the country their parents or grandparents had arrived into.

When the boys and girls filed through the doors of St. Francis de Sales School on Beach 129th Street, they walked under the words *Pro Deus* and *Pro Patria* chiseled into limestone. Being a good

Catholic and being a good American went hand in hand. Here and in St. Camillus—as in immigrant parishes across the city—the parish, FDR, and the *Brooklyn Tablet*, the fiercely parochial diocesan newspaper, combined for a secure and cohesive whole. The ascent of John F. Kennedy, the first Catholic US president, was the better part of a generation away and Catholics were still strangers in much of America, but by the 1940s the church in which Maura Clarke was growing up was shedding its defensive stance and engaging the world, albeit in a way that might look unfamiliar to modern eyes. Francis Cardinal Spellman, prelate of the Archdiocese of New York and sometimes called the American pope, was a power broker, chaplain to the US Army in Europe during World War II and a liaison between occupied Rome and Washington, DC. His brand of aggressive anticommunism looked simplistic and reactionary by the Vietnam era, but in the 1940s it was buying respectability for Catholic immigrants and their children who had been distrusted as suspicious foreigners, incapable of assimilation a generation earlier. In New York City, Spellman commanded the Catholic vote—or thought he did—and turned the annual Alfred E. Smith fund-raising dinner for Catholic Charities into a required stop on the Democratic political circuit. Candidates for mayor, Congress, and president attended to get his nod. There were Catholic nurses' associations, Catholic Broadway associations, Catholic guilds in municipal departments and on Wall Street. These existed in an interesting tension: a desire to be integrated into all parts of secular civic life, and yet an instinct to protect or hold back, to remind night-shift nurses and chorus-line girls alike that they came from "good Catholic homes" and that their souls were more important than the glittering material world.[27]

In the nineteenth century, Catholic sisters had been objects of prurient fascination and suspicion. By 1945, when Maura was fourteen, the image of a Catholic sister had been replaced in popular culture with glamorous Ingrid Bergman as the iconoclast young nun in the movie *The Bells of St. Mary's*—a simplistic and reductive image, but nonetheless one that revealed a broader acceptance of Catholics in America. Meanwhile, the booming voice of Fulton Sheen, auxiliary bishop of New York, entered 4 million American living rooms

every Sunday evening on *The Catholic Hour*, a national radio broadcast. More than 30 percent of letters to the radio program were from
non-Catholics drawn to Sheen's dramatic intonations and mix of
folksy and theological lectures. Walking along a residential street in
the Rockaways in summer, a person could hear Bishop Sheen's entire
sermon. Every home was tuned in and every window was open.[28]

While the bishop's talks generally focused on personal piety and
theological issues, a conspicuous theme of patriotism ran through his
lectures. He was the most visible embodiment of American Catholic
anticommunism. In the winter and spring of 1947, when Maura was
sixteen, he devoted eleven weeks of *The Catholic Hour* to lectures on
communism. Maura's family sometimes listened on Sunday evening
after a midday dinner. Maura often made those dinners, scrubbing
potatoes over the sink with her mother, laughing or telling stories
before Mary Clarke left for the evening shift at the hospital. After
dinner every night, summer or winter, the three children kneeled,
forming a semicircle around their seated parents—or if their mother
was at work, around their father—and recited the Rosary. The repe-
tition of prayers the children knew by heart long before they could
read was meant to free the mind for contemplation, not unlike a
Hindu mantra. In Maura's youth, the family prayed for neighbors'
sons fighting in World War II, for the family still in Ireland, for
work. It was one more way the prosaic was infused with the divine.[29]

The words the Clarke family spoke with every Rosary and at
every Mass were rote, the background noise of devotional Catholicism in the early twentieth century. But they were also a language.
Through the prayers and movements, through the specialized words
and a hundred little practices—blessing oneself when one passed a
church, bringing flowers to place before a statue of Mary, lighting a
candle—a Rockaway resident had access to a vast spiritual realm. A
simple life in a blue-collar neighborhood could be connected to the
creator of the universe.[30]

Most evenings after dinner, John Clarke stretched his legs on
the boardwalk. When Maura joined him on his strolls, he told stories
of the Irish revolution and instilled his thoughtful daughter with an
understanding of the world from the perspective of the person on

the bottom: the native, not the colonist. The peasant, not the land-lord. Irish and Irish American culture is rife with songs and stories of brave, principled rebels, of people who stand against the prevail-ing power and for the underdog. They lose. They are hanged or shot or exiled to Australia. But their tribute is immortality in memory. Maura ingested the message. As a teenager figuring out her place in the world, she drew inspiration from the inheritance of all those ro-mantic revolutionary stories—even if she looked like a demure young lady. She placed herself in the history. Sitting in a Rockaway bar as a teenager when a band played one of those rousing rebel songs, she confessed to her cousin James: "I'm a rebel."[31]

But first she was a student. Weeks after World War II ended, Maura began high school at Stella Maris Academy, an all-girls school in Rockaway. On her first day of classes, a bishop visiting from Pan-ama urged the girls to consider becoming missionaries and to pray for the people in Central America. It was something Maura was al-ready thinking about. At home she pored over *Columba* magazine, a publication of the globe-trotting Irish Columban fathers. Maura read about priests who faced malaria-infested jungles and crossed raging rivers in makeshift rafts, marveling to her cousin James at the brav-ery and sacrifices of the missionaries. At a time when social conven-tions were so strictly enforced that St. Francis de Sales gave etiquette class during school days, the missionaries must have seemed like ex-otic people who led intense and exciting lives. Maura wanted to help people and she wanted to do something big. Her romantic father and expansive mother raised her for something beyond a job at the tele-phone company and marriage to a boy from the neighborhood—the path of so many Stella Maris girls.[32]

There were other influences on Maura's Catholicism outside of school. One was an older sister of John Clarke's who was a nun in the Franciscan Missionaries of Mary in Rhode Island. Sr. Oswald spent her life as a direct fund-raiser for her order—a begging nun. The tra-dition dates back to the mendicant beggars of the medieval era and to Saint Francis of Assisi's radical rejection of his family's wealth in favor of living with nothing and relying only on Providence, or the hand of God, to sustain himself and his order. Sr. Oswald lived in the city of Providence, visiting the rich on one side of town and, with charm and authority, relieving them of excess wealth. She would literally fill her voluminous wool habit with cash and then dispense it on the other side of the tracks to individual families in need. She raised tens of thousands of dollars over the course of her life. Grandchildren of families she aided still remember her name. When they were children, Maura and Buddy visited and accompanied Sr. Oswald on her rounds to the sedate Yankee law firms and businessmen's clubs. Sr. Oswald was not like other people. Maura was inspired by her aunt's confidence and sense of humor. To Maura, Sr. Oswald seemed animated by her relationship with God and lived outside the narrow boundaries of the 1940s society.[33]

A few days a week, Maura worked at the Little Art Shop on Beach 116th Street, selling greeting cards, jewelry, figurines, and other gifts in the tiny store, to earn her school tuition. Miss Mattern, the owner, was strict. She wanted the jewelry boxes stacked just so and didn't appreciate customers who only came to browse or kill time as they waited for the train. Maura smiled excitedly whenever the door opened, greeting customers as though she was delighted to see them, striving to earn Miss Mattern's approval and make the customers feel appreciated. It was not uncommon for Stella Maris students to pay or contribute to their tuition. One of Maura's friends worked at a hot-dog stand on the boardwalk. Another began working as a waitress in an all-night diner on Beach 105th Street at age fourteen.[34]

Maura was a striking young woman. Her glossy, dark hair hung in thick waves to her shoulders and her brown eyes were soft and emotive. She smiled easily and walked with a grace she had learned from her mother, carrying her lean frame straight and tall. But in place of Mary's regal bearing, Maura had a coltish energy and long legs. She joined her friends nearly at a gallop and paid close, intense attention to whoever she was talking to, inclining her head as she listened, smiling encouragingly, as though the speaker were the only person in the world. When a friend needed help with a school assignment, Maura devoted her lunch break to helping her write the paper—at the expense of her own, acting as if her friend had done her a favor by asking for help. Maura played on a basketball team with the sister of the McGuire brothers Al and Dick, who were later inducted into the National Basketball Association's Naismith Hall of Fame. The boys attracted hundreds of spectators to their Catholic Youth Organization basketball games outside their father's bar. She played Ping-Pong in Betty McCann's garage in upscale Neponsit and babysat the Keiley children when their mother needed a hand, playing school and speaking gently to the children whose life was sometimes harsh. In the summer Maura and her friends lingered outside the bars of Irishtown, rushing in to dance when they heard their favorite songs. As they got older they sat inside with her cousin James and his friends, the boys drinking beers, everyone dancing the steps Cromwell had failed to stamp out.[35]

Events at the parish attracted big numbers. Maura attended feast day processions and nine-day novenas. At the end of each summer, the bars sent their house bands to a giant all-day fund-raiser at St. Camillus's hall and neighbors turned out. She acted in her church's community theater productions, drinking up the limelight and pretending not to like it. At Maura's basketball games, the Sisters of St. Joseph from St. Vincent de Sales and Stella Maris, wrapped in yards of billowing black, their stiff white wimple holding up a black veil, their heavy wooden rosary belt swinging, would climb the bleachers in the Stella Maris gym to watch their girls play. Maura and her friend Betty McCann went to parish dances nearby and in Brooklyn. Mary sewed most of Maura's clothes herself, but for dances she brought Maura to a shop in Rockaway whose owner went to Manhattan to buy the latest styles. The girls wore white gloves. By senior year, Maura was dating Joe Barry, a friend of Vinnie Melvin, whose family hers had lived with all those years earlier in the Bronx. Joe, tall and handsome with a square jaw and rugged smile, was a few years older, returned from the army and thinking about medical school. She took him to her senior prom and they went on dates in Manhattan.[36]

On nights when she wasn't working, Mary's friend Nora Cleary and Nora's husband, Paddy, came over for dinner. Nora and Mary worked up a feast in the kitchen and Paddy tried to wind Maura up, picking an argument with the sincere teenager just for the joy of argument. Maura played right along, flexing her mental muscles, good-naturedly outraged at Paddy's retrograde positions on integration or women's education.[37]

While her mother worked the three to eleven p.m. shift in the hospital, it was Maura's job to grocery shop and make dinner. She came home from school and settled into homework—or sometimes read a magazine in the living room. When she heard her father's footsteps on the stairs of the apartment, she leaped up, banging pots and pans together to make it sound as if she'd been hard at work for ages. John Clarke had an easy and teasing relationship with his daughter. He'd step in the kitchen and ask what was for dinner and Maura would shake her head slowly. "We're on Pound Street tonight, Dad," she'd wink to her father, referring to the sign he and his brothers had hung outside their home in Sligo—which doubled as a neighborhood shop—when they didn't want to work.[38]

Maura was growing up in a world so different from that of her parents, who had lived on land their ancestors farmed for generations and whose church was unyielding. By the twentieth century, the inward-looking faith of her parents' childhood, concerned primarily with personal piety and holiness, was beginning to engage with the flesh-and-blood matters of the world. In 1919, a committee of American Catholic Bishops had issued a blueprint for rebuilding society in the wake of the World War. It was a response to the dramatic social changes ushered in by urbanization, industrialization, and the rise of radical political movements from anarchism to communism afoot in the United States. Titled "The Bishops' Program for Social Reconstruction," it presaged many of the elements of the New Deal, calling for collective bargaining, the establishment of a minimum wage, and unemployment and disability insurance.

Through the 1920s and during the Great Depression, a new ethic and a new understanding of the role of Catholic faith began to bubble up through diocesan charities, Catholic colleges, and parish social halls. Called Catholic Action, it argued that the Church's work ought not only to be concerned with the souls of the faithful but also, crucially, to engage ordinary Catholics—laypeople, not just nuns and priests—in the important work of building the kingdom God—a world of justice and fairness. In the Rockaways, it meant St. Vincent de Paul Societies visited poor families, assessed their needs, and delivered shoes or groceries or financial help. A labor study group gathered at St. Francis de Sales to advocate for worker rights and assert a Catholic—not atheist, communist—influence on the burgeoning labor movement. Mission societies were formed to study conditions in South America or Africa and to support the work of missionary orders of nuns and priests. Animating the movement was a commitment to bring specifically Catholic answers to social problems and a belief that Catholics needed to be part of the public conversation. For them, advocacy for the weak and struggle for a fairer world were essential *spiritual* parts of being Catholic.[39]

This expanding notion of faith was part of Maura's experience at Stella Maris. She joined the school's Catholic Students' Mission Crusade, a club with chapters across the country that met to study the work of missionary orders and learn about conditions in mission countries—just like those magazines about dashing missionaries. In the club, Maura learned about the Maryknoll Sisters. It wasn't just men adventuring into the distant world to help people in poverty. Here were sturdy women, setting up hospitals for abandoned baby girls in China and treating malaria in South America. Helping those in need—and connecting with people different than her—attracted Maura. She wasn't necessarily interested in being a nun, but Catholic Students' Mission Crusade helped her imagine a life beyond Rockaway.

So did Fr. Curley, a parish priest at St. Camillus, who came often to the Clarke home for dinner. He saw potential in Maura. Many Sunday afternoons, he took her and a few friends on drives to Long Island or out to dinner at restaurants with white tablecloths, several steps up from the boardwalk concessions. They talked about vocations, about the life the girls might have if they became nuns. For one thing, they would be educated. At a time when few women, and even fewer working-class women, went to college, nuns were getting advanced degrees. They would be part of something vast, foot soldiers in a worldwide organization and dedicated to something beyond themselves.[40]

Maura's conversations about vocation with Fr. Curley piqued her interest. On January 21, 1950, shortly after her nineteenth birthday, she wrote to Maryknoll's mother superior. Maura had been out of high school since the previous January, taking classes of St. Francis College in downtown Brooklyn and working as a clerk at Saks Fifth Avenue.

> My thoughts about entering the convent came to me within the last year and a half. I was very interested in the missions through reading books like "When the Sorghum was High" and "White Fire" before I really thought of being a nun. A few of my friends have entered St. Joseph's order and I felt for a while that my interest in Maryknoll, which I didn't know too much about, might be the glamour of being a missionary. I am not sure how I decided but during the past summer my mind gradually became surer that God had given me a vocation.[41]

In June 1950, after she submitted letters of recommendations from Fr. Curley, a nun from Stella Maris, and her pastor at St. Camillus, along with forms certifying that she was healthy and strong, not anemic, with no tuberculosis in her system, Maura received a letter from Maryknoll.

> Your application to Maryknoll has been considered and approved and we are happy to count you among our candidates for this year. May God grant you many and fruitful years of service as a Maryknoll missionary sister.[42]

But before she entered the convent, Maura, Judy, and their mother would spend the summer in Ireland. The girls had never seen the country that shaped their parents and their neighborhood. Just before Christmas 1949, Mary Clarke's mother, Lizzie, died. Mary wanted to bring her daughters back to meet the cousins, aunts, and uncles they had read about in so many letters and to see the landscapes that served as the settings for so many of Mary and John's stories.

They sailed on a Cunard Line ship, sharing a cabin in second class with a single New York woman. Mary made friends with someone in first class early in the crossing and the mother and daughters took most of their meals in the stylish top dining room, the girls wearing dresses their mother had sewed for them. But they also spent time in the lower decks, dancing to fiddle and accordion with a crowd of Irish workers who were going home.

In Ireland they traveled by train to stay on the dairy farm Mary's brother Barney now ran in County Antrim. Twilight lingered in the Irish summer until close to midnight. Maura spent the evenings mixed in with her uncle Barney's teenage daughters, who were given rare permission to attend dances with their American cousin. During the day she sat at the farmhouse tables of her aunts and listened to half whispered family stories or hiked through the farmland and helped her cousins with their chores. Many days were spent visiting, simply walking from house to house to sit with the family over endless cups of tea and listen to stories.

From high points in Ballymoney, where Uncle Barney lived, she could see the flat-top, ancient volcano Slemish, where Saint Patrick was held as a slave in the third century. Patrick had been freed, but returned to Ireland to convert the Irish. This is where this religion of Maura's inheritance originated: a missionary far from home, in a brutal land.[43]

After a few weeks in Antrim, Mary, Maura, and Judy arrived in Sligo to stay with John's brother Michael in the Clarke house at the crossroads, beside the schoolhouse. Maura fell in easily with cousins in Sligo, too, and dated Gerry Gibney, a boy from the area. She told only one cousin that she was entering the convent at the end of the summer. That cousin was doing the same, but until then they didn't want everyone asking them questions or treating them funny.

In Sligo Maura heard the stories that filled in the gaps in her father's tales. Among the most exciting were the stories of Linda Kearns, a cousin of John Clarke's who during the Easter Rising, the 1916 precursor to the Irish Revolution, set up an impromptu field hospital in a bar a few blocks from the fighting in Dublin. She treated both British and Republican soldiers, but by the end of the few days, she'd become convinced of the justice of the revolutionary side. When the uprising ended and most of its leaders were executed, Kearns became a clandestine operative for the rebel organization. Unmarried, with the same tall, lean physique as Maura and the same disarmingly sweet smile, she transported messages, grenades, and rifles in her Model T car, driving from Dublin to Sligo. The Black and Tans, ruthless counterinsurgency soldiers rumored to be released convicts from British prisons, let a woman pass their checkpoints. But on one mission in November 1920, carrying a group of IRA men in the back of her car, she was stopped. The car was searched and Kearns arrested. She was imprisoned for much of the war but escaped from Mountjoy Prison in Dublin by climbing over a high wall after creating a diversion during an inmate football game; she jumped down the other side and was ferried away with two other female revolutionaries on the back of motorcycles supplied by Michael Collins, a key IRA leader. Kearns was a few years older than John but was a first cousin, and a cousin of Anna Melvin, the friend John and Mary Clarke would live with in the Bronx. After the Irish Civil War, Kearns became a politician, a member of the Republic of Ireland's nascent parliament and a close confident of Eamon de Velara, the Irish prime minister. In Sligo she was a native daughter everyone loved to tell stories about, a romantic fugitive who'd made a fool of British jailors.[44]

Maura's father's family had been thoroughly involved in the war, and indeed were leaders in the area. John's eldest brother, Tom, was a Sinn Féin man, organizing subsistence farmers in his region behind the political movement for full independence. Family lore attests that Countess Markievicz, the storied Irish revolutionary from an aristocratic family in Sligo and a confidante of W. B. Yeats, snuck out of her family's estate one night, riding on horseback down the dark beach, to listen to Tom Clarke speak at a rally. Tom had gone to the seminary as a young man, intent on becoming a priest. But after several years of study, just days before ordination, he left the seminary. Priests at the time were required to take an oath of loyalty to the British Crown. He refused. Serving God couldn't mean vowing obedience to an unjust power. Instead of joining the clergy, he organized for revolution.

Evenings that summer of 1950 when Maura was nineteen often ended at the Gibneys' or Corcorans' house, with card games and music. As her father and Linda Kearns had done a generation before, Maura crowded into the Corcorans' house, expanded now to a few more rooms. As Annie Corcoran prepared tea on the imposing coal-fed stove, the Corcoran children were called out to share a tune on their accordions and fiddles. During the day Maura and the other teenagers took walks to Strand Hill, the beach where the Atlantic Ocean beat the rugged coastline. Other times, as her father had when he was in Ireland, she walked by herself, covering miles between Dromard and Port Royal where her father's younger sister Babsy lived.

At the end of August, just before the Clarkes left to return to America, the Corcorans hosted a massive send-off party. Everyone from Dromard and Coolany, all the cousins and aunts and uncles and friends from scattered settlements along the hilly Sligo coast, were there. Linda Kearns, the revolutionary and prison escapee, by then an old woman, pulled up to the party in a Rolls-Royce. She'd come to meet the daughters of her old comrade John Clarke.

CHAPTER 2

Into the Silence: Novitiate

The Clarke women were home just a few days before Maura was due to report to the Maryknoll Sisters convent—the motherhouse in Ossining, New York. Maura, who all her life was racing to do one more thing and running late, either didn't have time or didn't consider it important to collect the prescribed wardrobe: the black dress and cape, the ugly low-heeled shoes, the undershirts and black slips and particular nightgowns and stockings prospective nuns were supposed to bring packed in a trunk, like the trousseau of hopeful brides, when they arrived at the convent. Instead she piled into a car with her family, wearing stylish black heels and a green suit her mother had made. Another carload of family friends followed. They would make an outing of Maura's departure, laughing and posing for pictures on the leafy convent campus, a slice of boisterous, communal Rockaway. A friend of Maura's brother joked that the girls arriving to enter the convent were too pretty to become nuns. All around them, young women were hugging their parents good-bye, trying not to cry, the parents proud and heartbroken. These daughters were beginning a life apart. It was a scene not unlike the ones many of the parents themselves had enacted, clutching good-bye at train stations and on shipping piers in Ireland or Italy, Germany, or Poland, setting off for something brave and necessary, uncertain they would ever return. For the rest of their lives these daughters would visit them only in brief snatches of time. If Maura was sent to the missions overseas, she would return to the United States just once every ten years—and then to this motherhouse, not her childhood home. Except at another church property, she would not be permitted to sleep overnight anywhere but here. She would not attend her brother's wedding. She might or might not be given permission to attend a parent's funeral Mass. In fact, the strictures of religious life would loosen dramatically in the next fifteen years, but as they delivered their adored oldest daughter to this convent in the country, the Clarkes didn't know that. Mary Clarke had told her daughter if it didn't work out, she shouldn't feel bad; she could come home and be a teacher.[1]

Maura walked up a few steps and through the heavy wooden door of the Maryknoll motherhouse. Here silence reigned and rules governed every aspect and movement of the day. From now on Maura was separated from the world, her relationships and activities determined by an exhaustive code of behavior that dated to medieval Europe. She was led to the fourth floor of the convent where a row of cots and footlockers were lined up one after another, each separated from the next by a curtain. There were more recruits every year and the motherhouse was running out of room. Maura changed out of her fine green suit and into the simple black postulant's dress that had been left for her. She pulled her thick chestnut hair under a short veil. She wouldn't wear her own clothes again for close to twenty years. As they caught sight of one another within the motherhouse, Maura and more than seventy other young women, dressed all alike, were beginning to realize the enormity of their decision. One of the regulations in the thick convent rulebook instructed the young women to "learn to move noiselessly. This will come with practice and thought." But Maura's fancy shoes clicked smartly down the halls that first day, and she had to suppress her instinct to hurry along at a near gallop. Whereas Maryknoll had been founded just forty years earlier as an emphatically active order dedicated to spreading Catholicism to foreign countries, its novitiate was adapted from traditional contemplative orders. Prayer, silence, and discipline were the operating principles. For Maura, who grew up in a house full of visitors and laughter, was comfortable in the middle of a party, was used to her mother's long leash and had always been something of a star, the novitiate was difficult. She began to doubt herself under the weight of so many rules. She felt her confidence wilting. She worried she wasn't good enough, reproached herself for breaking any of the thousands of rules, and longed for the approval of the convent superiors.[2]

But she kept these feelings to herself, endeavoring instead to be cheerful, turning her attention to the young women around her, more than to herself. Maura marveled that her fellow postulants came from all over the country, Kansas and Wisconsin, and several from Brooklyn. Two were from the Philippines, where Maryknoll sisters ran girls' high schools. She was buoyed by the other girls and appreciated that there was something to do every moment of the day, all the work directed toward a goal. If surviving the strictures of novitiate were what was necessary to get to the wide world, to be a Maryknoller helping people in need, Maura would persevere. Like many of the other young women, Maura was becoming a nun not primarily to draw closer to some idea of God, but to do good, to be of use in the world. She wanted to dive in, not lock herself away. Like the other postulants who were setting photographs of their families in their makeshift cells (only two photos allowed), Maura was here because of what she'd studied in Catholic Students' Mission Crusade, read about in *Columba* magazine, and seen in movies about heroic missionaries.[3]

The newcomers endeavoring to move noiselessly through the halls of the Maryknoll motherhouse were among the top students in their high schools. Several had a year or two of college behind them, a rare accomplishment for working-class women in 1950. In a time when career and life options were still tightly circumscribed for women and particularly for nonwealthy women, becoming a nun offered a divergent and exciting path. With the college degrees—and later master's degrees and doctorates—they would earn through the convent, Maura and her fellow postulants would become the most educated people in their families.

The attitudes of Catholic Action that led Maura to want to devote her life to God were in tension with the age-old purpose of the convent. The point of monastic life was to perfect a soul for its own sake and for God's sake. But Catholic Action and the liberation theology it presaged are built on a different concept altogether. Like the Jewish idea of *tikkun olam*—to repair the world—the goal in Catholic Action is to remake the temporal world into a better place, to build the city of God on earth by healing the sick and feeding the hungry. Later, fermented with liberation theology, the imperative would be to build the City of God by tearing down unjust social structures and replacing them with a society of love. These graduates of Catholic Action clubs and Catholic Students Mission Crusade troops were ready to roll up their sleeves and get to work. It's an understanding of vocation quite at odds with a life behind convent walls dedicated to personal piety.

The religious formation Maura would go through in the next few years was more traditional than she and the other postulants expected, given Maryknoll Sisters' mission. Three years earlier, Maryknoll's gregarious and open-hearted founder had stepped down. In her place rose Mother Mary Columba Tarpey, who had opened the Maryknoll missions in the Philippines and whom sisters nicknamed "the General" for her authoritative manner. Maryknoll training came to more closely resemble that of other religious orders and Mother Mary Columba ran the organization like an executive, focusing on growth and efficiency. By the time she left leadership in 1958, Maryknoll Sisters missions had expanded to British East Africa, Mauritius, the Caroline and Marshall Islands, Formosa, Ceylon, Bolivia, Chile, Peru, Panama, Guatemala, and Mexico, often following closely on US military and diplomatic expansion.[4]

Novitiate was a two-and-a-half-year training regimen in which young women were formed as religious sisters, a sort of boot camp for the soul. The young women were meant to align their life to God, to shed attachments to the world and their own sense of self, so as to exist ever more closely in tune with the divine. The goal was holiness. Their task as missionaries would be to share their love of God and God's love of the world with new people in strange lands. After six months as a postulant—an applicant on a trial basis who lived in the convent and learned the ways of the community—Maura would be accepted, or "received," as a novice: a trainee nun. After a year as a junior novice and a year as a senior novice, she would take temporary three-year vows of poverty, chastity, and obedience. After three more years she would take a second set of temporary vows, then finally permanent vows, lifelong oaths from which only permission from the pope could release her.[5]

Postulants and novices prayed and took classes, learned to live as part of a group, were closely monitored by their religious superiors, and developed the skills of self-control and the habits of faith that would serve them when they were sent to open a health clinic on an island 1,000 miles off the coast of Korea or establish a school for indigenous children in the Andes. There was a rule for everything: a proper place to put your stockings, a proper place for your shoes, a proper way to close a door, and rules on how to address your superiors. It was a setup not unlike what their brothers might be experiencing in basic training in the army, except here they were learning to serve not the army for a few years, but the Church for their whole life. In the convent Maura had just entered and the church it reflected, the very understanding of the world was hierarchical. Everything had its place, from the spoon in a table setting, to the sister in the classroom, to the priest at the head of the congregation, the worker in the mine, and the political leaders in power. The social order was not in question. The challenge was to reach God by slipping into one's place in the existing setup, not to disrupt the world. The women would stay on the campuslike grounds of the Maryknoll motherhouse, making only very occasional forays into the village of Ossining, New York. Their focus was on the vast landscape of their interior selves. The two and a half years of novitiate were meant to be a time for each woman to understand her personality and straighten out self-destructive behaviors that separated her from God. The depth and intensity of the prayer life begun in these years at the novitiate were a source of strength and stability. They would constitute the center of Maura's life.[6]

The day was wrapped in prayer. Maura woke to a ringing bell at 5:15 a.m. She joked in a letter to a high school friend that if she failed to make it through novitiate, it would be because she couldn't get out of bed so early. She had twenty minutes from the bell until she needed to be in chapel for silent and then group prayers, morning Mass, and meditation, all before breakfast at 7:30 a.m.[7]

As she washed her face, Maura said, "Cleanse me, Oh Lord, and purify my heart, that being made white in the blood of the lamb, I may have the fruition of everlasting joys." As she dressed she prayed, "O Jesus, take from my heart the love of worldly pomp, which I renounced in Holy Baptism, and clothe me anew with thyself." As she put on her shoes she prayed, " O Jesus, teach me so to walk in love and in conformity with thy Holy Will, that though my feet must tread the earth, my mind and my heart may dwell in heaven."

The line of young women walked, as quietly as possible, downstairs to the first floor chapel to join the older nuns in the morning prayers of the Divine Office, itself a set of psalms and hymns recited at specific hours of the day by monks and priests throughout the world. Maryknoll was the only women's order at the time that prayed the Divine Office. The prayer swept its adherents through the day in a spiritual raft, with posts every few hours from morning to night. After prime, at an hour when she still would have been asleep in Rockaway, Maura moved on to the next prayer.

> *Of myself indeed I am nothing. I have nothing. And can do nothing worthy of thee. But since, by a wonderful device of thy wisdom and love I may approach thy majesty through Christ my savior, humbly offer thee in union with Him and through his sacred heart whatever I possess, my body, my senses, all the powers of my soul.*

Then, the prayer of St. Joseph.

And the litany of saints.

There was a prayer before meditation and a prayer after meditation.

They prayed the Angelus.

They prayed the Anima Christi, written five hundred years earlier by Saint Ignatius Loyola.

There was Mass, sung in Latin and celebrated by a Maryknoll priest who walked to the convent from the priests' red brick, Chinese pagoda–style monastery across the road. The silence and intense seriousness were unnatural, particularly for a crowd of teenagers. Sometimes a fit of giggles swept through the row of young women kneeling in chapel and Maura had to stare hard at the floor to resist breaking into laughter.[8]

After Mass, the women filed in silence to the dining room for breakfast, eaten in silence as someone read from the Roman martyrology, a catalog of the early Christians who had lost their lives at the hands of a militaristic and rapacious state. Stories of martyrs were pervasive. Maura had been raised on them at Saint Francis de Sales and Stella Maris and in her father's invocation of political martyrs. In the convent they were held up as ideals. In a lecture a few months after she entered Maryknoll, Maura heard the order's founder, by then in retirement, make an offhand reference to everyone's desire for martyrdom. "Is there any one of us who has not at sometime or another envisioned herself as a heroine, a notable public figure, beloved of all, doing good, heroically serving Christ, being gloriously martyred? We can smile at our own presumption."[9]

The Catholic imagination of Maura's day was fed on sacrifice, from stained-glass images of Christ selflessly submitting to his fate to daring missionaries entering hostile lands and winning glory by dying for their belief. During her time in the convent, Maryknoll sisters who in the past decade had been interned with Japanese Americans they worked with in California, held as prisoners of war in Manchuria, or tortured in Japanese camps in the Philippines, now sat in chapel with the young nuns. The stories of Sr. Hyacinth Kunkel, who had died on a death march across the Philippine mountains in 1945, were still fresh. A month after Maura arrived at Maryknoll, Sr. Agneta Chang, who had been leading a group of Korean nuns ever since American Maryknollers were expelled from Korea at the beginning of World War II, was kidnapped and disappeared into North Korea. As Maura began her training, Maryknoll priests and nuns were imprisoned by the communist government newly at the helm in China and the order's leadership was working its connections, trying to get them released to Hong Kong. Being willing to suffer or die for one's belief were part of the mind-set.[10]

So was a fear and resistance to "Godless communism," the same enemy invoked in the Rockaway of Maura's girlhood. Like many American bishops, Mother Mary Columba supported Senator Joseph McCarthy. She brought in speakers and reading material that supported a vision of Catholicism as being engaged in a good vs. evil battle with worldwide communism, in which the United States was solidly on the side of the angels. During that first year in the convent, Maura would listen to lectures on the scourge of communism and the importance of US and Catholic resistance. Ngô Đình Diệm, future president of South Vietnam, lived part of his early exile from Vietnam with the Maryknoll fathers and brothers. Maryknoll marketing material proclaimed, "The Maryknoll Sisters are a part of our own twentieth-century America and have gained immeasurable good will for America."[11]

After breakfast, Maura worked on household chores, polishing furniture or scrubbing floors for a few hours. With more than seventy postulants and another hundred or more novices cleaning each day in a building they hadn't exactly made filthy the day before, the work struck some as absurd. But it was another way to keep them busy, a method for teaching obedience and sacrifice. The work and silence were also meant as fodder for meditation: simple work for the hands so that the mind and soul could concentrate on higher things.

By midmorning, Maura was on her way to classes. Half of the novices studied in the morning, the other half worked in the laundry or kitchen. They switched roles in the afternoon. Maura took classes on Scripture, theology, the history of religious life. Before she was through novitiate, she earned a degree at the Maryknoll Teachers College, an accredited school of education. Others studied nursing, leaving the grounds to study at secular or Catholic nursing schools. In addition to academic classes, the young women were assigned to read spiritual and mystical books, meant to nourish their relationship with God.[12]

Unlike in Maura's home where there were few expectations except hospitality and being generous, in the convent there was a regulation for everything. The motherhouse rule book adopted in 1946 has eighteen pages of dos and don'ts, many pertaining to minute cleaning details or Victorian levels of propriety.

> Do not remain at any window where you can be seen by visitors
>   or outsiders.
> Never stare at, nor turn to look after passing a stranger. To do
>   so borders on the vulgarly curious.

Do not gaze about in chapel, even to see if others are in their
place.
When escorting a guest to the dining rooms in St. Joseph's Hall,
make sure that the doors of our cloister are not open.
Sisters may not urge visitors to remain after they have signified
their intention to leave.

There were rules on how to wash stains out of a habit and rules
on which soap to use for which purpose.

Do not loll about or lean against walls. Do not stand with
hands or arms resting on chair backs.

There were instructions on how to clear one's throat or blow
one's nose without making noise.

Turn the pages of books from the upper right hand corner.
Never wet the fingers or push pages over with the thumb.[13]

There were 114 words on how to arrange a place setting and specifics on how to hold a vinegar cruet. Many of the rules were simply meant
to standardize activity, to ensure smooth operation of the institution.

One afternoon, the nun in charge of the new recruits took them
out to the forest on Maryknoll's campus. She spread a white sheet on
the ground and instructed the young women to sweep leaves onto it.
They believed, having run out of things to clean indoors, they were
being made to tidy the woods. In fact, they later learned they were
collecting leaves to make mulch for rhododendron, but given the rigidity and the busy work expected of them, the first impression was
conceivable.[14]

Many of the world's religions have a monastic form—a strain of
the faith dedicated to purification and communing with God in isolation from the material world. It's particularly robust in Hinduism and
Buddhism. In Christianity the monastic tradition developed a few
hundred years after the death of Christ, when men and women began
striking out into the Sinai desert to be alone in prayer and penance.

By the year 400, Saint Augustine established a code for Christian monastic life. Known as the Rule of Saint Augustine, it was the foundation for life in the convent Maura entered and in all convents and monasteries. It had five elements: life in community, prayer, fasting, vows, and works. Saint Augustine's document is a succinct few pages, a very basic guide for people living together in a community dedicated to prayer.

In the twelfth and thirteenth centuries there was an explosion of monastic life as convents and monasteries were built all over Europe and an elaborate religious life developed in these fortresses of prayer. In the 1,500 years between Saint Augustine and Maura's entering the Maryknoll novitiate, the Rule remained constant but other traditions and habits were embroidered around it, from the distinctive costume each religious order wore, to elaborate ceremonies of penance. The Rule and the endless regulations that grew up around it in the medieval period were meant to clear the novice's mind from worldly distractions, the frittering details of daily life that T. S. Eliot decried. From their founding until the nineteenth century, religious orders for women were like monasteries—places that existed solely for prayer. They were meant to sanctify—make holy—the church by virtue of being a place filled with prayer, where the divine was respected. Becoming a nun expressly meant denying the world, nearly exiting it, so as to commune with God. Some convents did some works, running an orphanage or hospital, for instance, but it was peripheral to, not the heart of, their purpose.

In the 1800s as the United States grew and its burgeoning Catholic immigrant population needed to be educated and cared for, American bishops appealed to European orders of nuns to come serve the new country. French, Italian, Belgian, Irish, and other orders of sisters came to the United States as missionaries. They flowed into the cities and followed the western expansion, building schools and hospitals, following Catholic Europe into a new land. In many ways, they are responsible for building the American church, establishing and then staffing the structures that had existed in Europe for a thousand years. Whereas traditionally sisters were divided into two classes, contemplative nuns who lived in near total separation from the world and active ones who exited the convent during the day to teach or nurse, in the new country where so much needed to be done, active orders of working sisters became the norm and their work teaching or caring for the sick became a more significant part of their life.[15]

From the time of the first Catholics in the colonies that became the United States—from the landing of Francisco López de Mendoza in Saint Augustine, Florida, in 1565 and the incursions of priests riding behind conquistadors in the American Southwest to the ships full of sisters arriving at Ellis Island to minister to the Catholic immigrants flooding new American cities—the Catholic Church in America was a mission, a satellite of the mother churches in Europe. In 1908, an act of the pope made the Church in the United States its own entity. Just as the nation in the first decade of the twentieth century was asserting global power through Theodore Roosevelt's expansion of the Monroe Doctrine, the newly independent American Church was beginning to turn outward and looked to spread its influence. Almost immediately it established its own missionary operations. The Catholic Foreign Mission Society, the body that eventually became the Maryknoll Fathers and Brothers and the Maryknoll Sisters, was founded in 1911. No longer the little brother of the European Church, the American Catholic Church would send its own missionaries to establish or reestablish Catholicism in more distant lands. Founder Fr. James Walsh and Mother Mary Joseph (Mary Josephine Rogers) recruited a small group of women dedicated to the idea of supporting the foreign missions. They would live in a community down the road from the men, maintain a simple lifestyle, practice celibacy, and assist in the publication of a magazine, A Field Afar—at the time the central project of the young organization. A key part of their "support" for the missions was cooking and cleaning for the male seminarians.

By 1920, the group of women was transformed into the Foreign Mission Sisters of St. Dominic, an official congregation of sisters. The first missionary, Sr. Gemma Shea, was sent to California to work with Japanese migrants almost immediately. By September 1921, six sisters were on their way to China. Their assignment was to work with women and girls, and they soon established orphanages for the many Chinese girls who were abandoned by families that valued sons over daughters. Until at least the 1950s, stories of nuns' caring for orphan Chinese girls were a centerpiece of American Catholics' conception of Maryknoll missionaries.[16]

To become a Maryknoll sister was a very particular thing. While entering a religious order was not an uncommon choice for a young Catholic woman in 1950, becoming a Maryknoller denoted a certain worldview. It meant acknowledging that all of humanity was related, that all people were children of God, and that it was worthwhile to go far away from home to connect with some of those distant brothers and sisters. In an era before the height of the civil rights movement, before the 1965 immigration reforms brought large numbers of Asians, Africans, and Latin Americans to the United States and well before any notion of globalization or a global family was commonly understood, Maryknollers preached and practiced a kinship with people who looked and lived very differently from those assimilating children of firemen and civil servants in the Rockaways.

When they came home for their once-a-decade visits and spoke in schools or parishes, Maryknoll sisters brought a piece of the wide world with them. They returned to the United States speaking Chinese and Japanese, brought Polynesian art into their chapels, told stories of the feast day celebrations in Chile and the Christmas *paradas* in Mexico. They were part of a big, wide world, not the close, familiar, and sometimes claustrophobic one bound by the bay and the ocean or the *Brooklyn Tablet* or even the United States. It would be anachronistic to say they advocated multiculturalism, and the very notion of a missionary, even one concerned with humanitarian issues, is rightly critiqued as imperialistic. Still, signing up with Maryknoll was a declaration that one shared concern with people of other races and religions.

To the young postulants and novices, Maryknoll sisters, like the Irish Columban fathers whose magazine Maura had pored over in high school, seemed daring and brave. They went to places you couldn't get to on the nascent commercial airlines, riding freighter ships and pickup trucks and writing letters home about tropical fruit and monsoons and bugs as big as your hand. While her classmates from Stella Maris who entered other religious orders could expect to be teachers fairly close to their childhood homes, by joining the Maryknollers Maura was signing up for life in an utterly foreign country. In an age before the Internet or even reliable telephone service, going away truly meant going away. It was a religious order for the adventurous.

What drove Maura toward the convent was not a desire for safety or rigidity, but a sense of purpose, a desire to do practical good in the world and to lead a life that was big, significant, meaningful. Maryknoll was known for its relative openness and forward-looking orientation, a good fit for Maura, who had always been allowed independence. Raised on the ocean and her mother's open door, she wasn't a girl who wanted to be locked away safe. The young women who entered the Maryknoll novitiate did so in part because they wanted to see the world, to find adventure, to know people not like themselves. Maryknoll was leery of taking in overly serious or meek young women. An April 1955 cover story in *Time* magazine reported that the order believed, "High spirited girls make the best sisters. The ones that enjoy parties and have dates." Elsewhere the article says, "The Maryknoll sisters know how to drive jeeps (and repair them), how to administer hypodermics and do major surgery, how to teach Christian doctrine."[17]

As much as their training conditioned sisters to fit in and serve the group, the order always appreciated space for the individual. It was founded very much as an American congregation, with the windows open to new ideas, a basic respect for practicality and a robust sensibility. This relatively modern orientation was a result of its missionary status—rules and regulations had to be practical and flexible enough to work even in communities where there were just two sisters in a house on stilts in a farming village in central China. It was also in large part the impact of the personality of the congregation's founder, Mary Josephine Rogers.[18]

While it is inaccurate to use the word *feminist* for early Maryknoll sisters, the fact that Mary Rogers was a graduate of Smith College, an institution on the forefront of women's empowerment, and that the early efforts of the Maryknoll Sisters were directed at serving abandoned girls can't be overlooked. Even in the very beginning there was a place for women and an acknowledgement of women's worth in the Maryknoll understanding of the world.[19]

At the same time, there is a danger in an anachronistic reading of Mother Mary Joseph. To be clear, she believed in salvation only through Christ, that souls of "pagans" needed to be saved, and that men were the natural leaders of the church. While she lectured plainly and convincingly on love and instructed novices to respect the customs of the people they would encounter, in all the lectures and retreats in the novitiate she was entering in September 1950, Maura heard not a word on justice, fairness, actual poverty, or the rights of human beings.[20]

In 1946, answering a plea from the Capuchin Franciscan friars, another Catholic order, Maryknoll sent a group of sisters to Siuna, Nicaragua, a mining town in the mountains. Sitting at a right angle to the long table in the basement dining room as two hundred other young women ate with minimum of silverware clinking, Maura listened as sisters read aloud from the reports of fellow Maryknollers in the field:

"Five sisters went by mule and horse on a mission trip to El Dorado, a little pueblo in our mission territory about a two-hour ride from Siuna," the sisters in Siuna wrote in January 1951. They wrote about Doña María, who walked two hours on an ulcerated foot to have her bandages changed at the sisters' clinic and who paid with flowers because she had no money. In March 1951, the sisters in Siuna wrote about a strike at the Canadian-controlled mine. Workers wanted their pay increased by thirty-five cents because the prices of food and clothes at the company-run store had increased. The workers were quickly ordered back to work by Nicaraguan president Anastasio Somóza García, who had a financial stake in the mine and in all other economic activity in the country. The mine owners were ordered to pay twenty cents more, but it meant nothing: they simultaneously raised the price of rice and beans in the company story by 100 percent. The sisters wrote about visits to families where the children had no clothes and of a man who came to the convent asking for clothes for his wife who wore only rags.

Subsequent diaries spoke about a malaria-eradication campaign and related the ongoing relationship between the sisters and Adela, a local woman dying of tuberculosis. "She was so weak she can only sip a few mouthfuls of milk through a small piece of bamboo in a bottle," Maura heard as she sat at lunch. Adela told the sisters that they were the only people who visited her. "No one else in the village would visit or care for her because they so feared tuberculosis." The sisters visited daily, bringing food and flowers. They bathed her in water kept warm in a thermos bottle.[21]

As she went about her afternoon classes or work, Maura's head was filled with these stories of life in Nicaraguan or Chinese or South Pacific villages. Thinking that she would soon be in the jungle, comforting people with tuberculosis, teaching children how to read, changing bandages, and bringing the sacraments to families who hadn't been to Mass in years, allowed her to survive the regimentation and rigidity of the motherhouse.[22]

For Maura, there was still much to enjoy at the convent. She loved the rolling hills and the woods of its grounds, writing to her mother that she felt lucky to be in such a beautiful place. The grass in the courtyard was so vividly green it reminded her of Ireland. At night she fell asleep to the sound of crickets, the tiny symphony transporting her back to Baker Camp where she'd spent summer weeks exploring caves with a boyfriend and slept in a cabin with her family. On afternoons at Maryknoll she and friends went for walks under the trees. They always had to be in groups of three or more. There was a prohibition against forming close friendships with an individual girl—a guard against lesbianism. In the woods they could let their voices out, shout or call loudly. Sometimes they sang, as much for the joy of making noise as for the music. They climbed trees, picked apples at a nearby farm and cleared a field behind the motherhouse to play baseball. In the winter they walked to Echo Lake, nearly 2 miles away, to shovel off the snow and ice skate.[23]

And as with kids at camp or their brothers in the army, there was an esprit de corps. While they peeled potatoes or dug up a garden, the girls would sing, to the tune of "Home on the Range":

Oh give me a spot
and a neat little cot
With a chair and a bed as my home
Where never is heard an uncharitable word
'cause silence reigns all alone[24]

Maura wrote every week to her family, the maximum allowance, asking about news from Rockaway, cheering her little sister as she finished high school, thanking her mother for encouragement. For her first Mother's Day in the convent, Maura sent Mary Clarke a small book she'd made from folded paper. In it, she recounted her mother's sacrifices and love, mentioned her blue eyes and horn-rimmed glasses. Maura illustrated the homemade card with tiny watercolors she'd painted in her free time: a mother bird feeding three chicks, the ship on which Mary had sailed to America, a loaf of Irish brown bread. Similar letters decorated with simple watercolors would become a hallmark across the years. Phone calls were prohibited and beyond the letters to family, she was permitted to write just three letters a month. But her parents and siblings visited as often as the convent permitted; they missed her painfully. One Sunday a month, they drove up to Ossining to walk on the campus with this new young woman, now wearing a white veil and signing her letters Sr. Maura John.[25]

As evening fell, the sisters filed into the chapel to sing vespers, the restful, meditative prayers that greet the end of the day. After supper (in silence) they had "recreation," an hour or two in which they could sit in a parlor and chat quietly. They weren't to speak of their life before they entered the convent; they were to ward against gossip and to discipline themselves about complaining. They weren't to talk about the young women who disappeared, leaving the convent without explanation or good-bye. Maura waited with expectation for these hours, hungry for a chance to ask about her friends' ideas, eager to connect.[26]

She wanted to be friends. Maura rushed to do favors for other sisters, sometimes promising more than she could deliver. She signed up for any extra work and then sometimes had to beg favors to get the work done when she realized she was overcommitted. She volunteered

for overnight hours of silent prayer before the Eucharist in chapel—
the same devotion her father was a part of at home. In the deep quiet
of the sleeping convent, she slipped into the high-ceilinged chapel
where rows of pews face each other, relieving the sister who had the
previous shift. She settled herself before the tabernacle and dropped
her tired head to her folded hands, whispering the prayers. God was
in that tabernacle, in the form of the transubstantiated bread. It was
her duty to keep him company through the darkness.

On Wednesday, May 7, 1953, Maura walked into the chapel with all
the young women who had survived novitiate training. Several had
left in the past year and a half, packing up quickly while others were
in class, asked to leave by the novice mistress or deciding themselves
that they weren't meant to be nuns. Their names were not spoken,
there were no good-byes. But now on a warm spring day, Maura was
about to take first vows, to become a Maryknoll sister. Professed sisters in their black veils and the veteran nuns home from the wide
world in their gray wool habits rose above the young novices in tiered,
center-facing, wooden pews, watching as Maura's group advanced to
the altar in a solemn processional.

Maura and the others lay prostrate, their forehead pressing
against the chapel's stone floor. The priest on the altar asked the
women what they sought.

"I ask God's mercy and yours," Maura said in unison with the
others who were becoming her sisters.

"Do you wish to make profession and to observe the constitution of this congregation of the Maryknoll Sisters of Saint Dominic?"

"Yes, your excellency, this I wish and desire by the grace of God,"
Maura answered.

She raised herself from the floor and walked carefully toward the
priest, who now sat on a small stool on the top step of the altar. She
kneeled on a lower step and extended her left hand, the one that ran
to her heart.

"I, Sister Maura John, do hereby vow poverty, chastity, and obedience for one year to God, to the Blessed Virgin Mary, to our Holy

Father Saint Dominic in presence of you, in the hands of the Mother General of the Congregation of the Maryknoll Sisters of Saint Dominic, according to the Rule of Saint Augustine and the constitutions of this congregation."

The priest slipped a ring on her long fourth finger.

"Receive the ring of fidelity to God, given in the name of the most holy trinity, that wearing it you may be armed with the strength of heavenly protection."[27]

CHAPTER 3

The Bronx Is Mission Territory

Maura's first assignment as a missionary was called out as she sat in the dining hall one evening in the winter of 1953. Maryknoll sisters were now serving in British East Africa, Mauritius, the Caroline and Marshall Islands, the Philipines, Formosa, Hong Kong, Ceylon, Bo-livia, Chile, Peru, Panama, Nicaragua, Guatemala, and Mexico. She, however, would be going to the Bronx. It felt a little like being called to the junior varsity team. But as she would quickly learn, there was plenty to do.[1]

The neighborhood Maura arrived in was dense with six-story apartment buildings, laundry drying on fire escapes, music blaring from radios, dominoes played in the park, police sirens wailing, and fights on the sidewalks. St. Anthony of Padua, the parish where Maryknoll sisters taught school, was located in Morrisania, one of the poorest neighborhoods of the Bronx and getting poorer. The federal government had labeled the area a bad bet for investment, noting the high percentage of families on government relief and the mere presence of African Americans and Puerto Ricans. Morrisania was a classic redlined neighborhood. Many families were without fathers. Heroin was a major fact of life. Joblessness was common, families showed the effects of social dislocation, and kids were tough. To Maura and other sisters arriving from the order and regimentation of the novitiate, the neighborhood looked chaotic. This wasn't like Rockaway where everyone knew her name.[2]

A broad, three-story yellow brick building, St. Anthony of Padua Catholic Church rose from sidewalk, close upon the street at the corner of 166th Street and Union Avenue in the Morrisania section of the Bronx. Founded in 1903 by German immigrants, it lay just a mile and a half from the parish where Maura was baptized and about the same distance from the neighborhood where her parents lived when she was born. Maura was now one of eleven Maryknoll sisters assigned to staff St. Anthony of Padua elementary school, manage the after-school religious instruction of huge numbers of public school children in the neighborhood, help in the sacristy, and be part of a robust parish that was recruiting and converting waves of adults.[3]

When Maura arrived in January 1954, Maryknoll sisters had been running the parish school for nearly ten years. They lived in a broken-down convent building that would be condemned by the New York City Department of Buildings a few years later, on the same block as the school. It was part of a parish plant of church-school-convent connected by paved playground that was replicated every half mile or so across Brooklyn, Queens, and the Bronx. The sisters lived a semi-cloistered life largely contained to the three buildings of the complex, their routine dominated by the prayers of the Divine Office, morning Mass before school, and evening compline. The women lived separately from the neighborhood, keeping the traditional convent routines and experiencing the sounds of the street as very much outside. They weren't part of the community and did little to try to understand it.[4]

St. Anthony of Padua was different from the parishes Maura knew from Rockaway. While 75 percent of the people who lived within the parish boundaries of the St. Camillus of her childhood were Catholic and the vast majority of those were active in the parish, Morrisania was just barely Catholic in 1954. During the Depression and World War II, African Americans, overcrowded in Harlem, fleeing the terrorism of the rural South or those who, after experiencing comparative freedom in the military in World War II, refused to return to Jim Crow, moved into the neighborhood. As they arrived the remaining Germans and Italians moved out. It was the beginning of white flight that would remake the city. In 1944, the previous religious order had pulled out of St. Anthony of Padua. It no longer recognized the neighborhood.[5]

Cardinal Spellman had recruited Maryknollers to take over the parish school. Their training for mission meant they would be able to serve in a neighborhood that appeared foreign to other orders of sisters. The thinking went that Maryknoll sisters, veterans of China and Japan, could manage in the Bronx. As she would again and again in her life, Maura found herself serving in a place filled with displaced people, where the communal ties that had made her Rockaway childhood so pleasant, even though it was poor, were frayed. During the course of her six years in the Bronx, the parish would see an influx of Puerto Ricans after a failed revolution and economic displacement drove tens of thousands off their island. Discriminated against in most New York City neighborhoods, they found their way to the Bronx.[6]

Life was difficult for African Americans and Puerto Ricans alike. A teenager was shot by police in front of the church. The father of several students had become a heroin addict. He was shot in the head and his assailants attempted to throw his body off the roof of a building. When Maura's brother, Buddy, and his wife came to say hello on their way out of town for their honeymoon—Maryknoll rules prevented Maura from attending the celebration—their wedding gifts were all stolen from their car. Someone broke into the church and stole the relic of St. Anthony, a tiny fragment of bone stored in a solid gold reliquary. The sisters wryly added a prayer to their litany, asking the saint popularly venerated for finding lost items to find his own relic. One morning, students were late for choir practice because two people had overdosed and were sprawled on the church steps, blocking their entrance. The violence of the neighborhood wounded Maura. She suffered to see the poverty and suffering around her. She was aghast to witness the fatal plummet of a woman who'd been clinging to a window ledge as her husband beat her fingers. When one of her second graders told her he couldn't accept the idea of God as father because he didn't want God to be anything like his brutal father, Maura, was distraught, talking about that admission for days.[7]

But as in any poor neighborhood, the majority of people were simply trying to get by, navigating a society that didn't want to rent them an apartment or hire them for a job and yet making progress: raising their children, finding ways to send them to high school and college, establishing hiring systems in civil service, saving for a house in Queens.[8]

The sisters understood that their purpose in being at St. Anthony's was to give the children a strong education and the habits of discipline they hoped would lift them out of poverty. The goal was to arm the students with enough skills that they would be able to make some headway in a world that was racist and hostile to them. Maura taught second grade at St. Anthony's, and she threw herself into the work. It would take some time before she learned to do it well, though. At first, she struggled to maintain control of her fifty students, who would stand on their desks, shouting. She was loath to raise her voice, so as the year progressed she developed a habit of standing solemnly at the front of the room when the class got out of hand. She would very slowly raise her hand to her forehead and bless herself. The children would follow along and order was restored. Other times Maura would wait for Sr. Richard Marie, the music teacher, to arrive. She'd rush to the door breathless and thank her colleague for coming. When she came back after a break, the children were singing and orderly and Maura would say, "Now I can go on all right."[9]

Maura's schedule at St. Anthony's was nearly as demanding as it had been at the convent. Sisters rose at 6:00 a.m. for morning prayers and Mass before breakfast, then taught from 8:50 until 12:40. At lunch they supervised close to 250 children who stayed for lunch (others walked home). In the afternoon Maura and other sisters collected hundreds of public school children from their schools in the neighborhood for afternoon religion classes that ran until 4:30 p.m. Afterward came evening group prayers with the sisters who lived at St. Anthony of Padua, dinner, then laundry, night prayers and rosary with the group of sisters in the chapel. By 8:00 p.m., Maura began correcting homework and planning her lessons, unless it was Tuesday, in which case she was on her way to the rite of Benediction and Adoration in the church, the same ritual that had greeted the end of World War II in Rockaway. Other nights, there were meetings at school or parish events. School holidays and weekends were filled with conferences on new teaching methods at nearby Cardinal Hayes High School. Additionally, Maura visited neighboring schools, public and Catholic, for ideas.[10]

She spent long hours at night preparing for class, applying the techniques she'd learned in teacher training college, carefully writing out lesson plans and correcting homework. She worried the children were not learning as well as they should. She feared she was letting them and her superiors down. As she would do throughout her life, she gave teaching everything she had but feared constantly that it wasn't good enough. That she didn't measure up. When a sister who had taught elsewhere insisted the young teachers learn a new phonics method, Maura buckled down in nightly study sessions and struggled to master the new system. The two other young sisters assigned to learn the technique rolled their eyes. They had their way of teaching and didn't want to jump through hoops for a new fad, but Maura wanted to get things right, even if it meant working all night.[11]

But more than the other sisters she enjoyed the children, really played with them in the schoolyard, listened to their stories. She laughed easily with them, patiently helped them on with their boots and mittens. She painted the scenery for the school play, impressing her superior with her quiet generosity. When children came to school hungry because there was no food in their apartment, she discreetly brought them into the school kitchen and quickly make an egg or some other simple breakfast. They were children she cared about, not just students to be formed. Christmas her first year in the Bronx she took her class to Rockefeller Center to see the massive Christmas tree and the lights of the city. Many of her students had never been out of the Bronx and she wanted them to feel that the city belonged to them. The other sisters warned her it was too much, that she would need half a dozen parent volunteers to come along, that she might lose a child on the subway or in the crowds. But Maura moved in great waves of trust. She didn't want to lean on the parents and she had faith that the trip would be fine. With fifty children she boarded the subway, the seven-year-olds ducking under the turnstile while Maura fished in her pockets for the fare. They all made it down and back without incident.[12]

Because they were in New York, Maryknoll sisters arriving from around the world frequently stopped in on their way to the mother-house, or sisters taking classes at nearby Fordham University stayed with the sisters at St. Anthony's.[13]

The nuns and the parish priests believed a strong enough parish and faithful parishioners living within the church strictures would overcome the hardships of the neighborhood. St. Anthony's tried to build a strong parish life, a thriving Catholic village like the one Maura had been raised in at St. Camillus and St. Francis. She worked closely with mothers in the Parent Teacher Association (PTA), hundreds of whom came to PTA meetings. She had a knack for connecting with parents in the parish. She spoke quietly, but with ease, about the meaning of First Communion when she told the parents of her second graders their children would now be participating in the central rite of Catholicism, taking in God's body.[14]

In her first years, Maura and the other sisters spent Thursday afternoons visiting families in their homes, checking up on students who'd been absent, or families not at Sunday Mass—but also simply attempting to forge a relationship. The apartments were crowded, two or three rooms for families with five or six children. The TV was always on and Maura began to understand why it was difficult for her students to complete homework. At one home, the entire family gathered to greet Maura and another sister. An older girl sat at the piano and played a song for the visiting nuns. Then Maura's student did the same, using just his right hand. Finally a little brother in first grade picked out a tune with one finger. The three children sang while their father, who was teaching himself and his children, played. It was a little like her own home, the father putting on a show for guests—or like the Clarke home in Sligo, where everyone was expected to share a tune with visitors.[15]

The parish and school were a haven of activity. There was a parish credit union. A Fathers' Planning Committee was formed to run activities for boys. There was a youth social group for teenagers. Maura started a Sodality of the Virgin Mary, a service club for junior high school girls, like the one she had been part of as a teenager. A girls' choir that regularly swept city and national competitions gave birth to the famed doo-wop group the Chantels. The group sang after every basketball game, complex multipart harmonies they'd perfected studying, Gregorian chant bouncing off the gym walls and wooden bleachers. The girls' basketball team regularly dominated city-wide championships, and the sisters joked that the school would need a new trophy case to hold all their awards. In her first year at St. Anthony's, Maura brought a few of the girls to Brooklyn to learn to be referees. She'd played basketball as a girl at St. Francis de Sales and knew how good it felt to run, to be part of a team. In the fall of 1954, Maura was with the St. Anthony's girls' team when it went to an exposition match in Manhattan that was covered by NBC. But the victories were hard won. The girls were terrified to play against white teams and the Maryknoll sisters lined up at the entrance to hostile white parish gyms, forming a barrier against screaming racist parents.[16]

Maura found a kindred spirit in Gerald Ryan, a young assistant priest at St. Anthony's and another first-generation Irish American. He had the ascetic, gentlemanly look of Maura's father and the refined, slightly formal bearing of her mother. In the years he overlapped there with Maura, he tried to build a community, a place where the people of the parish could find succor from the hostile society. He'd been assigned to St. Anthony's pending a teaching job at Cardinal Hayes High School. The appointment never came. Instead he became among the first priests in the archdiocese of New York to learn Spanish, spending his vacation weeks in Mexico and Puerto Rico. He was an early advocate for the Puerto Rican migrants who were remaking the parish and the borough, and was focused on adult religious education. He was also a member of the NAACP, a rarity for a white man in 1954. A decade later he would take students to the march from Selma to Montgomery in support of the Voting Rights Act. He and Maura got along easily.[17]

Fr. Ryan and all the sisters at St. Anthony's loved the frequent visits of Maura's family. Arriving on Sunday afternoons with freshly baked Irish soda bread and a dinner of roast chicken for all the nuns, they quickly became like adopted parents to the group. Often her brother or a family friend would arrive with a car and bring Maura and several sisters out to Rockaway for the weekend, to stroll on the boardwalk and taste the salt air. Maura was friendly with the other nuns, at home with people right away and easy to talk to. She would lose herself in a joke, cracking up and forgetting the punchline more often than not. The group generally got along and Maura's instinct was always to seek resolution to potential conflicts. "I'm sure she didn't mean it," she would say if anyone's feelings were hurt. At St. Anthony's as in the novitiate, the sisters felt that they were working together in a big project. They joked about students' erroneous answers as they corrected papers together in the parlor, but apart from shared experiences at school, they didn't really know each other well. The self-denying practices of convent life were still in effect, so the women were discouraged from speaking about themselves and focused instead on being their best, on forming their lives to God.[18]

Maura interpreted this as doing everything for everyone who needed help, even when she should have been taking care of her own responsibilities. She committed herself to more projects and favors than she could fit in a day, and would then realize that she had conflicting obligations: basketball practice, First Communion rehearsal, and teen youth group. At a prescribed time each week, the sisters sat in their parlor, detaching the starched white cuffs from their voluminous wool habits and pulling the white frame from their peaked veil, carefully replacing them with freshly laundered ones. The cuffs, yellowed with sweat and soot, were supposed to be washed once a week. The fabric tape that collected dust and grime along the wide hem of the bell-like gowns had to be replaced each week as well. Maura frequently spent the time helping older sisters whose stiff hands struggled with the dexterous tasks, leaving no time to do her own. The tape at the bottom of her robe was frequently dragging and her veil was often askew. The difference in Maura's appearance was so evident that the woman who came in to take the sisters' laundry admonished them for mistreating her. "Why doesn't she get proper clothes like the rest of you?" the laundress asked.[19]

Sometimes Maura's self-forgetfulness frustrated her housemates. One day in the schoolyard as she breathlessly described some crisis of overcommitting she'd gotten into, the other sister looked at her— exasperated—and urged Maura to use her head. When she knelt long in the chapel, her head bowed and hands folded other young nuns teased her—"God can hear you just as well when you sit, Maura."

But in her years at St. Anthony's she started to emerge from the shunting self-abnegation of the novitiate and allowed herself to bloom. She took an art class at Fordham, then wrote to the rest of the sisters in the convent inviting them *not* to visit the end of semester art exhibit. But she was a good sport (and maybe even proud) when her work was displayed in the shared living room. She became a stronger teacher and made costumes for school plays, convincing a fabric shop on Union Avenue to donate their remnants.[20]

In March 1959, Maura returned to the chapel at the Maryknoll motherhouse to make her final vows of poverty, chastity, and obedience, pledging herself to a life of mission. She finished the school year as a senior member of the St. Anthony convent. In the fall she would receive her assignment: another poor parish in need of care, this time in the jungle of Nicaragua.[21]

CHAPTER 4

Siuna: Away in the Jungle

Maura packed hurriedly for her new life as a foreign missionary. She'd known since the end of the summer that she would be going to Siuna, Nicaragua, and had been reassigned to the motherhouse in Ossining to prepare. But now, suddenly, the day of departure was fast arriving. On Tuesday, October 6, she learned that she and another sister would leave that Friday. On the morning of the ninth, Maura rode to Idlewild Airport, a few miles from the neighborhood she grew up in. Her parents were at the airport to say good-bye. While they waited for the flight, an airline captain approached them. He, too, had a daughter in Maryknoll and recognized the gray wool habits. He thanked John and Mary Clarke for giving their daughter to Maryknoll.[1]

Maura cried and hugged her parents. She was always more demonstrative than the rest of her family. Somehow she hadn't inherited the stoic Irish aversion to emotional displays. As she said good-bye, she knew she wouldn't see her parents for five years. Many of her Maryknoll sisters had been far from their family since the day they walked through the convent doors in Ossining, but the Clarkes, just a little over an hour away in Rockaway, had visited at every opportunity. Now, nine years after she first entered Maryknoll, she was actually leaving home.[2]

Travel policy had liberalized dramatically in the few years since Maura had taken her vows. When the first Maryknoll sisters went to China in 1921, they'd set out for life. They bid farewell to their parents the way many of those parents had said good-bye to their own homeland: with hope and excitement for a new life colored by the finality of death. They would not return again. In Ireland in the early years of mass immigration a tradition developed called the immigrant's wake. On the night before daughters or sons sailed for America, the village would gather to celebrate them with bonfires and stories and dancing—an approximation of the wake they wouldn't have when they died in a strange land. The Atlantic Ocean might as well have been the River Styx. Similarly, the girls who told their mother they wanted to be Maryknoll sisters were saying good-bye forever. But in 1952, with the advent of increasingly accessible commercial air travel and an emerging appreciation of the need for professional and theological updating, the rules at Maryknoll changed: sisters would return to the motherhouse—and could make a stop to see their families elsewhere in the United States—every ten years. Those at certain missions deemed hardship assignments would be given time home every five years. Because of its remoteness, Siuna was one of these. Maura would be back in 1964—after 260 Sunday afternoons.[3]

That day, Maura wasn't thinking of 1964. She was excited to finally be beginning the work she signed up for: overseas missions. This is what she'd dreamed about when she wrote to Mother Columba as a nineteen-year-old, saying she first wanted to be a Maryknoll sister because of the books she'd read about missionaries' bringing God to people who were without him. This was the life she talked to her cousin James about when they were teenagers, her eyes growing wide at stories of the daring missionaries. She would not be going alone. Maura had met her traveling companion, Kay Kelly, just once before, at the Maryknollers' beach house in Watch Hill, Rhode Island, a few weeks earlier. They hit it off, forging a deep connection almost immediately. Maura and Kay would spend much of the next fifteen years together and be each other's closest friend.[4]

From New York they flew to Miami and stayed overnight. At six a.m., when they would ordinarily be saying morning prayers, they departed for Managua on a six-passenger flight with the mother-in-law of General Anastasio Somoza Debayle, the head of Nicaragua's national guard and the real power in the country. The shared trip was coincidental, though Maryknoll sisters in Nicaragua at the time had a cordial relationship with the Somoza family. As she sat on the plane terrified of flying, Maura distracted herself by focusing on Kay. The two sisters stumbled through the Hail Mary and Our Father, using the little Spanish they knew.[5]

Maura knew almost nothing about the country she was going to. In fact, Nicaragua had played a vital role in US business and foreign policy for more than a century. Both the US and the Nicaraguan government enjoyed having the Maryknoll Mission in the country. For the Americans, the Maryknoll Sisters acted as goodwill ambassadors of American largesse. For the Nicaraguan elite, the sisters provided services the government was too corrupt or callous to provide. Since the establishment of the Monroe Doctrine at the time of Central American independence from Spain in the 1820s, the United States claimed the prerogative of intervention anywhere in the Western Hemisphere. The notion of the United States as Big Brother with the right or duty to intervene in hemispheric affairs was robustly enhanced under President Theodore Roosevelt.[6]

As early as the mid-nineteenth century, the political fortunes of Nicaragua were of special concern to the United States. Its northern neighbor eyed the country as a profitable place to build a cross-isthmus canal that would revolutionize hemispheric trade and make American merchants rich. A massive inland lake on Nicaragua's western edge meant there would be fewer miles to dig than elsewhere. In 1849, with the support of the US chargés d'affaires, railroad magnate Cornelius Vanderbilt negotiated a contract with the Nicaraguan government, gaining exclusive access to the land and water route for twelve years. The idea was to build a canal, but in the meantime Vanderbilt would make money transporting across Nicaragua goods and forty-niners desperate to join the gold rush in California. The British, who retained colonies in the Caribbean and up the Atlantic coast tried to disrupt Vanderbilt's Accessory Transit Company. The United States intervened. Eager to preserve the chance of digging a canal, but unable to finance such a project yet and hoping to avoid continual conflict, the United States and Britain signed a noncompetition treaty in 1850. They didn't consult the Nicaraguan government. Four years later, when officials in the city at the eastern edge of Vanderbilt's route sought to oust company officials, the

US Navy bombarded the city. In 1855, William Walker, a US citizen who had previously attempted to establish a personal colony in Mexico, invaded Nicaragua with a band of mercenaries, allied himself with one of the two dueling elite political parties, and took over the country. He installed himself as president, reinstituted slavery, and declared English the official language after attempting to wrest the cross-isthmus trade route from Vanderbilt. He suggested adding Nicaragua to the United States as a slave state. President Franklin Pierce recognized his government as legitimate and Walker enjoyed near mythic status in southern states.[7]

There had been US military interventions in the early twentieth century, invasions intended to protect US agricultural, logging, and mining operations, or to ensure the election of governments that would do so. US Marines occupied the country three times between 1909 and 1934. During the last occupation, Augusto César Sandino led a nationalist rebellion, gathering bands of dispossessed rural people to oust the marines and achieve Nicaraguan control of Nicaraguan gold and copper. He failed, but poor Nicaraguans still whispered his name. Sandino riled the United States enough that the US Marines established the National Guard in Nicaragua, an internal army trained to fight Sandino and designed to protect American commercial interests.[8]

Anastasio Somoza García, who had attended college in Philadelphia, became head of the National Guard. He ordered Sandino's assassination while the guerrilla was in negotiations with the American-backed regime in Managua, and became president two years later. As head of the National Guard, Somoza used soldiers to stamp out the flickering embers of Sandino's rebellion and instituted a regime in which dissidents were regularly imprisoned and tortured in dark warrens of cells winding beneath the presidential palace at the highest point in Managua. For the next twenty years he ran Nicaragua more as a business enterprise than a nation. He confiscated land and sold it to himself at deflated prices. He owned textile companies, sugar mills, and rum distilleries and set high tariffs against competitors. As an individual and not as head of state, he controlled the old cross-isthmus transport route that had caused so much trouble in the

1850s. He owned the railroad that ran across it and collected the fees for crossing it. He owned La Salud dairy—the country's only pasteurized milk facility, getting richer every time a Nicaraguan bought milk. Franklin Delano Roosevelt said of him, "Somoza may be a son of a bitch, but he's our son of a bitch."* Roosevelt believed he could control Somoza and his sons after him and use them to advance the US agenda of anticommunism.[9]

When he was assassinated in 1956, his son Luis Somoza Debayle took over. Luis and his brother Anastasio Somoza Debayle would rule the country, whether in office or through puppet governments, for the next twenty-three years. Educated like their father in the United States, the Somozas enjoyed easy and warm relationships with US diplomats and military. In fact, this Anastasio, head of the national guard and son-in-law of the woman sitting on the plane with Maura, was a graduate of the US Military Academy at West Point. It would be difficult to imagine a regime with closer ties to the United States.[10]

Maura knew none of this, only that the people she was going to serve were desperately poor, died of preventable diseases, and were barely educated in the Catholic faith their ancestors had professed for over four hundred years. In that era, missionaries received only the most cursory briefing on the places to which they were being sent. From her Catholic Students' Mission Crusade and Maryknoll training, Maura viewed the Nicaraguan people as part of the family of God, her brothers and sisters. Her assignment was simple: teach school and spread the Gospel.[11]

As the plane doors opened on the runway in the Nicaraguan capital of Managua, she felt a blast of heat, utterly different from the crisp New York autumn she'd left behind. She was relieved to see, in the crowd of people speaking a language she didn't know, a familiar gray habit: Sr. Margaret Therese, the mother superior of the Siuna mission, who had flown in the day before to collect the new recruits.[12]

Maura was amazed by Managua, a sophisticated city with a grand opera house, office buildings, colonial-style government buildings, and a soaring cathedral. As a young novice sitting in the dining

---

* Scholars of US Nicaraguan history believe this quote is probably apocryphal.

hall listening to the mission reports from Nicaragua read aloud, Maura had pictured arriving in a jungle. During the drive through the city to temporary accommodations she looked out the car windows at beggars; children with drawn, hungry faces; and women carrying trays piled high with tropical fruit on their head.[13]

Sr. Margaret Therese took Maura and Kay to the convent of the Assumption Sisters, an order of Nicaraguan nuns who ran an exclusive girls' school in Managua. The graceful, formal Assumption Sisters, drawn from the light-skinned, land-owning aristocracy, and the roll-up-your-sleeves, blue-collar Maryknollers were a funny mismatch. But the two groups were close. The Assumptionists had greeted the Maryknollers when they first arrived in the country in 1944, escorting the first sisters to Siuna and playing host to later Maryknollers whenever they were in Managua for doctors' appointments, yearly shopping trips, or on their way home to the United States. As Sr. Margaret Therese spoke in Spanish to the Assumptionists, Maura listened carefully to the conversation, trying to pick out a familiar word now and then. It was a bewildering experience that made her feel like an infant. But she was keenly open, trying to absorb everything. She stretched to bridge the language gap, smiling with interest, focusing on the faces of people near her, nodding, her lean frame tilted toward them, laughing when she fumbled a word. The Nicaraguan sisters fell in love with this eager, intensely available American.[14]

Maura, Kay, and Sr. Margaret Therese did not stay long; after a few days, they boarded another plane to finish their journey to Siuna. The C-46, a two-engine plane operated by LANICA (Líneas Aéreas de Nicaragua), the national airline, was controlled—like every money-making enterprise in the country—by the Somoza dictatorship. The LANICA planes had flown in World War II and were gifts from the United States government to its ally. Maura and Kay climbed into the plane, and following Sr. Margaret Therese's instructions, settled themselves into scooped-out indentations of seats, their back to the airplane's outer wall. It was like a rounded subway car: two rows of seats ran down the sides of the plane, passengers facing each other over a center aisle. Maura's heavy wool habit felt oppressive in the stuffy cabin. She was terrified of flying. But Siuna was reachable only by plane or arduous mule ride through the Amerrisque mountains that run down the center of Nicaragua like a spine, separating Managua and the populous cities of the western coast from the rugged and sparsely settled Atlantic region. There was no road into town, only a landing strip a few blocks long, a slice out of the dense, green foliage.

Siuna is often called jungle. The term isn't exactly accurate. It isn't rainforest. But it is thick, lush, mountainous forest, filled with palm trees, coconut and cacao, parrots and snakes. Peeking out the window, Maura was enthralled by the deep green below. The flight from Managua was only forty-five minutes. She listened intently as the plane approached Siuna and Sr. Margaret Therese shouted over the drone of the engines to point out the little town as it emerged from the wilderness: the tiny wooden houses tumbling down the hillsides, the church, the school, the single dirt road from the airport. Sr. Margaret Therese also pointed to the wreckage of a plane that had crashed into the mountain on takeoff. They landed without a problem.

Maura stepped out of the plane onto a staircase and into the punishing light. The sun felt like an assault and its clarity made one squint. She was sweating. The runway was lined with what looked like the entire population of Siuna. Children, barefoot and ragged, jumped up and down to see the new sisters. Students in blue and gold uniforms, their brass buttons glinting in the sun, played John Philip Sousa songs on fife and drums—Sr. Miriam Aloysius, who Maura had known from the Bronx, now ran an ambitious marching band at the Siuna school. The rest of the Maryknollers in Siuna, the women who would become Maura's friends and closest companions for as long as she lived in this outpost, stood together as a unit in gray wool and starched white collars and cuffs. Maura was struck by how jaundiced the sisters looked. In contrast with the people of Siuna, who were shades of warm brown from mahogany to coffee, the Americans—of Irish, French, and Polish heritage—appeared sickly. Led by the marching band, the throng of nuns, children, and adults walked along a muddy dirt road from the airport to the convent. Maura, Kay, Sr. Margaret Therese, and a few other sisters rode in the back of a pickup truck. On either side of the road Maura saw mud-floor shacks, their walls constructed out of discarded shipping crates. Chickens and gray pigs ran across her path and boys lined up at the town's single water spigot to wash their mules. There were two other roads (also unpaved) with rows of houses on either side. The rest of the settlement consisted of scattered houses on tiny plots at shifting elevations, connected just by footpaths. Few homes had any furniture. The kitchens were stone fireplaces outside. As Maura passed a woman clutching an anemic baby, flies circling its head, one of the other nuns explained that the sisters would provide a First Communion dress for one of the daughters of this family. Maura was alarmed by the poverty, but quickly tried to recast it so it seemed less terrible. The woman with the weak child possessed "a lovely serenity," she thought. At first she wondered how these poor people could stay in such rough conditions, but she told herself that they knew nothing else and were probably very happy. It was a common instinct, particularly among religious people, to make reality less horrible by attributing noble qualities to people in wretched situations. The Catholic Church taught that God rewarded forbearance; that the poor would be rewarded in heaven.[15]

When the pickup truck rattled to a stop in front of El Señor de Esquipulas church, Maura saw her new home: a convent, chapel, and school complex built around an open courtyard up to the left of the church. Eventually she would have a narrow room to herself, big enough just for a single bed and a desk. For now she shared with another sister. Her mornings here, as in the convent and in the Bronx, would begin early, with morning prayer at six a.m., Mass before breakfast, and then school. She would wake under a mosquito net to the cacophony of the forest: toucans and parrots, roosters in nearby yards, humming and chirping insects, and chilly morning air that didn't warm until the sun made it over the mountains. Her room was in a row stacked along the short side of a squarish U. Along one long side were a porch—with eight wooden rocking chairs, a staple of Nicaraguan repose—the parlor, the chapel, the dining room where the sisters ate their meals together in silence, a bathroom, and a kitchen. On the other leg of the U, separated by an open courtyard, were the classrooms, large spaces with solid wooden desks built by men in the village and blackboards from the United States outfitted with pull-down maps just like in the Bronx. Additional classrooms were a few yards away, down a hill from the original building.[16]

As she climbed out of the truck Maura passed a grotto dedicated to Saint Francis and the rectory where the priests of Siuna lived, Capuchin Franciscan friars from Wisconsin and Michigan.*

The priests were tall, laconic midwesterners with heavy Nordic names and gray robes. A few served in Siuna, but others spent their lives on horseback or on a river raft in an unending cycle of visits to remote clusters of families, bringing God with them, they believed, in sacraments and the Eucharist.[17]

The division of labor in the mission was strict: priests administered sacraments and preached; nuns worked with children or the sick. There were no newspapers in Siuna, no radio in the convent, no newsreels at Saturday movies, no interaction with Managua. When the biweekly plane roared down the runway and clamored unsteadily up over the green mountains, the little settlement was cut off.[18]

Maura wrote to her parents as soon as she could, describing the trip, the town, the convent. She asked her parents to send clothes for the people of Siuna who had so little, and cookies and chocolate for the sisters. She asked her sister, Judy, to make a list of birthdays and anniversaries of friends and family to send to her so she wouldn't forget. Maura kept a continuous correspondence with many friends, but her birthday and anniversary cards were usually late. She was delighted and relieved when letters arrived from her parents, full of news about Rockaway and about Mary Clarke and Judy heading off to work in the mornings together. It all seemed very far away.

On one of her first nights in Siuna, a powerful storm descended on the town, knocking out the electricity and flooding the convent.

---

* The Capuchin Franciscans had been on the Atlantic Coast only since 1938. Before that the Catholic mission was run by the older Spanish branch of the Capuchins, but decimated and nearly bankrupted at home by the Spanish Civil War, they passed the mission to their American counterparts. They had arrived in 1913 after being expelled from Mexico in the anticlerical Mexican Revolution, one of a series of early twentieth-century revolutions in Latin America in which the Catholic Church hierarchy, aligned with the landowning aristocracy, saw its power encroached upon.

Maura struggled in the dark to find a kerosene lamp, as thunder and lightning shook the building. Within minutes, 3 inches of water had risen in the bedrooms. Maura and the other sisters used brooms to sweep the water out. But she was thinking about the rest of the people of Siuna, soaked in their awful huts. Their roofs often came off in storms like this, the other sisters told Maura. She was shocked that chickens and pigs lived in the houses with the people, but equally shocked that most of the couples weren't married.[19]

A few days after Maura arrived in Siuna, the mission hosted a going-away party for Sr. Roseanna Tobin, who was being reassigned to Guatemala. Like the members of a military service, Maryknoll sisters served a strictly hierarchical organization; they could be sent to a new base at any time and served in one location only as long as it suited the needs of the operation at large. If a new mission opened in another country or on another continent or a death or decennial leave created a need for a skilled teacher or a nurse tested by battles with malaria and gangrene, a telegram would arrive from the motherhouse with the new charge. So, Sr. Roseanna—who knew the idioms of Nicaraguans' quirky Spanish and had grown accustomed to the smelting smell from the gold mine and understood the fourteen stanzas of the song the leading men of Siuna declaimed outside the doors of the church on the all-night observance of the patronal feast—would now go to Guatemala to open a new school. She would learn the language of the indigenous people of Huehuetenango, grow accustomed to the way that ground smelled when the rain came, learn to like those black beans.

Since they couldn't speak Spanish and didn't yet have any duties in the school, Maura and Kay were recruited to come up with entertainment for Sr. Roseanna's send-off. They picked out one of the convent's dozens of popular records and choreographed dances to go with them. Maura built costumes out of crepe paper and scraps of fabric and, as in the Bronx, decorated the school gym with scenery she painted. When she needed a word in Spanish, she asked the veteran sisters for translation and pantomimed. At the end of the week most of the people of Siuna crowded into the gym for the party.[20]

Sr. Roseanna had been in Siuna since 1944, part of the first group of Maryknoll sisters in Nicaragua. They were invited by

Bishop Matthew Niedhammer, a Capuchin Franciscan from the Midwest who was bishop of Nicaragua's Atlantic coast region—a church staffed all but entirely by foreign missionaries. In a sense, the sisters were a gift congratulating Niedhammer on becoming a bishop. After a ceremony at St. Patrick's Cathedral in New York, he visited Maryknoll founder Mother Mary Joseph. She gave him an ornamental mitre, the silver shepherd's crook bishops carry, and asked if he wanted anything else. "Yes. Give me six Maryknoll sisters for a school and dispensary for my vicarate in Nicaragua," he replied.[21]

That first group of Maryknollers to arrive in Nicaragua were welcomed by the Somoza government. In fact, on their first day in the country, the Maryknoll sisters paid their respects to both the American ambassador and Anastasio Somoza García, dining with the dictator and his wife in one of their mansions. The sisters admired the giant sunflowers growing in Somoza's garden and the strongman gave them seeds, encouraging the nuns to try to grow bigger ones in Siuna. Explaining their work and purpose in the country, Sr. Estelle Coupe assured Somoza they hadn't come to reform his country. "We won't be any trouble," she promised. When they arrived in Siuna four months later, national guardsmen from the Siuna post stood at attention and instructed the people of the village to shout, "Viva las Madres de Maryknoll."[22]

Siuna was a sorry place in 1944. La Luz Mining Company had been operating the mine that was the reason for the town's existence since 1938. Most of the inhabitants were transplants, drawn to Siuna by the promise of work in the mines, and as a result there was little sense of community or shared purpose. Drinking was the main recreation, few could read, and brutality against women was rampant. The Maryknoll mission built a sense of community, longtime residents said. In May 1945, the nuns opened a school serving 280 children. The health clinic began operating immediately. By 1959, the mission was humming along.[23]

The Maryknoll mission sought to improve the lives of people in Siuna by giving them some skills to ascend the existing social structure. The sisters didn't question the justice of the structure itself. Their goal with the school, hospital, and mission was to make people holy, to teach them to improve their lives through proper morals and discipline. They believed that with proper religious instruction and a little academic opportunity, the people of Siuna would be able to escape their poverty. To a certain degree, this was happening when Maura arrived. One graduate of the Maryknoll school, Mercedes Steiner, worked in the office of La Luz as a secretary, something that would have been impossible a generation earlier.[24]

Maura and Kay were sent to Guatemala for language scholl. By April 1960, they were back in Siuna with enough Spanish to begin teaching. Maura took over the second grade class, the same class she'd had in the Bronx. This time she knew what she was doing. As in the Bronx, Maura had fifty students in her classes. The school day started at eight a.m. with the children—almost all of them barefoot—filing into the Colegio Maryknoll courtyard in blue and white uniforms. Maura had perfected the quietly powerful teacher gaze that made students stop in their tracks. She also carried a 6-inch rubber strap that she'd slap on the blackboard or a misbehaving student's knuckle if disorder threatened to take over the class. She spent her evenings with the rest of the sisters, drawing up lesson plans and grading student work. On days when the academic classes and religious instruction were going well, Maura told the students to gather up their papers. She'd lead them out of the courtyard, up the hill from the church, past the general store, and into the forest. Then, in the vivid sunlight, using watercolors sent by her sister and mother, Maura would give an art class, translating the techniques her mother taught her and the ideas she'd learned from an art class at Fordham for the children of miners. They painted still lifes of mangoes and oranges, or landscapes of bougainvillea and palm.[25]

Despite her use of old-fashioned discipline techniques, Maura was usually calm, gentle. In the classroom she could keep students focused by dividing up the lessons, calling individual students to the chalkboard, or playing the trump card: she knew their parents. On Friday afternoons, teams of sisters walked the narrow lanes of Siuna and popped their head into the makeshift houses, asking how the children were behaving at home and reporting on their school progress. Maura excelled at this part of the job, connecting readily with parents, listening carefully. The other sisters started to tease that they couldn't afford to walk through town with Maura if they had anywhere they needed to be. Every few steps, someone stopped her to talk—and she never rushed.[26]

Seven sisters staffed the school, which ran from kindergarten to sixth grade and was accredited and supervised by the Nicaraguan government. The mission and the gold mine formed twin hubs of public life in the settlement. The Maryknoll fife and drum band marched with the National Guard in the parades on September 15 to commemorate Nicaraguan independence from Spain. In the first years of the school, attrition due to illness or the need to work was steep. By the time Maura joined the staff, the dropout rate had fallen off somewhat, though children of all ages sat in each grade. Twelve- and thirteen-year-old second graders were not uncommon. More than one hundred girls and boys had finished school able to read and write, having studied geography, biology, rhetoric, algebra, sewing, woodworking, and agriculture. By 1962, there were 785 students in the school and another 300 came to a new night school, mostly adults hoping to learn to write their name. School fees were the equivalent of seventy cents a month, although only half the students paid that. Sr. Jude Christine and Sr. Marysia gave weekly religion classes to the public school children. A few boys had entered the seminary, a fact the sisters considered their crowning achievement.[27]

The school Maura joined was a replica of the parish schools that hopscotched across American cities. The school library had eight hundred books that children could borrow on a weekly basis, a brand-new idea in rural Nicaragua. There was a choir, a glee club, and, as in Rockaway, a Legion of Mary group for the girls, a Catholic Action club for boys, basketball and volleyball teams for girls, baseball teams for boys, and a gym erected on the grounds of the mission, paid for with of weekly donations from the parents. The school had a newspaper and a safety patrol. The sisters used the same religion books as the New York Archdiocese, translated into Spanish.[28]

Fr. Roderick Brennan, pastor of El Señor de Esquipulas, tried to develop entertainment beyond the ubiquitous cantinas where mine workers frequently spent much of their meager paychecks. Once a month, round tins the size of pie plates, filled with tightly rolled 35 mm film, were flown in from Managua on the La Luz plane. Young and old came to the mission to watch movies, mostly westerns, projected on the wall. When Maura and the other nuns walked into the darkened impromptu theater to enjoy a movie, whoever caught sight of them first would bellow out the greeting they were taught to use when addressing the sisters: "Good evening, Queen of Heaven," and on cue all the teenage girls would shift out of the arms of their boyfriends.[29]

Those teenagers and children were skinny. When Sr. Jude Christine gave medical exams at the beginning of the school year, she found a common health profile: the kids had worms, parasites, antibodies for malaria, a variety of vitamin deficiencies, and very often anemia. The meals cooked on stone fireplaces behind the students' houses had to stretch far enough to feed the father who'd worked eight to ten hours in the mine, several children, and grandparents. Mothers cooked rice, beans, and starchy chayote and plantain—when they had it. There was little variety in the diet and meat was scarce. Siuna soil was metallic and not particularly good for agriculture, and most families had just the tiniest plot of land cleared from the forest. The sisters lined up the most malnourished children at the beginning of the school year and gave them vitamin injections and malt shakes.[30]

The well-stocked mission, its pantry filled with American products, such as Campbell soup, cookies, ham, sausage, jars of jelly, and canned vegetables, made the children's eyes bulge. The priests had wine and beer, all of it imported without paying duty taxes and circumventing the customs process—a favor from the regime to the mission. Some of Maura's students served as altar boys at El Señor de Esquipulas, attracted as much by the chance of being given food as by any spiritual inclination.[31]

Because their tiny plots yielded such paltry harvests, almost all food that people in Siuna ate was purchased at the La Luz Mining Company commissary—flown in on the Somoza airline and priced at a steep markup. Week after week miners, took an advance on their paycheck—with interest—to buy food. It was an income distribution method with the income flowing up, from worker to mine owner in interest on the advance of his small paycheck and from mine owner to Somoza family in the form of mining concession fees and "executive levies" or "presidential commissions" on the gold.[32]

As Maura's students came to school hungry and their fathers dug for gold deep beneath the ground, the Somoza government and its friends grew richer. Every Tuesday and Friday, a few of her young students watched as the LANICA plane touched down on the sun-baked airstrip in the middle of Siuna. On the edge of the airstrip, Gustavo Martínez Mendoza and other Siuna men slowly, laboriously rolled a flat wooden cart about the size of a king-size bed toward the plane, the muscles on their shirtless backs straining. National guardsmen, whose salary was partly paid by the mining company, walked alongside. The cart moved, burdened by the weight of ten or twenty 100-pound bars of gold stacked in a pyramid. It glinted in the sun. Twice a week. Every week. Once loaded, the plane raced down the runway and clambered over the mountains, bound for Puerto Cabezas on the Atlantic Coast. From there, the gold from Siuna was loaded onto ships bound for the La Luz parent company in Canada.[33]

The Siuna gold made many people rich. But not Nicaraguans. The mine abided by the nation's minimum wage laws, such as they were. There was no union to push for better wages—it had been smashed in 1954. Workers who had organized a strike were run out of town. They never worked in mining again and no one attempted to form another union.[34]

Maura was shocked by the discrepancy between the wealth of the mining company and the poverty of her students. But questioning La Luz wasn't her job or the job of the priests and nuns. They were in Siuna to instill faith, to cultivate a love of God and obedience to the precepts of the church. And anyway, they would remind themselves, the company provided electricity. Its dam upstream on the Rio Coco generated power and pumped water to the town. At Christmas, La Luz donated presents to the school and the sisters were able to hand out one gift per child, which would have been impossible without the company's generosity.[35]

Even as Maura's sympathy was with the children of miners, she made time for Lucy Plecash, the La Luz Mining Company manager's young, homesick wife. Lucy regularly invited the sisters up to the zone, the private community where the Canadians lived in a little re-created slice of suburbia with green lawns and a golf course, a swimming pool, and homes far more comfortable than any Maura had ever lived in in the United States. Like the rest of the sisters, Maura was uncomfortable amid such wealth. Her stomach clenched when the servants, parents of her students, served her steak. But the Plecashes were friendly and polite to their staff, and it was difficult for Maura to see them as the enemy. Lucy left the zone often, coming down to the mission to talk to Maura, to help in the clinic or sort secondhand clothes sent in big donation barrels from the United States. Maura called Lucy Plecash "dear heart" and appreciated her instinct toward good deeds, accepting Lucy as she was.[36]

Maura hated that the people of Siuna were so poor. She was forever giving things away, frequently her shoes, hoping to ease the poverty a tiny bit. But she wasn't in Siuna to make waves, and she believed that as a Christian she should be focused on the kingdom of heaven, not the world. Religious practices to underscore that point filled Maura's week. In the evenings she joined Kay and Sr. Jude Christine, Sr. Marysia, and the other sisters for Rosary and night prayers in the cavernous El Señor de Esquipulas, the church darkened and damp from rain and humidity, waxy candles flickering in the thick equatorial night. Just as in her parents' home, Maura knelt to pray the pattern of Our Fathers and Hail Marys. She was no longer with Buddy and Judy, but with the miners' wives and the children she taught during the day. The monotone hum of long-memorized words, the pauses when everyone in the church drew a breath together, were like gentling lolling waves, easing a release of the consciousness as Maura transported her mind to the incidents of Jesus's life. When, on Tuesdays, the assembled contemplated the Fifth Sorrowful Mystery, the Crucifixion, Maura brought her imagination to the scene of Christ's death. She looked at the battered and bloody body and understood it—from years of catechism instruction—not as an object of horror but as a gift of love. The son of God, becoming human, offered his life as a way to free humanity from sin—that is what she had been taught at St. Francis de Sales and what she was teaching the children of Siuna.

On Friday afternoons, the devout came to the church to pray the Stations of the Cross, a participatory prayer in which one contemplates fourteen episodes in the trial, torture, and death of Christ. Maura moved around the inside perimeter of El Señor de Esquipulas, gazing earnestly at the painted pictures of each episode: Jesus is lashed by the soldiers, Jesus falls the first time, Jesus is laid in the tomb. As she processed from station to station with the group—mostly old women, some pious girls—she put herself in Jesus's place. "How would I feel being whipped by the Roman guard? Would I be brave enough to be Veronica and jump up to wipe the blood and sweat off Jesus's face?"

The physicality of Jesus's death was a major part of Maura's prayer and of her Catholic imagination. For a religious culture famous for shaming the body, the Catholicism Maura grew up with was tremendously corporal. The moments of Jesus's life and the imagery in the prayers Maura had been reciting since childhood formed a rich backdrop to her daily existence. She wanted to instill that same deep and personal connection to the life of God in her students.[37]

Maura's faith, that depth of conviction and closeness to God, had been fostered when she was a teenager in the Legion of Mary service group in Rockaway. In Siuna she took on direction of the same club, recruiting girls to meet after school. They talked about Mary, Jesus's mother, whom the girls were supposed to try their best to imitate. Mary was the patron saint and namesake of the Maryknoll sisters, who took particular inspiration from an account in the Bible in which an angel tells Mary she will become the mother of God. Shocked and uncertain, the teenager accepts the commission and acknowledges that she will participate in the work of God, telling the angel, "I am the handmaiden of the Lord." Maura inscribed that phrase at the top of all her letters, the Latin words floating over whatever news or encouragement she was writing: "Ecce Ancilla Domini."

Maura encouraged the Siuna girls to think of themselves the same way, as assistants, actors on behalf of God. It was, in its own way, empowering. They saw themselves as a kind of battalion of service. They brought food to families poorer than themselves, visited women who were sick and confined to their homes. Under

Maura's direction they learned that sometimes a struggling woman just wanted to be acknowledged, to be talked to, to have someone pay attention. In the meantime, the girls learned that they had something to offer, that being generous was its own kind of power. She talked to the girls about a metaphor in the New Testament in which Paul, an early Christian and writer of many of the letters in the Bible, compared the church to the body of Christ. "We are all connected, brothers and sisters," Maura told the girls. "You are responsible for each other." The work instilled a deep instinct for solidarity, a sense that what happened to the family down the road mattered to them, too.[38]

Maura was close to the girls, forming real friendships. In the classroom she might have needed to be strict, but with the Marianistas, as the girls were called, she could be soft and open-hearted, building them up, encouraging them to think of themselves as capable and worth something—beloved as a part of God's body. The girls, in turn, were proud to be involved in the club, their confidence mounting as they offered assistance to their neighbors. And Maura's instruction imparted the idea that each girl's faith was something distinct, something that belonged to her and could be felt anywhere. It need not only be something that happened inside El Señor de Esquipulas as the Latin words washed over you.[39]

Maura's instinct may have been for emotional intimacy, but life in the convent was formal. Sisters were required to use the distancing salutation of "Sister" for one another, never "Kay" or "Maura" or "Christine," and they always addressed Margaret Therese as "Mother." Maura's primary relationship was with God. As she had in Ossining, she said the prayers of the Office throughout the day and prayed before the Eucharist once a week in the small green private chapel built within the convent. Maura was often in the chapel, kneeling, her head inclined on her folded hands. It was a habit that struck some of her sisters as overly pious. There was so much to *do*. But Maura needed solitude, time alone with God.[40]

Still, the sisters were good friends. At night when the school work was done, they gathered over the kitchen table, pouring one another cold drinks and talking over the day. There was often an air of cabin fever in the Siuna convent. One sister said she was getting dressed to see the opera, the notion of such a thing delightfully absurd in a tropical outpost. Fr. Brennan's movies only happened once a month. So, the nuns reenacted scenes from famous movies or wrote slapstick skits, Maura cracking up as she swept into the parlor in an improvised cape or bustling through the house to find bedsheets and linens that could be jerry-rigged into costumes. She danced the Irish dances she learned as a little girl, lifting herself onto her toes and bounding across the room in leaps and toe-kicks, a broad smile breaking across her face.[41]

Maura wrote constantly to her parents, upbeat notes full of endearments and questions, with a scriptural quote at the top margin and maybe at the end a line or two about what was happening in Siuna, usually accompanied with a "pray for me." Maura's mother wrote often to keep her in the loop about the birth of her brother Buddy's children, about Judy and her husband being transferred from Fort Benning, Georgia, to a military base in Germany. She heard all about her parents' trips to Ireland and about the news from Beach 115th Street and how the turnout had been at the St. Francis de Sales parish bazaar. In the summer of 1960, as Maura settled into the rhythm of teaching and after school activities, the letters were full of news about Jack Kennedy, an Irish American—and a Catholic—who looked like he might have a real chance of becoming president of the United States.

To Maura's parents and to Catholics and Irish across the country, it was a heart-swelling honor. Jack Kennedy's becoming president meant they were no longer strangers or guests in the United States. It meant, as Fulton Sheen and Cardinal Spellman had been preaching for a decade, that one could be a good American and a good Catholic at the same time.* In fact, given the Catholic Church's allergy to communism (and communist regimes' hostility to religion), being a Catholic was accompanied with certain anticommunist bona fides.[42]

---

* Certainly the 1960 campaign provided a prominent target for anti-Catholicism and revealed that anti-Catholic prejudice still existed. But the fact of Kennedy's election evidenced a culmination of Catholic assimilation, a development, as discussed in Chapter 2, that had been under way for a generation or two already.

In Rockaway, Kennedy posters were hung behind the bars and his progress was tracked in the *Brooklyn Tablet*. People delighted that his mother went to daily Mass. His big family of brothers and sisters looked like the families that clogged the pews at St. Camillus and St. Francis de Sales. The delight and personal affection for the young candidate reached all the way to the mission in Siuna. When the Maryknollers read about his inauguration—and when their parents back home watched it on fuzzy little television screens—they believed their country was a force for good. Against the totalitarian and dictatorial Soviet Union, with its gulags and silenced dissidents, its food lines and drab colors, under this vital young president the United States would be on the side of truth and hope.

Kennedy's call for service resonated with Maura and the other Maryknollers. They, too, had an optimistic, can-do attitude about their work, a belief that through discipline and correct habits, they could remake Siuna and lift up the Nicaraguans.

But there were other machinations at work. Among the guests at John F. Kennedy's inauguration was Anastasio Somoza Debayle. His brother Luis had been president since 1956, when their father was assassinated by a poet, but Anastasio held the reins of power. The new president's father, Joseph Kennedy, had invited Somoza to the celebration. While in Washington, Somoza met with Allen Dulles, director of the Central Intelligence Agency. Somoza asked Dulles if the attack on Fidel Castro's Cuba that had been in the works during the Eisenhower administration was still on target. Dulles walked across the office to make a phone call, then put down the phone and turned to the Nicaraguan, cigar in hand. "It will happen," he said.[43]

Somoza was asking about the covert attack on Cuba because Nicaragua was playing a key role. Whereas the Cuban exiles at the center of the Bay of Pigs invasion trained in US-friendly Honduras, the naval vessels that carried them to Cuba, as well as the air force planes that Kennedy did not engage, set off from Nicaragua. Puerto Cabezas, the Atlantic coast port the mining companies used to ship their gold out of Nicaragua, was upgraded and improved by the United States so that it could host US naval carriers and aircraft. When the boats set off from Puerto Cabezas for the Bay of Pigs in April 1961,

Fr. Roderick Brennan, Maura's pastor from El Señor de Esquipulas, was with the American soldiers and Cuban exiles. A chaplain to the Nicaraguan National Guard, he blessed the mission, praying that the ill-fated invasion would spark a rebellion in Cuba and topple Castro. The Catholic Church and the Somoza regime were so closely linked that Fr. Brennan sometimes wore a military uniform.[44]

It's hard to overstate the fear Fidel Castro and the Cuban Revolution engendered for the United States, the Somoza regime, and the rest of the military dictatorships in Latin America. By ousting a brutal and corrupt American ally with a makeshift guerrilla army, the Cuban Revolution showed that a different trajectory was possible for the masses of poor and abused people across Latin America. Castro represented hope to a small cadre of leftists in Nicaragua who wanted to see a society in which people beyond the Managua elite and the foreign mine owners could live with dignity.

Most ordinary Nicaraguans, however, knew very little of Castro and the Cuban Revolution. The newspapers that eventually found their way to Siuna reported only fantastical tales meant to frighten the children. That Castro was covered in hair. That he was a cannibal. That if he saw a child in the street, he would grab him and eat him. The newspapers said Castro was a communist and this, it was understood, was what communists were. They were trying to take over Nicaragua and the whole world.[45]

Maura might not have believed Castro was a cannibal wolfman, but she understood that communism and anything like it was dangerous. Communists had killed Maryknoll missionary Francis Xavier Ford in China and imprisoned Maryknoll sisters in labor camps. When Maura was in the novitiate, visiting speakers warned the sisters about the dangers of communism. Throughout her childhood, Fulton Sheen and the *Brooklyn Tablet* railed against its evils, its brutality, its way of stripping the humanity from people and making them just units—numbers—subjugated to the all-powerful state. But above anything else, one word was associated with communism: *godless*. It was almost axiomatic. Communism was always called godless. By implication, the other political and economic systems must be godly.

In June 1962, a telegram arrived from Ossining announcing a change of personnel. Sr. Margaret Therese would be reassigned to work at the motherhouse. Sr. Maura John would take over as sister superior in Siuna.

Maura was shocked. So was Sr. Margaret Therese. The older woman had suggested to headquarters that Maura had potential to be a superior, but she thought she'd be able to mentor the young nun for another few years. Maura was one of the youngest sisters in Siuna. She didn't see herself as a leader, certainly not as an authority figure. True, she had come into her own as a teacher, able to manage the classroom full of antic second graders and confident that she knew what she was doing. She loved teaching the First Communion classes after school, explaining the Eucharist to the children in down-to-earth language about sharing and love and urging them to be reverent, to make space in their mind for quiet. She managed warm relationships with the older girls in the Marianistas, talking easily about a friendship with God and in a million ways telegraphing that they were precious and lovable. She allowed herself the pleasure of teaching art to students who were interested. But to be in charge of her friend Kay Kelly, who was always ready to smirk at authority? Or of Rita Owczarek and Bea Zaragoza and all those sisters who had been walking the dirt roads of Siuna for years while Maura was still a young nun in the Bronx trying to master the art of putting on her veil? She didn't think she was worthy. She didn't think she was good enough. She feared—she knew—she would disappoint.[46]

Maura wrote to her mother, asking Mary Clarke to pray for her and writing that God uses the foolish. The assignment came without any explanation. She hadn't been interviewed. She hadn't been mentored, told that the order needed her particular brand of gentleness and fidelity during the next few years as radical changes were about to sweep through the entire church. She wasn't consulted or given any advice, a book on staff management, or a workshop on communication strategies. Like the assignment to mission, read out in the midst of the dining hall as she sipped her soup, the announcement that Maura would be the boss was simply handed down. It caught her off balance. Orders came down, obedience went up, just as it did between the bishop and the priests, the priests and the people, the nuns and the families in the school and clinic. The only option for Maura was to take on the new responsibility and hope she grew into it.[47]

Now management of the convent household was up to her. Maura would be in charge of ordering food, of maintaining the schedule of trainings and vacations and trips to Managua. It was her job to remind the sisters of the need for decorum. When Kay made a crack about the privilege of talking during meals, a right granted when a Maryknoll sister anywhere in the world died, Maura would need to remind her that she shouldn't be happy someone was dead, even if Kay had never known the sister. If someone laughed too loud or was on the verge of disagreeing publicly with one of the priests, it would be Maura's job to discreetly rein her in. The monthly stipend paid by the Capuchin Mission for the sisters' upkeep was her responsibility. She was principal of the school. Arrangements with the Capuchins over work and parish activities and new initiatives were now up to her. When mothers came to the door of the convent with a whispered prayer and an entreaty for some help from the priest, it was now Maura's job to gather up the requests and try to mention them subtly to the pastor, in a way that ensured he didn't realize his strings were being pulled. This last was a task Maura excelled at, though she would never have admitted it. The other sisters teased her about her soulful, brown eyes and their effect on men. "Take off your glasses," Kay would say, "and run up to the zone to get us fabric for the sewing class, some money for sports equipment, help with a scholarship." Communication with Bishop Niedhammer in the provincial capital, Bluefields, was now her bailiwick. She would travel frequently, flying out on rocky LANICA flights, rosary in hand, to meetings and conferences in Bluefields and Managua.[48]

Maura never got used to her new role. To make matters worse, Sr. Margaret Therese had been a staunch and mighty mother superior; a woman with an analytical mind and an air of precision, she ran the mission like a well-oil machine. How could Maura follow that act? She was always late, her veil a little crooked, her hems a little yellowed. But like getting some kind of dinner on the table in Rockaway when her mother was working the night shift, she managed.

She kept time for the habit of sitting in the kitchen in the evening to gab with the other sisters, staying up late into the night to finish her own work. On the eve of someone's birthday, she still painted place cards for the table. When she felt she needed to impose order, she did it collegially. It was an approach to authority that was just right because the whole nature of power in the church was about to be entirely reimagined.[49]

In the fall of 1962, a gathering began in Rome that would utterly change the shape of Maura's life. Called the previous year by Pope John XXIII, it brought hundreds of bishops and cardinals to the Vatican for a panoply of discussions on how the ancient institution should interact with the changing world. Something like a board meeting for the worldwide Roman Catholic Church, the group convened committees to come up with topics, then brought those topics forward for discussion and approval by the assembled princes of the church. That first fall, only one topic made it through the quasi-legislative process to even be considered: a suggestion that the Mass, the central exercise of Catholicism, be celebrated in the language of the people in the pews. That alone was a radical proposal, but something even bigger and more transformative was afoot. For the next three autumns, the church leadership would meet at the Vatican and discuss nearly every aspect of church life. Pope John XXIII compared it to opening the windows to let fresh air into an institution that had grown stuffy and cramped over two thousand years.[50]

In the beginning Maura was only vaguely aware of the council. It was something far off in Rome for bishops and cardinals, something that she couldn't imagine would affect her daily life in Siuna. But as proposals and documents from the assembly trickled out of the Vatican, Maura opened the windows, too. The sisters would be asked to redefine their role, to articulate why they were nuns, and to reconsider just how they interacted with the world. As their superior, Maura would be at the helm of a changing mission.

CHAPTER 5

A Changing Mission

Anastasio Somoza Debayle, director of the National Guard, inheritor of his father's dynasty, strutted to the front pew of the hushed El Señor de Esquipulas church in Siuna. Surrounded by bodyguards, he sat for a service held in his honor. Maura rose and all the Maryknoll sisters rose with her, a cloud of gray wool and starched white. She began to sing, her voice unsteady, but gaining strength in the gentle waves of the familiar Latin, its wide vowels and elongated syllables a comfort. The nuns sang together in their chapel every day, their voices blending to a single act of prayer in Gregorian chant. Now they sang the Te Deum, a hymn of adoration used to mark momentous occasions: the election of a pope, the signing of a peace treaty, the coronation of a king.

> *We praise thee, O God: we acknowledge thee to be the Lord. All the earth doth worship thee: the Father everlasting. To thee all Angels cry aloud: the Heavens, and all the Powers therein.*

The hymn continued for many verses of awe-struck praise, the sisters' voices imitating those of the angels.[1]

Later the dictator sat in the convent courtyard. Maura served him tea in delicate Belleek Irish china sent by her parents at Christmas. She knew a visit by so important a man to an outpost like Siuna was a great honor. Not everyone agreed. Eleven-year-old Ramona Arroliga was among the crowd that had greeted Somoza at the airport. One of her father's arms had been torn off when he fell forward into a machine at the La Luz mine. He received a one-time payment for the accident and now farmed on little slivers of land rented from neighbors. The family had no land of its own. After school Ramona and her six brothers and sisters helped their father harvest corn and yuca, rice and beans, a patch here, a few feet growing at the corner of someone else's field there. Her mother patted corn masa together to make tortillas she sold by the side of the road. Even by the standards of Siuna, they were poor. On a shortwave radio Arroliga's father tuned in to broadcasts from Cuba. He knew of Somoza's rapacious deals with the mining company and his brutal National Guard, the political prisoners tortured in his prisons. But for now, he kept silent. Anastasio Somoza Debayle and his brother Luis would hold power between them and through proxies for another generation. Anastasio had come to inspect the battalion, enjoy the hospitality of the gold mine officials and cut the ribbon on a new school building being added to Colegio Maryknoll.[2]

The main focus of Maura's work remained the Colegio Maryknoll, of which she was principal. As more families put a value on education and attendance rose, the classrooms began to get crowded and the building constructed in the 1940s started to sag, the years of rainy seasons taking their toll. In 1963, new classrooms were built. The money came not from the government in Managua, but from the United States, part of the Alliance for Progress, a concerted effort on the part of the John F. Kennedy administration to improve living conditions in Nicaragua and other poor countries with US-friendly governments. The school already received what the students called Kennedy milk, powdered milk in packages stamped with two hands in a hardy clasp. That handshake, meant to evoke friendship and cooperation between two nations, was stamped on every bag of rice, jug of cooking oil, and packet of oatmeal the program distributed.[3]

The Alliance for Progress was strategic, to be sure, intended to improve material conditions in places such as Siuna, so that people would be less tempted to push for wholesale change in the way Nicaragua was run. It was a response to the Cuban Revolution, an attempt to counteract Fidel Castro's influence. Even still, interest in the well-being of peasants in the mountains of Siuna was a departure for American policy and the sisters embraced it. For Maura, Kennedy embodied something hopeful and generous about the United States. Many Nicaraguans agreed; they regarded him as a US president who took the concerns of poor people seriously. In his inaugural address in January 1961, the young president addressed nations far from the United States. "To those people in the huts and villages of half the globe struggling to break the bonds of mass misery, we pledge our best efforts to help them help themselves, for whatever period is required—not because the communists may be doing it, not because we seek their votes, but because it is right." He then went on to re-iterate the Monroe Doctrine, warning that the United States would oppose "any aggression or subversion anywhere in the Americas."[4]

Maura knew that many of her students came to Colegio Mary-knoll in part because families whose children attended the school received health services at the Maryknoll clinic as well as Alliance for Progress food. Under Maura's direction, all seven of the Arroliga children attended Colegio Maryknoll for free. But as the time for her First Communion approached, Ramona was concerned. First Communion is a major celebration in Catholicism, marking the inclusion of a child into full participation in the church and mystical body of Christ. It is especially important in places like Siuna, where so many children died at birth or as toddlers, from infections and disease; being able to celebrate the milestone was significant. But there was no money for a beautiful white dress for Ramona, no money even for fabric that her mother could turn into a confection of ruffles and lace for Ramona to wear. Maura knew Ramona's worries. She made sure the little girl had a beautiful dress. She looked as much a cross between angel, bride, and princess as all the other little girls as they processed through the doors of El Señor de Esquipulas to receive for the first time the transformed Body of Christ.[5]

The meaning of that phrase, the *Body of Christ*, was taking new shape for Maura. She believed and had always taught in the First Communion classes that through the crucifixion, Christ made him-self a sacrifice. He was like the lamb on the altar in the Hebrew Tem-ple. As the people gather together at Mass, the bread is transformed into Christ's body. By the middle of the 1960s, drawing on the let-ters of Saint Paul, Maura understood the phrase the *Body of Christ* to describe the people gathered in the pews as much as the wafer held in the tabernacle. For Maura, this meant the Arroliga family, the children of a one-armed farmer barely scraping by on land filled with gold, were part of the body of God.[6]

Marta Carmen Davilla Lumby, a little girl who lived up beyond La Luz with her parents was part of that body, too. Maura and another nun hiked up the rocky hill to Marta, whose parents were too poor to send her to school and too sick to be left alone. Maura visited often, bringing first grade school books so Marta and her siblings could learn to read, coming back to visit and care for her parents.[7]

In 1963, Maura's first full year as sister superior, she received a book from Mother Mary Coleman, head of the entire order. Written by a Belgian cardinal, Leon Joseph Cardinal Suenens, who was a major participant in the Vatican Council in Rome, it was called *The Nun in the World*. Mother Mary sent a copy to every Maryknoll convent in the world, and urged her sisters to read it. The book examined the history of religious orders, most of which had been formed hundreds of years earlier in Europe as simple communities of unmarried or widowed women doing good works. Cardinal Suenens questioned the rigid traditions that had attached themselves like lichen to congregations and recounted how many religious orders had been driven away from direct engagement with poor people and into a cloistered existence by early modern bishops alarmed at these women's freedom, their tendency to act outside male authority. The history of communities of nuns was often the history of women gathering expertise and reaching out to marginalized people and of bishops reining them in, erecting walls and laws to lock them away. The cardinal decried the subjugation of women and criticized church leaders of the nineteenth century who had resisted feminism, praising the accomplishments of postwar women in government and in scientific research, in media, and arguing that nuns should experience the same liberation as lay women.[8]

The Nun in the World urged religious orders of women to reexamine their mission, to question their role as flowers of the church, as pious adornment. Instead the book presented a new metaphor: sisters should be like yeast in bread, completely mixed in with the dough and pushing and expanding to make the bread rise. The work of the church, Suenens argued, was in the world. The role for nuns should be among the rest of the people, leading and moving with them for a more perfect world.[9]

This new concept matched Maura's instincts and was bolstered by the original aim of the Maryknoll order. Maryknoll sisters had always been concerned with the physical well-being of the people they served. That's why they set up health clinics and built schools. But the Incarnational—the Christ in the world—emphasis emerging from Vatican II and from Latin American theologians and pastoral workers put the spiritual and corporal together. The people in Siuna suffering physically were the Body of Christ. This is where Maura's God was, in the people.

Maura realized that the mission in Siuna needed to do more to address the needs of the people. As sister superior she began working more closely with a dynamic new American Capuchin priest named Gregorio Smutko, a tall, lean young man with an intense gaze who was learning the new theology. Fr. Smutko, who later became a sociologist, was full of ideas on how to improve life in Siuna and the rest of the Atlantic Coast. He began a program to train teenage girls in the basic principles of the Catholic faith and then send them to teach what they had learned to their families and their neighbors in remote areas. Maura asked Guadalupe Maireno Estrada to be one of those girls who rode into the countryside on horseback.[10]

Maura was deferential to the priests in the mission and assented to most of their plans. And this one seemed like a particularly good idea. It was an effective way to spread knowledge of the faith. But it was also empowering the girls, demonstrating that knowledge of the Church was not something reserved to the priests and nuns. Guadalupe grew in confidence and the work made her admire the nuns. When she was in sixth grade, sisters from another congregation, the Carmelites, came to Siuna looking for girls to join their convent. To Guadalupe, a life of prayer and caring for children in the Carmelite orphanage was attractive. She wanted to be like Maura, to have the same grace and smile. She'd already been taking care of her little brothers and sisters and teaching children in the countryside. Maura wrote her a recommendation, telling the mother superior of the Carmelite nuns that Guadalupe was sincere and eager, that she wanted to serve God and help people in need.[11]

Training girls like Guadalupe to be leaders was part of a larger realignment beginning to take place in the Maryknoll convent in Siuna. The work expanded to include more community development; the sisters looked for ways to involve laypeople in the religious life of the church. Maura, the sisters, and the Capuchin priests met frequently, laughing over shared dinners, beginning to translate these new ideas percolating in Rome into their patch of Nicaragua. Beyond strictly religious activity, Fr. Smutko was committed to developing local leadership and infusing new energy into the farmers' cooperative that had been operating for a decade, developing a leadership structure of local farmers and aggressively seeking out new agricultural techniques for Siuna's difficult soil. Building up capacity for farming would provide an alternative to working in the mine and enable farmers to have some control over their own destiny. By the middle of the decade, Maura had launched a high school adjacent to Colegio Maryknoll and the church and people of Siuna were pressing the government to establish an agricultural school in the town. The watchword was shifting from *assistance* to *empowerment*.[12]

That's what Maura had in mind when in the fall of 1963 she answered a query from the motherhouse about how Siuna was finding a role for women in development. Maura noticed that Santos López, who repaired the sisters' habits and took care of anything that needed to be sewn in the convent, was talented. She hired her to teach sewing in the young grades and to train several older girls as dressmakers. It was a minor project, but it was empowering for López. Hiring López was an extension of a quality Maura had had all her life: the ability to notice someone who might be overlooked and to foster a woman's confidence.[13]

Maura also noticed that three girls in the graduating sixth grade class one year had great potential. Brunilda, Emperatriz, and Luisa were bright, but their families couldn't afford to send them to Bluefields for high school. After graduation, the girls would return to the mountains around Siuna to cook for their fathers and brothers.

Within a few years would come the first of many pregnancies and a husband or companion they could expect to beat them when he drank too much.

But Maura had a plan for Brunilda, Emperatriz, and Luisa. She spoke to their parents, explaining that the girls could work in the convent kitchen for six months. Maura would pay them a small amount. She'd be able to keep an eye on their work ethic and attitude. They would lose their rough edges and learn valuable cooking, budgeting, housekeeping skills. At the end of six months, Maura would start them out as teaching assistants in the lower grades. If they did well there, the Maryknollers would find a way to send them to Bluefields to train as teachers.[14]

The girls' families were convinced. Emperatriz's mother let her daughter spend as much time with the sisters as she wanted. For Emperatriz it felt like liberation: These women were different. They respected one another, joked with one another, and made plans for the future. They moved outside the sphere of men, cultivating their own authority. The three girls began the training and eventually went to high school. With Maura as boss, people felt closer to the sisters. Rules of decorum still infused life at the convent, but Maura made the sisters' courtyard and parlor places anyone from Siuna was welcome to visit. She treated each guest with care, even formality, offering thick coffee in demitasse cups and presenting even a simple glass of water with a napkin folded around it to catch the condensation, delivered on a tray. On Sunday afternoons the other sisters, Kay, Rita, Bea, and Laura, gathered in the parlor to spend time with whoever was visiting. The women moved as a group, like first-year college roommates: when one went to sit in the parlor or decided to hike to the swimming hole above the town, soon the rest followed. But on the weekends, a steady trickle of people visited the convent. Maura found it impossible to set boundaries. When a knock came at the door, she always answered, even if it was dinnertime or the sisters simply wanted some time to themselves. Often the other nuns watched their dinner get cold as Maura stood at the door speaking to someone. They couldn't eat until the sister superior sat down, and Maura was constitutionally unable to turn anyone away. It was the same when someone came asking for money: Maura gave from her own small stipend, sometimes borrowing against next month's to be able to accommodate a mother in need, a miner in crisis. On Saturdays she paid a little boy with a shoeshine kit to shine her shoes, paying twice what the other sisters did and upsetting the micro-economy. Was it charity or empowerment? the other sisters asked Maura. Wouldn't the other shoeshine boys find it unfair that this one child had been paid extra?[15]

Attitudes about how to interact with the people they served in the mission and the work the sisters should be doing were beginning to change. Since the mission in Siuna began, outreach and preaching had been the purview of the priests. Then in 1964, Srs. Bea Zaragoza and Laura John Glynn joined Fr. Loran Miller on one of his trips, riding nine hours on horseback into the remote village of Silbi. The settlement was just three houses and a bamboo structure built especially for the visitors. Bea and Laura set up a medical clinic so they could treat the ulcerated wounds, malaria, anemia, and parasitic intestinal infections that were rampant. When they had free time, they sat on the riverbank telling children and adults the stories of Jesus's life. Each day the nuns led the people in the Stations of the Cross, pointing out the incidents in the death march, encouraging them to consider how Jesus felt as he struggled up the Mount of Olives. Some of the people who came in from La Bu or Alo, other settlements an hour or two away by foot, brought gifts of bananas, corn, cheese, moist tamales wrapped in banana leaves, or tomatoes.[16]

This was a new kind of mission trip. Sisters had trekked into the hinterlands before, but as nurses, never as preachers and never for dialogue. The Capuchin priests had been traveling to isolated communities on horseback or mule and afloat a wooden raft down the Prinzapolka River since they'd arrived in 1938, making a biennial circuit to people who lived far from the church and without a priest. The project was all about transferring into the people the knowledge and grace possessed by the priest. It was a strictly one-way exchange, with priests holding grand ceremonies, giving a crash course on catechism and the Mass. They paid little attention to how and whether their teachings were understood. Gathering all the children who'd reached the age of seven since his last visit, the priest explained that at Mass, the bread the priest held became the Body of Christ. But the children had never seen bread. Their mothers make flat tortillas from corn flour and Mass was something celebrated only when these priests were present. So, Fr. Augusto Siebert, one of the missionaries, carried a large poster of Leonardo da Vinci's *Last Supper.* Unfurling the picture, he pointed to the yellowish circles scattered on the table on the fifteenth-century Italian painting and told the Nicaraguan children living in dense forest: "That is bread. It becomes God." When the children could repeat it, they were ready for First Communion. Then, after a long day of teaching and paperwork, Fr. Siebert or another priest would celebrate the Mass in Latin, a language no one understood. When the priest left, the church left with him. The people returned to being latent Catholics. Certainly people prayed the rest of the year and there were devotions like the Rosary and veneration of saints, but these were private. The people didn't meet as a community again until a priest returned in a year or two.

But in 1964 it was all changing. A few years earlier, Frs. Siebert and Miller had left Bibles written in simple Spanish with adults in a few of the scattered settlements in the mountains, encouraging them to see themselves in the stories they read. When they returned a few months later, they found that the families had begun meeting in the empty chapel every Sunday, reading the Bible stories together and praying. It was a significant act of self-determination.[17]

Working with adults on the 1964 mission trip to the camp and spending so much time close to people in their homes was a new experience for sisters Bea and Laura. Seeing how Nicaraguans lived, watching a woman cook a meal on a few stones, realizing that many people did not even have a hammock to sleep in, was far different than greeting children as they came into the school in Siuna. The spring mission, traditional as it was, marked a turning point for the nuns. When they returned to Siuna they wanted to do more work of the same sort. Sr. Laura John pushed against the constraints of the school-based mission. She wanted to be in people's homes, working with adults.

At the end of February, as Bea and Laura set off for the jungle, Maura and Kay Kelly flew home for their furlough: three months of rest and renewal at the motherhouse. Maura would be able to visit her family easily. It had been nearly five years since they arrived, wide-eyed and green in Managua. Now Maura was returning to her family as a sister superior, a school principal and leader. This was the homecoming the Clarkes had pinned their hopes on when Maura hugged them good-bye at Idlewild Airport that morning in 1959.[18]

During her time away, Maura had written frequently to her parents and siblings, quick letters with questions about the children and little bits of news from Siuna. She asked her mother and her sister, Judy, to send donations to Siuna, sometimes making long lists of supplies the school needed and requests for clothes. Judy collected clothing from friends and other women in her parish, running clothing drives and sending brown paper–wrapped packages to Nicaragua. Maura set aside baby things for families in particularly great need and discreetly sent the most tattered children home with new outfits. The Clarkes and Keoghs sent checks as well, money Maura used to keep the school and after school activities running and to offset tuition for families like the Arroligas. Maura's family was part of the work in Siuna and always on her mind. Likewise the Clarkes and Keoghs felt connected to Maura's work in Siuna. The nieces and nephews grew up hearing about Aunt Maura continuously and knew she was out in the world doing good work. Now she was back.[19]

Maura dropped back into life in New York as smiling and effusive and loving as ever, but something was a little different. Her center of gravity was shifting. It was a little unclear which place was home, Nicaragua or Rockaway. In the years that Maura was away, Judy had returned from a stint in Germany with her husband, Peter, who had finished his army service and was now working through law school. Judy was raising young children and working as a nurse, like her mother, and spending a lot of time caring for her parents, who were starting to show signs of aging. Buddy and his wife, Carol, were nearby, raising their sons on Long Island. That spring Maura spent as much time as she could with her parents, her siblings, and the nieces and nephews she had only read about in letters. She brought other nuns to the beach and spent time near her ocean. Being back in the comfort of the Rockaways was strange after years in Nicaragua, but she tried to explain her work and the life of the people in Siuna to her old neighbors. She spoke at her childhood parish St. Camillus one evening, a program meant to raise money for the Maryknoll Sisters. It was the sort of event with which churchgoing Catholics were familiar: a nun or priest back from the missions in the wide world gives a talk about the poverty, simplicity, and godliness of the people in whatever country she or he is working. Maura had heard talks like this when priests from St. Camillus returned from their visits to the Hopi reservation and on her first day of high school at Stella Maris when a missionary from Panama addressed the assembled girls. Now she was standing in front of the room, nervous and eager. Betty McCann and another classmate came out to listen to their old friend. As they watched Maura they were struck by how joyful she seemed. Here was a woman who loved her work. McCann turned to her friend and asked, "Why can't we be that happy?"[20]

Just two months after her daughter's return to the United States, Mary Clarke had a heart attack. The crisis terrified Maura who, even in her midthirties and having been away from her parents for years, was very close to her mother. Through all the tumult of Maura's childhood—the lost jobs, the constant moving, and her father's struggles—Mary had been the solid center of the family. She held it all together, minimizing any trouble and marching forward with a strength and grace she tried to impart to her children. To see her weak and in need was unnerving. Maura dreaded her parents' death, telling friends she didn't know how to let go of them. Mary Clarke survived, and Judy took over her mother's care, moving her into her home and making sure she stayed off her feet. Maura felt inadequate, but she was good at sitting with Mary, spending unhurried time. Too soon, her sojourn in New York would be over.[21]

While Maura was in Ossining, a great deal of energy and excitement was roiling through the Maryknoll order as a result of what was taking place in Rome. The order was preparing for a general chapter, a meeting in which regional superiors from every part of the world where Maryknoll sisters worked convened to discuss these new ideas emerging from the second Vatican Council. The Maryknoll sisters were beginning to hash out a new mission for themselves. How could they best be like yeast in the bread of society?[22]

The headline innovation in the Constitution on the Sacred Liturgy, an official item of church teaching published the previous fall, was that the Mass, which had been celebrated in Latin since the time of the Roman empire, would now be said in the language of the people in the pews. The local language decree was accepted enthusiastically by the Capuchins in Siuna. Holy Week 1964—while Maura was still in New York—was celebrated in Spanish. In the next few years, all over the world, people heard the ritual they'd always witnessed largely as guests declaimed in their own language. It was revelatory, opening up a whole panoply of possibilities for the faithful to more deeply embrace what was happening on the altar. After the publication of the Constitution on the Sacred Liturgy, the priest turned to face the congregation. Mass was to be understood not as a solemn and mysterious ritual in an ancient language, but as a shared meal among friends. The goal was to reclaim the spirit of the early Christian communities in Palestine, Greece, Egypt, and Rome, small groups that convened organically to talk about Jesus and reenact the Last Supper.[23]

Maura's order wanted to do the same, not just in the way Mass was celebrated, but in every approach the sisters took to their mission. Was it enough to be teachers and nurses to people who needed schools and hospitals, or should they be doing something even more transformative than education, something to invite the laypeople into full participation in their church?

One of the presenters at the Maryknoll chapter meeting was Sr. Mary Xavier O'Donnell. Sr. Mary Xavier shared a curriculum she'd developed with a Chicago priest to teach adult catechism and encourage newly arriving Puerto Rican migrants to get involved in the church there. Called Family of God, it was, in its way, revolutionary. Using Socratic method, the Family of God curriculum relied on the people's own experience of God, not the authority of the instructor. In the sort of exchange of information and tactics that would later make governments across Latin America suspicious, Sr. Mary Xavier shared her technique with Sr. Estelle Coupe from Chile and the rest of the sisters. It was adopted by Maryknoll communities all over the world.[24]

The Family of God curriculum would inspire Maura's work for the next several years and set the stage for the rest of her life. Because the entire course emerged from the participants' own analysis of the story of Christianity and their role in that history, Family of God profoundly shifted the participants' relationship to authority. Instead of transferring knowledge from the expert teacher, it drew out— and validated—the interpretive power of the adult learners. It asked people not only to believe, but to think and act. Nothing would be the same again.

A new type of church community was already being formed in nearby Panama, a result of the Family of God approach. In 1963 Leo Mahon, Sr. Mary Xavier's coauthor, had relocated to Panama, where the Archdiocese of Chicago was beginning a mission. There, Mahon and the Maryknoll sisters who worked with him used the Family of God curriculum in San Miguelito, the parish he established in a poor neighborhood in Panama City. It was a new kind of parish, modeled on the early Christian communities, with the full engagement of the laypeople.[25]

San Miguelito was the first of many such communities— eventually called Christian Base Communities—that emerged in Latin America in the 1960s and 1970s. The trend can be traced back to 1961 when, in response to an endemic shortage of priests in Latin America and fearing the advance of Marxist ideology, the pope urged US religious congregations of nuns and priests to send 10 percent of their members to Latin America. The resulting influx of young, idealistic, and highly educated sisters and priests reordered the direction of the church in Central and South America. The goal of the "reevangelization of Latin America" was to bring Catholicism to people like those in the mountains around Siuna who had called themselves Catholic for five hundred years but knew almost nothing about the faith. The influx was less violent than the original conquistadors; this time the missionaries came with schools and malaria medicine instead of swords and spikes. The clergy who flooded into Nicaragua and Panama, Peru and Brazil, Guatemala and Chile may have been sent to reclaim the countries for Catholicism, build a barricade against the spread of communism and to deepen the roots of a church that had long been the redoubt of the wealthy and powerful, but they brought with them their own motivations and ideas. These new missionaries were influenced by their own experience of growing up Catholic, usually in blue-collar immigrant parishes, such as Maura's St. Camillus in Rockaway, where the priest was as much social worker as divine intermediary. They also carried with them strong union traditions, the memory of the New Deal, and sympathy for the US civil rights movement, with its harnessing of the power of religion in a struggle for human dignity. And after immersing themselves in Latin American communities, these new missionaries were irrevocably transformed by the people they served.[26]

Maura returned to Siuna in April 1964 inspired by the new ideas she'd encountered at the motherhouse. Her fellow Maryknollers were just as excited. Sr. Laura John, who had been a close friend in novitiate, greeted her with stories of the February mission trip and her desire to focus on adult education and community building. Sr. William Aurelie, a young, headstrong sister who arrived directly from the motherhouse at the beginning of 1964, had just undergone a novitiate training that had been much more about questioning than obedience. Sr. William Aurelie carried with her a copy of the Family of God text. By summer Maura implemented the program. The Maryknoll sisters began gathering married couples to start the first ten-week session. Maura and the sisters walked out from the convent-school-church complex after school, visiting different sections of Siuna and nearby La Luz, talking to women and encouraging them to learn more about their religion and take a more active role in the church. This was the sort of work Maura would do for the rest of her life, visiting people in their homes, asking them questions about their lives, encouraging them to think more deeply about what their religion meant, inviting them to share their ideas with a small group of neighbors. She was good at it. Maura was taller than just about everyone in Siuna but she was gracious, unassuming. She inclined her head and smiled when she listened. She touched people, a gesture that went a long way in Siuna, where white people were considered cold and remote.[27]

The sisters met with six to ten couples, asking them to share their ideas about what baptism meant, what Eucharist was about, what marriage entailed, what it meant to be people of God. The theme was that all people are the family of God and therefore need to treat one another with love and concern. The format called for the sisters to ask questions, not to preach. They weren't standing in front of a classroom or officiating from an altar. They were sitting beside laypeople as guests in their homes. The goal was to shift the balance of power, to communicate the idea that the nuns weren't heavenly creatures who existed on a rarified plane above the people and closer to God. They were sisters.[28]

The curriculum was ordered around the Catholic sacraments: baptism, reconciliation, communion, confirmation, marriage, holy orders, and last rites. Ramona Arroliga paid close attention when her mother and the other women talked about what marriage could mean. The sisters spoke clearly against domestic violence. Brunilda watched her mother's understanding of her worth shift as she began to speak with these visiting nuns. The older women started to believe that they could seek better treatment from their husband, expect their spouse not to get drunk, not to have affairs. Soon there were meetings and gatherings all the time. Ramona's family became much more involved in the parish.[29]

The concept of the church as the family of God meant that people had a responsibility to care for their neighbors. It also meant they had rights. They were God's beloved family. God wanted good things for them, not suffering. Maura found the ferment, the connections formed between previously suspicious neighbors inspiring. "The people in the pueblos are beginning to unite and to make their voices heard. Siuna has been abandoned for so long but there is an awakening of hope," she wrote home to Judy after several Family of God workshops were up and running.[30]

When Maura set out for Nicaragua in 1959 she thought she was going to bring Christianity to the people of Siuna. It was the mindset of the era. But in living in Siuna, she learned that God was already there. What the sisters had to do, she realized, was listen to the people they were serving, to understand how the world worked from their perspective at the bottom. The shift meant casting off the role of savior or authority with all the answers. Instead of working for poor people, Maura would work with poor people. It was, in effect, an act of changing sides.[31]

As she embraced that new role, Maura saw more and more keenly the injustices people were subject to, the effects of low wages at the mine, the lung illnesses and metal poisoning, the arrests for failing to kowtow to the National Guard, the alcoholism and family violence that sprang from hopelessness. If this was the Body of Christ, it was being tortured. Her instinct was to make herself more available to people, to give more material assistance and to pray that God would help her understand her role. While she and the other Maryknollers were realigning themselves with the poor of Siuna, a new organization was growing in Nicaragua. The Sandinista National Liberation Front (FSLN), named for Augusto Sandino, who led a rebellion against US occupation of the country in the 1920s and 1930s, was still tiny, and it is likely Maura wouldn't hear its name for a few years. But as it grew, it would pose a dire threat to the Somoza government, whose abuses Maura was just beginning to see clearly.[32]

A new consciousness was dawning on the Maryknoll community in Siuna, born from the sisters' deeper engagement with adults through Family of God. The nuns began to reexamine their own part in the hierarchies that condemned so many people in Siuna to poverty, and it was rarely an easy or flattering process. Sr. Laura John, who had advocated for the mission to be involved with adults, was likewise at the forefront of this push. She told Maura it wasn't right that the sisters got their food shipped in by virtue of a favor from the dictatorship. She said that while the people of Siuna lived in such poverty, it wasn't right that the nuns lived in a comfortable house with running water, bathrooms, a car they could borrow from the priests, medical care when they needed it in Managua. Maura didn't have answers. She wasn't comfortable with the disparity, which was why she was forever giving bits and pieces away at the convent door. But she didn't know how to change the situation, either. The sisters needed to stay healthy with good food and medical care to be able to be of use in Siuna, didn't they? While she often lacked clear answers, she did appreciate the questions, the straining for clarity. "What do you think? There is something wrong. Keep asking questions, even though there is no answer," she told Laura. Maura met Sr. William Aurelie's unending questions and challenges with openness, even when the most basic elements of the life she'd been trained for were put under scrutiny. It was an attitude that pervaded the Maryknoll community in Siuna. The sisters had tremendous confidence in one another, which allowed them to move forward with confidence and tremendous trust in the possibilities unfolding before them.[33]

The process wasn't as smooth elsewhere, as Maura witnessed at meetings with other Maryknollers in Central America. As the changes tentatively embraced at the 1964 chapter took effect, there was upheaval and difficulty throughout the order. By 1967, the nuns were wearing short veils, white blouses, and below-the-knee civilian skirts in bland colors. These were halfway to regular clothes: still distinctly nunnish, but a far cry from the heavy drapery of the old gray habits. But the changes in Maryknoll cut far deeper than dress. Scores of sisters were leaving the order. As enhanced roles for lay-women in the church emerged, many sisters realized they could lead lives devoted to their faith but not circumscribed by vows. Dozens more fell in love as they worked more closely and freely with priests and laypeople. There were 1,430 Maryknoll sisters in 1966; 993 just eight years later.[34]

It was happening in Siuna, too. In the spring of 1966, Maura had a sticky problem. Sr. William Aurelie was in love with a teacher at the school. The man had been to seminary and left to become a teacher. He was intelligent and warm; Sr. William Aurelie could talk to him forever, sharing ideas, thinking about how to solve the problems of the world. The friendship between the two was obvious—and threatened to become scandalous. Sr. William Aurelie had made initial if not permanent vows to chastity, after all, and had promised to foreswear worldly romance. It was Maura's job as superior to rein her in or dismiss her. Maura called the young nun in to discuss the matter. She was gentle, though it was difficult for her to be direct. Sr. William Aurelie told Maura she didn't want to leave the convent, renounce her vows, and return to lay life, so Maura decided it would be best for her to leave Siuna instead. Sr. William Aurelie was reassigned to Guatemala but would leave the order a few years later.[35]

None of the other Siuna sisters considered leaving during those years, but at regional meetings and in letters from friends in different missions, Maura heard of many of the women she trained with and studied with leaving to marry or simply find another life. To the sisters like Maura who stayed, those departures felt like a loss, a rejection. One nun described it as like watching your sister go through a divorce. And then your next sister. And your next. And worse, those who stayed weren't sure what it was, exactly, that they were sticking with. The daily schedule of prayer and work had been uniform in every Maryknoll convent in the world, from the motherhouse to Siuna to a few sisters on an atoll in the Marshall Islands when Maura made her vows in the 1950s. Now communities could make their own schedule, decide when and how to pray together, keep the Divine Office or not. Instead of appointed superiors named by the mother superior and some divination of the will of the Holy Spirit, there would be elected leaders and a central governing board in New York.[36]

That most of the changes were welcome made them no less jarring. Moving from a system of obedience, where decisions were made at the top and simply pronounced to one of discussion and discernment was rocky. Sisters who had been trained to obey had to learn to advocate, to hash out concerns, to engage in dialogue. It was difficult for Maura. She wanted to be a good superior, to embrace the changes, to keep peace, to make sure no one felt rejected, all at the same time. At a meeting in Guatemala with the superiors from Maryknoll communities across Central America, she listened as the women asked one another questions, reflected on readings, discussed the latest church teachings, and sounded out their feelings on what it meant to be a nun in the world and what they should be doing. Why were so many leaving? How could the superiors acknowledge the agency, the adulthood of the sisters in their houses, without letting the group descend to anarchy? The documents all those cardinals and theologians in Rome had assembled called for a complete renewal of the role of nuns and a reordering of the church. But interpreting and implementing those changes was more difficult than reading a fine treatise. "We are going through quite a soul searching study of trying to find out who we are and what is wrong in religious life. You may laugh at this but because of so many problems and lack of real love we see much weakness in our life, so pray for us," Maura wrote to her parents in the fall of 1967.

Like Maura, the majority of these women had entered the convent as innocent teenage girls, now they were middle-aged women learning how to make decisions in a group. Not everyone welcomed the changes. Many older sisters thought Maryknoll was moving too fast, watering everything down, losing its purpose.

Maura found it plenty painful, but embraced the difficulty. She wrote to Judy about the soul searching: "It is for our good because in all growth or change there has to be pain. Religious communities and the many other structures in the Church need renewal and perhaps a revolution in order to give new life and to help us all to be Christians meeting the needs of today."[37]

The new attitude about authority—an approach that called for collaboration between peers instead of obedience to superiors—was breaking out everywhere. In the spring of 1967, Fr. Loran Miller and Srs. Kay Kelly and Marian Aileen formed a parish pastoral team, with the goal of a more collaborative and democratic parish. It was one of the requirements set out in the Vatican II documents promulgated from Rome. The team would be responsible for identifying and finding ways to meet the pastoral needs of the people.

Maura loved the meetings with the priests, the hashing out of ideas, the long conversations over shared dinners about how best to build this new kind of church in which all the faithful contributed their personality, their energy, their concern and cooperation into becoming the Body of Christ. The prayer and discussion groups flourished. It was as if the Nicaraguans, so long treated as subjects by both church and state, just needed the smallest bit of encouragement—permission, even—and then they emerged as actors, full of energy and ideas, making the faith that had so long been preached at them their own. By 1966, there were sufficient numbers of these lay-led church communities that the diocese sponsored a conference, gathering all the groups together in Rosita, another mining town near Siuna, for a weekend course.[38]

In March 1965, in the midst of all the unfolding changes, the Clarkes came to visit their daughter. It was exceedingly rare for someone from home to visit sisters in the missions, even rarer for anyone to visit as out-of-the-way a place as Siuna. Maura was delighted to have her parents with her. She had written to them every few days since she came to Siuna and felt terribly connected to them, as though she hadn't loosened the tie of childhood the way most people do as young adults. It was a closeness and interdependence friends noted all through her life. But her roots in Nicaragua were growing deeper. She arranged for her parents to stay in a house in the zone, a comfortable place with a good refrigerator and stove. Mary and John both involved themselves with her work. Her mother helped with the clothes and donations. Her father played with children at the school. The convent celebrated St. Patrick's Day with Irish dancing and John Clarke sang old Irish ballads. Kay, Bea, Rita, and the other sisters adopted the Clarkes as their own parents and later on when back in the United States for renewal at the motherhouse, they would make a side trip down to Rockaway to visit them.[39]

Maura herself was traveling more frequently. There were meetings all the time now, training courses for her and the others in Bluefields, seminars on the new pastoral methods, on how to run a meeting or help interpret Scripture. And there were meetings with the superiors of other orders of nuns that Maura attended, and check-ins with the bishop. She was at the Siuna airstrip frequently, waiting beside the grass runway for the LANICA flight to board, then coming back home a week or a few days later as kids ran to meet the plane. Before long she was away again. Sr. Rita Owczarek often accompanied her to the airport, waving a white handkerchief as Maura's flight lifted off.[40]

Beginning in 1967, Maura started making more frequent trips to Managua. Sr. Estelle Coupe, one of the original Siuna sisters, was living in a poor neighborhood of Managua, working with a small group of people who didn't have a church building. They met in an unused warehouse and celebrated Mass with a Spanish priest named José de la Jara who made the nascent community his home beginning in 1966. Sr. Estelle and three other Maryknoll sisters used the

Family of God method to establish a Christian Base Community, a new model of church formed by the laity, as in San Miguelito in Panama. This community would be like the apostles who followed Jesus and carried on his message after Pentecost, more a gathering of friends united to build the kingdom of God, than a franchise of a worldwide institution devoted to order. It was electrifying for Maura. She brought the energy from her trips back to Siuna and absorbed it herself, learning to act with confidence and hope. In 1967 she wrote to her parents with news: she'd led a Eucharistic service at a large gathering of all the rural church groups up in Rosita. It wasn't Mass; rather, a liturgy that could be performed without a priest: readings, a discussion homily, and prayers over the already consecrated bread. That fall she and the rest of the Maryknoll sisters in Siuna met weekly to study the new theology emerging from Vatican II. As Maura read the papal documents that called for a church engaged with the modern world in the study group, she was seeing that vision take shape in Managua.[41]

Jenny and Luciano Sequeira had been among the first members of the community. As a child Jenny had learned to fear God, to dread his punishment. She attended Mass all her life, but never understood the ritual. Now she was learning a new way to see God. God was a loving parent, not a bolt of lightning. Luciano invited people from his job in a workshop to the meetings. He played guitar and set poetry to music; the gatherings were full of songs about a Christ who lives in the world and like Nicaraguans rides a mule in the mountains. Jenny, Luciano, and their neighbors met and talked and prayed together. They made connections, wove their lives together, claiming their inheritance as children of God, building back the Body of Christ that Saint Paul had written about. Those around her, Jenny realized, the other working people of the backstreets of Managua, were her brothers and sisters. They quickly recruited others in the neighborhood and soon helped forge a vibrant community, a church of the people, inspired by the early Christians who lived under the oppression of the Roman empire and met to pray in the catacombs. They called their little church San Pablo Apóstol (Saint Paul the Apostle). Maura spent hours and hours in the homes of San Pablo members, typing song lyrics and meeting notes on an old Olympia typewriter in the home of another member, Gloria Cannillo, and talking to the women about their right to fair and respectful treatment by their husbands. They met frequently without a priest, hosting their own Eucharistic services in which Jenny, Luciano, Gloria, or another member read a passage from the New Testament. The group reflected on its meaning together and then shared consecrated bread, not in a Mass in the cathedral but in a discussion in their homes.[42]

By 1968, the community of San Pablo had been meeting and praying together for two years. As their numbers grew and their ties became stronger, they started to engage more directly with the problems of life under Somoza. Jenny and Luciano along with the other members began to focus on what responsibilities they had as children of God, what duties they inherited to make the world more just. They'd been trained to read the stories of the Bible and apply them to their own lives, to insert themselves into the narrative. Now they looked again. Christianity was commitment, they told one another as they sat on folding metal chairs in the warehouse or around tables in their adobe courtyards. At meetings they read the stories in the Old Testament: about the prophets who decried a wicked world and demanded justice for the poor, about the Exodus when God delivered the Israelites from slavery. Defense of the people was important in this Bible they held in their hands. Assenting to this faith carried with it a social and political commitment.[43]

As the community of San Pablo Apóstol shifted to take on political concerns, to be involved with civil organizations protesting against the detention of political prisoners, the parish leadership team made up of Fr. José de la Jara, Sr. Estelle, Fr. Félix Jiménez, and two other Maryknoll sisters was divided. Fr. de la Jara and Sr. Estelle wanted to keep the focus on the Family of God method, on community building within the church community. They'd been inspired by the spiritual life, the lay leadership of religious activities at San Miguelito in Panama. Fr. Jiménez and the younger Maryknoll sisters were ready to move into a more public and outward facing commitment. Leadership team meetings were tense and fraught. Fr. Jiménez and the younger Maryknoll sisters faction argued that the role of the Church was to be in the world, to look outward to the society, not inward. Family of God, they contended, had been a great innovation and a revolutionary change a few years earlier. But time had progressed.

Maura was still in Siuna, but on her frequent visits to Managua she sat in on many of those fractious meetings. She listened, attentive and receptive to what everyone had to say, but she was firmly on the side of deeper engagement with the wider society. She managed to be kind and collegial even when others weren't, but she was certain. They needed to be nuns in the world, priests in the street, and people utterly engaged in the society's struggles. It wasn't enough to develop a strong spiritual community where people could pray together and understand that God loved them. The times called for more.[44]

Even as Maura and the Maryknoll sisters in Siuna were enthusiastically implementing the reforms of Vatican II, Bishop Niedhammer was getting nervous. Seeing the nuns adopt a new stance as leaven rather than foot soldiers for the church was disorienting. In April 1968, Maura flew to Bluefields to present the new contract she'd written to reflect the goals and principles the Maryknoll sisters throughout Central America had adopted the previous November. The aim was to realign the Maryknoll mission with the imperatives of Vatican II. Each statement was carefully footnoted to the Maryknoll Constitution or the November statement of mission. It was explicitly collaborative. The sisters wouldn't be taking orders. They would make decisions in consultation with the priests, whom they understood to be peers, not superiors, on the parish team. These were strong words from the Maryknoll sisters who had been presented to Bishop Niedhammer a quarter century earlier as gifts on the occasion of his ordination. He wasn't prepared to see them rewriting their terms of service. He rejected the new contract.

Maura had been raised to be polite and deferential, and while she believed strongly in the contract she and her fellow Maryknollers had carefully crafted, confronting the bishop would prove to be difficult. As a Maryknoll sister and as superior, she had always avoided conflict. Her instinct was to seek agreement, to keep looking for ways a puzzle could be solved. "We'll figure it out," she would tell Srs.

Laura John and William Aurelie. "There must be an answer." Even so when it came to a central belief, she was staunch. Just as in parish team discussions at San Pablo Apóstol, Maura was adamant that the new contract represented the work the sisters needed to be doing. After nearly twenty-five years, they had trained enough Nicaraguans to run the school. Most of the classes were taught by lay teachers now. It was time to hand the school over to the people and for the sisters to focus on working with adults, to develop leaders and build up the popular church.[45]

In July, Sr. Mildred Fritz came to help sort out the impasse. Over the course of the summer Maura, Sr. Mildred, the mother superior in New York, and Bishop Niedhammer exchanged increasingly tense letters. In August, Bishop Niedhammer wrote to Mother Mary Coleman, asking that she end the Maryknoll mission in Siuna. He'd brought the sisters there to be teachers. If they were finished being teachers because they'd trained a generation of Nicaraguans, he reasoned, then their work was done. His letter praised the Maryknollers' work over their quarter century in Nicaragua, but he emphasized that their most important role had been as examples of holiness, as images of sanctity. It was as though he hadn't read the Vatican II Decree on the Adaptation and Renewal of Religious Life, the official church teaching that stirred all the changes in the lives of nuns, from shedding the habit to reimagining their work. Maura knew that nuns' power was not in being holy creatures on a pedestal, reminding the world of heaven. It would be in working closely with the people they served to build God's kingdom in this world.

It seemed as though Bishop Niedhammer would get his way, but Maura didn't want to leave. She loved Siuna, loved seeing the children she'd taught in second grade graduate, go to Bluefields, and come home as capable adults. She loved the women she'd spent so much time learning from and the men she's seen step into a leading role in the parish. She loved the feeling of being out on the edge of the world in Siuna. At midsummer she wrote to her parents, "Keep Siuna especially in your prayers as we are thinking seriously that it might be best to leave this community for the good of the church. Missionaries are supposed to work themselves out of a job. Pray that God's will be done. It is so hard to go."[46]

By then, the convent had emptied out. Her good friend Kay Kelly had left nearly a year earlier, in August 1967, walking up the steps of the LANICA plane in a blue polyester skirt suit and short veil, clutching a traveling case and waving good-bye. Sr. Rita Owczarek had gone home on renewal. Others left for new assignments or to study the new theology. Arrivals and departures were always part of life in the Siuna convent, but this time as sisters were moved elsewhere, no one was sent to take their place. Maura, as sister superior of Siuna, would be tasked with closing the convent in December, at the end of the school term.

The fall of 1968 was a particularly heart-wrenching time to leave Siuna, because the very future of the town was in question. In August, an earthquake in Managua caused a disaster on the Atlantic Coast. The force of the earthquake burst the hydroelectric dam on the Rio Coco that supplied energy to the La Luz mine. A wall of water had barreled downstream to Siuna, wiping out farms and outposts and swamping the mine pit. The underground tunnels were flooded, and without an electric source, it would be all but impossible to empty them. The price of gold was too low for La Luz Ltd. to invest in the expensive repairs the earthquake and flood necessitated. The company diminished operations to just a skeleton crew and withdrew most Canadian and US staff from the zone. Maura asked her parents for donations. People had lost what little they had in the flood and now were struggling to survive on one or two shifts a week at the mine. The Clarkes sent enough money to buy rice, beans, and bread to feed the whole town for a week.

Maura and Sr. Lois Lorden sat by candlelight in the mostly empty convent and mapped out a strategy for getting donations and an emergency relief work program. Eight hundred people had been laid off from the mine, the payroll shrinking to two hundred. Those who still had a job worked only one or two days a week. Maura was cheered by the fact that a group of men were traveling together to Managua to demand disaster assistance from the government. Perhaps the parish work, the discussion and reflection groups, were making inroads against the fatalism that had always held Siuna in its grip. "Pray that we can awaken the government to help their own people in a more stable way," she wrote to her parents.[47]

Maura already felt terrible about leaving the people of Siuna. Now, with the town in tatters, pulling out felt like abandonment. But the reasons for leaving, for turning over the school to Nicaraguans, for stepping into the new work of being a nun in the world, hadn't changed because of the flood. It was time to go. The work of the parish and of empowering lay leadership would continue under the Capuchins. Maura's mission was calling her out of the convent and into the backstreets of Managua. At five p.m. on December 16, Maura, Phyllis O'Toole, and Bea Zaragosa climbed onto the LANICA flight for the last time. A crowd gathered at the airport to see them off, a reversal of the marching band and jubilation that greeted Maura and Kay when they arrived in 1959. Mercedes Steiner and Luisa, who was by then a teacher in the school, stood and cried. The plane lifted off into the green expanse. This time, Sr. Rita Owczarek's white handkerchief wasn't waving. It was Siuna itself saying good-bye.[48]

CHAPTER 6

Into Managua

Maura spent 1969 at Maryknoll headquarters in Ossining, back in the halls she'd entered as a nineteen-year-old novice. Now she was a thirty-eight-year-old woman. The coltish energy of her youth had mellowed into something like poise, though she still tended to bustle as she walked, a certain urgency in her movements. Freed from the veil, her chestnut-colored hair was brushed back from her high forehead and rested thick and wavy in a cloud around her head. One evening in Ossining, one of the younger sisters styled it for her. But Maura was too embarrassed, thought it too vain, and hurriedly brushed it out before coming down to chapel for evening prayers. Having spent her adulthood in a uniform, she was beginning to navigate what to wear and how to present herself. As a teenager she had dressed carefully, inheriting her mother's air of sophistication, but two decades in the gray habit had eroded her affinity for clothes. Her mother and sister tried to help, keeping an eye out for pretty, but not showy, dresses to buy or copy. Her mother sewed most of what she wore now, sending over midcalf-length shirtwaist dresses or dresses with long sleeves and simple patterns, which Maura always wore over neutral-colored stockings. She never wore pants.[1]

The Maryknoll Sisters had changed tremendously since 1950, both in the structure of how they were organized and in how they regarded their work. They were now led by an elected central governing board, not a mother superior, and most of the nuns had reverted to using the names their parents gave them, not the ones they were assigned when they took their vows. Maura's view of her work and role in the world had evolved, too. She saw herself as an adult, an individual with responsibilities for making her own decisions, not a subordinate responding to dictates. In the few years since Vatican II, her understanding of her vocation had shifted from teaching people to be better Catholics to helping those who were suffering recognize their dignity and worth, and with it their own responsibility to build a better world. The goal was no longer to strive to be worthy of a reward in heaven. It was to build heaven on earth.

She arrived back at the Sisters Center, as the motherhouse was now called, while the congregation was in the midst of a fraught and intense general conference. The 1968 chapter, which stretched from November 1968 until February 1969, was convened at the instruction of the Vatican, as a time for the congregation to decide how to formally implement the changes brought by Vatican II. Delegate sisters arrived from every corner of the world where Maryknollers worked, some with very divergent ideas on how thoroughly or cautiously to adjust their missions. The sisters from Latin America (Chile, Mexico, Guatemala, El Salvador, Nicaragua, and Panama) were already far along in a transformation. They argued for closer identification with poor people, for less formal living arrangements, for organizing and pastoral work to replace hospitals and schools. Maura wasn't a delegate to the conference, but her good friend Kay Kelly was, as was Sr. Mildred Fritz, who'd mentored her through the difficult shuttering of Siuna; both sat on important committees. Some older sisters feared the congregation was watering down what it meant to be a nun, that it was too eager leave behind the formal structures, the group prayer and rituals that made the sisters distinct in the communities they served. Conversations and arguments played out at dinner and in small clusters in hallways. Sisters circulated articles and books on emerging theology.[2]

But the most exciting reading moving through Ossining in the fall of 1968 and winter of 1969 was a set of documents written not in Rome but in Medellín, Colombia. In August 1968, bishops from across Latin America gathered in that city to discuss the new ideas generated by Vatican II and apply them to their local work. The resulting papers on poverty, justice, and peace would define Maura's work for the remainder of her life. They laid out a blueprint for a Catholic church explicitly engaged in the problems of the world, codifying and giving official sanction to notions that had erupted in a hundred San Pablos up and down the continent. Condemning inequality of wealth and power between classes and nations, the bishops argued that the earth was created for all people and all nations and that Jesus came to liberate humanity from hunger and injustice. They called for a social order "where a man is not an object, but an agent of his own history." The document on justice expanded the notion of sin from a matter of personal behavior to one of societal structure. The society that kept its citizens in poverty and ignorance was far from God. Therefore, the church "will lend its support to the downtrodden of every social class so that they might come to know their rights and how to make use of them." It was as if the bishops had been listening as Maura and Fr. Félix Jiménez hashed out their ideas of what it meant to be the church and as the Delegates of the Word in the mountains beyond Siuna gathered their neighbors to speak of God.[3]

But Maura's focus in 1969 was often on her family. That summer she traveled back to Ireland with her father, seeing again all the cousins, aunts, and uncles she'd met as a teenager and with whom her parents kept in constant correspondence. From the Sisters Center in Ossining, she could visit home easily. She was a frequent presence at her parents' house in Rockaway and got to know her young nieces and nephews well. Maura was interested in everything about them and listened to their stories with rapt attention. The kids liked her; she was easier to be with than most adults, less interested in rules. Maura often came down to the city on a train from Ossining to spend the weekend with her parents, her brother, Buddy, driving her into Manhattan for the train or all the way back to Ossining on Sunday nights. On weekends he and his wife and sons, her sister, Judy's family, and cousin James and his wife and sons piled into the grandparents' house, the whole clan together in a constant din. Maura's father muddled sugar and bitters with Irish whiskey to make old-fashioneds, and the adults sat outside, close enough to the ocean to feel the salt air and while away a Sunday afternoon. Nan and Pat Cleary visited often and conversation moved freely, Maura telling stories but more often listening, asking questions, deflecting attention even as she absorbed it.[4]

Mary Clarke had had a series of heart attacks beginning in April 1968 and spent much of the summer of 1969 at Judy's house in Glen Cove, New York. Maura struggled to keep her father's spirits up and to find her own place in Judy's home. She felt ineffective sometimes, deeply worried about her mother's health but not a skilled and confident nurse like her little sister who seemed able to keep on top of everything all the time. In Maura's absence Judy had assumed primary responsibility for their parents, taking them to doctor's appointments, monitoring her mother's medicine, sweeping her into her home for extended visits whenever Judy thought the older woman needed a break from housework and cooking for their father or simply to keep an eye on her. Mary had recovered from her heart attack of 1964, but with this series of attacks in 1968 more responsibility fell to Judy. Whenever Maura was home she was the star, the celebrated firstborn returned from the wide world, but her personal gifts of showering her mother with affection and sitting for long cups of tea seemed pale in comparison to Judy's whirlwind ability to keep a house of young children running, maintain a stylish Long Island home, work in the county public health department, and provide skilled nursing care to Mary. And Maura had a habit of disrupting the quiet rhythms of her parents' home, not quite realizing that they were twenty years older than when she'd left.

One day Maura met a Spanish-speaking woman on the bus in Manhattan. She was excited to speak her adopted language and felt connected to the woman, who must have reminded her of the women in Siuna. Maura brought the woman home to her parents and began making a pot of arroz con pollo, filling the tight little house with the smell of garlic and spices foreign to her Irish family, assuming John and Mary Clarke would entertain the stranger. She had learned her open-door approach from her mother, but to Judy the unannounced visitors and the steady stream of nuns visiting Rockaway looked like an imposition on the generosity of her increasingly elderly parents.[5]

And there were other challenges to being home. During the years in Siuna and especially the past few, dipping into work in San Pablo Apóstol had shifted how Maura saw the world. When she was a teenager in the 1940s, prayer services at Stella Maris Academy concluded with the students singing "God Bless America." Being a good Catholic and a loyal American were wrapped together. But the Catholicism Maura practiced in the past few years and the brutality she saw in the government of her country's great ally Anastasio Somoza had made her more critical, skeptical of the rightness of the American military. Life with Rafael and Carmen, Jenny and Luciano, and the neighbors in Managua was more real to her now than life in New York. Back in the United States now, she marched in protests against the Vietnam War. A year earlier, a group of Catholics, among them a former Maryknoll priest and a former Maryknoll sister, had broken into a draft board in Catonsville, Maryland, and destroyed draft records with homemade napalm, a sensational act that landed them in federal prison and drew attention to a rising strain of antiestablishment Catholics. Across the country scores of other draft offices were raided by antiwar protestors, with Catholic activists among them. The country was at a fever pitch after Martin Luther King's and Robert F. Kennedy's assassinations, urban riots, the violence and repression at the Democratic convention in Chicago and persistent protests in Washington, DC. While Cardinal Spellman, who had played such a large role in shaping the Catholicism of Maura's youth, called the war in Vietnam "Christ's war against the Vietcong and the people of North Vietnam," Maura saw it as an extension of the same sort of American imperialism that made life miserable in Nicaragua. Her sister's husband had left the army to become a lawyer, but the family was still close to many friends in the military and the certainty of Maura's stance against the war was jarring. On a car ride with their mother, the two sisters argued sharply about Vietnam, Maura adamant and unyielding. It was an indication of how different the two sisters' lives had become.[6]

Maura spent another Christmas with her family, then in February 1970 returned to Nicaragua to begin her new work. She took a circuitous route, visiting friends and attending regional meetings along the way in Mexico and El Salvador, finally arriving in Nicaragua by the end of the month. She wrote chatty, detailed notes to her parents at every juncture, reaching to stay close even as the miles between them lengthened: a postcard from the airport in New

Orleans while she waited for the plane to Mexico, just hours after she left New York; another letter a few days later from Mérida, Mexico, where Maryknoll sisters ran a prestigious girls' school and where her old friend from the Bronx, Mary Malherek, was stationed. Maura phoned home several times during the journey, expensive, echoey long-distance calls, such that her mother felt the need to remind her that they were together always in their hearts, despite the distance. She missed Nan Cleary, missed the cups of tea and the cocktail hours, begged Mary to give the grandchildren hugs.[7]

The few days in El Salvador allowed Maura to visit her mentor Sr. Estelle Coupe, the progenitor of Christian Base Communities in Nicaragua. Sr. Estelle was old-fashioned and a bit severe, a mother superior of the old cut, but throughout Maura's life she was something like a big sister. Maura sought her out when she needed reassurance and felt that Sr. Estelle really knew and understood her. During her brief visit to El Salvador, Maura sat in on meetings with the Christian Base Communities and women's groups the sisters ran there, listening quietly but intently, encouraging the poor peasant women to find their voice, cheering their analysis of the Gospel.[8]

She arrived back in Managua on February 20, 1970, and was met at the airport by her old friend Sr. Bea Zaragosa, with whom she'd worked in Siuna. When Maura had landed in Managua eleven years earlier, the country was completely foreign to her, she spoke no Spanish, and she knew nothing about the lives of the people she'd come to teach. Now she was a seasoned missionary, part of a percolating movement of Catholics critically involved in resistance to the regime. She was ready for the next adventure. But she was also apprehensive, worried that she wasn't skilled enough at running meetings or working with adults or giving talks. In Siuna in 1959, she joined a community of sisters who had been embedded in the town for a generation and she was assigned straightforward, if challenging, work teaching schoolchildren. The group of sisters she joined now in the slums of Managua was brand new to the city. The nuns were strangers to the people there and Maura's initial work was amorphous: developing relationships with her neighbors and inviting people to be more actively involved in the parish of Santo Domingo.

The parish covered a sprawling encampment of rural Nicaraguans displaced by draught and insecure land rights and drawn to the city in hope of finding work. The people collected on the shore of Lake Managua, not far from the center of the capital, built houses with whatever they found, often cardboard and crates, and tried to scrape out an existence. Maura moved into a precariously built two-story house she would share with Bea, Sr. Rita Owczarek, another alumna of the Siuna mission, and occasional visiting sisters. On the first floor was the kitchen and a health clinic, a communal meeting space for the neighborhood, and an open library. From her small room on the loft-built second floor, Maura could gaze at the shimmering lake two blocks away. The neighborhood was called Miralagos (Lakeview), but the pretty name belied the fetid, ripe stink of the place. Managua's sewage—both industrial and human waste—had been draining into the lake since the 1920s.[9]

Some squatters managed to build concrete or clay houses a few blocks from the shore, but much of the neighborhood was built out over the lake, houses held up on stilts like a Vietnamese fishing village. Filthy water sloshed against Maura's shoes when she stepped into the street and seeped through the floors of neighbors' homes when it rained. The Vatican II document on priests and nuns called on them to leave their safe and separated convents to live just like the people they served, not ministering to them from above but sharing their struggles and joys. Maura was in it.[10]

She was part of a parish team, led by a trio of Basque Jesuit priests, intent on implementing the Christian Base Community model Maura had helped pioneer at San Pablo Apóstol. The work was knitting a community from people tossed together by misfortune. Her friends from San Pablo Apóstol, Jenny and Luciano, Rafael and Carmen, and Gloria Cannillo and her husband helped organize courses and meetings, inviting cradle Catholics to learn their faith in a systematic way, beyond the rituals and prayers they'd imbibed since childhood. Maura worked, too, with youth groups and clubs for younger children. Fr. Pedro Miguel García, the pastor, ran a woodworking and carpentry workshop to provide job skills for teenagers. There were also literacy classes. Mary Hamlin, the Peace Corps coordinator for the country, had spent time with the sisters in Siuna, working in Rita's health clinic. A US government employee assigned through the State Department, she was chafing at the orientation of her Somoza-friendly supervisors. She came to the Maryknoll house often, finding sanity and solidarity with these warm and encouraging sisters. Hamlin was drawn to Maura and her housemates by the emotional closeness the nuns shared and their deep commitment to improving life in the slum. Hamlin brought National University students to volunteer in Rita's clinic and lead classes on sanitation and public health. Working in public health, seeing the illnesses and degradation suffered by the people of Miralagos, prompted the upper-class college students to ask critical questions. Why were these people made to live so terribly? What could change their circumstances? Running through all the work was an effort to empower the people of Miralagos to make their own decisions and stand up for their needs, worthy children of a loving God.[11]

Initially the work was simple: knocking on doors, or rather poking one's head past the tear of fabric that served as a door, and like a magazine salesman, asking to come in. Maura hesitated in the first moments, unsure what to say to the young woman with her black hair braided down her back she found sitting at a sewing machine in the dark room. But Maura smiled broadly and began to explain, she was a sister, from the church, she was getting to know the neighbors. Miriam Guerrero, like many other people the sisters visited, was happy for the company and thought Maura's approach was so friendly, so warm. She'd been watching as this tall, thin *gringa* with cat-eyed glasses came walking through the tangle of shacks, accompanied by Fr. Valentín Martínez, one of the Spanish Jesuits. Miriam had never seen the priest outside of the church, but now here they both were, simply asking about her life, making conversation, treating her as if she mattered. It was a new sensation.

Week after week Maura came, sometimes with Fr. Martínez. They were getting to know Miriam, asking about her family, her work as a seamstress, and listening to her sorrow and worries. Within a few weeks Maura invited Miriam to join a group of neighbors who would read the Bible together and talk about church. Miriam thought it an attractive invitation, because while she lived cheek by jowl with neighbors, she didn't know them. And while she went to Mass and prayed to the Virgin, she understood little of Catholicism. She'd learned as a child that God punished and she learned to beg him for safety, for enough food, for the health of her children. This was different. Talking to other women, listening to stories from the Bible, and relating them to her own life made her feel less alone. But what was most exhilarating, most thrilling was being asked for her own opinion. She'd never been asked what she thought—about anything. Now she sat up straight and laced her fingers together as she considered what it meant when Cain asked whether he was his brother's keeper. The curriculum was the same that Maura and the other sisters had used in Siuna and in the early days at San Pablo Apóstol, Family of God.[12]

The members of the group, sometimes just women, sometimes men and women together, sat in a circle in one of the members' homes, bringing chairs if they had them, or crates. Maura opened her Bible in her lap, holding her knees together and crouched forward a bit, casting her eyes around the circle before she began. Before the meeting, she'd marked the verse she wanted to read with a slight pencil line, so it was easy to find.[13]

She gently passed the open Bible to whoever volunteered to read. If no one was feeling confident—few people had gone to more than a few years of school and many could not read—Maura read from the Gospel of Saint Luke: "He has sent me to bring glad tidings to the poor, to proclaim liberty to the captives, recovery of sight to the blind and release to prisoners, to announce a year of favor from the Lord."[14]

"Now, what is Luke telling us? What does that mean for us today?" she asked. Maura settled into her chair, letting the women speak. She wanted to hear their ideas. In a successful evening several people would speak, explaining where they saw God, what they thought God was asking of them, laying out their understanding of the stories, applying them to life in Managua in 1970. During the day most of the women sold tortillas or fruit in the open-air market. Children played in the muddy lanes of Miralagos in tattered rags, the youngest ones naked. But here at night, these women were respected

members of a group, their thoughts mattered. This Gospel, these stories of prophets were written for them.[15]

At Miriam's house, Maura helped make the coffee before meetings and sat happily with a child on her lap, a familiar presence, ready
to laugh, quickly a friend. Quoting Saint Paul's letter to the Corinthians to explain that church was more than the big stone cathedral
and more than the institution of bishops and pope, Maura stressed
that every person had a vital role. Together they made a whole, the
Body of Christ in the present.[16]

The idea appealed to Angelique Rodríguez Alemán, a young
woman in her twenties, who sold what she could in the market and
had moved to Managua so her children might be able to go to school.
She was taken by Maura's openness. She, too, had always gone to
Mass, but church was mostly about obedience and fear of God, until
the day a small crowd of people came to her door, fifteen of them:
Maura, Fr. Martínez, and others from Miralagos. They were singing,
the priest playing a guitar. In the front was this tall woman, very
beautiful, smiling. Who could deny her?

Angelique loved the study sessions, called cursillos, the meetings and retreats that grew out of them. She looked forward to the
weekly sessions, to the bustle of sweeping up the house and setting
out chairs for these neighbors who were fast becoming friends. They
celebrated birthdays together; when a relative died, the community
visited and sang with the grieving family. It broke the loneliness. As
in Siuna, Maura talked to the women about marriage, said their husband should treat them as a partner, not beat them, not drink too
much, not have affairs. She insisted that the stories Angelique and her
neighbors read in the Bible were about love, not judgment, that God
wanted not obedience and fear, but love.

Angelique, who had stopped school at third grade, was not a
confident reader. But Maura encouraged her, insisting that she was
capable of thinking on her own, of interpreting God's stories. Angelique felt herself growing more confident. She and her husband,
Manuel, had married in Masaya, a then-rural area outside Managua,
when Angelique was twenty-four. They moved to Pescadores—the
fishermen's section—of Miralagos, hoping to find work and land of

their own where they could build a house along the beach. They were near the center of Managua and close to the market where Angelique could sell fruit, tortillas, or the clothing she sewed. She tried to think of the move as a good thing, even though she'd left her brothers and sisters in Masaya. The children would be able to swim—and bathe—in the lake. In Managua there was a better chance the children could go to school. Instead, Manual traveled near a hundred miles to work digging wells in Chinandega, a city near the Honduran border. He spent the week away and took a long, slow bus ride home on the weekends. The children swam in the lake, but the lake was a dumping ground and a sewer. It frequently overflowed. There were mosquitoes and flies and an ever-present smell of rotting fish and fetid lake water that never left the nostrils. Being part of this group of women conversing and celebrating together made her feel human. Life was more than the difficulties and the poverty. She was part of something growing between neighbors. And Angelique loved Maura, loved how eager and personable she was, how quickly she integrated herself into the barrio, becoming another neighbor.[17]

Maura never missed a Wednesday night meeting. She walked through the lanes of the barrio, poking her head into dark shacks, reminding people to come to the next gathering. If someone missed a week, she visited the next day to ask how they were, sit for a cup of coffee or keep them company a while. It was slow, emotionally demanding work. The parish team had divided the neighborhood into zones. Maura had been flattered when the stern Fr. Martínez asked her to work with him in his zone. She mentioned it in several letters, expressing how impressed she was that he was so confident and sure of himself, relieved to follow the lead of someone who seemed to know what they were doing. Between various groups in Santo Domingo and ongoing work with adults and young people in San Pablo Apóstol, Maura was busy almost every night, often arriving home after ten p.m.[18]

In the mornings she sat with her Bible, read from the psalms or letters Saint Paul had sent to early communities of Christ's followers, and closed her eyes. Letting her chin drop to her chest, she contemplated the meaning of the verses and how they could draw her closer to God. Her greatest goal, even as a teenager ducking into Mass during lunchtime at Stella Maris Academy, was to pull herself closer to Christ, to model her life on God's until they were joined. It was her primary relationship. As a young woman she had vowed to love and serve, to seek and follow God. This is where her God had led her, to the fetid edge of a polluted lake where families discarded by a rapacious world struggled together. As the noise and stench of the neighborhood enveloped her, she prayed to make herself as open and as giving as the divinity who loved the world enough to suffer with it. Maura was endlessly open-hearted, tuned to the needs of people she encountered. But she required these spaces of solitude to replenish and prepare to meet her Christ suffering in the barrio.[19]

She dressed quickly in a blue or brown skirt her mother made, buttoning a white blouse, and pushing her hair back, before she left the rickety house a little before eight a.m. to catch a bus. She taught English to elementary school boys at the Colegio Centro América, a Jesuit school in another part of the city. The priests in Santo Domingo could only pay a tiny salary, and even living so simply the sisters each needed other jobs to support themselves. In the afternoons she taught religion in a public school. The public schools were deplorable: dark, crowded, and hot, and students sat at broken desks. But Maura enjoyed being with children again.[20]

She carried a brown accordion file folder under her arm everywhere she went, pulling out half-finished letters while standing in the street waiting for a bus, while waiting for a meeting to begin, in the few minutes before she fell into her bed at night. Her letters constituted a running conversation with her parents. She reread her parents' letters several times throughout the week, unfolding the thin, onionskin paper to remind herself of her mother's words or to read portions aloud to Rita and Bea. She responded quickly; letters often crossed each other in transit. Maura's letters were chatty and breezy, but their sheer preponderance revealed her homesickness, her uncertainty in this new role, her longing to be part of everything at home. Her mind wandered to her parents at different times throughout the humid Managua days. She finds herself trying to bridge the miles to Rockaway, wondering what they are doing at any moment.[21]

From 1,500 miles away she tells her mother to be careful on the stairs when she returns to her own house, worried that they would put a strain on her weakened heart. She notes that Judy's younger son would soon be a year old and tells her parents that Sr. Estelle would be in Nicaragua in a few days and then would visit the Clarkes in New York. Maura's parents kept in touch with several of their daughter's fellow nuns, writing letters and hosting her friends for dinner whenever they were in the United States. The day before Mary Clarke's birthday, after Maura had been gone for little more than a month, she phoned home. The conversation was quick, just long enough to hear her mother's voice and learn her father was marching with his IRA comrades up Fifth Avenue in the St. Patrick's Day parade. Maura was proud of John, thinking he must look handsome in his suit, garnering cheers for a cause he committed to a half-century earlier.[22]

In another week Maura celebrated Easter at a religious retreat with teenagers from Santo Domingo and San Pablo Apóstol parish. They prayed and talked about Jesus's arrest, torture, death, and resurrection not as a remote, spiritual event—something depicted in statues or medieval paintings—but as something that happened when God became a human who lived and who suffered under military occupation. The Jesus of Good Friday and Easter knew what it was to fear the National Guard. He wasn't locked up in the sky or laid flat on the pages of a holy book. This Jesus belonged to the people, came alive again when the people were united. The critique Maura developed against the Somoza regime and the growing public opposition of the Christian Base Community groups wasn't reducible to a political platform. It was, for Maura and her friends building this new kind of church, an attempt to follow and be loyal to God. Finding Christ in the contemporary world was an act of prayer.[23]

The group left the city for a few days of reflection and discussion at an estate formerly used only by nuns. In the bucolic and peaceful retreat house, the teenagers were asked to think about what Jesus Christ's death and resurrection meant to them, what role they would have played if they had been with him in Jerusalem. They sang, played games, and did icebreaker exercises. The atmosphere was casual and warm, encouraging the teenagers to see themselves not as subjects of a royal God, but as friends, beloved children of God, and agents, participants in a message of love and liberation. They needed to work together to build a society with less suffering, one where children didn't swim in fetid lakes and fathers didn't have to travel halfway across the country for work while a small elite lived in great comfort.

Teenagers gave talks on Jesus's life, relating the story in which Jesus's followers fed a crowd of fifty thousand by pooling and sharing what they had to their own reality or considering what it meant when Jesus said whoever saw someone hungry and fed them or saw someone homeless and made them welcome, was serving God. Maura and the priests and other nuns organizing the retreat used a methodology called See, Judge, Act that had been in place in Catholic church work since the early 1960s. It called on participants to consider a problem, ask why the situation existed, what its root economic, social, and historical causes were, to evaluate the problem in light of what they learned from the Bible and Catholic social teaching, and finally to decide what actions needed to be taken. It is the method the people at San Pablo Apóstol used as they stretched beyond their initial community building and became active in the opposition to Somoza. Maura would participate in dozens of retreats like these in the next several years, with teenagers, with women and married couples, with groups of other Maryknoll sisters, and with nuns and priests from across Nicaragua.[24]

The practice of social analysis was critical. So was empowering retreat-goers to speak their mind and develop their own leadership skills. Christina Suoza, a teenager from San Pablo's youth group, was to deliver a talk at one of the retreats for priests and nuns, on the poverty and oppression of most people in Managua. She was apprehensive about speaking in front of dozens of teachers, principals, and doctors, people far more educated than herself, worried that she would stumble or look foolish. "No, no, you can," Maura said as she put her hands on the girl's shoulders. She loved listening as Christina and the other women found their voice, was energized by learning how they made the story of Jesus their own and found themselves in it. "You know the reality, you walked the barrios, you know well that religious reality that is being lived in Nicaragua. You can, you can."[25]

When Maura was supposed to give a lecture on women in the Christian community at another retreat that April, she was as nervous as Christina, worried about the quality of her Spanish and whether she could say anything worth listening to. She fretted over it for a week, stayed up late making notes, filling, and reordering index cards. She asked her father to pray for her and confessed, not the first time, to feeling inadequate. In the event, she was poetry, discarding her notes and speaking from the heart about God's love. She fought machismo in her frank and unquestionable regard for the women of Managua's slums, and likely drew upon stories of women in the Bible who had valued roles, who sat and discussed with Jesus, carried Jesus's message to others, comforted him. She pressed that all the people gathered together for the retreat, all the people in the barrios, the women sitting at sewing machines and pounding masa were beloved by God, indeed that together they constituted the church, God's body in the world. She underlined the verse in her Bible: "Love then, consists in this: not that we have loved God, but that He has loved us."[26]

After the talks and the prayers and songs sung with guitar, often pieces from the Misa Popular Nicaragüense, a folk Mass written and recorded by the people of San Pablo Apóstol a few years earlier, there was dancing. The community was high on love and Maura was part of it, moving to the music, singing the folk songs that weren't so different from the ones her father sang. When the talks were over, she could relax, sit on the grass with her legs drawn up beneath her, and soak up the company of these new friends she was growing so close to. God is Love, they told one another, and Maura agreed.[27]

But all these meetings—the gatherings in people's homes and poor market women climbing on rented buses to spend the weekend at retreat houses; the guitars, the songs about a liberator, the priests and nuns who spent more time listening to poor people in the barrios than praying in the Cathedral—it attracted the attention of the Somoza regime at a time when protests and demonstrations were frequent in the streets of Managua. Somoza and his National Guard had a name for the new nuns and the people working together: *comunista*.[28]

Several prominent clergy in Nicaragua—though not the official leadership of the Catholic Church—had in the past few years publicly criticized Nicaragua's economic system and its resulting poverty and condemned the repression and violence visited upon any who resisted. Opposition to Somoza was broad by 1970, yet most of those who opposed the regime were not members of the Sandinista National Liberation Front. The group, formed in the early 1960s and invoking the name of the nationalist rebel Sandino from the 1920s, had staged a few doomed battles with the National Guard in the countryside at the beginning of the last decade. A dedicated cadre continued to conspire against the regime. Many Sandinistas were serving long prison sentences. Now the group was quietly and steadily building strength, finding allies in unions, farm cooperatives, and student associations. The Somoza regime hunted these dissidents. Meanwhile news trickled into Managua of raids and arrests in the countryside: the massacre of dozens of peasants in the mountains, the killing of nineteen members of the same family in the department of Jinotega, the National Guard raping suspected Sandinista sympathizers and arresting others in the north. As the summer of 1970 wore on, the church groups became more intermingled with the political opposition to Somoza. In Maura's Nicaragua, opposition emerged from the conversations on retreats, from the women and men rereading the Gospels, parsing Jesus's words, and poring over the actions of his followers. Plenty of people in Nicaragua were reading Marx, but in the Christian Base Communities Maura and the others were organizing; they read the Bible and looked around. It was enough.[29]

That fall, tensions between student activists and the state only fanned the flames of dissent against Somoza. And here, too, priests and nuns played a role, in particular a Jesuit priest, Fernando Cardenal, who was involved in the new kind of religious organizing Maura was part of. Fr. Cardenal came from a prominent Nicaraguan family and had worked in poor neighborhoods in Colombia in the 1960s, shocked and angered by the misery he saw. In 1970, he returned to his home country, vowing to work always for the liberation of the poor. Appointed vice president for student affairs at the Jesuit-run University of Central America (UCA), Fr. Cardenal was quickly caught between the administration and student activists demanding greater say in the operation of the school—the same sort of campus protests that had riven US campuses throughout the 1960s. He sided with the students.

Then on the night of September 19, the Office of National Security, an arm of Somoza's sprawling surveillance state, rounded up more than twenty students and teachers from neighborhoods across Managua. Among them were five student leaders from the Jesuit university. The student government, Fr. Cardenal, and a few other priests signed a statement protesting their arrest, but knew they needed to do more to protect their friends now held in Somoza's notorious prison beneath the presidential palace. On the morning of September 26, ninety students and six priests walked into Managua's Catholic cathedral in a nonviolent protest. They gathered in the soaring neo-Gothic building that anchored downtown Managua for the same reason refugees and wanted men run to sacred space: the army wouldn't pursue them into the sanctuary. Sitting under images of Jesus's torture and execution they demanded the release of political prisoners, the end to torture, an accounting for the arrested students.[30]

Soon everything was moving quickly. Maura heard of the sit-in as teenagers she knew rushed to replicate the protest. She admired their passion and discipline and was proud that priests were with the students, separating themselves from the government. Young people took over churches across Managua and across the country. They sat in the pews and slept in the aisles for three days, until one of the UCA priests was permitted to see the student prisoners.[31]

Less than two weeks later, Maura was with the teenagers of Santo Domingo and San Pablo Apóstol at a national youth congress she was helping Fr. Cardenal run in the Pacific coast city of León. Catholic youth groups from all corners of Nicaragua met at a retreat house to pray together, analyze the situation in their country, and make a commitment to work for change. Maura joined them as they sat in clusters talking with the teenagers she loved, listening as they invoked Christ's commandment to love their neighbors, to provide for the poorest, to claim their dignity as children of God as reasons for building a new Nicaragua. They reminded her of her father pining for freedom for his country and taking the Irish Republican Brotherhood pledge to liberate his people.[32]

The sit-ins and demonstrations were covered in the US newspapers, where they took the form of stories about violent leftists taking over the churches. In their next letter Maura's parents asked about the riots they had read about. "Actually there really weren't any riots when they took over the churches and the Cathedral in protest against injustices to human rights," their daughter assured them, praising the six priests who had stayed with the students. It was late, her housemates were already asleep, but she pressed on, hoping to help her parents understand. "Don't worry dear hearts, I'll be careful and stay out of the riots and fights but we must do what we can to lend support to those who have the courage to give themselves for a change as surely this can't continue on the same much longer."[33]

But while the Maryknoll sisters and many Jesuit priests and the homegrown church communities of San Pablo Apóstol and Santo Domingo were wholeheartedly in favor of the protests and participated in them, many in the church hierarchy saw the political agitation as dangerous and disrespectful. The bishops and the pope's representative in Managua took offense at the use of the cathedral as a place of sanctuary by activists and denounced this mixing of politics with religion. Student demonstrators were threatened with excommunication.[34]

But protests continued to roil Managua. In mid-October, the school teachers threatened to go on strike over the government's refusal to negotiate various demands. Maura thought their claims were legitimate. She found it shocking how weak the unions were in Managua, nothing like the muscular municipal unions of the New York City of her youth. She joined a demonstration with her public school colleagues, marching through the streets of Managua in a throng with the teachers' union. Although she didn't often miss the Maryknoll habit—it was hot and constricting and separated her from people, made them think she was some kind of an angel instead of an ordinary woman trying to follow God—she wished she had it to wear now, so that bystanders would recognize that a nun was in the march. Still, she felt a little tentative, remembering the scandal three years earlier when Maryknoll sisters and priests in Guatemala were caught conspiring with guerrillas. They had been forced out of the country and several left the Maryknoll order. Sr. Mildred Fritz, Maura's regional superior during the end of her time in Siuna, blamed the Melville incident, as it was called, for derailing Maryknoll's ability to do the slow, steady work of raising consciousness. It had made the whole congregation suspect.[35]

Maura cared what people thought of Maryknoll and valued her relationships with other orders of nuns. Partly for this reason, partly because she had more patience than the other Maryknoll sisters in the country and could be more diplomatic with traditional and conservative orders, she was appointed the Maryknoll delegate to the Confederation of Religious of Nicaragua (CONFER), a professional organization of nuns and priests. She pushed, along with Fr. Cardenal and Luz Beatriz Arellano, a Nicaraguan Franciscan sister, to get the organization to take a stand in the movement for human rights and political justice. Nuns and priests working on the ground and in the neighborhoods were inspired by Medellín and the Christian Base Communities, but the older members, the presidents and mother superiors, were skeptical. The younger sisters at CONFER meetings and those excited about the emerging role of sisters in building up an active and engaged church talked about Maura after meetings. She exemplified the new idea of a nun as a person who reflected her deep relationship with God through her engagement with the matters of the world.[36]

As rainy season began, mosquitoes circled the damp rooms in Miralagos, buzzing in everyone's ears. Maura slept under a mosquito net and neighbors poured into Sr. Rita Owczarek's health clinic with skin infections and deep, persistent coughs. Many of the homes were flooded, filthy water rising on the wooden floors. There was no respite in the slum, no break from the din of neighbors whose lives Maura heard through the walls of the cramped houses. Someone was always fighting in the barrio; someone was always at the door asking the sisters for a favor; the communal room downstairs always full with meetings or women seeking counsel. Maura could hear Rita snoring when she went to sleep at night under photos of her parents, siblings, and nieces and nephews pasted to the wooden wall. She woke to the busyness of the narrow streets: peddlers hawking wares, children shouting, roosters crowing. She climbed out of bed each morning early—to steal some time for herself.[37]

Meanwhile, Lake Managua continued to rise, washing out the ragged homes in Pescadores and Miralagos. The residents, squatters really, were transferred by the government to an empty plain, a former cotton plantation outside Managua called Operación Permanente de Emergencia Nacional #3 (OPEN 3). Fr. García, the pastor at Santo Domingo, began to build a house there where the sisters could live to be close to those they loved and struggled with. Maura and the other sisters relocated there. Maura traveled in from OPEN 3 to Managua proper to work with the people who still lived in the other parts of Santo Domingo. New nuns joining the Nicaragua mission would also live in OPEN 3.[38]

At the end of her first year in Managua, Maura broached a topic with Bea and Rita. She wanted to go home for Christmas. It was just so hard to be away from her parents, and with her mother not well, couldn't she take a quick trip back to Rockaway? The strict orders of the old convent are no longer in effect; she didn't have to beg permission anymore for an extra piece of paper from a sister superior. But her time wasn't exactly her own, either. They were supposed to be living a life of radical simplicity, in total solidarity with the poor people they served, Bea and Rita reminded her. It's not as if the people of Miralagos could hop on a plane. But her friends wouldn't stop her. Maura was intent on going home. She needed to see the family, to be with Judy and Buddy and the children, to look at her mother herself and take a walk with her father. But even though she didn't exactly need their permission, Maura wanted Bea and Rita's approval. Couldn't they understand why she wanted to see her family? Did they think maybe she shouldn't go? It was a dance Maura often performed. She knew what she wanted, but she desired not just acceptance but approval of her wishes from her friends. Contemplating that they disapproved or even merely weren't enthusiastic made her anxious. It drove her friends a little nuts. "Maura, if you are going to go, go." "Do you think so, should I?" Living so closely together, on top of one another really, working in overlapping roles in the neighborhood and sitting together for joint prayers and reflection in which they discussed their deepest feelings, the three women were close with one another and with the other Maryknoll sisters in the country: there was a house in León and another in the countryside. They knew the ins and outs of one another's personality, knew the games each played, her insecurities and needs. Mostly they strove to accept one another openly, to let their guard down, and when conflict arose, discuss it in a healthy way. But Maura hated conflict. If someone offended her, it was her instinct to turn inward and manage her own reaction, saying, "It's okay, it's nothing. It will be fine."

She went home for Christmas 1970, arriving two days before the holiday, ready to soak up her parents' affection. Sometimes it was as if she'd never left home, never quite separated from Mary and John—and yet she had chosen a missionary order, knowing that life would send her far away. After she went back to Managua, and as time wore on and she grew accustomed to her work, Maura sent fewer letters home; now a week or two might pass between missives. But initiating meetings, gathering new groups, and building leadership was draining, sometimes disappointing work. Fr. Martínez was away for most of 1971, back in Spain visiting his family. The parish wasn't the same without his leadership. And the work was hard. In June 1971, Maura returned to her hot little house exhausted and dejected one night, in need of comfort from Bea and Rita. A meeting for a new cursillo group attracted just a tiny number of women, and she'd been organizing for ages. When the groups came together, relationships blossomed and the community stayed together as a cell, a unit of connected believers pursuing God together, it was beautiful. But plenty of times it was like pulling teeth to get any numbers of men to come, or there were jealousies and squabbling between women. Maura tried to put it in perspective: Jesus's whole life looked like a failure: an itinerate preacher whose friends abandoned him when he was arrested.[39]

She didn't want to abandon him—and didn't want anyone to feel forgotten. A few months earlier, when university and high school students again took over the cathedral and other churches, staging a three-week-long sit-in to demand the release of political prisoners who had served their time, Maura visited to pray with the teenagers she knew and offer emotional support. She sat with the mothers of the young political prisoners, student activists, and teenagers rounded up by Somoza's National Guard or Office of National Security and locked away in the brutal prison. When the mothers went on hunger strike, refusing food for twenty-one days, Maura visited them, sharing their fear and hope. Mary Clarke, always full of praise, told Maura she should continue, and compared it to work relatives of hers had done during the Irish revolution. "They worked for the language, culture and the improvement of the young," Mary wrote to Maura. "But your people are so distressed I'm glad you can give them some moral support."[40]

Maura joined marches and demonstrations but stayed out of the most dramatic actions because, as a foreigner, she didn't want to risk deportation. Already some Jesuits had been refused reentry into the country. The small group prayer meetings and retreats bled into planning meetings for political action. By 1971, the Nicaraguan bishops were beginning to take notice, issuing an official document in May that argued Christians had a moral obligation to be engaged in public life. The hierarchy still didn't approve of the church takeovers and were deeply suspicious of the Marxist orientation of many of the activists, but they were acknowledging that Nicaraguans lived under an oppressive regime.[41]

In September 1971, Maura's parents were again in Ireland, visiting family. But the north of Ireland was in turmoil. In 1969, after violent repression of a Catholic civil rights movement and renewed IRA guerrilla activity, the British government sent troops to impose order. The soldiers were meant to keep peace, but with searches, arrests, machine-gunned checkpoints, and troop carriers rumbling through little towns, the peacekeeping felt like occupation to Catholic Irish. At dawn on August 7, 1971, the British Army descended on Catholic areas, armored trucks disgorging helmeted British soldiers, guns in hand. They knocked in doors, smashed windows, and tore men from their homes. Anyone could be arrested. Charges weren't necessary; subversives needed to be dealt with forcefully: detention on suspicion of terrorism. The jails filled up, 342 people arrested the first day. Most were not violent, many not IRA members, a few not even political.

They were tortured. There were marches and protests in Belfast and Derry, Molotov cocktails, and IRA gunmen. So much tear gas was discharged by the British military that the dogs were going blind. Mixed Catholic and Protestant neighborhoods purged their minority members. Maura's family wasn't directly affected yet watched in horror, Mary praying for the thousands of people driven from their homes. At night in humid Managua, Maura prayed for her cousins; theirs was the same struggle as the Nicaraguans, she thought. People aching to be the authors of their own history.[42]

In December 1972, Maura hosted a dinner. She pulled out a recipe book her mother had sent and chopped potato salad, roasted steaks in the oven, and beat eggs and condensed milk into flan. Sr. Melba Bantay, a young Maryknoll nun who'd arrived in the past year, and Kay Kelly, her old friend from Siuna, were working all day, so Maura hustled around the kitchen herself. In the continuous musical chairs of assignments and living arrangements, Melba and Kay had replaced Bea and Rita as Maura's roommates in the city when Bea and Rita decided to stay in OPEN 3. The whole group were close friends, confidants who devoted real energy and consideration into their relationships with one another. Maura cooked rarely. Putting on a dinner put her in mind of those high school afternoons when she rushed to get dinner on the table. This time she was cooking not just for Kay and Melba but for Frs. García, Marciano Mercerreyes, and Martínez, the last of whom Maura always mentioned with fondness and excitement in her letters. He had returned from his long sojourn in Spain and Maura was glad he was back. She admired his commitment, his passion for the work of building up the small church groups, and told her mother that he sang well. The other sisters teased that she had a crush on him.[43]

A week later Maura hosted another party, this time to celebrate Fr. Martínez's birthday. She invited everyone in the parish to dine on the roof of the parish house. The sisters had just that fall moved back into the city from OPEN 3, where they'd relocated after Lake Managua rose. Now they were living above the parish office in a three-story fortresslike concrete building close to the church of Santo Domingo. Up above the neighborhood the air was lighter, Maura could see the twin spires of the Catedral de Santiago and the lights of Managua sparkled in the dark night. The party reminded Maura of the shindigs of her youth when her father's old Sligo friends would pile into the house and the evening would wear on with dances and stories, ballads recited and old songs declaimed. It was the same at a Nicaraguan party: everyone offered a poem or a song and everyone left happy and late. It would be the last lighthearted evening for a long time.[44]

As Christmas 1972 approached, the church communities and political organizations began to agitate for the release of political prisoners—an amnesty before the holiday. And they were disgusted by the opulent Christmas preparations in the wealthy quarters of Managua, advertisements for Christmas duck and luxury gifts, when people in the countryside were struggling to scrape food out of the land in the seemingly unending drought. On December 22, hundreds of people, led by Fr. Cardenal, with Luz Beatriz Arellano and many of the Santo Domingo and San Pablo people, gathered at the Catedral de Santiago in the heart of downtown Managua. They planned to camp out for three days, holding vigil until midnight Christmas Eve, when they hoped their demands would be met and scores of their comrades released from Somoza's prisons. Maura wasn't at the demonstration. Following Fr. Cardenal and Sr. Luz Beatriz's advice, the American sisters stayed home. They believed the protests should be led by Nicaraguans: if Maura and the other Maryknoll sisters were deported, they'd be no help raising the consciousness of people in the barrios.[45]

Soon after the protestors bedded down for the night, a mighty rumbling sound swept through the plaza. In seconds the marble pillars of the cathedral splintered. The paintings above the side altars jumped from the walls. The cross that sat atop one of the spires tumbled off and clattered to the ground. A clock atop the edifice, its mechanism disjointed, froze at 12:29 a.m. Managua had been hit by an earthquake of 6.2 magnitude.[46]

Maura's bed was rolling, the floor buckling beneath her. Her few books flew off their shelf. Her dresser careened across the room.

She woke up to the house shaking violently. It felt as though the three-story concrete tower was being pulled apart. With fearful cries Maura, Kay, and Melba leapt from their beds and met in the hall-way in their nightgowns. Their eyes wide and prayers on their lips, they ran down a flight of stairs, the walls waving and cracking beside them—hoping to escape the building before it tumbled down upon them. But on reaching the second floor, they remembered the iron gate at the front door was locked from the inside and the windows on the first floor were barred. Where was the key? Standing in the dark building, hearing the crashing and screaming of the neighborhood around her, Maura thought death was near. She struggled to compose herself, to meet God at this chaotic end. Where was the key? Then she remembered precisely where it was, tucked away upstairs. Melba ran back up. Calmer now, the sisters tried the key in the lock. But the earthquake had shifted the building and the door was jammed, the weight of three stories bearing down on the iron gate. Across the street was a gas station. They knew it could explode at any moment, sending flames into them. The wind was blowing steady and strong.

The building was still shaking from aftershocks as the women ran up to the second floor. They broke a window. The Jesuit priests who lived across the street—Frs. Martínez, Mercerreyes, García, and others who worked in the university—found a ladder and leaned it against the building, but it didn't reach the window. Melba tied sheets together and she, then Maura, slid down into the arms of the priests, who stood at the top of the ladder and guided the women's feet onto the rungs. Maura was barefoot. With shattered glass ev-erywhere, one of the priests lifted her to the middle of the street. Fr. Martínez shouted to Kay, who was still at the window, to go back to the third floor and find some shoes for Maura and clothes for all of them. Amazed that she was spending a second longer in the unstable structure, Kay bolted up to the living quarters. She emerged again with shoes but hadn't stayed inside long enough to find clothes in the mess of furniture, overturned suitcases, and broken dishes.[47]

Around them Miralagos—all of downtown Managua—lay in ruins. The devastation was Dante-esque, as families wailed for loved ones trapped under rubble, people crushed by their zinc roofs screamed in agony, and fires ignited by knocked over candles and lanterns set the wooden structures ablaze. Fire rushed through the row of shacks across the street from the sisters' apartment; the families of several members of the parish youth group lived there.

Few in Miralagos had electricity, but the lights of the cathedral and the palace and the streetlamps of central Managua usually diluted the darkness. Now there was nothing but night. It was difficult to get one's bearings and Maura and her sisters moved by sound, not sight. Dazed but recognizing that they were uninjured, they pushed themselves into the ad hoc rescue efforts around them. Kay went with a crowd of neighbors to look for injured. Melba walked to the other side of the parish house where a young husband and wife from the parish were pinned at opposite ends of their home. Maura heard a man shouting. It was Sergio, a member of the Christian Base Community, trapped under the full weight of his house. His wife was in the street, crying. No one knew where their eighteen-month-old daughter was. Maura climbed over to Sergio and began praying with him, her voice keeping him from isolation, as friends struggled with crude jacks, endeavoring to lift the house off him. "Sister, thank you for staying with me. But could you pray in Spanish?" Sergio said from under the pile, his voice constricted with pain. In her excitement Maura had slipped into English. She switched to Spanish and stayed with him for several hours, keeping him conscious, protecting him from despair. Finally his neighbors opened a passageway wide enough for Sergio to crawl out. He emerged with a broken leg and broken arm, but intact. His daughter was dead.[48]

For the rest of the night Maura and the other sisters stayed in the chaos, comforting survivors, praying with the injured, providing triage medical attention. In the morning, realizing that the nuns' house was still standing, Melba and one of the priests climbed in and fetched clothes. Maura had spent the night in a nightgown and light robe. She stayed in Miralagos the next day, consoling people and trying to help. Neighbors sat dazed in front of their ruined homes, their few salvaged possessions clustered before them. Families wept for dead children, parents, siblings, and friends. Dead bodies littered the street. The market was utterly destroyed, as was the water infrastructure. In the evening the sisters retreated to OPEN 3 for a shower and meal and a night's sleep. Too frightened of aftershocks to sleep indoors, they strung hammocks in the courtyard behind the house and whispered good night to their neighbors doing the same. Like everyone else in the barrios, Maura closed her eyes under a dome of stars, rocking gently beside her friends.

The next day, Christmas, she returned to the earthquake zone. She didn't want to abandon the people she loved when they were in such crisis. Everyone was being evacuated to temporary camps in another part of the city or returning to the rural villages they'd left years before. She wanted to say good-bye, to keep track of everyone. There could be no Mass for Christmas Day, no celebration of God's birth in the world as a poor child. The big stone church of Santo Domingo stood empty and there was no wine to transform into the blood of Christ. Maura went with Fr. Mercerreyes as he walked through the remains of the parish. Each time they found a crowd clustered, they hugged people together and cried with them, held a prayer service and shared the Eucharist. It was Christ's broken body for a ravaged people.[49]

Maura at her First Communion at St. Rose of Lima Parish, Rockaway, New York, 1938.

Maura gazes at the mountains from a diving board at Baker Camp in Harriman State Park, New York, where the family vacationed, late 1940s.

Maura, on top step, smiles with her brother, Buddy, and a family friend, on her sister Judy's First Communion, early 1940s.

Maura *(second from left)* poses with Kay Keiley, Maura's boyfriend Joe Barry, and Patricia Thorpe, 1949.

Maura *(center)* laughs with her Stella Maris High School friends Lucille Callahan and Kay Kieley, 1949.

Maura with her mother, Mary McCloskey Clarke, on the Ireland coast, days before entering the convent, 1950.

Judy Clarke, Mary McCloskey Clarke *(obscured),* John Clarke, and cousin James Clarke visit Maura during her first months at Maryknoll, 1950.

The reception into the Maryknoll order at the end of the postulant period. Maura is among the sisters in white veils in the Maryknoll chapel, Ossining, New York, 1951.

Maura speaks to a member of St. Anthony of Padua parish during a picnic at Maryknoll, late 1950s.

Maura (left) and other sisters, along with students of Colegio Maryknoll, inspect a snake in Siuna, Nicaragua, early 1960s.

John and Mary Clarke visit Maura (kneeling, right) in Siuna, Nicaragua, 1963.

While Maura was working in Miralagos, the squatters' encampment in Managua, her parents sent money so the sisters could go out to dinner. *From left to right:* Sr. Bea Zaragoza, Sr. Peg Dillon, Sr. Rita Owczarek, and Maura, October 1971.

An outing at the beach with young people from Santo Domingo parish, Managua, and Fr. Valentín Martínez SJ, after Valentín returned from Spain, before the earthquake, December 1972.

Maura *(center)* with members of one of the Christian Base Communities in Santo Domingo parish. Fr. Marciano is at left. Managua, December 1972.

Maura with a close neighbor
in OPEN 3, mid-1970s.

Maura dancing during a celebration at the end of a retreat with a
Christian Base Community from
Santo Domingo parish, before
the earthquake, ca. 1971. *Photo
courtesy of Angelique Rodríguez
Alemán, Managua, Nicaragua.*

Maura *(center)* beside Fr. Marciano, with Fr. Valentín *(crouching)* and members of the
Christian Base Community of OPEN 3, just before she returned to the US, October 1976.

Maura with her parents at their home in Belle Harbor, New York, when she was working with the World Awareness Program, late 1970s.

Maura *(left)* with three of Judy's children—Peter, Patricia, and Deirdre Keogh—at Judy's Long Island home, June 1980.

Maura on the first anniversary of the Nicaraguan revolution, wearing a Sandinista scarf, Managua, July 1980. *Photo courtesy of Cynthia Arnson.*

Maura on the coast of County Sligo, Ireland, August 1979. *Photo courtesy of Sr. Gerri Brake, MM.*

Sr. Terry Alexander MM, Sr. Maddie Dorsey MM, and Sr. Elizabeth Kochik SC, kneel as the bodies of Maura, Ita, Dorothy, and Jean are recovered in Santiago Nonualco, El Salvador, December 4, 1980. *Photo courtesy of Susan Meiselas, Magnum Photo.*

CHAPTER 7

The Convent Is in the Street

Managua was rubble. Tectonic plates ran straight through the center of the city and now the entire downtown was a mass of twisted metal and piled concrete. Maura thought it looked as if the city had been bombed. Earthquake survivors were still pulling the bodies of their loved ones out of the rubble days after the quake. There were 8,000 to 10,000 dead, 20,000 injured, 101,000 suddenly without homes. Four hospitals had been destroyed, along with 95 percent of the capital's small factories and workshops. The water mains had ruptured. The central market had burned down, leaving the city without food. In the first days, the parishioners of Santo Domingo walked their streets dazed and shocked, breaking down in gales of tears when they found a friend or relative alive. A meager and difficult life had become infinitely harsher: dead children, lost relatives, no market at which to sell handmade tortillas, no cement house laboriously built by pennies saved. Aid poured in from the international community, but lack of organization stymied efforts to get it to the people; a week after the quake, many still had no food, water, or shelter. The government instituted martial law and announced the formation of the National Emergency Committee. Anastasio Somoza Debayle, who everyone knew really held the reins of power but who was not at the moment president, was now officially in charge.[1]

Three days after Christmas, Maura and Melba moved into a displaced persons' camp the government established with the aid of US military personnel. It was named, cruelly or optimistically, Campamento Esperanza: Camp Hope. Maura and Melba hoped they could be of use to people there. It seemed important to stay with the people in greatest need, to be part of the camp so as to really understand what was needed—and to help the people organize. There was no shade from the punishing tropical sun but in airless canvas tents where whole families clustered. The slightest breeze lifted the topsoil, coating hair, clothes, and sweaty skin with a layer of grit. In the mornings, Maura lined up with everyone else at the food tent for a breakfast of rice and beans with hot powdered milk, her face and arms filmed in dust. She and Melba offered to help in the government-run kitchen but were rebuffed. They assumed it was because the Nicaraguan military was skimming the food allotted to the camp to sell on the black market. Everything was an opportunity for self-enrichment. At night the temperature dropped and everyone shivered inside the tents. The hastily dug latrines were rank, attracting incessant swarms of flies and making dysentery and typhus a serious risk.

The sisters coordinated with the bevy of international aid organizations and nongovernmental organizations (NGOs) that rushed into Managua to help, trying to find immediate assistance and to set up more permanent solutions. Maura distributed blankets and clothes, heartbroken that life had become yet harder, yet more precarious for Managua's poor. She wanted to cry, seeing so many families dislocated and grieving. All her work knitting together a community in Miralagos and Santo Domingo was scuttled by the earthquake, the people scattered throughout the country. No one would live in that jumble of rubble where she'd known such love. Maura was uninjured and would have a place to live whenever she wanted to move out to OPEN 3 with the other Maryknoll sisters, but the people in the camp had nothing. God must have spared her so she could carry on working, she thought, and tried to feel grateful. With each tent she visited, Maura focused on making the people feel cared for, asking them questions about themselves and smiling gently at the traumatized children. It was always easy for her to relate to kids. They craved attention and she had it to give. They had no shell of self-protection, no cynicism, and neither did she. Nearly half the camp's inhabitants were children.[2]

Maura and Melba wanted to organize a Christian Base Community at Camp Hope so that the people who flooded in from various parts of the city and were strangers to one another, would begin to work together and bond. But among the more than 1,200 camp dwellers were the families of forty-five national guardsmen and military personnel loyal to Somoza and suspicious of the new ways of being Catholic. A Christian Base Community would have to operate clandestinely, under a different name.[3]

Months earlier, Maura and Fr. Martínez had agreed to attend a six-week class on pastoral methods in Guatemala, joining dozens of other priests and nuns from up and down Central America. But now, with the destruction of Managua, leaving felt treasonous. The other Maryknoll sisters convinced Maura it was worthwhile to go. So much of Managua, both church and state, had been destroyed. It was horrendous, but also presented an opportunity to build back a new society, fairer and more loving. The horror of the earthquake's devastation had presented the Nicaraguan Church with a chance to truly stand with its poorest members, to commit itself to alleviating the hardships of the people while expressing God's love for each of them. The purpose of church was not to bolster the institution but to build the world Christ demanded, the sisters argued. Maybe now that would happen. Maura was already a veteran organizer, but she was doubtful of her own abilities and always eager for more training. There would be seminars on how to elicit authentic discussions, how to overcome interpersonal divisions, how to gracefully shut up a loud mouth and draw out an introvert. What she would learn in Guatemala would be useful in the next project, in building a new kind of postdisaster Church.[4]

And so, on January 5, Maura and Fr. Martínez left for Guatemala City. The course was led by Fr. José Mertens, who circled throughout Latin America leading similar workshops focused on harnessing the innate power and talent of the people in the pews. He was heavily influenced by education theorist Paulo Freire, who argued for teaching methods and philosophy that specifically sought to overturn unjust social structures. Maura, Bea, Kay, Rita, and the other Maryknoll sisters had been talking about Paulo Freire since their days in Siuna. Melba was hoping to use his methods as she set up literacy classes in Camp Hope. Freire pioneered a literacy program in Brazil that used interaction between teacher and student, a rejection of hierarchical relationships, to teach literacy while empowering the students. He argued against charity or a mind-set of the teacher or social worker or priest saving the people from ignorance. To teach liberation, one needed to share common cause with the oppressed. The methods of the system that created oppression would not dismantle it. The third week of the Guatemala course was devoted to studying the economic and political landscape of Central America. These priests and nuns had to know what they were dealing with to be able to fight it. How different it was from the bare-bones training Maura had received after leaving the Bronx for Siuna. Fr. Mertens asked the workshop participants to write a brief autobiography, a statement of self, articulating their personal history and motivations for their current work. Maura wrote hers in Spanish, a series of pared-down declarative sentences. "I was born the first of three children to Irish parents, revolutionary and poor," it began. "My father fought and consequently suffered a great deal in the Irish revolution."[5]

She sat in small groups with the other participants, taking personality assessments, such as the Myers-Briggs test, to better understand how she handled conflict, how she responded to stress, how she harnessed or shrank from authority. Maura put on a habit, the old uniform, to examine how it made her feel, the power and distance the old costume created. Everything was followed by conversation aimed at helping the participants understand and accept themselves so that they could be better leaders and animators of the people they hoped to reach in their parishes. Maura soaked it up, eagerly taking notes and joining in the late-night conversations. She was excited to be getting to know Fr. Martínez better, delighted to see the stoic Spaniard opening up. She was having a great time with all the other participants, happy to be with people doing similar work and able to lose herself in the conversations and games. At night they sang songs and often danced. At the end of the first week Maura celebrated her forty-second birthday. Someone played a waltz and everyone danced with Maura. She didn't mind the attention. She was touched when Fr. Martínez celebrated a Mass in her honor.[6]

By the beginning of March, Maura was back in Managua, sharing a tent with Melba in Camp Hope. The camp had developed while she was away, the thrown-together collection of people becoming organized into the beginnings of a conscious community. She was amazed by what Melba had accomplished in six weeks. Melba had made a connection with the Colgate Palmolive company, which now supplied soap, toothbrushes, and toothpaste to the camp and built a swing set for the hundreds of school-age children who lived there. Melba had recruited boys from the youth organization of Santo Domingo to begin Freire-style literacy and consciousness-raising classes, first arranging to have them trained by Edgar Macías, who worked with Kay Kelly at the Institute of Human Development doing organizing and popular education with farmworkers. The priests from Santo Domingo came twice a week to celebrate Mass and initiated a Christian Base Community, but called it Religious Action so the military wouldn't be suspicious. Families wanted their children to make First Communion, but Melba had nowhere to teach, so she set up a classroom in the corner of a US Army medic's clinic. She organized meetings at night to which hundreds came, ready to make demands, to agitate for their needs. Most important, she brokered a deal with a Nicaraguan nongovernmental organization (NGO) in which men in the camp, many of whom were carpenters, would begin building prefabricated houses. Finally, jobs. She'd made friends with the Nicaraguan colonel in charge of the camp, somehow convincing him to permit classes, even though the government was opposed. He jokingly called Melba the real *commandante.*

Maura fit herself in teaching math and literature classes for fourth, fifth, and sixth graders. There was no other school. Walking though the camp, she often thought of all the progress that had been destroyed in Santo Domingo. And she entertained the idea of going home, writing to her parents as she sat in the little tent with Melba. She wasn't due for a trip to the United States for another year, but she was homesick. Maybe she could convince the community of sisters that she could slip away for her father's birthday in May. As she lay in her tent at night, inches from Melba and able to hear the sounds of all the displaced families just a few feet away in their tents, she thought of all the times her family had moved when she was young, driven from one home to the next by rising rents or changing fortunes. It had been good practice, she thought.

The community was coming together to solve its problems. Maura tried to grasp onto the hope that represented. The latrines were a mess, breeding an army of flies that infested the tents. So, Melba and Maura went with the people to the office of a public health official responsible for conditions in the camp. It wasn't his job to keep the latrines clean, he said. He called the people Maura and Melba lived with degenerates and illiterates unused to living like civilized people. No wonder the latrines were disgusting. Fuming, the sisters helped the camp residents organize into work crews for several days. Men took turns digging better latrines from 8:30 a.m. to 9:00 p.m. Women cleaned the existing latrines and the kitchen, using detergents donated by Colgate Palmolive.[7]

And then suddenly it was over. The US State Department was nearly ready to move into its new embassy, which was being constructed on land abutting the encampment. The US government wanted the eyesore removed. The people had three days to evacuate. The United States was paying for the construction of a new encampment, a development of five thousand dirt-floored, wooden houses in another part of the city, but the people would have to pay rent. Maura thought this absurd since there was no paid work to be found and the plan for the prefabricated homes factory was now scuttled. She was outraged that the people had no say in their future. As usual, the powerful were treating people she cared about as a nuisance, as objects to be dealt with, rather than human beings. She complained about it to her brother, writing him a long letter about the cruelty of the decision, in what was ostensibly his birthday letter. Like most she sent to her family, it was late. She made a card for him out of cardboard she scrounged from somewhere in the camp, carefully writing out a quote about happiness. "There is a time for laughter," it began. She hoped so. The swift eviction, the generally wretched treatment of poor people, the emerging reports of earthquake relief money and

supplies disappearing into the maw of Somoza's corruption strengthened her conviction that organizing the people to unite in strong protest was the only way to truly help.[8]

Maura and Melba moved back to OPEN 3, where Rita, Bea,
and Peg Dillon had been already for a few years, working in the parish there, running a health clinic, and attempting to build a sense of
community. Maura had lived in OPEN 3 temporarily after Miralagos
flooded at the end of 1971; many of the people she spent time with
in those first years in Managua, beside the lake, had fled to OPEN
3 then and had remained. Now they were reunited. The house she
moved into had been a storage shed, close enough to the street that
a fine layer of grit from the bus and the dry wind settled on dishes,
clothes, books. When she climbed out of her thin-mattressed bed in
the morning, Maura covered it with a heavy plastic sheet. She pulled
plastic over her desk and the clothes her mother made and sent from
New York. Everything in the house was perpetually sheathed in grit.
The little house reminded her of the cabin the Clarkes vacationed in
when she was a child: a basic square with tiny bedrooms divided by
walls that didn't reach the ceiling. The roof was a sheet of metal, the
rafters open to let in air. She might have felt as though she was on her
own when she retreated to her room to write letters at night or to talk
silently to God, but every sound was still audible to her roommates
just inches away and neighbors leaned in the windows to say hello as
they walked along the street. In Siuna, the convent represented an
oasis, a special place for the nuns, so different from the rest of the
town that Maura felt compelled to invite visitors in on Sundays to
topple the barriers between the nuns and the people. In OPEN 3,
there was no separation. The sisters lived the life of everyone else.[9]

It was April 1973. Sr. Peg Dillon, a young intensely intelligent sister whom Maura called "Freckle Face" and gushed about in her letters
home, ran a youth club and gathered mothers together to share ideas
about child development. Sr. Kay Kelly, who worked in the countryside up near the Honduran border, training small farmers on human
rights and democratic action at the Institute of Human Development, came to OPEN 3 on the weekends. Fr. Marciano Mercerreyes

and Fr. Valentín Martínez, who'd served at Santo Domingo, moved to the barrio, too, joining Fr. Pedro Miguel García, who had been there since the settlement's founding.

Maura tried to keep up a positive attitude, but she felt dejected. The people in OPEN 3 were even poorer, somehow, than those in Santo Domingo. She wondered if she had anything left to offer. The job of building a community, of truly helping the people make something better, seemed insurmountable. Even the international relief flown in after the earthquake from generous countries around the world was sucked up by the dictatorship. All functions of government and all aspects of disaster relief were under Somoza's direct control. Somoza's men met the shipments at the ports and hustled them to warehouses. Aid meant to be given free to people sleeping on dirt floors showed up on the black market run by national guardsmen. International loans intended to spur reconstruction were awarded to Somoza family and friends and construction contracts went to connected firms. Somoza, other top government officials, and their families began buying up formerly public land in an area slated to be the new center of Managua, since few wanted to rebuild on top of the fault line. They quickly sold the land back to the government at high prices, getting paid with international development funds.[10]

Meanwhile life in OPEN 3 was meager. The unincorporated settlement was just a collection of shacks on a flat, treeless plain—a former cotton plantation. The years of cotton production had stripped the soil of nutrients and now it was mostly dust. There were no services: no electricity, running water, or governance and only limited transportation to Managua. Men set out to the earthquake zone in the morning to work at banging concrete off iron girders so they could sell the metal. Their wives stayed in the barrio with the children and the fathers came home late, never able to eat with their family, never able to spend any time together before dropping into bed.[11]

There were two Maryknoll houses in the settlement, sardonically named the white house and the dusty house. Maura's, the white house, was across the street and down the block from the dusty house and near the building the neighborhood used as a church. That church, a simple building the size of a school gym, constructed of concrete blocks with a tin roof, was topped by the huge metal cross that once adorned the church of Santo Domingo. Fr. García salvaged it in the days after the earthquake. It was as though their cross had followed the Santo Domingo people who fled to OPEN 3. The new church was known simply as Cruz Grande (Big Cross). In lieu of a bell, Fr. García leaned a broken piece of railroad metal beside the church. For many years, the people of OPEN 3 were called to Mass and to meetings by a clanging on that piece of railroad.[12]

Cruz Grande would be the site of neighborhood empowerment and rising resistance to the Somoza regime as well as the locus of a tug of war as the priests and nuns argued over the orientation of faith. Was a religious commitment about interiority, a personal relationship with God, and a quest for holiness? Or was it about the relationships between people and building the Kingdom of God, the society of love and justice Jesus called for? Fr. Martínez and Maura might have pondered that question on their long rides out of Managua to reconnect with Angelique Rodríguez Alemán, Maura's friend from the old parish. Angelique cried when Maura walked into her new neighborhood, amazed that she mattered so much to Maura that the nun would come looking for her. But she did. Unready to let the work of building the Christian Base Community in Santo Domingo completely unravel, Maura and Fr. Martínez drove every week to where Angelique was staying in Masaya and helped gather a new community of people to pray and talk together. Here Maura was comfortable. When meetings went late, Fr. Martínez drove back to OPEN 3 and Maura stayed with Angelique's family, sleeping in a simple wooden bed and eating breakfast with the family she adored.[13]

In OPEN 3, Maura took her turn sweeping the wooden floor and wiping the kitchen shelves with a damp rag to keep down the dust. It was never truly clean, but eventually she stopped seeing the dirt on the floor and got used to the gritty feeling when she rested her arm on the table. Water was delivered by horse cart once a week; a large barrel stood beside the house. It was a precious commodity parceled out judiciously for cooking, washing, and bathing. A scoop of water powered the outhouselike toilet. Maura used coffee cans to approximate a shower: one canful to wash off the soap, another to rinse her hair. She used the recaptured water—what remained in the tub from the shower—to sprinkle on the dusty plants outside. They made her think of her mother, now planting flowers in her own garden.[14]

Hundreds of families, displaced by the earthquake, were flooding into the settlement and erecting makeshift houses on land they mortgaged from the government. Just as in the Bronx when the Maryknoll sisters knocked on the door of each of their students to assess the family's needs, Maura and the other nuns organized a census of the burgeoning encampment, assembling school-age children and young teenagers from Peg Dillon's youth group and recruiting the newly arrived kids to identify the families that needed food, clothes, help with their children. They used the information gathered and the cadre of kids to disperse donations. Walter López Jirón, Humberto Bolaños, Roberto Somoza (no relation), and Henri Norori, who everyone called Frijolito, "little bean," were twelve- and thirteen-year-olds who spent their days playing soccer in the alleys of the shantytown. The work Maura and the other sisters gave the boys kept them out of trouble. It taught them to put the Christian commandment to love their neighbor into practice, underscored for them a link between religion and social action. The children's parents were happy they were doing something with the church, loosening their oversight of their sons and daughters as long as the kids were with the nuns.[15]

Roberto and Frijolito were intrigued by these strange new nuns who didn't wear black robes and who spent all their time talking to people. They loved being in their company. Maura could take a joke, her laughter hoarse and easy as she surrendered to it. She made them feel adored, as did Peg, who was forever asking them *"porqué?"*—why are things this way?—goading them to articulate what they saw, what they thought. Carmen García and Gloria Cannillo and other old friends from San Pablo trekked out to OPEN 3 to help make the census and to distribute goods. This was work Maura had always excelled at, establishing relationships, forming deep emotional connections. Just as in Miralagos and the other parts of Santo Domingo parish, she spent her days paying attention to people who were in a bad way. Meetings were important and there were many, but it was in the one-on-one home visits that she did her best work: communicating God's love, drawing people into connection with their neighbors, establishing relationships that would build a vibrant church and a strong neighborhood. But it was slow going. So many were traumatized by the earthquake, skittish and preoccupied with putting together their houses, usually shacks made of salvaged crates and boards. Those a little better off built with plywood. Maura felt the effects of the earthquake, too. She found herself jittery and tender. She reminded herself of a letter written by Saint Paul to some early Christians, exhorting them to fight the good fight. As the spring wore on, the sisters acknowledged to each other that they were feeling unsettled and anxious. They'd survived the earthquake and kept right on working, barely pausing to feel or admit that they were surrounded by death.[16]

Maura realized that the other sisters needed her here, and while she was disappointed she wouldn't be going home to celebrate her father's birthday, she knew it wouldn't be fair to leave again. Instead she painted pastel designs on a birthday card for John Clarke and wrote across the top a quote about memories allowing her to close her eyes and see all who she loves and who love her. Sitting late at night in her tiny room, aching for her parents, she wrote to them several times, apologizing that she couldn't be home. In each return letter they invited her anyway. They would send money to cover the ticket. Couldn't she consider it? They were so looking forward to having her. In June, Maura mentioned her vocation. She had chosen the life of a missionary, after all. This is where she belonged, even if she missed them terribly. She needed to stay. But the sideways entreaties continued: Cousins from Ireland were visiting and wouldn't it be nice to see them? If you could come like you thought you would, we would be so happy indeed, her mother wrote. Finally her father spelled it out. "Mom is not too good. She feels she would love to see you. You should try and come soon." Her sister, Judy, called urging her to come home right away. Maura wrote to the Maryknoll Central Government Board a few days before she left, announcing she'd be in New York on July 22. Meanwhile her Maryknoll sisters from across the region would be convening in Panama to sort out some questions with Sr. Laura John, Maura's friend from novitiate and Siuna. Sr. Laura John ran a radio program, pushing leadership training and consciousness-raising programs for rural people. For the past two years she'd been asking questions and failing to find answers about the disappearance of a priest, Fr. Héctor Gallego, she'd worked with. Laura suspected he had been killed by Panama's military government because of his advocacy for human rights.[17]

But being home was delicious. Maura and her father took a road trip to Providence, Rhode Island, to visit his sister, Sr. Oswald. Mary Clarke, who didn't seem to be in bad health at all, sewed a new white dress for Maura. Judy and Carol, Maura's brother Buddy's wife, bought her stylish sandals and pulled together a family party at Judy's house. She was embraced, adored, encouraged, able to take a real shower. In the late afternoons she sat with her parents in their backyard and admired the clean grass until her father carried out the tray of drinks, tall old-fashioneds. It was heaven to be home. Maura returned to Managua laden with Mary Clarke–made dresses for the sisters and shirts Carol had bought for the priests and the handy-man, and a tin full of cookies, a preserved ham, yards of pretty fab-ric, pots and pans for the kitchen, and a beautiful tablecloth from Judy, to brighten up the house. It was difficult to live in OPEN 3, but she would buck up, she told herself. There was good work to do. She set out the china tea set her mother had sent years ago to Siuna. A small luxury would make the tea taste better. There was no need to go to the dogs just because the street turned to a river of mud when it rained and she sometimes slopped into meetings with mud up to her knees.[18]

Being with the larger group of Maryknoll sisters, seeing what the whole set of them were doing in sites throughout the country, made Maura happier in those first months after the earthquake. Some were working with small farmers in the northern part of the country. Sr. Estelle had returned to Nicaragua to begin a planned community for earthquake survivors in the city of León, working with Miguel d'Escoto, a Nicaraguan Maryknoll priest whom she had worked with in Chile on a similar project in the 1960s. The Nicaraguan Founda-tion for Integral Community (FUNDECI) would offer simple but dignified houses with proper sanitation and open spaces for children to play in, a departure from the squalor most people lived with. Sr.

Estelle brought her sense of order and propriety to the project. There would be activities for families and an active parish. She screened families, insisting that couples be properly married and checking into their reputation. It struck some of the younger sisters as a bit rigid, but Sr. Estelle had her ways. She had invited Maura to join the project, but Maura declined; she wanted to be near the group she'd been working with in Managua.[19]

By late August Maura was happier. After heavy rains tiny blue and yellow wild flowers sprouted from the dirt and what was gray a month earlier turned spring green. Work was coming together. On Saturday afternoons she sat with María Luisa Urbina, a friend from Miralagos who had fled to OPEN 3 after the lake rose and now was the first lay person to teach First Communion classes in the barrio. María Luisa and other women met with Maura in the white house or in their own ragged homes each week, planning the lessons they would teach seven-year-olds the next day. By August one hundred children were enrolled in these community-run classes. It gave Maura energy to see María Luisa proudly asking the children what it meant that Jesus gave his life, what they shared when they celebrated Mass. Maura had been teaching First Communion classes since her first days in the Bronx, but now she was giving neighborhood women the power to be their own experts, the authority to share their faith. And María Luisa was so solid, a woman the neighborhood could depend on. She lived next door to the white house. They called to each other through open windows, talked as they hung laundry or washed in the heavy concrete sink in the center of the yard. Maura loved stopping into María Luisa's tiny house to chat at the end of the day or to check on some business with the parish. María Luisa made her a cafecito and Maura asked her about her day, about the news in the neighborhood. She smiled and asked María Luisa how she felt, what she was thinking about. When María Luisa and her husband returned to the shack late at night having been away all day visiting María Luisa's mother-in-law, Maura whispered over to her neighbor, "You must be hungry. Let me bring you something to eat."[20]

Mercedes Taleno, whose teenagers Lesbia and Edgar were finding their voices in the youth group, became a good friend to Maura, too. They prepared meetings together and went through the labyrinth of OPEN 3's shacks to invite more neighbors to join their discussions. Mostly they simply enjoyed one another's company, Maura's face breaking into smile when she saw Mercedes. Just as in Santo Domingo, the visits were a way to build up the confidence of the women oppressed by a machismo culture and unrelenting poverty. For Maura it was instinct. She couldn't not connect.[21]

Women stopped by the house constantly asking Maura for help or sympathy or to prepare for a meeting or march. The *sala*, the central room of the white house, was forever occupied by some neighbor. And Maura loved being with them, loved hearing the utterly new ways they interpreted the Gospel, was happy when a new group came together and they filled the Cruz Grande with songs. Something was alive in the barrio. The people were coming together, building a new kind of church and a new kind of community. The group dynamics and meetings, courses, and outings were all a way to suggest to the women that they had worth and dignity, even if they weren't treated that way. The men from San Pablo Apóstol came to talk to the men in OPEN 3. Maybe a husband didn't need to always be in charge of his wife, they suggested. Maybe these nuns were right in what they told the women, that marriage was a partnership.[22]

Visiting people in their homes let Maura feel precisely the contours of her neighbors' lives. She was sure each person in the neighborhood had something to offer the group, some personality trait, some way of seeing the world that would strengthen the whole. She spent her days walking the dusty lanes of her sector of the barrio, smiling, asking questions. One day she got lost. Standing on a corner she looked around in confusion, disoriented by the unending rows of shacks and dirt lanes. Then she saw Denis Sandigo, a young man who lived beside Rita's health clinic. He opened his arms wide and so did she, effusive and grateful to be found. Denis led her to his house, where Maura sat and drank coffee with his mother and admired Denis's artwork. He painted Nicaraguan primitives, small, brightly colored scenes of a country house or a farm. They were beautiful, Maura told him. Where did he get such talent? What a gifted artist he was, bringing beauty into the barrio. Denis led Maura home to the white house. At the home of Rosa Blandón she sat outside the makeshift cardboard shack and laid down the food she'd brought. Rosa's many brothers and sisters had little to eat so Maura did what she could, often taking food from the cabinets of the house she shared with the other sisters. Visiting Rosa's mother made the overburdened woman feel loved. She was surprised by how natural this tall *gringa* acted, as though sitting in a wobbling chair beside a plastic-sheeted home and drinking pulpy jicama juice out of a battered plastic cup was what she enjoyed most. When Maura looked at her, it was like she was the only person in the world, as though Maura wanted to drink her in. Rosa looked forward to Maura's visits. This *gringa* nun made the shy girl feel as if she had something to offer the barrio.[23]

Maura returned to the white house every evening sunburned and covered in a film of dust. She slipped off her shoes and rolled down her tattered stockings to walk barefoot in the house. The days of strict decorum and formality between sisters were long gone, which was a relief to Maura. It had never suited her instincts. Inside the house Maura sang (not very well) and sometimes danced a few steps, mussing her fingers through her sweat-dampened hair before sitting in one of the curved metal deck chairs to fill Peg, Melba, Bea, or Kay in on the day's work. There was a near constant rotation of sisters in and out of the neighborhood; someone went home for leave and another came to visit for a few weeks. Kay left for Chicago in 1974. Peg Healy, a young nurse practitioner, arrived in 1975. Maura herself would leave to work at the Sisters Center in Ossining in 1976. All the sisters traveled frequently to visit the other Maryknoll houses in Nicaragua and for meetings in Guatemala, El Salvador, and Panama. They shared books and teaching materials, hoping the customs officials at each border wouldn't look too closely at these prayers that called Christ a liberator and talked about Eucharist as the manifestation of God in his organized people.[24]

Maura loved these women. They knew one another intimately and treated the friendships as valuable relationships to be cultivated and maintained. When tensions arose, they analyzed their feelings and tried to confront problems. Certainly, sometimes they got on one another's nerves, and not every personality was suited to the next.

Did Maura really need to leave her dainty china teacup in the concrete outdoor sink? The younger sisters had heard the older ones tell stories about Siuna so often they considered banning the name of the town. Maura still shied away from confrontation, tried to brush off any difficult feeling, but she loved and was loved by these women. They knew her.[25]

It was in conversations with her roommates that Maura began to admit her feelings for Fr. Martínez were more than a crush. Most of the sisters had experienced something similar or had some layperson they worked with profess his love. Dozens left to marry. Maura didn't want to leave. And she had no indication the priest shared her feelings. But still, this set of emotions was new and powerful. Feeling her heart swell in the presence of this man after twenty-five years of celibacy was confusing. She'd dated plenty in high school and even that last summer before she entered Maryknoll, but those were the flirtations of a teenager. This desire for Fr. Martínez was destabilizing. She told her mother, whispered it to Judy. On one of her many visits home to the United States she shopped for cufflinks for the priest, excited to be thinking of him. No, her mother told her gently. Don't buy the man cufflinks. That's too much.[26]

She was in the midst of work at the white house one day when she announced, "I'm going to tell him." It seemed important—and important to be honest. She and Fr. Martínez were close enough friends and colleagues that she owed it to him, or herself, to be forthright. Her friends drew in their breath quickly. "No, no, Maura. Don't." They were mystified by the attraction. Fr. Martínez was brusque, severe, and traditional; Maura was opposite. They couldn't understand what she saw in him and feared he'd cut her down, trample her sweet openness. Despite being ten years older, Maura engendered a certain protectiveness from the younger nuns. Her guilelessness, her radical openness to each person she met, was disarming, but it also made her vulnerable. There was nothing hard about Maura, no protective shield of irony or world weariness. In the end she took her friends' advice. She didn't tell him.[27]

Once a month, all the Maryknoll sisters in Nicaragua met for a day they called Play and Pray. The sisters in rural towns in the north of the country; Pat Murray and Julie Miller, who worked in Tola; and the OPEN 3 gang drove out to León, the stately colonial city on the Pacific Coast, to meet Sr. Estelle Coupe and Sr. Margarita Jamias. The crowd of sisters walked on the beach at Point León, bought fresh fish from the vendors under palm-thatched stalls, and soaked up the sun and the company of peers. They teased one another and laughed, made space to uncoil from the demands of their work. At night they sat in a circle and told the stories of their work: Fr. García Laviana and the Christian Base Community in Tola were helping girls escape from the brothel there. They suspected the National Guard was behind the operation. Girls came to the sisters' house at night, thirteen- and fourteen-year-olds from rural villages who'd thought they were getting jobs as maids or cooks. The next night, Gaspar hid them in a box in the trunk of his jeep and drove to a priest in another town who'd bring the children home to their parents. The teenagers in León were getting ready to march again for the release of political prisoners. Maura and the OPEN 3 sisters talked about their fear for their teenagers and their pride. These kids knew what it meant to be Christian, to struggle for one's neighbor.

At these the monthly gatherings Maura and the sisters also tried to understand what goals they were stumbling toward. The prayer services were intimate, beginning with a song from Carlos Mejía Godoy, the protest singer whom Maura and the others knew from demonstrations at OPEN 3 and around Managua. Then the sisters asked God to be with them, called him into the circle. One of the sisters opened a dog-eared paperback Bible to a psalm or a piece of the Gospels, or increasingly as repression grew more intense, to the story of Exodus, of God's freeing the Israelites from slavery in Egypt. What was God asking of them? How could they respond with love to the endless demands of the life they'd chosen? What were the challenges to being authentic in their relationship with one another? Where did they see the Holy Spirit at work? Prayer services ended with singing, the women's voices, some harsh and gravelly, some light and sweet, finding one another's tune. Although 5,000 miles from the Latin prayers at dawn Maura had sung each morning as a novice, it was the same quest: a life in community directed at the transcendent.[28]

In OPEN 3, Maura, Peg Dillon, and Peg Healy ate at least one meal together every day, pulling the metal chairs around a rickety table and teasing one another over rice and beans—the silent, somber meals of the old convent a distant memory. They prayed the Divine Office at night, the sounds of the neighborhood mixing with the ancient prayers. Thursday nights they celebrated their own Eucharistic service, just the three sisters breaking the bread to re-create Christ's last meal—a reminder that Jesus was a person who lived and loved and was willing to lay down his life for his friends. But most nights were occupied with meetings.[29]

A few people from each sector met regularly to talk about their obligations as Christians to improve the situation in the barrio. Human beings, loved by God, shouldn't have to live this way. In the summer of 1974, some were engaged in a campaign for bus service, organized by Melba, Peg Dillon, and Maura. The women and men of the Christian Base Communities met in Cruz Grande to plan and strategize. They sewed banners and made signs, then marched in the streets of OPEN 3, demanding reliable transportation to the city where the people might earn a living. Too many men had lost their jobs in Managua because they'd arrived late. The existing service was unreliable and brought them home well into the night. It made it impossible for a husband to spend any time with his children or to talk to his wife. At the end of the summer the sisters held a meeting about the bus problem. They garnered great attendance, but Maura was worried. A strong communist element existed in the barrio. She didn't want to see the people used as tools for someone else's agenda. It wasn't political, she thought, to demand basic services. It was simple justice.[30]

That's what she told the teenagers in the Christian youth club Peg Dillon organized. The kids got together to play guitar and prepare for Mass. They put on socio-dramas, little plays that shed light on some problem in the community: disrespect for women, drunkenness, the high price of food. Peg led and Maura often helped out in exercises in the Paulo Freire style meant to get the kids thinking about equality, cooperation, or trust. When Frijolito and others printed the youth club's newsletter on the sister's mimeograph machine, highlighting the needs of the neighborhood—the poor people who did not have electricity, the lack of clean water—it wasn't being political. It was loving their neighbors. That's what Maura and the other sisters had taught them when they distributed earthquake relief: love your neighbor as yourself.[31]

But the political and the religious had merged. On Thursday nights, the teenagers came to the sisters' house to celebrate Mass with Fr. Fernando Cardenal, the Jesuit priest who dressed in a T-shirt and jeans. He and Maura had coordinated a national youth retreat months before the earthquake, asking the young people to commit themselves to building a society of justice. Maura had been impressed with the students' fervor. They reminded her of her father as a young man and she wrote to tell him so. After the earthquake, as the greed and brutality of the regime became ever more apparent, Fr. Cardenal founded the Christian Revolutionary Movement, dedicated to struggling more explicitly against the dictatorship with the college students who'd been part of the demonstrations of the past several years. In early 1973 he joined the Sandinista National Liberation Front (FSLN). He believed it was the best way available to build the kind of society Christ demanded.[32]

In his Masses in OPEN 3 in 1974, Fr. Cardenal didn't preach a homily. Roberto and Frijolito, Rosa, Lesbia, and dozens of other OPEN 3 teenagers sat on the floor with rich university students, members of the Christian Revolutionary Movement, many of whom joined the Sandinista front in 1973 and 1974. Fr. Cardenal asked them questions about the Bible readings, what Jesus wanted them to do about the disease and hunger around them, about the violence of poverty. It was the same rubric as in the old Family of God courses Maura had instituted in Siuna: See, Judge, Act. The actions were what made a religious conviction real. OPEN 3 was developing a reputation as a place of subversives. Tensions were bound to boil over. An afternoon in October 1974 was one of many boiling points. Maura heard shouting through the open windows of the white house. The National Guard was digging bodies out of the ground. There was no proper cemetery in OPEN 3, so families buried their many dead, the children killed by malnutrition, sepsis, tuberculosis, and diarrhea, in fallow fields at the edge of the settlement. She raced to the field with Peg Dillon and Bea. There she found the family of Carolina Calero, a five-year-old whose mother had buried her that morning. The day before, the landowner, the same one who sold the land for OPEN 3 and promised but never delivered improvements, wanted to sell this next field as well. So, he called the National Guard to clear the field of bodies. Even in death, the poor people of OPEN 3 were disrespected and discarded—an impediment to the designs of the wealthy. It infuriated Maura. She shouted at the guardsman, pointing her sharp chin toward the soldiers, her soft brown eyes hard and open wide, red rising in her cheeks. She had a way of getting taller and straighter when she was angry. Roberto and Henri were shocked to see their gentle friend and the other nuns confronting the National Guard. No one ever did that. Fr. Cardenal was there as well, and was stunned by the ferocity of the three women. It was the first time he saw the National Guard back down.[33]

For the young people, run-ins with the National Guard were common. But it was remarkable to see the sisters taking on their fight directly. The day after Mother's Day, May 1974, a message arrived at the white house. Roberto and some of the boys from the youth club were in the jail. Maura and Peg Dillon rushed to the dreaded building, terrified the boys had been harmed. They were fine. The teenagers had been out walking from house to house, serenading their mothers, the night before and ended up at the home of one of the girls, singing until midnight. But then the National Guard stormed into the house, arresting them. Any public gathering was suspicious to the regime by 1974, and a gathering of young people doubly so. Maura and Peg pleaded with the police. These are good boys, Maura said. They're not delinquents or troublemakers. She and Peg paid the bail and brought the kids home.[34]

Again and again, Maura and the others would step in to protect the children of OPEN 3. After the earthquake, a curfew had been imposed and never lifted. Now members of the National Guard swept the streets at night, picking up any young person they found. Many nights Maura would rush into the street to shelter the kids, hustling them into the white house before the soldiers came. The teenagers would hurry into the sisters' house when the guardsmen broke up meetings in the Cruz Grande, sneaking through back paths to get away. The nuns were their protectors and their house a center of action.[35]

Now the soldiers sneered when they saw Maura or the other sisters. They whispered to the teenagers, "Why are you hanging out with Sr. Comunista?" Maura was aware of the allegation and equal parts sensitive to it and dismissive. She wasn't a communist or even a Marxist; she was a Catholic. Plenty of priests and nuns as well as everyday church members were studying Marx in the 1970s and hashing out a sort of interreligious dialogue to create a Marxism with room for religion—Jesuits and other theologians across Latin America had been doing this since the early 1960s. But that sort of dense reading and wrestling with theory wasn't Maura's style. She far preferred to sit with Juana Rosa Duarte as she embroidered doilies and tablecloths. The woman had arrived from the Atlantic coast and she and her husband had no way to feed their five children. Maura suggested she start this micro-business. It was the same thing Maura had started with the Casita María in Siuna, the sewing workshop for girls. Maura kept running into people from the Atlantic Coast. Former students from Siuna frequently came to OPEN 3 to visit her and Rita, bringing stories of the difficulty of life in the undeveloped western half of the country and the beatings and disappearances of church workers there. By this time the Capuchins with whom Maura had worked in Siuna were spearheading a vast network of lay church workers, people in the scattered rural settlements who led weekly Mass-like services in the absence of a priest and who drew the community together to interpret the Bible and apply it to their lives. Called Delegates of the Word, these community leaders often carried messages for the Sandinista guerrillas massing in the mountains. The goals seemed analogous. Some were members of the FSLN.[36]

Maura was walking through the barrio one day when she caught a glimpse of Ramón Rodas Martínez. She'd taught him in elementary school in Siuna and seen him off to secondary school in Bluefields, the regional capital, nearly ten years earlier, hoping he would escape the servitude of the mine. Now here he was a grown man. She flung her arms wide and shouted to him, "*Mi niño, mi niño!*" He wasn't the only one. Guadalupe Maireno Estrada, the little girl Maura encouraged to go out riding into the campo on one of the first mission trips with Maryknoll sisters in Siuna and whom she'd recommended to the Carmelite convent was here, too. Guadalupe had been asked to leave the convent, unable to maintain the rigid decorum the mother superior demanded. She was ashamed. But Maura was glad to see her. Guadalupe's sister worked as a cook for the sisters and now Maura would be able to see her former student more. She hugged the young woman. "God isn't only in the convent," she assured Guadalupe.[37]

Maura knew it was true, but finding her way as a sister in tumultuous Nicaragua was a daily struggle. She became a nun to serve God and care for people in need, but the ground had shifted so much since 1950. On retreat days at a borrowed house near the Pacific Ocean, she sat on the beach with her knees pulled up to her chest and listened to the waves. The ocean was restorative. It was the same vast, unending sound that comforted her as a girl growing up by the sea. Here she could think. She didn't want to be sucked into a violent political movement. But she loved these people in OPEN 3. She admired the mothers struggling to figure out a way to live and the fathers risking emotional vulnerability to speak up in meetings. The young people, these university students and the scrappy and brave youth of the barrio, were an inspiration, their idealism palpable. And she trusted her Maryknoll sisters and was energized and inspired by the gatherings when those who were serving in Central America came together to talk and pray about their work. There were years, after the Melville incident in Guatemala and after so many nuns married the priests they worked with, when Maura was nearly embarrassed to be a Maryknoller. But it made her proud to be part of a roomful of women committed to building a better world, endlessly ready to analyze their own motivations and forever orientated toward the experiences of the most marginalized people. The departures of the past decade were blows, but at the regional meetings she remembered there were still tremendous Maryknoll women groping through to do God's work in the difficult world.[38]

A quarter century earlier when she'd entered the convent, Maura had been assigned to the Corpus Christi group, a clutch of sisters who were encouraged to find particular inspiration in the concept of the Body of Christ. What did it mean that the God who created the universe became human? In the 1950s, the emphasis was on gratitude for God's taking on lowly human form and suffering at the hands of human sin. By her time in OPEN 3, dwelling on what Catholics called the mystery of the Body of Christ meant considering the very physical realities of life. God was here. These people uniting for their rights in OPEN 3 were the body of God. And if that were so, being faithful to Christ meant building a world that was safe for him. The goal wasn't a worldwide proletariat, it was a world that fostered and respected the holiness of each person. But the goals of the Sandinistas and the goals of the church seemed close enough to intertwine. The Jesuits in Managua ran a think tank analyzing the social reality. At monthly talks quietly publicized to friends, they put the question in terms of Somoza vs. Sandinista: which holds the possibility to offer the signs of the reign of God, when the poor will be fed, the homeless sheltered, when justice reigns?[39]

Kay Kelly came home with a story one weekend at the end of May 1974 that made this question even more urgent. A farm woman up in the countryside had been raped. This happened all the time, Maura knew, but this story was horrible. Someone had told Amada Pineda that the National Guard was coming for her. She was a member of the Nicaraguan Socialist party and a farmworkers' union, enough to justify arrest. Friends told her to flee, but she had a four-year-old and a fifteen-month-old baby. Her husband was away in the Soviet Union, training with other farm organizers. That night Amada slept in a house farther up in the mountain, under a sheet of plastic with her daughters and another woman. At four in the morning she heard the dogs. She rose, opened the door, and looked out. The house was surrounded by soldiers, one knee on the ground, guns hoisted to shoulder: firing position. They took Amada to another house for interrogation and asked about the union, about her husband, about the guerrillas. Then the guardsmen took her, bound, to another nearby house, where they raped her. She struggled until her arms were black and blue and her legs battered. It lasted for three days, the men coming in and out of the room whenever they liked. Three of them were officers. Amada counted seventeen rapists.[40]

Maura knew it wasn't unusual treatment for a dissident woman. Men were tortured. Women were tortured and raped. What made Amada Pineda different was that she complained. She came into Managua and told her story to *La Prensa*, the Somoza-critical newspaper. No one had ever done that. The publication of her story marked a rupture in the tacit silence Nicaraguan women suffered. Here was a poor, peasant woman accusing Somoza's National Guard of a crime everyone knew from sisters and mothers and aunts was common. But everyone had always been too frightened and ashamed to speak out loud. Amada reported her rape to the judiciary and brought a case against the National Guardsmen. Now she needed the sisters' support, Kay explained. There would be a trial in a Managua courtroom. Kay wanted to pack the benches with women to show Amada solidarity as she took the stand and pointed to her torturers. Maura agreed. The poor woman needed them. The judge needed to see nuns and their perceived moral authority when he looked across the bench. But it wasn't a project without risk. Showing their faces before the judge and the National Guard effectively meant the Maryknollers were publicly criticizing the regime. Kay went to CONFER, the federation of religious orders, to try to gather supporters. Many other congregations demurred at first, worried what it might look like to support a communist. The answer was simple for the Maryknoll sisters. It didn't matter what Amada's political beliefs were or what kind of agitation she might have engaged in. They spent their days preaching that women had value. Kay was trying to organize ahead of the International Year of the Woman in 1975. How could they do that if they didn't stand up for this woman brave enough to stand up for herself?[41]

In the end, the courtroom was filled. Maura was happy to see Carmen García from San Pablo Apóstol among a large group of women from the Christian Base Communities. When Maura first started organizing in San Pablo with Sr. Estelle in the late 1960s, inviting people to the Christian Base Community there, Carmen was so timid. It took Maura weeks of visits to get her out of her kitchen and she rarely spoke at meetings. Now she was here, standing bravely with the frank authority radical Nicaraguan women were beginning to adopt. Carmen and the women of the Sandinista women's organization came every day and organized vigils and rallies on Amada's behalf, brave enough to show their own face, whatever the risk. The editor of *La Prensa* marched and Maura, Maryknollers from across Nicaragua, and so many people from OPEN 3 marched. There was joy in standing together.[42]

The abuse continued during the trial. Amada was made to stand, as were the nuns and other supporters. The guardsmen who raped her, meanwhile, testified while sitting in a chair provided by the court. They said she was lying, accused her of slander, called her a whore. Amada's head ached. When she returned to the house where she was staying, she lay awake at night, alert to every noise in the neighborhood. The Maryknoll sisters visited the safe house and brought her medicine. When the soldiers accused her of not being a peasant woman, claiming that she had no children, the Maryknoll sisters drove to the countryside to bring her young children to Managua to be with their mother. They brought milk to feed the toddler and clothes for Amada to wear to court.[43]

Maura was struck by Amada's stately bearing in the face of shocking attacks. There was something regal in it. In the evenings, she visited the safe house to talk to Amada, listening, encouraging. She tried to make Amada feel less alone. Maura assured her that nothing more was going to happen to her, and wished she could guarantee it. She told her she had done something brave for all the women in Nicaragua, that it was important to denounce what was happening in the mountains. Amada looked forward to Maura's visits. With this gentle nun she felt human again.[44]

Maura wrote to her mother about Amada, but otherwise most conversations with her parents were light. Whether for fear of the government censors the sisters suspected read their mail or a desire to protect them from worry, Maura rarely got into specifics of the work in OPEN 3. Instead she asked about the grandchildren, soaked up

John and Mary Clarke's careful description of weeks spent at Judy's house and all the ways Buddy's children were growing up. She took out her watercolors to paint cards for birthdays, then almost without fail sent them late. New York was always on her mind. She wished she could be part of the lives of Judy and Buddy's children who were the same age as some of these kids she was watching grow powerful in OPEN 3. But always there was one more thing to do and she struggled to keep on top of thank you notes to all the people Judy and her mother recruited into sending money and clothes to OPEN 3. Her parents' financial situation was better now than it had been when she was young. Her father sent checks every few months. So did her siblings.[45]

Maura made out long lists of supplies the parish needed and asked her mother and sister to send them down with whichever Maryknoll sister visited Rockaway next. The parish needed a bigger coffee percolator. Kay needs new shoes. Rita needs a girdle. Could she send nylons; Maura's were mostly runs. It was as if the extended Clarke family was part of the mission. They received an endless stream of visitors, Maura inviting any of her roommates to stop in for a dinner at her mother's house and occasionally sending Nicaraguan friends to stay for a few days while they toured New York. She directed Fr. Martínez to visit her parents when he had a layover in New York after going home to Spain to visit his own family, but he didn't call. Maybe it was a way to include her parents in her work, to make the distance shorter. There were so many people to try to make feel better, Maura thought. She gave to beggars, even when her Maryknoll sisters pointed out that sort of charity was useless, maybe even harmful. They were working to change the system, the whole structure that left people destitute. Borrowing against next month's $10 personal allowance to give to some family in crisis wasn't really a fix. But how could she say no when someone came to the door? She had so much. Even the spartan white house the sisters shared, where dust blew in through the slits between boards and they had to boil their water before drinking it, was the nicest one in the barrio.[46]

Maura wrote a quick note to her parents in the Christmas card the parish printed in 1974. It reworked the passage in the Gospel of

Matthew in which Jesus tells his followers to feed the hungry and clothe the naked, adapting it to life in the barrio of OPEN 3: "Because I was hungry without a home, without a school, without light, transportation, or a hospital, without culture, without work and without recognition of my rights and dignity and YOU helped me."

The previous year, Maura's father had been with her at Christmas. He came in the end of December 1973 and stayed for a week, walking with her on her rounds. It wasn't as bucolic as Siuna and there was no Canadian zone to escape to for first world luxuries, but John was relieved to see Maura gung ho in her work and surrounded by friends who loved her. He was stunned by the rank poverty, writing to his wife of the rows and rows of shacks and the malnourished children who loved their daughter.[47]

Now, a year later, Christmas week 1974, Maura couldn't believe what was coming out of the radio in the white house. She could hear it in stereo all over the barrio: an accounting of all the crimes of the regime. The rapes in El Cuá in 1968. The young men bound and tossed down the hillside near Lake Managua. The dungeons under the presidential palace. The people thrown from airplanes into the volcano. On and on, decades of horrors, all the arrests, tortures, midnight murders that people suspected and whispered about, were now pouring into the air. Days earlier, just after the American ambassador left a Christmas party at the home of Chema Castillo, one of Somoza's close allies, ten Sandinista operatives burst in. They held dozens of Managua's most prominent citizens hostage, demanded $5 million in ransom, the release of fourteen Sandinista prisoners, and a plane to take them to Cuba. (The FSLN accepted $1 million in ransom, but got all the political prisoners they demanded, and passage to Cuba.) But their last demand was the most fantastic. The regime would be required to air on state radio and television a list of its crimes of the past many years. The partygoers were Somoza's relatives and business associates. He had no option but to comply.[48]

All over the neighborhood Maura heard shouts of recognition and joy as secrets long harbored were broadcast out loud. It felt like liberation just to know the dictatorship could be forced to meet the Sandinista demands. And the operation was so bold. Maura and the sisters couldn't help being cheered by the swagger of it. They were impressed by these young men and women filled with audacity and hope. The Christmas raid meant the Sandinistas were more than a dead-end handful of ideologues in the mountains. Often it felt as if they were hopeless, a tiny band of rebels making madcap bank robberies to fund a long fight against a dictatorship with the backing of the most powerful nation in the world. But this highly coordinated and flamboyant raid showed there was more to the Sandinistas than everyone feared. Maybe it really would be possible to build a new country.[49]

Somoza responded to the humiliating raid by doubling down on repressive tactics. He called a state of siege and released an elite counterinsurgency force within the National Guard. The goal was simple: eliminate the FSLN. That would not be so easy. As FSLN militants set off for Cuba, people in tattered clothes lined the road to the airport and cheered, revealing for the dictator just how much his people had been infected by the rebel ideas. At the same time, Somoza had to deal with opposition from Managua's business class, which was frustrated by gross corruption after the earthquake. "We need to eliminate the contaminated peasants," a national guardsman told a journalist. The United States upped its military aid to Nicaragua by 80 percent and taught counterinsurgency techniques at the School of the Americas in the Panama Canal zone.[50]

Now when Kay came back from trips to the country with her farmworker rights organization, she brought with her tales of terror. The National Guard had redoubled its actions against guerrillas and suspected sympathizers and collaborators. The Capuchin priests in Siuna began keeping a tally of the peasants they trained as church workers who disappeared or were found dead.

The protest singer Carlos Mejía Godoy, always beloved, became a champion of the opposition. He joined some of the OPEN 3 marches, slinging his guitar like a rifle and leading the crowds in songs everyone knew the words to. Maura had been running into him at protests and demonstrations for years. The burly and garrulous songwriter was active in the opposition to Somoza, but not yet a member of the FSLN. His recordings, banned in Nicaragua, were smuggled in from Costa Rica and played secretly by everyone who wanted a new Nicaragua. The lyrics were fierce. They were upbeat and eminently singable, integrating classic Nicaraguan folk rhythms and indigenous instruments. Nicaraguans weren't playing John Philip Sousa anymore.

In 1975, Fr. Fernando Cardenal and his brother and fellow priest Ernesto Cardenal, a poet and artist who'd founded a commune on a string of islands in the massive inland Lake Nicaragua, recruited Mejía Godoy to write a new popular Mass. Like the liturgical works of Beethoven and Bach, it would be both a work of art and an act of devotion. And in a country where the majority of people were illiterate, it would be a method of education, a way to teach the new theology that emphasized that Jesus was a poor person who came to preach liberation. For months Mejía Godoy holed up at Fr. Ernesto Cardenal's commune at Solentiname, composing the Mass, rewriting each of the prayers to be relevant to the harsh realities of life in Nicaragua. Finally, in early 1975, it was finished. But a Mass is only a Mass if it is performed, or celebrated. A people's Mass needs to be unveiled somewhere outdoors, somewhere thousands of people could gather to pray and sing. The wide, flat Plaza de Cabros at the center of OPEN 3 was perfect.[51]

Hundreds of people began streaming in from Managua in the morning, gathering at the plaza as the Cardenals and men from OPEN 3 set up a stage and altar and brought amplifiers and microphones to the plaza. By noon it seemed as though most of the population of OPEN 3, along with thousands of faithful and activists from Managua, had crowded the plaza. Maura came with the rest of the Maryknoll sisters, nervous and excited that such a momentous event was happening in their sorry barrio. National Guard troops rolled to the edge of the plaza, first one battalion, then another, then another, forming a ring around the crowd. Frs. Fernando and Ernesto Cardenal donned the robes and stole priests wear to say Mass and took to the stage as Carlos Mejía Godoy began to sing the first strains of the opening song.

"You are the God of the poor, the humane and simple God, the God that sweats in the street, the God with a tanned face. For that reason I speak to you in the way my people talk, because you are the worker God, the laboring Christ."[52]

Maura knew perfectly well the National Guard was going to intervene. But she wanted to be there, part of the communal prayer. She noticed the military vehicles arriving. The guardsmen stepped out of their jeeps and trucks and mounted their guns on their shoulders. Several walked through the crowd toward the soundstage. Another soldier cut the microphones to stop the music. They arrested Mejía Godoy and several other men, hustling them into a vehicle. It was the first time the songwriter was ever arrested. Terrified, he imagined the torture he would soon be subjected to, thought about the possibility he would be dropped out of a helicopter into the volcano as Sandinista activists had been.[53]

The congregation—the thousands of OPEN 3 residents and Sandinista activists in from Managua who had come to this despised, disregarded, dusty plaza to celebrate a miracle of divinity present in the physical—joined hands around the whole plaza. This, Maura realized, was collective. She reached for the hands beside her. With the rest of the Maryknoll sisters, she was part of the crowd, a body of Christ. And they were singing. Mejía Godoy and the other musicians who were arrested were released within an hour. The Frs. Cardenal escaped through the shantytown maze, running in their priestly robes.[54]

While Maura was expanding her understanding of serving God by serving people, learning that she found this suffering Christ in each person before her, the young men and women she adored were taking the church teaching to love your neighbor and the critical thinking and social analysis taught by the Maryknoll sisters to further conclusions. In September 1975, Frijolito, Humberto Bolaños, and Walter López Jirón became the first crop of young recruits from OPEN 3 to join the Sandinista front. In doing so they were making a commitment to the clandestine organization, promising to be part of the struggle for a new Nicaragua. They remained in OPEN 3 for the time being, part of the broader struggle for basic rights and services, as they waited to be called up to join the guerrillas training in the mountains. In the idiom of revolutionary Nicaragua, the young men and women joining the fight for a new way of life went to the mountain—like Moses or Muhammad.[55]

The courtship of potential young militants was not unlike the recruitment process Fr. Curley had practiced with potential vocations in Rockaway a quarter century earlier. Beginning in 1973, Sandinista members had been in contact with Frijolito, scoping him out, measuring his commitment, his trustworthiness, his usefulness to the organization. It wasn't a single invitation; it was long assessment. Maura and the other nuns were dimly aware of the recruitment process. They knew their altar boys and youth group members were being visited by Sandinista operatives and agents. But they protected themselves and the young people from knowing the particulars. Still, they held the Sandinistas in high regard as people struggling for a better Nicaragua. These guerrillas were not strangers to Maura. They were the kids she'd trained to think freely, using Paulo Freire's methods. They were the teenagers she'd sung and prayed with and nurtured for years in the youth group. They remained involved in all the neighborhood struggles, continued to be part of the prayer groups and protest strategy sessions. In OPEN 3, the church members moved seamlessly from Mass to protest march, all of it of a piece.[56]

The water fight crystallized everything that was wrong and everything that might be possible in Nicaragua. A few years earlier, the first set of sisters in OPEN 3 had organized to get water delivered, so that people wouldn't need to spend their day waiting at the well that Fr. García had dug when the area was first established. Now water was delivered by a private company and customers charged by volume. The wealthy had swimming pools and bathtubs in the neighborhood just adjacent to OPEN 3, but in the shantytown every drop was precious. When research revealed that the company charged lower rates—half the price—to the wealthy community, the people of Cruz Grande swung into action. That families struggling for their next meal had to pay so much for something as essential as water was outrageous to Maura and the other sisters. María Luisa, Mercedes Taleno, and the rest of Maura's women's group met in the white house to make a plan. The teenagers argued about justice. Everyone had a point to make, seemingly everyone wanted to hear his or her own voice in the long sessions. Maura tried to encourage women to speak, or men who didn't usually hold the floor. And when they noticed new faces in the meetings, Peg Dillon put finger and thumb to her own earlobe and cast a quick glance at the stranger. Was this an *oreja*, an ear, a spy for the National Guard or the water company? Or was it a newly engaged neighbor?[57]

Confronting the water company brought on the fury of the National Guard. Now its soldiers disrupted meetings in the Cruz Grande. Activists from around Managua flowed into OPEN 3 to join this struggle of the poorest people for dignity and justice. Each day was occupied with strategy and meetings. In June 1976, the women of the Mother's Club signed a letter to the water company, demanding a lower price. A thousand people showed up to a meeting at the church. The priests argued meetings should be open to members of the Christian Base Communities and the parish only. But the sisters acknowledged there were others in the barrio who were interested in this struggle. The Christian Base Community groups and the youth group met to lay out a plan to negotiate for better prices. After a series of letters garnered no response, the community agreed that a public march would be best.[58]

Carrying signs and singing Carlos Mejía Godoy songs, activists marched from the Cruz Grande to the Red Cross, where they conducted a hunger strike. For eight days the protestors stayed in the Red Cross. Frijolito grew even skinnier. Maura wasn't inside, but she fasted along with the protestors and agreed with their efforts. She remembered her father's stories about the Irish revolution and his part in a hunger strike in a Dublin prison. The demands in OPEN 3 were clear: ten cordobas a month for water, not twenty.[59]

While the protestors remained in the Red Cross, Maura joined the rest of the neighborhood in daily rallies and marches to let them know they had support. The Cruz Grande was transformed into a nerve center for information and planning. Peg Healy helped set up a local radio station to keep the neighborhood informed on negotiations. Students printed a clandestine newspaper. Sympathizers came from across Managua to support the demonstration. The bishop tried to negotiate, asking the water company to come down to seventeen cordobas, but the neighborhood rejected that plan. The Red Cross sit-in ended without resolution, but the fight continued for months, cementing OPEN 3's reputation for militancy. The priests initially offered tentative support but were apprehensive. It seemed to them the nuns spent more of their time marching than praying.[60]

It was during the water fight that five Sandinistas—three of them local leaders who had known the sisters since they were boys—met in the white house to hash out plans for their next month. Humberto Bolaños was assigned the door, keeping watch for the National Guard. If any soldiers came, his job was to alert the people inside. The militants would race out the back door and through the yard behind the sisters' house.[61]

The guardsmen came, an elite antiterrorist unit from Managua, formed after the Christmas raid of 1974.

Humberto ran into the house to warn his friends. Maura and the other sisters—several were visiting from various parts of the country—refused to let the soldiers in. They hadn't been part of the meeting; they just allowed the young men they knew to meet in their home. Time passed, frantic and tense. Finally it was decided Humberto would go back outside. What could they charge him with? He wasn't even part of the meeting. But as he stepped out the door, two guardsmen grabbed his arms.

Humberto was arrested and taken to the National Guard station in OPEN 3. For three days he was beaten. The soldiers forced his head into the toilet, and kicked, punched, beat, and electrocuted him, running charges through his ears. It was typical treatment. Maura, Peg Dillon, Peg Healy, Melba, and the other sisters of OPEN 3 kept vigil in the jail for the entire three days, taking shifts so that someone was always in the station. They organized others to visit and complain so that Humberto's captors would know they were being watched. This way, the nuns hoped, at least he would not be killed. At the end of the three days, Humberto was released. He couldn't walk. The sisters embraced the broken body of this boy they'd helped raise and kept him at the white house for two weeks, caring for him until he could walk again.[62]

Before young men and many women journeyed to the Sandinista training camps in the northern reaches of the country, they came to the Maryknoll sisters to say good-bye, to pay respects. What could Maura say to these beautiful teenagers she'd instructed on their confirmation and sat in weekly Masses with? She didn't teach them to raise arms, didn't want them to be killed or to kill. But she respected their moral education. She'd provided it. And their decision to fight could be justified by the long church tradition of Just War theory and the Pope's teaching in "Populorum Progressio" (On the Progress of Peoples) in 1967. That document conceded that after long struggle against insurmountable injustice, armed rebellion could be moral. Frijolito and Walter and Humberto had tried praying. They had tried putting their skinny bodies against the dictatorship in sit-ins and hunger strikes and marches. It hadn't worked. There were thousands more Amada Pinedas. Thousands more Humberto Bolañoses. Maura respected that they'd made a choice. *No greater love is there than this, to lay down one's life for one's friends.* It was a verse on so many people's lips in the barrio.[63]

What's more, Maura recognized these teenagers. They were her father during the Irish Revolution. That year, after Irish revolutionaries made a spectacularly disastrous attempt to overthrow the British Empire on Easter Monday 1916, by taking over the General Post Office in Dublin, John Clarke traveled from New York to Boston to make a similar commitment. He pledged allegiance to a banned, secret society, the Irish Republican Brotherhood. He promised to fight for an Ireland free of oppression, an Ireland where the Irish could breathe and shape their own future. It was a story Maura had heard hundred times in a crowded Rockaway apartment or in her uncle's house in Ireland filled with old Sligo partisans sipping their whiskey and singing the revolutionary songs. They weren't so different from Ernesto Cardenal's poems and Carlos Mejía Godoy's anthems.

The teenagers came to the sisters' house to say good-bye. "Sister, I am going to the mountains. Give me your blessing." What do you say? You ask them whether they really think they are ready. You ask what will happen to their mothers. You don't tell them not to go. They've already made their decision. It's not theoretical. So, of course, you say you will pray for them. You tell them not to forget their prayers, not to forget their faith.[64]

Los muchachos (the boys)—that phrase was said with such affection. Los muchachos were meeting at the sisters' house when the National Guard came, grabbed one of them. Maura saw and rushed to the street with the other sisters.

"What are you doing to that boy?" Maura shouted at the guardsmen. "Why are you harassing your own people? They are simply asking for a fair price for water." Her voice was loud and the words came in an angry torrent. "Water is a human right. It is given to us by God! People have the right to ask for water!"

The soldiers wrestled the teenager into the back of the truck. Maura lunged. She grabbed the lieutenant, wrapping her narrow fingers around his arm, and tugging at him, her face close to his. She threw her arms against the front of the truck, banging on its metal hood. The rest of the sisters stood in shocked silence. Maura was touching the lieutenant of the National Guard.

He was amused and bewildered by this tall, ferocious white woman in the midst of the wretched barrio. "Who . . . are . . . you?"

Maura straightened herself. Still seething, she pulled up to her full height, probably taller than the lieutenant. She tilted her chin up and fixed her dark eyes on the soldier.

"I am Sr. Maura Clarke."

He sneered. This was no threat. This was just a harmless nun.

"Oh, sister," he said, as though talking to a child or a pet. "Go back to your convent."

For ten years Maura had been learning that the convent—her life as a nun—wasn't a fenced-off space safe from the agony of the world. Her vow to be faithful had taken her further and further into the bitter experience of people she loved, people she believed embodied the God she had knelt before and made her vows to in that chapel in Ossining.

"THIS IS MY CONVENT!" she shouted, thrusting her finger toward the dusty, dry street. "This is my convent!"⁶⁵

CHAPTER 8

Mission to the United States

Maura woke in her dusty room on October 22, 1976, the cries of the neighborhood roosters and the rattletrap buses already noisy on the street a few feet from her window. A meeting with the youth group was planned for the evening. She and the other Maryknoll sisters had spent much of the past several months in an activist campaign, organizing meetings, helping speakers articulate their points, sharing ideas on how to encourage participants to speak their mind and how to avoid having one voice dominate a discussion, making banners, planning rallies, and marching in the streets. Maura placed her feet on the wooden floor. Between her toes she could feel the grit blown in during the night. She said her morning prayers as she dressed. It was her last day in OPEN 3.[1]

After seventeen years in Nicaragua and almost four in the barrio, she had a new assignment. Sisters were required to come home and work temporarily for the congregation after many years in the field. Maura would spend the next three years in the United States, talking to American Catholics about the church's teachings on social justice and about life in the third world. The Maryknollers called the work reverse mission. Instead of being missionaries in a poor country, preaching Catholicism and working to alleviate poverty, sisters and priests on reverse mission came back to the first world as missionaries to educate middle-class Americans about poverty and its causes, in an attempt to influence US foreign policy. In this new assignment in the United States, Maura would take what she saw and experienced in Siuna and OPEN 3 to church halls and college classrooms, seminaries and high schools. She was more worried now than she had been as a young nun boarding a plane for unknown Siuna. She'd been away a long time, living in Nicaraguan slums, praying and working with peasants and squatters for longer than she'd ever worked in the United States. Now it was the American suburbs that seemed foreign.[2]

She spent this last day walking the streets of OPEN 3, making teary farewell visits to as many friends as possible. At María Luisa Urbina's house, next door to her own, she put her arms around her old friend as the woman cried. When she began training the women in the neighborhood as instructors for religious education, Maura had compared them to Jesus's first recruits. He hadn't chosen powerful and influential people; he had picked fisherman. But humble people could do tremendous things, she had told María Luisa. In turn, María Luisa had prepared dozens of children for First Communion, telling them God created the world for everyone to share. María Luisa's welcome and acceptance of her had helped Maura accept herself. Now she was leaving, uncertain she would see her friend again. Miriam Castillo cried as Maura approached her house. Maura had made her feel that she mattered and encouraged her to speak up, to court her own counsel in the church reflection and study groups the nuns ran. Miriam would miss Maura's unhurried and attentive visits. The tightly packed rows of shacks in the shantytown were thick with dear friends with whom Maura's life had been entwined for the past four years. Tearing apart felt like opening a wound. These were the people she'd lived with, trying to make her life as much like theirs, to understand the world from their position.[3]

Neighbors clambered onto a minibus to accompany Maura to the airport. They crowded the departure gate, giving her last hugs, promising to write, crying openly. Once she was seated, she pressed her face against the window, smiling and waving a white handkerchief, just as Sr. Rita had always done as she left Siuna. As the plane lifted off from Managua, Maura was—for the first time in years—alone. The warmth, frenetic energy, and deep emotional intimacy of OPEN 3 was behind her. Before her lay a winter in the northeast, work she had never done before and a new partner—a sister who'd spent her years of service in Hawaii.

After a brief visit with her old friend Kay Kelly in Chicago and a reunion with her family in Rockaway, Maura spent eight days at a Jesuit retreat house a little north of New York. She'd been looking forward to a directed retreat for years—time out from life where she could ponder deeply her relationship with God. After the past few years in Nicaragua, from the drama of the political movement, to her unsettling feelings for Fr. Martínez, to the daunting challenge of a new assignment, she wanted time to slow down and try to hear what God was asking of her. Between prescribed times for prayer, Maura met with her retreat director, a Jesuit priest who would guide her through the week of contemplation. She turned her attention inward and experimented with different styles of prayer: meditation, close recording of emotional reactions to the Bible readings, imagining herself as a character in a familiar Gospel story. She didn't speak to anyone outside the retreat house, use the phone, or write any letters. Sitting in the small, comfortable room of the retreat house, she wrote of fear: her fear of pain and death, the need to face fear, her fear of not being liked, her need to please people. She needed to be more courageous, she told herself, in standing up against injustice. Friends saw an ever-smiling and selfless woman, deeply committed to a life of prayer and justice, but Maura considered herself mediocre and admonished herself for not trusting God. "Oh, if only I could allow Him to be all in me," she wrote in a small notebook. She scolded herself for living among poor people in OPEN 3 but not living as poorly as the people she was trying to unite with.[4]

As the aching strains of a Brahms violin concerto filled the room where retreat-goers gathered for evening reflection, Maura wept until she shook. Leaving Nicaragua had been awful. Being in the United States now felt like living in exile. But maybe she'd been in exile in Nicaragua, too, she wondered. She had been deeply engaged in important work she loved, but perhaps, given the urgency of her daily tasks, she had remained removed from a more profound relationship with God. There was the question, too, of reconciling her faith with the brutality she had witnessed in OPEN 3. But she told herself to trust God, even though she couldn't understand how he could let the death toll mount in Nicaragua.[5]

She thought about Carlos Fonseca Amador, one of the three central leaders of the Frente Sandinista who had been killed during the summer, and of the dossier that priests she'd worked with in Siuna had compiled of crimes committed by the National Guard against lay church workers.*

It was a list of three hundred people who'd been killed or disappeared.

In the middle of the night Maura sat in the chapel, an echo of her days in the novitiate when someone had to be in the chapel at all hours to pray near the exposed Eucharist, keeping Christ company. Contemplating the night before Jesus was crucified when he prayed alone on the Mount of Olives, begging God to spare him but also submitting to what was to be, she understood Christ's fearfulness. She would be strengthened, she told herself, if she trusted and did what God called for.[6]

Reading the Bible passage about Jesus brought before the high priests and the Roman judge Pontius Pilate brought to mind the people of OPEN 3. Somoza and the National Guard were the Roman soldiers taunting Jesus. The people of OPEN 3, the men willing to die for the freedom of their people, were the tortured Christ.[7]

It was a trying week, but by the end of it Maura felt more at peace, forgiven and embraced by God.[8]

---

* The Capuchin Franciscan priests on Nicaragua's Atlantic Coast had been collecting evidence of the disappearance and killing of three hundred Delegates of the Word in the provinces around Siuna since 1974. They published it in June 1976 in Nicaragua. The following March, the Nicaraguan bishops endorsed it. Delegates were lay people trained by the church to lead prayer services and facilitate discussions among far-flung communities in isolated rural areas that were only rarely visited by a priest. The Delegates of the Word—as people who heard the concerns of their neighbors and were involved in trying to improve their lot—were often sympathetic to the FSLN, sometimes provided food or shelter to them and sometimes carried messages. Others drew a strict line between church work and the nascent revolution. Because of the impression of collaboration, they were frequent targets of National Guard repression. [From Philip Berryman, *Religious Roots of Rebellion* (Maryknoll, NY: Orbis Books, 1984, 71.)] The Capuchin report, along with testimony before the US Congress by Fr. Fernando Cardenal, SJ, in June 1976 dramatically increased international attention on Nicaragua.

Since their earliest years as missionaries in China in the 1910s and 1920s, part of the Maryknoll congregation's mission had been to alert Americans to the struggles of life in the places they worked. Through *Field Afar* (now called *Maryknoll Missionary Vocations*) and later *Maryknoll Magazine* and visits to parishes, Maryknoll priests and sisters told American Catholics stories about the work they did and the people they lived with in poor villages around the world. These trips to US parishes were primarily fund-raising operations. A sister or priest would speak after Mass about finding converts and digging wells, and urge the Catholics in the pews to think of these foreigners as brothers and sisters—and to give money to support the work. They didn't ask the Americans to consider the larger structural, economic forces that made the people poor, or challenge them to consider the role of the US government in the countries where they worked. But as the sisters'* understanding of the causes of poverty and their commitment to changing the social structures that built misery was transformed during Vatican II and after the publication of the Medellín documents in 1968, they rethought the purpose of these visits. Maryknollers returning to the United States were shocked at how little their own families and other American Catholics understood about the world and the social forces reshaping life in so many of the countries where they served—or the sisters' role in those movements. In the mid-1970s, Maryknoll established regional teams of nuns tasked with educating American Catholics about the problems of third-world countries. They built an educational program based on the popular education methods many had already been using with peasants and urban slum dwellers in the missions.[9]

Maura and Jean Burke, her new partner, spent the end of 1976 making contacts at parishes and colleges throughout the Northeast, looking for people interested in hosting one of their workshops. They wrote quizzes on world poverty and hunger, used pictures from Paulo Freire and group dynamics exercises to prod people to consider their relationships to one another and to the broader world. On colorful

---

* And priests, clearly, but we'll focus here on the nuns.

poster board Maura carefully wrote quotes from official papal teachings on poverty and the right to unionize and the right of all people to share the resources of the world. She drew up charts illustrating American military support for dictatorships and printed out addresses for the members of Congress and US senators who represented the regions they would visit.[10]

In March 1977, Jean and Maura drove to Virginia Beach to run a two-and-a-half-day workshop for forty people at St. Nicholas parish. They took turns leading presentations and facilitating conversation and reaction afterward. Just as in the group meetings in OPEN 3 or Miralagos, Maura listened attentively to each person's thoughts, nodding encouragement and smiling brightly when someone shy spoke up. She pushed gently to get people to think more deeply. The Virginia parish members took a multiple choice quiz on world hunger and malnutrition, then tried to match a list of names with a series of quotes. Was it Karl Marx or Pope Paul VI* who said: "No one may appropriate surplus goods solely for his own private use when others lack the bare necessities of life" and "If certain landed estates impede the general prosperity because they are extensive, unused or poorly used, or because they bring hardship to peoples or are detrimental to the interests of the country, the common good sometimes demands their expropriation?"[11]

At lunch Maura sat with Elaine Hruska, who'd seen a notice about the workshop in her church bulletin and been curious. Elaine's comments had been so helpful, Maura said as the two women ate. She should really share them in the next session. Maura asked for Elaine's address; she would love to write to her, to keep in touch.[12]

At the end of each workshop, Maura spoke specifically about Nicaragua, carefully explaining the nation's history from Christopher Columbus's arrival in 1502 through the US occupation in the 1920s and current struggle against Somoza. Standing in front of a map of Central America, Maura described the staggering illiteracy rate, the deaths from malaria and malnutrition, and the brutality of the National Guard. She told stories about the millions of dollars of earthquake relief embezzled by the Somoza family, about the food

---

* It was Pope Paul VI, in "Populorum Progressio," March 26, 1967.

in the tent city of Camp Hope siphoned off to the military, and about her neighbors' efforts to improve life in OPEN 3. She talked about torture, about the church workers in the countryside around Siuna who had been killed or had disappeared, about sitting in the police station waiting for the release of Roberto, arrested for singing Mother's Day songs. She talked about Amada Pineda, raped by the National Guard for three days because she was part of a farmworkers' union. And she talked about Carlos Medija Godoy's Misa Campesina, and this new way of understanding Jesus as one of the poor people beaten up by the US-trained military.[13]

In Virginia Beach, a man raised his hand. "Does our government know this is going on?" he asked, his eyes wide. Maura pressed her lips together and gave a small nod.[14]

Just a few weeks before visiting Virginia Beach, Maura had spent a day in Washington, DC, listening as the US House of Representatives debated funding for Nicaragua. A month earlier, Jimmy Carter had been sworn in as president, promising he would make respect for human rights a component of US foreign aid. After more than a generation of strict cold war calculus under which any enemy of communism was a friend of the US, and a century and a half of Latin American policy shaped nearly exclusively by the interests of US businesses, Carter's approach was a dramatic break. And it presented an opening for Maura and other opponents of Somoza to make the case that the United States should not be supporting the dictator.[15]

Articles about the strife in Nicaragua appeared in US newspapers every few days. In March, the Nicaraguan bishops endorsed the dossier of National Guard brutality against church workers compiled by the Capuchin priests. An article in the *New York Times* began, "Nicaragua's Roman Catholic bishops have accused government forces of resorting to widespread torture, rape and summary executions of civilians in their battle against leftist guerrillas in this impoverished Central American republic." But as Maura understood it, the battle wasn't between "leftist guerrillas" and the Somoza government. It was the story of Humberto Bolaños and Angelique Rodríguez Alemán standing up to claim their rights as humans. The coverage of violence and torture in Nicaragua made Maura more determined to open Americans' eyes to what their country's ally was doing.[16]

As spring began, Maura and Jean traveled frequently to Boston to run a series of workshops with a Boston College theology professor. The two women were telling people uncomfortable facts, pushing them to take responsibility for the actions of their government and arguing that a country they'd barely heard of was in the midst of a struggle for fundamental systematic change. But she managed to be soft. The lectures she gave weren't harangues on imperialism. They were stories about María Luisa's bravely planting a flower garden in the dust pit of OPEN 3 and Rosa Blandón's learning to take pride in herself. She spoke of Henri Norori and Walter López Jirón and Roberto Somoza, teenagers who already had barely enough to eat, going on hunger strike to demand a fair price for water. It was always personal. She wanted these Americans in church basements and college campuses, these groups of nuns and diocesan employees, to fall in love with her Nicaraguan friends, just as she had.[17]

A letter from Peg Healy was addressed to all three of the OPEN 3 exiles stationed at the Sisters Center in Ossining: Maura, Bea Zaragoza and Melba Bantay. The news was bad. Lesbia Taleno, the daughter of Maura's close friend Mercedes Taleno, and another teenager had been arrested for hanging political posters in OPEN 3. "The ears have tripled in the barrio," Peg wrote, using the slang for "spies." The priests intervened and the kids were released from jail, but a few weeks later Lesbia missed her period. Finally, she told her mother: She'd been raped three times during interrogation. It was the thing Mercedes had always feared most, the reason she wanted to pull her precious daughter back in the house when Lesbia began to put herself in the struggles of the barrio. Peg and Peg Dillon went with the sixteen-year-old girl to an ob-gyn for a proper test, Peg explained, and the doctor confirmed that she was pregnant. They brought Lesbia to a notary public to make a formal declaration against the National Guard.[18]

"You can imagine what a suffering it is for them," Peg wrote. "At what cost liberty? It's hard to love one's enemies and it has been such a bad week with so many tragedies that I just had to sit down and cry one night to see such good people suffering."[19]

Maura had known Lesbia since she was a scrawny twelve-year-old, had sat in her house, telling stories with her mother. This was a girl Maura had bolstered with kindness and attention. She'd listened to Lesbia articulate her thoughts in countless meetings and prayer groups, her heart swelling as the girl grew confident and brave. Now Maura wrote to Lesbia and to Mercedes to give her strength for this new trial. When the baby was born, Lesbia named her Maura Margarita after the nuns who'd offered her comfort and support. Lesbia was the second woman Maura was close to who was raped as a consequence and as punishment for her involvement in the revolutionary movement. In both cases, the nuns supported the women as they stood up and named their attackers.[20]

In June 1977, the US Congress debated a Democratic amendment to a foreign aid bill that would have withheld $3.1 million from Nicaragua as a consequence of the regime's human rights violations. But the proposal was rejected. The Somoza regime retained its flow of US cash and loans.

Throughout the United States in churches, on college campuses, and in political circles, groups formed to support the liberation struggle in Nicaragua. Lectures and vigils were organized and groups that would later coalesce into the Nicaragua Solidarity Network and the Religious Taskforce on Central America began organizing protests and sharing information. The struggle of inspired, emboldened poor people and students against a powerful dictatorship was beginning to capture the American imagination.[21]

In San Francisco, where there was a large Nicaraguan immigrant community, high school students went door to door to raise money for the Sandinistas and supporters held rallies, published a newspaper, and wrote poetry in that city's Mission district. Sandinista solidarity marches were so common that the plaza around the 24th Street Bay Area Rapid Transit station was sometimes called Plaza Sandino. A cadre of Nicaraguan immigrants and Nicaraguan Americans—students, busboys, gas station attendants—met each Saturday morning for military training. They bought combat boots in Army Navy stores, guns at pawn shops, and ran counterclockwise up the Bernal Hill, a San Francisco park. They learned to fly small aircraft and prepared for the day when they would fly to Nicaragua to aid the revolution. A leader of these guerrillas-in-training was Roberto Vargas, a poet and professor at San Francisco State University. In 1977 he was traveling widely in the United States, drumming up support for the Sandinistas and figuring out how to bring attention to their cause. He visited Maryknoll priest Miguel d'Escoto several times in Ossining. Fr. d'Escoto, a Nicaraguan who worked with Maura's mentor Sr. Estelle in Chile in the 1960s and helped establish a community-centered housing development in León after the earthquake, was now director of communications for the Maryknoll priests. In 1970 he had founded Orbis Books, a Maryknoll-backed publishing house that steadily brought out works on liberation theology and the church in Latin America. Earlier in 1977 he had taken an oath as a member of the Sandinista front, a vow he was at the moment trying to keep secret from his Maryknoll superiors.[22]

In late July 1977, Anastasio Somoza Debayle had a heart attack. While he was in the United States for treatment, hope sprouted in Nicaragua that the regime might be coming to an end. Vargas wanted to capitalize on Somoza's weakness. He decided to make a bold move, a dramatic gesture neither Somoza nor his supporters in the United States could ignore. Anti-Somoza activists would take over Somoza's consulate to the United Nations. Vargas made his way to Ossining again and shared his plans for the consulate demonstration. They would need to act quickly, in just a day or two. D'Escoto called Maura and Bea.[23]

This was Maura's chance to do something brave for the Nicaraguans she loved. Finally, even though she was far away, she could be part of their heightening struggle. But her fear was powerful. She wondered if she'd be brave enough to go through with it. Bea would be returning to Nicaragua soon and didn't want to risk her ability to get a visa by having her name in the newspapers. They agreed that Maura would go into the consulate, while Bea would stay in Ossining and call the media once the operation was achieved. Maura waited outside the Sisters Center for Miguel d'Escoto to come with a car. He was a son of the Nicaraguan upper class. His father had been an ambassador to the United States and Miguel had grown up partly in the United States. Anastasio Somoza Debayle had attended his ordination at the Sisters of the Assumption's chapel in Managua in 1961 and the Maryknoll sisters from Siuna, though not Maura, had flown down to celebrate with him.* D'Escoto and Maura had actually spent time together in New York before they entered Maryknoll. As a student at Manhattan College, he and a group of young men would come out to the beach to visit a friend from Rockaway, where Maura joined them for picnics. Now he was devoting himself to toppling Somoza. With him was Jim Sinnott, a Maryknoll priest who'd recently been expelled from South Korea for protesting the regime there. They drove to Manhattan and parked outside the Nicaraguan Consulate to the United Nations. Roberto Vargas was waiting.

Jim, Vargas, Maura, and another Maryknoll sister entered the posh offices of the consulate. Vargas had scoped them out a few days earlier. They acted quickly now. Vargas, dressed in fatigues, with a black beret and bulging muscles, announced the office was being liberated in the name of the Nicaraguan people. The consulate staff called the New York Police Department. Maura, smiling and demur but certain of her task, hustled into the inner office and signaled to d'Escoto, who was watching from the street below, ready to call Bea at Maryknoll to alert the press. Maura lifted the phone to call the Nicaraguan embassy in Washington, DC, then convinced a consulate staff person to place the call. Vargas took the phone and told the embassy in Washington that a group had liberated their consulate to the United Nations. He demanded Somoza release the political prisoners held in Managua. "You should be aware until the dictatorship is gone people will not rest in Nicaragua or outside," Vargas said.

Soon the police arrived. Two officers began to strong-arm Vargas. Echoing her role in the confrontations between National Guard and *muchachos* in OPEN 3, Maura stepped in front of the police. She was shouting now, her eyes bright and her shoulders back. They had

---

* The priest who celebrated d'Escoto's Ordination Mass was José de la Jara, who founded the community of San Pablo Apóstol a few years later.

no right to harass this man. He was fighting for his people. She stood between Vargas and the police, shielding him, giving him space to back up. She didn't yield. This was something she was certain about. The cause of the Nicaraguan people was just, she told the police. Really, the police should support it. If they knew what the people suffered in Nicaragua, they would protest, too. The police looked dumbfounded. Were they really being lectured about supporting revolution by a nun?[24]

Arguing that the NYPD had no authority to arrest them in the diplomatic space of a consulate, Maura and the protestors agreed to leave. The takeover was one more in a steady drumbeat of protest against Somoza, directed as much at his US enablers as at the regime itself. Bowing to US pressure on human rights, in September 1977 Somoza lifted the state of siege put in place after the Christmas raid of 1974.[25]

Not long after the consulate action, d'Escoto flew to Costa Rica. He and Fr. Fernando Cardenal, Maura's Jesuit friend from her Confederation of Religious of Nicaragua (CONFER) days, had been steadily recruiting a group of prominent Nicaraguan businessmen and academics to oppose the dictatorship. In October, the twelve of them met in Costa Rica to draft a statement calling for Somoza's resignation. They issued it from outside the country because they knew their public opposition would carry a prison sentence. The same weekend, Sandinista guerrillas attacked police command posts in several cities, sparking a vigorous crackdown and intense fighting. Fr. Ernesto Cardenal, Fernando's poet brother who lived in an artists' commune in Lake Nicaragua, left the island with other members of the community to attack the National Guard post in nearby San Carlos, then fled to a Sandinista camp in Costa Rica. In Ocotal, near the Honduran border, the Frente attacked another command post and ambushed guard troops. In Masaya, south of Managua, the FSLN attacked the heavily fortified National Guard post in the center of town. It looked as though the revolution was beginning.[26]

Throughout the fall of 1977, Managua and OPEN 3 were alive with demonstrations, often put down by an increasingly violent National Guard. In OPEN 3, the young people took over the church, holding meetings and marching boldly in the neighborhood. The sisters had taken to carrying baking soda and a little wet handkerchief wherever they went. It helped with the tear gas. Several times in recent weeks the National Guard had broken up meetings of the young people in the church and the nuns had intervened, telling the kids to go home, to resist confrontation. One night as National Guard trucks rolled through the dusty streets, the sisters huddled in their little house. Julianne Warnshius, a new Maryknoll sister who worked with disabled children in Masaya, pulled out a bottle of fine skin lotion and began spreading it on her arms. "What are you doing?" the two Pegs asked, incredulous that she could engage in such a luxurious act. Putting on her finest haughty tone, Julianne looked at them carefully. "But darling, tear gas burns my skin." They fell over themselves in laughter.[27]

Soon, however, not even the nuns and priests were safe from the soldiers' violence. Just before Christmas, Sr. Julianne and Peg Dillon were walking behind a march with one of the priests, trying to keep the protestors calm as National Guard troops again descended on the street. Roberto Somoza, the guitar-playing, broad-smiling youth group member, was among them. The priest and nuns told the young people to go home instead of confronting the guardsman. Then, they turned to the guards, arguing that they need not arrest the young people, who were simply coming from a meeting at church. One soldier began hitting Roberto with his rifle butt. When the priest grabbed the gun to stop the beating, the guardsman turned his ire on the priest, knocking him to the ground. He whacked the nuns with the gun, bludgeoning them on the head and drawing blood. News reached the Sisters Center quickly. The Maryknollers had been trying to unite with the experience of Nicaraguans. Now, like so many of their neighbors, they'd felt the wrath of the National Guard. On retreat in September 1977, Maura had pondered the injustice in Nicaragua and the madness of militarism and a world economy that created OPEN 3 and enforced its misery. "God should consume us, destroy us, because of so much selfishness in our world, in us—but yet He doesn't." She'd contemplated God's deep knowledge and embrace of her and came to some conclusion about her role. "We want God to vanquish the evil when He desires to use us as instruments on this task of changing evil in the world—but desires our full cooperation."[28]

Physically Maura was a long way from the conflicts in OPEN 3 and the rest of Nicaragua, but they were always on her mind. Soon she would be asked to turn her attention to different work: outreach in the Archdiocese of Boston's Office for Urban Affairs. Maura and Sr. Jean Burke had been traveling for the past year, taking their workshop to whoever would have them, but beginning in January 1978 they would have a stable post. They were hired to present the workshops in each corner of the archdiocese over the next few months. On their first day in Boston, Maura and Jean presented the outline of their program to Jim Hannon, the newly hired director of the archdiocese's Commission on Justice and Peace. A veteran of Boston's racial desegregation fights and a Vietnam War resister, he was excited to be organizing the church's justice work. The commission would have committees on peace, human rights, economic justice, family, and democracy in the church. But almost before it began, there was intrigue and disagreement over how far the work would be permitted to go. The diocesan brass were worried about alienating philanthropists or speaking too radically. Maura could tell the atmosphere was tense. She sat with Hannon at the end of their meeting and gave him space to talk about the troubles of the commission, the bad blood in the office. He thought it a little inappropriate that he was speaking so frankly with near strangers, but he was at ease with Maura in particular. She exuded interest and commitment. She and Jean brought a breath of fresh air to the office. But as the work began in Boston Maura felt angry, out of place, trapped.[29]

Maura and Jean lived behind the cathedral in a low-income residence for single women. For the past year, while living in the Sisters Center and traveling around the northeast, Maura had worried that she was growing out of touch with poor people. Now she was back in a community of the poor, confronted not with destitution and hunger as in Nicaragua, but with the loneliness and sadness of women who had no one. She wondered whether she could take it. When she returned from work in the archdiocesan office, she could have sat alone with Jean in a quiet corner of the dining room. But that wasn't her way. Instead, she took her seat at a table with the other women, ready to listen and care for them. These women mattered to her. Sometimes, she even took one of them down for a weekend visit to the Sisters Center or to visit her parents in Rockaway.[30]

Maura's parents were by now in their late seventies, and she wanted to spend as much time with them as possible while she was nearby. She dreaded having to say good-bye—perhaps for good— when she returned to Central America. Whenever she returned to the Sisters Center from Boston, often late on a Friday night, she got a ride to the train station in downtown Ossining and waited on the platform, the beginning of a two-hour journey out to Rockaway. Even a day and a half spent with Mary and John Clarke was precious. And for now, she could finally spend real time with the nieces and nephews she'd been keeping up with for years in her siblings, Judy and Buddy's, letters. The towheaded toddler twins in matching Easter dresses that Maura had gushed about from Siuna, Judy's daughters Patricia and Pamela, were elegant teenagers now, getting ready for college. Buddy and his wife, Carol, had moved to Florida with their boys, but Maura spent time with Judy's younger children. She soaked them up. Maura cheered when Deirdre walked to the center of the room in Judy's new house in a fine Long Island suburb to show off her latest ballet steps. As the adults sat with tea in proper china and talked of whatever it was American adults spoke about, Maura caught the eye of Scott Eoghan, Judy's youngest child. Maura was far more interested in him than in polite adult conversation. The ten-year-old pulled Maura into the sprawling backyard. She was the only adult allowed into his fort among the brambles. He had her entire, glowing attention and she never rushed to exit their imaginary worlds.[31]

Fear of leaving her parents preoccupied Maura more and more. She knew they might not live long enough to see her return from her next posting to Central America. It was frightening to think of death disrupting the close relationship she'd maintained with them all these years. When she spent an afternoon with Carolyn MacDonald, a Maryknoller whose brother lived in Boston and was dying, Maura cut through any niceties. She asked Sr. Carolyn how she felt about her brother's imminent death. One day, at the Sisters Center in Ossining, Maura ran into Kay Cussen, with whom she'd lived for years in Siuna. It was Kay who on cabin fever nights in the convent in the cacophonous jungle sometimes announced she was going to the opera. She'd been a singer before she was a nun. Now the two women were posted to the United States and both longed to be back in Central America. Sr. Kay had spent the past several years in Guatemala and wanted to return but dreaded leaving her brother, who had had a stroke. Maura sympathized. She dreaded leaving her parents. "But Kay, I feel sure God wants us back with our people down there. They need our support." They'd have to trust God to care for Sr. Kay's brother and Maura's parents, she said.[32]

In the spring of 1978, Sr. Margarita Jámias, whom Maura had spent happy days with on the beach at Point León in Nicaragua, replaced Jean on the Global Awareness Team. She and Maura worked well together. Sr. Margarita was detail oriented and organized, keen to run efficient programs and enthusiastic in telling the groups they trained about the struggle for justice gathering pace in Nicaragua. At the end of their presentations Sr. Margarita busily packed up the posters and worksheets while Maura lingered with the participants, seeking out people who seemed to have something more they needed to process. She asked questions, made immediate deep connections, and collected addresses so she could stay in touch, trade letters, and share encouragement. As they walked to their car at the end of the session Maura always apologized for not having helped clean up, for having left too much of their work to Sr. Margarita.

But Maura had formed relationships. She couldn't turn away when someone needed attention. When a participant resisted the nuns' analysis, she didn't argue, she simply asked more questions, invested more in trying to understand the speaker than in proselytizing her view.[33]

It was an attitude she brought to every workshop she presented. Seated at the edge of a circle of chairs in a church basement or parish hall, Maura would gently ask someone to say more about why he or she thought the United States should be more concerned with military defense than human rights. It wasn't a trap. She wanted to give people space to articulate their ideas and she gave them respect, even when she disagreed. Her own ideas had shifted radically but over a long period. In Siuna she served tea to Luis Somoza Debayle; in OPEN 3, Sandinistas met in her house.[34]

One of the exercises Maura and Sr. Margarita led was intended to help people feel firsthand the effects of imperialism. Participants were divided into two groups, one much larger than the other. The larger group, the majority of people in the room, were told to sit on the floor surrounded by chairs or overturned benches that created a pen around them. The members of the smaller group sat at a table and were free to move as they liked. Everyone was given a stick of chewing gum. Then Maura and Sr. Margarita told the people in the smaller group to take the gum from those in the penned-in group. Some simply asked for it; others ordered the penned-in group to give it up. The smaller group always ended up with all the gum, and the larger group ended up trapped and without gum. They would then tell the group in the pen to strategize and figure out how to improve their situation. The sisters were happiest when someone simply stood up and moved the benches aside, walking into liberation.[35]

Maura and Sr. Margarita were in accord. They had to use their time in the United States to do what they could to help the people they loved in Nicaragua throw off the dictatorship. Educating these middle-class Catholics, building friendships in each parish and town they visited, could lead to real change if the people they spoke to lobbied Congress and talked to their neighbors. It was important, Maura thought, to prepare conscientiously for these presentations and talks, workshops and meetings. But once they had begun, she needed to trust God to work through her, to make the work a kind of prayer. Otherwise all the activity was just an idol, a distraction from her deep quest for communion with God.[36]

Mary Heidkamp understood that quest. The young woman and her work partner (and future husband) Jim Lund ran the Catholic Church's Peace and Justice Commission in Providence, Rhode Island—a counterpart to Maura's employer in Boston. Sr. Margarita and Maura found reasons to visit Mary and Jim frequently throughout 1978. Together they could speak deeply and practically about the education and organizing work they were each trying to do. They could also simply relax. With Mary and Jim, Maura felt at ease, accepted. There was delight and energy in their friendship, a desire to soak each other up. Maura stayed over in Providence and bedded down on the younger woman's floor. The group took Maura's father out to dinner when he came to visit Providence, where his sister also lived, and spent the night singing in an Irish bar. Sr. Margarita, who is Filipina, convinced everyone she had an Irish grandmother because she could sing "I'll take you home again, Kathleen" and "Believe me if all those enduring young things," the same songs John rolled out. Maura regularly invited Mary and Jim to come share a weekend at the Sisters Center. There, they'd all be able to bask in one another's company and take walks together on the grounds. Maura sent them home with stacks of books from the Orbis bookstore: new translations of works on liberation theology and the church in Latin America—there was so much to learn. Standing together in the bookshop, Maura pressed a newly translated volume into Mary's hands. This is *The Gospel of Solentiname*, she explained. Written by Fr. Ernesto Cardenal, the book consists of long dialogues meant to be transcriptions of conversations about the Gospels between Fr. Cardenal and a group of Nicaraguan peasants and artists living on an island in Lake Nicaragua. It was the closest material available to explain the kind of work Maura had been doing since her days in San Pablo Apóstol, reading the Bible from the experience of poor Nicaraguans. The *Solentiname* members applied the Jesus stories to their own world, with a revolutionary analysis, seeing Jesus as a literal liberator and the promised reign of God as their wished-for freedom. A year earlier, Fr. Cardenal's group had joined the Sandinista attacks in October 1977 and fled to Costa Rica.[37]

Maura appreciated that people in Nicaragua were relying on their own conscience as they determined how to support the struggle for liberation. Some remained activists and church workers or supported the Sandinista cause through meetings and demonstrations, as Lesbia Taleno had done. Others, including many of the young men and women she'd loved in OPEN 3, joined the armed guerrillas. Fr. García Laviana, the priest two of Maura's friends worked with in Tola, rescuing trafficked girls from a brothel, decided to join the guerrillas. Calling Somocismo—the support of Somoza—a sin, he argued the Sandinista struggle was a just war, that joining the fight against the institutional violence and social structure of a sinful society was his duty as a Christian. Again reminded of her father's role in the Irish revolution fifty years earlier, Maura respected these decisions and admired the sacrifices so many were willing to make. It seemed familiar. No one could be motivated by a desire for violence, she thought, but having seen their country suffer, having seen the torture and the daily violence of poverty, she understood why they made the decisions they did.[38]

Julio López, a teenager from OPEN 3, had been writing to Maura since she left Nicaragua in 1976. He was unsure what he should do. So many of his friends from the barrio had left for the mountains to join the guerrillas. But Julio was uncertain. He wanted to be part of the struggle, but he didn't want to take up arms. Instead he was working on a farm cooperative in Matagalpa. Maura tried to offer comfort, she didn't really have advice. She painted a quote from Camilo Torres, a Catholic priest who had died fighting with the revolutionaries in Colombia, at the top of one letter to Julio.* She tucked Julio's picture, a teenager with an open, smiling face leaning against a farm fence, into her Bible. It greeted her every morning when she opened the Bible to pray for him and all her friends in Nicaragua. When nuns serving in Nicaragua came through the Sisters Center, she sent messages to Julio back with them, with instructions to give her love to Mercedes Taleno and others in OPEN 3. When fighting consumed Matagalpa, she fretted, worrying that Julio had been hurt, phoning mutual friends in Nicaragua to check on his safety. So many of the precious people she loved were dying or risking everything for hope of a better country. It reminded Maura of the sacrifice of Christ—a life laid down out of love for others.[39]

"I'm sure you are doing everything you can for the people you love so much. The lives of so many innocents have been sacrificed

---

* Camilo Torres quote was: "The highest measure by which human decisions must be measured is the all surpassing love that is true charity. I accept all the risks that this standard demands of me."

and offered for the liberation of Nicaragua and also for the whole world because the blood of so many brave people, as the blood of Jesus, calls us to a total change," she wrote to Julio. It wasn't only the people she loved in Nicaragua suffering and dying for a vision of a society where children didn't die from hunger and weren't buried in borrowed fields. These were the body of her God. The Christ she'd pledged to serve was being cut down, over and over.

In the fall of 1978, the guerrillas launched an organized insurrection in the capital and several major cities. In Managua, Lesbia Taleno's brother Edgar joined other Sandinista guerrillas outside the National Palace in stolen military uniforms, posing as presidential guards. Aware that even the country's politicians feared the elite National Guard unit, the Sandinista commander (dressed as a presidential guardsman) shouted, "The boss is coming!" The genuine soldiers at the door of the palace stepped aside and the Sandinistas marched unmolested into the legislative session being conducted inside the building, drew their guns, and took hostage the entire assembly. The guerrillas demanded the release of eighty-five Sandinista organizers and soldiers held in Somoza's prisons—and $10 million. Twenty-seven of the prisoners had already been executed. As he had during the Christmas raid at the home of Chema Castillo four years earlier, Somoza acquiesced.[40]

Now the war arrived in full force. Maura followed the news closely, reading coded news in letters from the sisters in Managua. She read in horror reports of National Guard massacres and guerrillas attacks, of fighting in towns she had visited, the continual aerial bombing of cities where her friends lived and the deaths of people she loved. It felt ridiculous to be in the United States, embarrassing not to be with the people she'd helped awaken, now that the revolution was coming. "Like Jesus' dying, the laying down of these lives of the poor Nicaraguan people must be the martyrdom, the gift of total and heroic love, a last desperate crying out to the world," she wrote to the sisters in Nicaragua as the violence exploded.[41]

Allies in the United States launched pressure campaigns in support of the revolution. It began to work. The Carter administration delayed some aid to Nicaragua as leverage for improvements in human rights in 1977, then restored it. Throughout 1978, the State

Department threatened and flirted with withdrawing or suspending aid. Carter urged Somoza to step down and pass authority to a governing junta the United States could find palatable. A solidarity group in Boston was planning a rally in front of the John F. Kennedy Federal Building there for the end of September 1978. The demand was straightforward: let the Nicaraguan people decide their own future; the United States should not try to manipulate. Maura and Sr. Margarita prepared eagerly, urging their colleagues in the Peace and Justice Commission to join them at the rally. Peg Healy, Maura's roommate from OPEN 3 who was now working with the Washington Office on Latin America, a pressure group formed by various Christian groups concerned about US policy toward Latin America, was slated to speak. Thousands of people gathered midday in downtown Boston, filling the plaza in front of the federal building named for the president whose Alliance for Progress food relief Maura had dispensed to her students in Siuna.[42]

When Maura was a child in the 1940s, being a loyal American and a good Catholic were intertwined, reinforced every day as she walked under those words "Pro Patria, Pro Deus" (For country, for God) inscribed in the limestone of St. Francis de Sales. At Stella Maris Academy as a high school student she sang "The Star-Spangled Banner" at the end of prayer services—the churchful of girls, the daughters of immigrants, attesting to their Americanness, promising in their Catholic anticommunism that they were loyal proponents of the American project. Now she was raising her voice outside a federal building named for the first Catholic president, decrying the relationship between her nation and one of its most enduring clients, endorsing the movement of the Nicaraguan people she'd fallen in love with—which was led by Marxist revolutionaries. Maura crowded into the plaza in Boston with activists and church members, lefty veterans of the anti–Vietnam War and disarmament movements, and Americans enchanted by stories of mustachioed, poetry-spouting Nicaraguan rebels and disgusted by their nation's long support of a wantonly corrupt and vicious dictator like Somoza. US Representative Paul Tsongas took the stage to speak. He had been arguing in Congress for the cessation of US aid to the Nicaraguan government.

Maura had expected to be just one of the crowd, but at the last minute, Peg Healy couldn't attend. The rally needed another speaker. Hastily, Maura was drafted. She knew the country, had seen the devastation of the earthquake and the vacuuming up of relief into Somoza's coffers. She knew the brutality of the National Guard, had sat vigil more than once as boys she'd trained to serve God by serving the most poor were held in jail cells—their convictions about dignity an affront to the regime. Now she took the stage, flustered but ready to do her bit. This is where her prayers for courage would be put to the test.

Her voice rose over the crowd, sweet and strong, battling with the midday traffic. She had no notes, so she talked about the people who shared her heart. She'd intermittently done her best to understand the big geopolitical issues, taking notes in seminars on economic imperialism and spending a day at a library at the New School for Social Research studying the structure of International Monetary Fund loans that somehow managed always to exacerbate the desperation of the landless poor. But these were not the ways Maura understood the world. As the crowd leaned in to hear, enraptured by this passionate, disarming woman, Maura spoke instead of the people in OPEN 3 and Miralagos, of the love she'd found in tarpaper shacks. She spoke of the recognition of people grasping to make God's promise real, recognizing in one another the possibility of something better than hunger and fear. She spoke of the many adults she knew who couldn't read and of the treatable illnesses that stole their children. There was wealth in Nicaragua, she assured the crowd. But it was held in the hands of the few. What the Nicaraguan people wanted was simple: a decent life, a reason to hope for their children's future. These people she loved would prevail, she told the audience, because they'd grown strong together.[43]

Over the next few months, Maura and Sr. Margarita continued their work to rally support for the Nicaraguan people as the Sandinista rebellion gained traction. In the spring of 1979, as they walked along the beach in Watch Hill, a retreat house the Maryknoll sisters maintained in Rhode Island, they shared their frustration at not being in their adopted country as the war unfolded, yet consoled each other that they were doing their part for its freedom. "We may not see the liberation of Nicaragua, but we're part of it," Maura said. Sr. Estelle Coupe who, upon arrival in Nicaragua in 1944, had promised Anastasio Somoza García, the current leader's father, that the Maryknoll sisters would be no trouble to him, analyzed the revolution in a detailed presentation. "How does a revolution begin?" she asked. There are many reasons, she continued, but the consciousness-raising that the Maryknoll sisters and others had been doing for more than a decade had been decisive.[44]

Somoza was increasingly isolated. After the assassination in January 1978 of opposition newspaper editor Pedro Joaquín Chamorro Cardenal, middle-class and moderate Nicaraguans abandoned the regime and formed various alliances for its ouster. Time was running out for Somoza.

In mid-July, at Riverside Church in Manhattan, Maura and Sr. Margarita joined a small group of people who shared their dream of a free Nicaragua. William Sloane Coffin, the civil rights veteran and progressive Christian pastor who built Riverside into a powerhouse activist congregation, opened his church to host a fast that would call on Somoza to step down. That weekend, Maura and Sr. Margarita and others slept at Riverside Church and prayed together, giving up food as a symbol of their conviction. Since childhood Maura had fasted on Good Friday and Ash Wednesday, days of penance in which forgoing food was supposed to bring the person fasting closer to Jesus's discomfort. The activists in the barrio used a hunger strike in hopes of forcing concessions from the water company in 1976. Maura's father went on hunger strike in an Irish prison during his country's civil war. Jesus had fasted in the desert for forty days. Now Maura was taking up the challenge, directing her discomfort, her body, to some transformative, Godly goal. She was relieved to learn the activists would allow themselves juice. She worried she wouldn't be able to go totally without nourishment. At the end of two days they celebrated a liturgy and took Communion, their first food in forty-eight hours. They'd offered their bodies as a sacrifice, albeit a brief one. Now they were sharing the ritual meal together, taking part in Jesus's body as they directed their prayers to the liberation of God suffering in Nicaragua.[45]

Two days later, Anastasio Somoza Debayle fell. The forty-four-year Somoza family reign was over. He fled to Miami and ceded power to the speaker of the parliament. Two days later the speaker, too, fled and on Thursday, July 19, the Sandinistas marched into Managua's central plazas. Work begun by radicals taking pledges in the mountains, by students occupying the cathedral in 1970, by Carmen García growing bold in San Pablo Apóstol, by Miriam Guerrero claiming her right to speak in Miralagos, by Amada Pineda naming her rapists, by the teenagers of OPEN 3 professing love for their brothers and sisters, had come to fruition. In the end, Maura's commitment to the revolution was expressed in prayer, in an old-fashioned exercise of fasting. The struggle of the past decade was complete. Her political convictions had been informed by her Christianity and her prayers directed to an outcome in the concrete, political world.

Maura was elated, awed. But she was also chagrined. After all the suffering and struggle, all the growth and hope she and the Nicaraguans she loved had experienced since she first alighted on that thin strip of dirt sliced out of the jungle in Siuna, she hadn't been there in the end. She worried she wouldn't be able to relate to her Maryknoll sisters who'd lived through the war, that they'd experienced something deep and profound that she wouldn't be able to understand.[46]

By the end of 1979, the new Sandinista government was beginning to rebuild from the vicious and devastating war—and Maura's three-year term of service to the congregation was over. She would soon be returning to mission in Central America. But the landscape had changed dramatically, and now she was needed elsewhere.

CHAPTER 9

Into the Darkness

As 1980 began, Óscar Romero, archbishop of San Salvador, issued two pleas. To Jimmy Carter he wrote a letter begging the US president to stop sending military and economic aid to his country. It only fed the military state that was butchering the impoverished people demanding their rights as citizens and humans. And he asked the president of the Maryknoll Sisters to send more of her order. For years Maryknoll sisters and priests—along with others—had been doing much the same work Maura had in Managua: leading Bible study groups in which people analyzed the story of Jesus from their own experience and put those ideals into action in the real world. Maryknoll priest John Spain had been working in El Salvador since 1971, long enough to see a nascent opposition emerge against the feudal conditions under which most of the country lived and long enough to see violent repression of that effort gather and rise. The repression fed armed resistance as previously peaceful activists, responding to electoral fraud that closed off avenues for protest, turned to various guerrilla units in a combination of self-defense and frustration. By 1980, life was a matter of struggling to stay afloat amid all the death.[1]

The people in these church groups, like the people in the unions and farmworkers' associations they sometimes made common cause with, wanted relief from the vicious poverty that circumscribed their lives. El Salvador's economy was built around export-oriented coffee and cotton plantations owned by a small circle of interconnected families descended from the Spanish conquistadors. In 1880, traditional agricultural lands—that indigenous inhabitants had farmed communally—were enclosed and turned over to a small number of wealthy families. The people who had lived on these lands became laborers on giant estates driven by guards who bore a certain similarity to plantation overseers. From the 1880s to the 1970s, the Salvadoran oligarchy built up a thoroughly militarized society. Most peasants lived under the power of these employers, patrolled by a National Guard that enforced the will of the landowners and ran a network of spies to report on agricultural workers. The result for the majority of Salvadorans was abject poverty. Diarrhea was the leading cause of death in El Salvador in 1980. Three quarters of the nation's children were malnourished.[2]

Archbishop Romero admired the way Maryknoll sisters made themselves part of the communities they served and he wanted reinforcements. The leadership of the Maryknoll Sisters sent an appeal to experienced missionaries, particularly those familiar with Latin America, asking them to consider answering the archbishop's call.[3]

In his plea to Jimmy Carter, Archbishop Romero told the American president that aid to the Salvadoran government was directed toward killing: "Your government's contribution, instead of favoring greater justice and peace in El Salvador, will undoubtedly sharpen the injustice and repression suffered by the organized people whose struggle has often been for respect for their most basic human rights." The president did not respond. The archbishop was referring to a $5.7 million request for nonlethal military aid. Congress approved it in March. The US had provided military training to 2,000 Salvadoran officers from the end of World War II until the late 1970s. Military aid under Carter started slowly but set the stage for continued growth. The Salvadoran military received cargo trucks, radio equipment, riot control gear, teargas, and more, in addition to economic assistance from Washington: $65.2 million between October 1979 and the end of 1980.[4]

The archbishop had some hope that Carter would be sympathetic to his pleas. The Democratic president had made human rights a component of his foreign policy, repudiating a generation of US practice that ignored gross human rights violations by allies in the fight against communism. With Directive 30 in February 1978, Carter ordered that US allies' record of human rights would now have some bearing on how the United States interacted with the country.

That same policy eventually suspended military aid to Nicaragua in the final year of Somoza's regime. After the US criticized its human rights record, in 1977 El Salvador's military government rejected US military assistance. But after a reformist coup in October 1979 aimed at reining in the military, the US resumed aid. But the junta established in October 1979 failed to achieve its reformist objective. Instead of isolating the most violent elements in the ministry of defense, hardliners, such as Col. José Guillermo García, took control. By January 1980, most members of the October junta had resigned in disgust. Several fled into exile.[5]

Organized leftist opposition to successive Salvadoran regimes had grown throughout the late 1960s and 1970s. Particularly after a fraudulent election in 1972 and the torture and killing of those who protested the fraud, many poor and middle-class Salvadorans were convinced that electoral politics were useless. A variety of guerrilla organizations formed in the early 1970s—some with far older roots—bombed government buildings, kidnapped prominent members of the oligarchy, and assassinated others. By the mid-1970s, each guerrilla group had formed a nonmilitary popular organization composed of already existing unions, peasant committees, and rural associations dedicated to deepening resistance to the oligarchy and its military. The links between the popular organizations and the guerrillas were not always clear to members of the popular organizations. One could be a member of the Popular Revolutionary Bloc (BPR), an amalgamation of unions and peasant associations, without realizing it was firmly connected to the Popular Liberation Front (FPL), a guerrilla group. Hanging over the steady and rapid work of peasant and urban organizing was a haunting memory. In 1932, indigenous people, spurred in part by communist organizers, rose up against the feudal condition and poverty of their lives. A few hundred people attacked police stations, killing six people. The response from the government was overwhelming. Within days, the forces of General Maximiliano Hernández Martínez, the nation's military dictator, had killed between 10,000 and 30,000 peasants—a significant portion of the population in a tiny country. The taste of La Matanza, the Massacre, was still in the mouths of Salvadorans rich and poor. To the military and the oligarchy with which it was aligned, La Matanza represented a policy success. Swift and overwhelming military response produced the desired result: forty years of compliance. To Salvadoran peasants, it was a haunting reminder of the price of dissent.[6]

In the winter of 1980, President Carter appointed a new ambassador to El Salvador to manage the increasingly delicate relationship with its military government. Robert White had spent his career in Latin America, with postings in Nicaragua, Colombia, Honduras, and Paraguay. He was a liberal anticommunist and an enthusiastic member of Carter's emerging human rights paradigm. The United States was trying to strike an uneasy balance: to prevent a repeat of Nicaragua in which a Marxist government comes to power, yet also to condemn and try to stop the brutality the right-wing Salvadoran government was visiting upon any opposition or perceived dissident. White believed keeping El Salvador out of Marxist hands was his highest priority and that killing civilians and torturing unarmed opponents—in addition to being wrong—weakened the government's position and drove it closer to all-out war. When White was briefed on his new assignment in Washington, DC, in February 1980, a member of the US National Security Council suggested he visit Rome on his way to San Salvador and try to convince the Vatican to muzzle Archbishop Romero. Instead, upon arrival in El Salvador, he visited the archbishop and suggested the two begin sharing information. White wanted the Salvadoran government and the leftist opposition to negotiate an end to the fighting. Archbishop Romero was beloved by the vast majority of the country—and loathed by the ruling oligarchy and military. If the US Embassy shared information, maybe the wary archbishop would trust White and the two could work toward fostering a negotiated settlement.[7]

While Ambassador White was getting his bearings, Maura was trying to figure out what to do next. The Maryknoll Sisters leadership had issued a call, asking sisters with Latin American experience to consider reassignment to El Salvador. She had visited the country a few times during her years in Nicaragua: once to sit in on a women's discussion group with Sr. Pat Murray; once while traveling in the early 1970s with women from San Pablo Apóstol in Managua to an international church group meeting in El Salvador. During the latter trip, they'd carried books and pamphlets about a Jesus who came to declare liberation for the captive and freedom for the oppressed. Maura and the women stood frightened as soldiers at the Honduran border searched their luggage. Literature about a Christ who had something to say about the physical conditions of life on earth was subversive, dangerous. Already in 1970, small gatherings of church people reading the Bible and farmworkers talking about fair wages were met with suspicion by the Salvadoran authorities.[8]

El Salvador was breathtakingly poor, even for experienced Maryknoll sisters who were used to dirt floors and hand-operated wells. And it was mean. Violence permeated the society, from the security services that patrolled the coffee plantations, to the work itself in which the necks of farm laborers sometimes snapped under the weight of coffee sacks, to families in which men regularly beat their wives and girls had little autonomy. The Christian Base Communities worked on people's hearts, little by little identifying this violence and working to change it. As in Nicaragua, the movement was personal as much as it was political. It called for individuals to change their own behavior as well as for a shift in national priorities. For this reason it was doubly dangerous, not only seeking to reform government policy, but in fact seeking a wholesale transformation of society.[9]

But Maura's visits to El Salvador had happened years ago, before OPEN 3, before the Nicaraguan Revolution, before her long sojourn in the United States. At the end of January, she began the Mission Renewal Program, a six-month course of updating, study, and reflection. The invitation to El Salvador preoccupied her. She wrote to Maryknoll sisters in Nicaragua and El Salvador in the end of February, asking how soon she'd need to make a decision. Her friends in the region encouraged her to take her time. Two sisters who had long worked in Chile, Ita Ford and Carla Piette, would be arriving in El Salvador soon. Maura need not rush.[10]

Three years earlier, when the first Catholic priest, Rutilio Grande García, SJ, had been killed by the Salvadoran government in March

1977, Archbishop Romero went out to Aguilares, a poor village where Grande had been pastor and part of the land reform movement. Fr. Grande's preaching on the rights of people to determine their own destiny and his work organizing farm laborers made him dangerous to the big plantation owners. It was his assassination that opened the archbishop's eyes to the brutality of El Salvador's security forces. A naturally conservative and bookish man, Archbishop Romero had been close friends with Fr. Grande but, until the priest's death, he had tried to stay out of politics. When Grande was killed, Archbishop Romero sat for hours, listening to the villagers tell their stories. Afterward in weekly homilies—broadcast throughout the country on the diocesan radio station—he condemned the killing, the torture, the disappearances of people who were struggling for their rights. From the pulpit each week he catalogued the murders that were engulfing El Salvador, repeating the names of unarmed peasants who'd been found dead, speaking out loud the names of the military battalions and police forces responsible, listing the villages and the dates. Archbishop Romero's data came from a network of human rights documenters throughout the country who brought written reports to the archdiocese's headquarters.[11]

In 1975, the archbishop had established Socorro Jurídico, a legal aid office to work on behalf of poor Salvadorans. As terror against peasants and suspected subversives mounted, Socorro Jurídico collected testimonies. Mothers walked into the office in the archdiocese headquarters clutching pictures of their children, beseeching the lawyers to find out what happened to them. They gave names and told the same stories in desperation: the son that didn't come home, the death squad that roared into the village in the night and dragged daughters out of their beds. The bodies found bloated in the ditches, stripped, beaten, shot through the head. It documented atrocities committed by the leftist guerrillas as well. And Archbishop Romero denounced these. But they were a tiny fraction compared to the military's campaign to eradicate dissent.[12]

Archbishop Romero's radio broadcasts were heard across the small country. Guerrillas in temporary encampments in the rugged mountains tuned in. In the northern province of Chalatenango,

Esperanza Tobar, a poor farm woman who was part of her parish council, listened with the volume turned low, lest a passing soldier or neighbor who was part of the right-wing civilian militia hear. In the military barracks, lieutenants and colonels listened to keep track of what this bothersome priest knew. In the market, a person could move from stall to stall and listen to the entire homily, just as a person walking along the street in Rockaway, New York, in 1948 could hear Fulton Sheen's voice emanating from every house.[13]

In his usual homily during the Sunday Mass on March 23, after recounting a list of the cases of arrest, torture, and killing that had occurred in the past week at the hands of the military, Archbishop Romero begged Salvadoran soldiers to disobey the orders of their superiors:

"Brothers, you come from our own people. You are killing your own brother peasants when any human order to kill must be subordinate to the law of God which says, 'Thou shalt not kill.' No soldier is obliged to obey an order contrary to the law of God. No one has to obey an immoral law. It is high time you recovered your consciences and obeyed your consciences rather than a sinful order." The words poured forth from a thousand radios in villages and barracks, in the luxurious San Salvador homes of the landowners and the guerrilla encampments in the forest. "In the name of God, in the name of this suffering people whose cries rise to heaven more loudly each day, I implore you, I beg you, I order you in the name of God: stop the repression."[14]

The next day, as the archbishop celebrated Mass in the chapel of the small cancer hospital where he lived, a Volkswagen pulled up to the curb. A man took aim up the center aisle of the church and shot him dead. Óscar Romero's body fell behind the altar, his blood staining the stone floor. Nuns who served at the hospital rushed to him, trying to staunch the bleeding. The car drove off. The assassination had been organized by a former intelligence officer, Roberto d'Aubuisson Arrieta, and financed by wealthy Salvadorans. That night, fireworks and the celebratory firing of shotguns filled the air in San Salvador's wealthy neighborhoods. No one was arrested.[15]

In letters from El Salvador, Ita Ford and Carla Piette, who had arrived in the country too late to work with Archbishop Romero, wrote of the chaos and violence at his funeral. Fifty thousand mourners—church leaders from across Latin America and the poor people who'd found comfort and hope in this archbishop who cared for them, popular organizations of students and farmworkers who'd been sitting in and marching for a decade to change El Salvador and militants of the left-wing guerrilla organizations—filled the Metropolitan Cathedral and the large plaza in front of it. The crowd was packed tight. Some fainted or fell from sunstroke or dehydration as the funeral began. Then a bomb exploded in the plaza. Suddenly, chaos: gunfire everywhere, shots fired on every side of the church, and explosions erupting at each entrance. Flames engulfed cars on the perimeter of the plaza. The crowd of people outdoors surged forward, thousands scrambling for safety inside the cathedral. Forty people were killed, most of them crushed in the panicked crowd.[16]

It was these things Maura pondered as she took the short walk each week from the Sisters Center to the Maryknoll cloister to talk to Sr. Grace Myerjack.* Maura's old friend Peg Healy had suggested she might benefit from Grace's calm, judgment-free counsel as she decided what came next.[17]

Maura wanted to make sure she was going to El Salvador for the right reasons. And she had some other troubles to work out: her persistent hunger for approval, her sense of never being good enough. She was wrong-footed around her sister Judy and feared abandoning her parents. So, each week, she visited Sr. Grace for spiritual direction.

---

* The Maryknoll cloister is and was a chalet-style house on the grounds of the Sisters Center in Ossining. A group of Maryknoll sisters, some returned from service abroad, some who have led a life exclusively devoted to prayer, live quietly, though not in the silence of traditional cloistered religious communities. The sisters in the cloister offer spiritual counseling and pray for the work of their active counterparts. Mother Mary Joseph, the founder of the Maryknoll sisters, considered a place devoted exclusively to prayer an important component of the Maryknoll project. [Claudette LaVerdiere, *On the Threshold of the Future: The Life and Spirituality of Mother Mary Josephy Rogers, Founder of the Maryknoll Sisters* (Maryknoll, NY: Orbis Books, 2011).]

Years earlier she might have had a relationship with a confessor, and she still went to confession with a priest on occasion, but the relationship with Sr. Grace was something different. Although it wasn't psychological counseling, it bore some similarities. Sr. Grace served as a guide and sounding board, a person to whom Maura could speak her deepest thoughts and fears, with whom she could discuss her most profound relationship. Sr. Grace would help Maura uncoil complex motivations and reactions, with the goal of freeing her to be closer to God.[18]

From the time she'd entered the convent as a nineteen-year-old that sunny September day in 1950, Maura's fundamental goal was to grow ever closer to God, to be united with Jesus. Kneeling in St. Camillus in Rockaway, teaching in that chaotic classroom in the Bronx, visiting families in Siuna, marching in Managua and sitting in at Somoza's consulate—each phase had been about growing closer to God, about being with Jesus in every frightful and hopeful place he existed. Now she was nearly fifty, a middle-aged woman, and before she made her next step she wanted to recommit, to make total her relationship with this Jesus. She told Sr. Grace she wanted to cement her dedication to Christ. To do that she had to work through everything that was holding her back, everything that smacked of fear or hesitancy, defensiveness or dread. She wanted to be free and open, to accept everything God offered and to give her whole heart.

They talked about love. They talked about Fr. Martínez. What had that been all about? Maura still found it unsettling that she'd fallen in love. She was happy she hadn't pursued it. She wanted to remain a nun. And she didn't feel guilty now. But why had those feelings emerged? What did they mean? What was God trying to tell her through the experience of falling in love? Sr. Grace helped her understand that the feelings were to make her more whole, more literate in being human. Being excited to see Fr. Martínez, infatuated, feeling her heart swell—this was another aspect of the love of God, the nun counseled. Maura could follow that love, not into a romantic relationship, but deeper into the heart of Jesus. Now maybe God was asking her to follow him to El Salvador. Could she respond freely, out of love instead of fear or guilt?

Going to El Salvador would involve the very real possibility of death. Thousands of church people and reformers, dissidents and priests had been killed in just the past few years. As crocuses emerged in the woods in front the cloister and tender green leaves began to sprout on the dogwoods and maple trees, Maura knew death was stalking El Salvador. It was a fear she couldn't shake. The assassination of Archbishop Romero meant the military and security forces had loosened the last bit of restraint. Anyone could be killed now. She checked Elisabeth Kübler-Ross's *On Death and Dying* out of the Maryknoll library.

Martyrdom, dying for one's faith, had been a consistent element of Maura's religious education and cultural upbringing. It was a frequent topic of sermons when she was a young novice in the convent. The many Maryknoll priests who had been killed in China, and Sr. Hyacinth, who disappeared on a Japanese death march in the Philippines, were held up as heroes and models to the young nuns. The way they were talked about made dying a martyr the highest honor, something to hope one might be lucky enough to face. It made a person important. In martyrdom one could test the depth of one's love of God. In the language of the Christian Base Communities in Nicaragua, the definition of martyrs included those who were willing to die for the cause of national liberation. Maura decorated some of her letters in those Nicaragua days with a phrase from the Gospel of John: "There is no greater love than this, to lay down one's life for one's friends." It was a passage the young men and women who joined the guerrillas embraced. When her father's Irish friends had crowded into the living room in Rockaway and begun telling stories, and stories gave way to songs, those were songs of martyrs, too: brave men who gave all for Ireland, their names were invoked like saints': Thomas MacDonagh, John MacBride, James Connelly, Pádraig Pearse. But Maura wanted to strip away any notion of romance and consider it soberly. She wanted to follow Jesus as far as he led her. Could she do this freely, out of love, not pride? The challenge was to be able to respond to the call for reinforcements in El Salvador not because going would earn her praise or make her worthy, but to be able to go calmly, out of love.

First, she and Sr. Grace dwelt on pain. With the horror of El Salvador as her next possible home, there was no sense avoiding it. Maura had the habit, acquired as a child, of taking on other people's pain. It was part of her relationship with her father, of her intense empathy, to seek a way to aid whoever she was with. Everyone said when she listened, it was as if she was taking in your whole soul. It felt that way to Maura, too, and she was injured by other people's pain. So, what would happen to her in El Salvador, where the bodies were piled on the road and barefooted mothers brought the pictures of their dead sons and daughters to the archdiocese? With Sr. Grace she talked and prayed about how to accept suffering, to acknowledge and take in the pain she saw in people who'd suffered, but not be done in by it. In being open to other people's injury, she was accepting her own pain and hoping to have the love and understanding she offered mirrored back to her, Sr. Grace said.

It was an asset, surely, that Maura was so empathetic. But if she could acknowledge her own pain, accept that whatever childhood traumas and family tension she felt only made her fuller, better able to be part of Jesus's suffering, she would be able to meet pain in others and yet know that she and they could survive. Sr. Grace believed that Maura was so focused on whoever she was talking to because she longed for acknowledgment. She wanted to be with each person, to make him or her feel noticed and valued, because she wanted the same for herself. Now she needed to take the suffering or injury not as something to be overcome, but part of the wide experience of life, something that could draw her closer to God, who knew the same rejection.

This is what all those scenes of Jesus's death on the cross that Maura had prayed over on Friday afternoons in Rockaway or Siuna were about. Jesus came to take on human suffering not to condemn humanity, but to be part of it. As a young novice she had meditated on the prayer of Saint Teresa of Avila: "Christ has no body now but yours, No hands, no feet on earth but yours, Yours are the eyes with which he looks compassion on this world. Christ has no body now on earth but yours."

Where was Christ most needed now? Maura asked herself. Where was his compassion most lacking? She wanted to go there, to be those hands and feet, to be that body. Maura and Sr. Grace talked about Saint John of the Cross, a medieval mystic who contemplated the wounds in Jesus's hands, feet, and side as depicted in Christian statutes and wrote that every wound when touched by God is transformed into a wound of love. This was Maura's task, to adjust her approach so that she wouldn't try to ignore her insecurity, but instead accept it and offer it to God as a way to grow even closer to him.

But she had to convince her family, too. Maura's parents had soaked up her years in the United States, delighted by her frequent visits to Rockaway, content when they had her in the house with the rest of the family. Michael Clarke, son of Maura's cousin James, was a sophomore in high school in 1980. He failed Spanish that year, so when his parents left for their annual trip to Sligo, he had to stay behind for summer school. He spent two weeks at the family's house in the Catskill Mountains, an Irish summer enclave north of New York City where Maura's parents visited as well. Maura went with him to the Catskills house. They took walks to Point Lookout on Hunter Mountain and breathed in the clean air at a nature preserve, the soft mountains green and lush around them. Over two weeks they declined Spanish verbs and stumbled through clumsy conversation. Maura had been speaking Spanish for twenty years, but she was patient with this American teenager, his life so different than the lives of the youth in OPEN 3.[19]

Maura's imminent departure hung over the family. Since the winter she'd been talking about which country to go to—Nicaragua or El Salvador? Her parents tried to be subtle, but they wanted her in Nicaragua. El Salvador was far too dangerous. It came to a head in the cousin's house when the elderly Clarkes came to visit during Michael's extended tutoring session. Michael was sitting in the living room, actually studying for once. His father, returned home from Sligo, was arguing with Maura while her parents reclined on chaise lounges outside. Maura's cousin was angry, insisting that she should stay close to home. Her parents were older now, James said. They needed her nearby. "I know," Maura said to him. "But the people there need me more."[20]

It was time. Her three years of service in the United States were complete. She belonged in Central America and the call for El Salvador seemed clear. Rose Gorman, whom she'd met while traveling with the World Awareness team, begged Maura not to go to El Salvador. But the people there were in such need, Maura said. "If we abandon the people when they are suffering the crucifixion, how can we speak credibly about Resurrection?" Maura asked. All those radical readings of the Gospel had taught her that Jesus was in the people, being shot and beaten beside them. She wanted to be closer to him.[21]

In June she spent three weeks with her parents, this time in their house in Rockaway. Just as he had when she was a child, John Clarke stretched his legs after dinner and asked her to join him for a long stroll on the boardwalk. It was a walk she'd taken hundreds of times beside her father. As a little girl she'd had to stretch to keep pace with him. Now her gate was sure and his a little slower. They walked past the places she'd played as a child, past the Jewish Nursing Home where her mother had worked, past the back of St. Camillus church. The ocean was the same vast power, dark and loud, waves steadily crashing beside them. It was the other side of the same ocean she'd gazed at the year before, when it seemed half of Sligo celebrated at the Beach Bar in Aughris. That party had felt like an American wake, the send-off for immigrants who wouldn't return.

John Clarke didn't want to beg. But he wanted his daughter beside him. Did she have to go? Hadn't she done enough? Maura was always patient. Gentle. But firm, too. This was her mission. She needed to go.

She wrote to her parents as the plane flew from Miami to San Salvador and then on to Managua on July 16, a chatty note recounting her few days in Florida with her brother Buddy and his family. She signed off as she arrived in Managua. She was apprehensive about what she would find, expecting the country to be devastated by the war and so many dead. But even in grief over the loss of so many idealistic lives, the country was full of hope, joyful, even, at the possibility people's efforts had created.[22]

A busload of friends from OPEN 3, now renamed Ciudad San-dino, greeted her with cheers and embraces as she entered the airport. These were the same people who'd traveled to the airport three years earlier, crying as she departed. Now she'd returned and the country was free.

On the morning of July 19, Maura rose with her neighbors in Ciudad Sandino before five a.m. They filled thirty-five buses to ride into the center of Managua for a celebration of the first anniversary of their revolution. Maura stood and sang with the throngs of people pulled in from all parts of the country. Children, now adults, whom she'd taught in Siuna, ran to her through the crowd to deliver jubi-lant hugs and kisses. A man shouted her name, then wrapped his arms around her, nearly lifted her off the ground. It was Sergio, who she'd refused to abandon the night of the earthquake eight years earlier, when he was trapped under a collapsed building. Now they stood together in the hot July sun, free to congregate, free to say the name "Sandino," proud that Nicaragua was writing a new history. She listened to hours of speeches, including one by Fidel Castro who pledged his support for the new Nicaragua. Maura's friends told her they didn't want to imitate Castro's communism, but as a Latin American who'd led a successful revolution he was an inspiration.[23]

As hundreds of thousands of Nicaraguans, Maura among them, stood in the wide, open center of the ruined city, the district that had been leveled by the earthquake and never rebuilt, shouting slogans, waving banners of their organizations and neighborhoods, sing-ing the Carlos Mejía Godoy songs that had once been banned, the skies opened up. Soaked with rain and giddy with delight, Maura piled into a taxi with Gerri Brake and several other sisters, weaving through the crowded streets and back to Ciudad Sandino. The neigh-borhood was hung with black and red bunting, the Sandinista colors. All the people from the Christian Base Communities, the women and men she'd spent her years in OPEN 3 falling in love with, the people who'd struggled together in the water fight and whose sons and daughters had steadily slipped out of the barrio to join the Sand-inistas in the mountains, the families who had secretly supplied food to the militants and who had taken first-aid classes so they'd be ready for the fight, who carried baking soda and wet rags to protect themselves from tear gas in the years of Somoza, they all gathered at Cruz Grande to celebrate a Mass, remember their martyrs and thank God for their new history. Maura noticed the monuments, everywhere in Ciudad Sandino and throughout Managua, to the beloved who had died in the revolution. She listened as old friends, such as Mercedes Taleno, shared their stories of heroics and death. Lesbia Taleno's brother Edgar had died fighting near the Costa Rican border. But in the midst of such pain, Maura observed, there was belief in Resurrection, in something new being born.[24]

People from the barrio had jobs in government and the Christian Base Communities filled the ranks of the new neighborhood associations that were starting to build proper roads, lay sanitation pipes, and plant trees in Ciudad Sandino. And some of Maura's friends were serving in the highest reaches of the new government. Her old friend Fernando Cardenal, the Jesuit priest who came to the barrio every week to celebrate Mass with the young people in the early 1970s, was leading a national literacy campaign in which tens of thousands of teenagers and young adults traveled to remote villages to teach, using Paulo Freire methods. Later he would be minister of education. Miguel d'Escoto, the Maryknoll priest with whom Maura had taken over the Somoza Consulate to the United Nations in 1977, was now foreign minister.

In the days after the anniversary, Maura made a date to talk to her old friend Luz Beatriz Arellano, the Franciscan sister she'd been friends with in the early 1970s. Sr. Luz Beatriz had needed to flee in 1975 after she'd received death threats for her opposition to Somoza. Now she was back. Sr. Luz wanted Maura to stay. The church needed people who supported the revolution, and there was so much to do, she told Maura. Conservative elements in the church hierarchy were already circling. Frs. Cardenal and d'Escoto would need the help of nuns and priests who backed them, Sr. Luz Beatriz argued.[25]

Maura had still not completely decided whether she would go to El Salvador or stay on in Nicaragua. She saw a role for herself in Nicaragua, a way to help Sr. Luz Beatriz and others build the society the people she loved had struggled so long to achieve. But she also felt out of place and knew that more was needed in El Salvador. The work she and thousands of others had begun ten years earlier, teaching about a liberating Christ and training people to work together, had paid off. Somoza was gone. The people were free to chart their own history. "We've won here," Maura told Sr. Luz Beatriz. "They still haven't won in El Salvador."[26]

At the beginning of August, Maura left for El Salvador. At the airport she was delighted to see a familiar face: Leila Rodríguez, Angelique's daughter, with whom Maura had spent so much time in Miralagos before the earthquake and whose family she had visited often in Masaya after the quake, was grown up now. Confident and strong, she worked for the new revolutionary government in its embassy to Spain. Leila embraced her old friend. What was she doing in Nicaragua? Had she returned? Maura explained that she was on her way to El Salvador. "No," Leila implored. "It's far too dangerous. Stay with us!" Maura smiled. "The people there need me more," she told Leila.[27]

CHAPTER 10

In the Valley of Death

The death squads came in the night: men with hard faces, standing in the back of a pickup truck, weapons slung over their shoulders. In Lamatepec, the cooperative housing development in the city of Santa Ana, El Salvador, where Sr. Maddie Dorsey lived and acted as pastor for the parish, she kept a long piece of railroad steel beside the church. In OPEN 3, Maura and the other sisters banged on a similar piece of broken railroad to announce Mass and meetings in the Cruz Grande as the community struggled together to build a new life. Here Maddie hurried to bang a spoon against the metal to warn of death. The death squad—usually off-duty soldiers and lower-level officers but also some nonmilitary thugs—targeted teenage boys especially, those suspected accurately or not of participation in the social movement or of being in sympathy with the guerrillas. Families knew to go looking the next morning in the garbage dump.[1]

Three young men from the parish were killed the day before Maura came to stay with Sr. Maddie in the second week of August 1980. In a different time there would have been a wake, flowers in the church, a chance for the mothers to wail, the bodies of the young men mourned. But the security forces had recently banned all public assemblies after a national strike was called by the left. No one was allowed to gather for any reason, even a funeral. Even if they'd been allowed to hold a funeral, few people might have come. In the circular logic of El Salvador's counterinsurgency policy, to be shot meant one was a guerrilla. Associating with a guerrilla carried its own death threat. People feared going to funerals of those killed by the security forces because it labeled them as subversives, meant they might be next. The walls had ears in Lamatepec and the streets had eyes. When Maddie and a teenager from the neighborhood, Guadalupe Calderón, gave public health classes on nutrition and hygiene, national guardsmen watched. When the Christian Base Community gathered to read the Bible, national guardsmen watched. So, instead of bringing the dead to the church this night, Maura and Maddie went to the families' homes and sat beside the grieving and frightened relatives. Archbishop Romero had spoken often of accompaniment, the act of simply being with the people suffering. There wasn't much to say, but Maura could be beside people in their grief.

During the day Guadalupe Calderón taught health classes and helped Maddie with work in the parish. At night she coordinated logistics for the guerrillas, managing medical supplies and figuring out where to bring children whose parents had been killed. She didn't get medical supplies from the sisters, but she confided in them about her work. Maura listened one night in the parish house as Guadalupe talked about her commitment to the revolution. "What faith," Maura murmured.[2]

Maura had arrived in El Salvador on August 6. The plane from Nicaragua left late and it took two hours to get through customs. Everything and everyone coming from Nicaragua was suspicious. The Salvadoran elites feared the revolution the Nicaraguans had achieved. Maddie and another sister, Terry Alexander, brought Maura to La Libertad, a port city on the southern coast, where several Americans from Cleveland worked in a parish and ran a large meals program for hungry children. A few Maryknoll sisters worked with this team. One of them, Joan Petrik, had just left that summer. Her mother was sick and death threats against Joan were becoming more common. Terry had arrived the previous spring, responding to Archbishop Romero's appeal for more Maryknollers. She lived in La Libertad, but now was moving to live with Maddie in Lamatepec. She, too, was getting death threats and thought it safer to be with another sister.[3]

The next day, outside the parish house in La Libertad, Maura joined the sisters and their friends as they shared horror stories. A journalist from the *National Catholic Reporter* was there as well, a woman who had been writing about El Salvador for four years, watching as the violence grew. She visited the Maryknollers whenever she could because they worked so closely with poor people. They knew what was happening in the country. John McAward, president of the Unitarian Universalist Service Committee in the United States, was there as well. He had been bringing delegations of church people and members of Congress to see for themselves what was happening in El Salvador since the early 1970s. After Fr. Rutilio Grande was killed in 1977, McAward brought Jesuit priest and Massachusetts congressman Robert Drinan on the first congressional fact-finding trip to the country. The Unitarians provided funding to *Paz y Justicia*, a tiny newsletter printed by Fr. Fabián Amaya, which used cartoons and drawings to make its points to illiterate farmers. The newsletter wasn't associated with the leftist guerrillas or any organization beyond the Catholic Church, but it was still dangerous to be caught with it. Some farmers buried their copies, rather than risk being found with them.[4]

At La Libertad Maura met the three other women she would work closely with over the coming months. Dorothy Kazel was an Ursuline nun from Ohio who had been working with Christian Base Communities for several years and helping run the parish food program that fed three thousand. She was contemplating returning to her order in Cleveland, where she had been a high school teacher, but worried that the transition to ordinary life and a comparably conservative order would be stifling after years in the mission. Jean Donovan was young, just twenty-seven, and had none of the inherited reserve the nuns carried with them from convent training. She broadcasted her emotions loudly and publicly. She'd been close to two young men from the parish who were killed a few months earlier and she was still grieving. She told her parents and fiancé that conditions were not as bad as they sounded and that she would be fine, but the nuns worried about her and thought she needed to go home. Maura had met fellow Maryknoll sister Ita Ford just a few months earlier, when they were both spending time at the Sisters Center in Ossining. The two had traveled into Manhattan together in February to hear a presentation on El Salvador at a parish on the Lower East Side. It was run by Tom Cornell, a radical pacifist and one of the first people to publicly burn a draft card in protest of the Vietnam War. Cornell worked for an interreligious peace group that Archbishop Romero asked to hold meetings and publicize what was happening to Salvadorans. Tom thought then that they seemed green.[5]

But Ita was far from green. She'd worked in poor neighborhoods of Santiago, Chile, before and after the military coup that brought right-wing dictator Augusto Pinochet to power. She knew about disappearances and guilt by association. Erudite, sharp-witted, and intense, she had a petite frame that was coiled with energy. Ita and her friend and fellow Maryknoller Carla Piette had been reading Archbishop Romero's speeches and following the news of El Salvador. When the appeal came that the archbishop wanted more Maryknoll sisters, Carla and Ita signed up. They arrived just after he was assassinated. Now instead of meeting him in the cathedral, they filed reports on torture and death at the offices of Socorro Jurídico, the legal aid service he had established.

When they'd arrived in late March, Carla and Ita looked around for a place to be useful. By June they were working under the direction of Fr. Amaya in the archdiocese's division of social services. They were assigned to one of the hottest part of the country: Chalatenango. The farmers and peasants there were heavily involved with the farmworkers' unions. Leftist people's organizations, such as the Popular Revolutionary Bloc, held sway, their graffiti sprayed on the concrete walls of Chalatenango town. Guerrillas of the Popular Liberation Front (FPL) maintained camps in the countryside and fought with the military. This meant that, under the security forces' "drain the sea" counterinsurgency policy, civilians in Chalatenango were subject to particular brutality. The military hoped to drain the region of any support for the guerrillas until, like fish without water, they were left gasping.* Ita and Carla spent much of their time ferrying people marked for death

---

* "Drain the sea" was a counterinsurgency policy developed by the United States and employed during the Vietnam War. The metaphor inverts Mao Zedong's instruction that the guerilla must move among the people like the fish swims in the sea.

from Chalatenango to the relative safety of impromptu refugee centers in San Salvador or bringing people without food massive bags of rice and dried beans donated through international aid organizations. Their frequent trips back and forth to San Salvador in Carla's jeep and sometimes with Dorothy and Jean in the La Libertad van drew the attention—and suspicion—of the security forces.[6]

Maura had only just arrived in El Salvador and already she would be offered a way out. As the Maryknoll sisters sat talking at La Libertad, one of them, Jenny McDonald, the regional superior, reminded them that everyone at the Sisters Center back in Ossining was worried about the nuns in El Salvador. She reiterated the message from the order's leadership: they didn't have to stay. They should feel free to stay or go, depending on their own conscience. Maddie, Terry, Carla, and Ita, who had been working in the country for several months already—in Maddie's case, several years—said they believed God wanted them here. These were women with deep spiritual practices. They didn't know why God wanted them in this horror, but they were searching for the answers. Maura listened, taking in the conversation and the sincere grappling of her colleagues. Finally she spoke up. She was at peace about being in El Salvador, she explained, content in trying to understand why God was calling her to this place. The other sisters nodded their head in agreement and relief.

After a few days in La Libertad, Maura and Terry Alexander returned with Maddie Dorsey to her home in Lamatepec, in the city of Santa Ana. Maura missed the intimacy of OPEN 3 and the coziness of Siuna. Terry and Maddie seemed like wonderful people, but she didn't really know them. Maddie had lived alone for more than a year and now there were three of them in the house. The newness of being in El Salvador and the journey from La Libertad to Lamatepec had kept Maura distracted for the first week. Now she was lonely and frightened. She wondered whether she'd made the right decision. "I want to believe, and hope that I do, that there is nothing to fear. 'Fear not, I am with you, be not dismayed,'" Maura wrote to her friend Mary Manning in Boston, quoting the prophet Isaiah. She'd stay a few weeks to see whether she could be useful.[7]

Maura arrived in Santa Ana just before a general strike. The popular organizations had called for all work in the country to stop, shops to close, and people to stay home on August 13, 14, and 15. It was a way of demonstrating to the government and the military that the people's organizations had power—and the strength of broad swaths of the population behind them. Because of the strike, the National Guard and the death squads were on high alert.[8]

Maura jumped into the work of the parish, supervising young religious instructors and visiting sick people. When a group of teenagers distributed food to families with young children, she helped fill bags with flour. Maddie kept a cabinet stacked with Bibles and medical supplies in the main room of the house. Maura had stood with her back against it, praying they wouldn't destroy the Bibles, when the National Guard burst in one day, searching for contraband. In the spring, after a few convents in San Salvador were raided by the military, Maddie had buried her copies of Archbishop Romero's homilies. To have them in the parish house was evidence of subversion. To Maura it brought back memories of the stories she'd heard from her McCloskey cousins the year before: of the Royal Ulster Constabulary charging into Mary and Ethna's tidy house in Belfast, of young men in the neighborhood being dragged away during the period of internment in 1971. In Northern Ireland, every Catholic was potentially disloyal. Here, too.[9]

In addition to the security forces, which told the same lie as in Northern Ireland of a neutral military attempting to establish order in the midst of fighting from opposing sides, there were, as in Northern Ireland, civilian militias to worry about. These patrolled towns and villages and kept information on suspected subversives. Salvadorans didn't know which of their neighbors they could trust. This Maura recognized from County Antrim, from her mother's habit of keeping her own counsel, and from the stories her Uncle Barney and cousins told of Unionist paramilitary groups and subtle and overt intimidation. Here it was far worse. ORDEN, the National Democratic Organization, was a civilian defense squad founded in 1967 to route out communism. It was ostensibly civilian, but was organized and directed by the military and comprised of reservists from the army and security forces. Disbanded after the reformist coup in October 1979, it was reconstituted in the winter of 1980 after the majority of moderates abandoned the ruling junta. ORDEN was active in every town and village. There was a unit in San Antonio Los Ranchos, where Carla and Ita spent much of their time.[10]

Maura still had some doubts about El Salvador, and she confessed her fears with openness to her friends back in Boston. At night she sat in the chapel in Lamatepec, asking God to make it clear to her what she was supposed to do. Before long, however, the decision to stay would become obvious.

On August 23, just three weeks after Maura arrived, Carla and Ita left their rooms behind the gleaming white cathedral in Chalatenango and walked across the town square to the barracks of the National Guard. A few young men from the nearby village of San Antonio Los Ranchos were being held there, and Carla and Ita wanted them released. Colonel Ricardo Peña Arbaiza, the army commander who told Ita that Catholic nuns and priests were subversives because they sided with the poor, kept a copy of Norman Vincent Peale's *The Power of Positive Thinking* and a loaded gun on his desk during their meetings. This time he released one young man to the sisters.[11]

They might have brought him back to the building where they lived, where several refugees from Los Ranchos were sheltering. But there was a rumor that he was an informant, that the military had released him only because he gave them the names of neighbors who were sympathetic to the guerrillas. Others said he wasn't an informer, simply a young man picked up like so many others. It was night and the weather looked ominous. Ita and Carla decided to drive him to his family; they didn't want the risk of him seeing the people hiding at the convent. As they started out in Carla's jeep, a seminarian and Alfredo Rivera Rivera, a high school student who was thinking about becoming a priest, both of whom lived at the parish house in Chalatenango, jumped into the back of the jeep to provide some protection for the sisters. Driving at night was dangerous. They headed out of town, up the steep, rutted road to Los Ranchos.

As they left Chalatenango town, the sky opened up. Carla had to drive hard to pull through the winding, lazy river that switched back and forth along the road to Los Ranchos. Ordinarily the river was nothing more than a simple stream, but in a rainstorm it swelled, growing violent and fierce. Sheets of rain beat down on the windshield and wind buffeted the jeep. They crossed the river, twice, three times. The young man, informant or victim, was let out and climbed up the bank of the river to his family. Carla turned the vehicle to return to Chalatenango. Then, suddenly the water was all around them. Alfredo and the seminarian broke the back window of the jeep and climbed out, trying to make way for Ita and Carla to follow. But a torrent of water forced the vehicle onto its side and pushed the young men toward the opposite bank. Ita and Carla were trapped in the spinning, sinking jeep. Somewhere downstream Carla pushed Ita out the partially open window and then the jeep was gone. It tumbled along in the torrent.

All night the young men and others from Los Ranchos searched for Carla and Ita. The rain stopped eventually and the river slowed, but as the sun began to rise the nuns were still missing. At dawn, people from Los Ranchos found Ita shivering and covered in mosquito bites in a field of corn. She had grabbed onto a tree root and with great difficulty, after many attempts, pulled herself up out of the water, then collapsed on the prickly ground. Carla was found dead several hours later, her body washed far downstream to where the river meets with another.[12]

Ita was devastated. She had lost her best friend and been traumatized by her own near drowning. But now Maura's role was clear: she would work with Ita and help her through the difficult months ahead. Maryknoll sisters converged in El Salvador from Mexico, Guatemala, Panama, Chile, Nicaragua, and New York to mark Carla's funeral. Hundreds of people from throughout Chalatenango and across the country filled the high-ceilinged, magisterial church the night before Carla's funeral. Some walked miles, some hitched rides, to be there.

For others it was too risky to attend. María Guadalupe Menjívar's son had been killed by the National Guard during the general strike on August 15. He was a member of the Union of Campesino Workers, aligned with the left, and a participant in the cursillo movement, a Catholic prayer group that emphasized lay leadership and personal closeness to God. Both made him suspicious in the eyes of the security forces. After her son's death, Maria feared the death squad would return for her as well as her son's widow and six children. On August 22, Ita and Carla had evacuated the family, bringing them down through the hills to Chalatenango town and into the convent behind the church. From the front door of the convent one could see the army barracks—and be seen. A year earlier, the military intelligence division had set up shop in the barracks as well. Now a soldier was always posted within sight of the parish house, watching, noticing who came and went. Maria stayed in the convent, surrounded by her grandchildren and daughter-in-law, all of them shell-shocked, as the wake took place a few yards away in the church.

At the wake Carla's friends read from the Bible and sang. A young man who'd begun seminary training when Archbishop Romero was still alive spoke at the end of the wake. In his last year of training, he and other seminarians were sent to assist the churches in villages in Chalatenango. After the funeral, he spoke for forty minutes from the altar, delineating the crimes that had been committed against the people of Chalatenango by the security forces and invoking the good work Carla had performed in her adopted country. As he spoke, the army, National Guard, and intelligence police drove their trucks close up to the steps of the church, filling the plaza between it and the military installation. Later that night, Maura and Maria left the convent to buy bread for Maria's family. Maura fussed over Maria, putting her arms around her and doing what she could to make her feel less hunted.

The man who had the unenviable job of filling Archbishop Romero's shoes, Bishop Rivera y Damas, drove up from San Salvador to celebrate the funeral Mass the next day. Among the mourners were Peter Hinde and Betty Campbell, a priest and a nun from the United States, whom Maura had met years earlier in Nicaragua. They were traveling throughout Central America collecting information on repression and the Church. As the funeral ended, Maura walked side by side with Peter down the steep streets of Chalatenango. The whole church walked with the casket, accompanying it down to the crowded, narrow cemetery at the foot of the town. They sang as they walked, more than one hundred people standing tall as they passed the National Guardsmen and carried their friend to be buried in Salvadoran soil.[13]

Since the order's earliest days, Maryknoll sisters have been buried where they died. Their graves dot the most distant bits of the planet: encampments in the Marshall Islands, remote jungles in the Philippines, rural villages in China, open plains in Tanzania, and crowded cities in Japan. Carla would be buried like her Maryknoll sisters, beside the people she served.[14]

After the funeral, Ita spent a few days in the hospital in San Salvador with a severe bronchial infection and Maura returned to the southern coast, where she'd spent her first days in El Salvador. The Maryknoll sisters—including some from Guatemala and Mexico, who'd come for the funeral—gathered at a hotel near the ocean to think and talk and decide what Carla's death meant for their efforts in El Salvador. Beside the sea, Maura felt calmer. She watched the waves crash against black volcanic rocks and send white spray into the humid air. The situation felt different than in Nicaragua, more angry and confused. In OPEN 3 there had been great swells of hope as well as fear. Knowing her parents were saying the Rosary together back home in Rockaway was a comfort. If they died, as she had so feared in her last year in the United States, or if she died in this nightmare of a country, it would just be God calling them home, she told herself.[15]

Death was everywhere. Bodies of people killed by the military and the death squads were left to rot on the side of the road or in fields where they were tossed—a judge's order required before a body could be moved. Some had their hands tied behind their back or their head chopped off and hung nearby. The lips were cut off the face of some and the skin removed from the body of others. Some were doused in acid and their fingernails removed. Many were naked. Maura was horrified to see buzzards feeding on the dead. These were human beings, families, children, "blessed temples of the Lord," Maura wrote to Peg Dillon. "It seems unbelievable but it happens every day."[16]

When Ita recovered a few days later, the two returned to Chalatenango. Maura settled into the parish house, a converted warehouse a few feet from the back of the church and just yards away from the

National Guard barracks. The priests and seminarians lived in one part; another was used for meetings and to house the people fleeing their villages. Carla and Ita had shared a small room tucked behind the others. Now as Maura took Carla's place, she unpacked her few possessions. She thought she'd have books. In July she had mailed a box of books from New York to Nicaragua. They hadn't arrived by the time she left for El Salvador. She'd pick the books up in November when she went to a regional meeting in Nicaragua.[17]

Now, in the spartan room she would share with Ita, Maura set a souvenir from Ireland on the small bedside table. It was a trinket, really: a wooden figurine of a donkey cart laden with turf. When she'd stood at the door of her Uncle Mick's house in Dromard, County Sligo, just a summer earlier, she could look across the sweep of fields and up the hill of the peat bog where logs of cut turf were stacked, drying in the sun. She had sat at the foot of that hill where people believed Saint Patrick had drawn water from a white stone well more than a thousand years earlier as he traveled through his adopted country. Some swore the water from the well cured arthritis and other ailments. Last August, Maura stood on the highest stone slab, cut like an amphitheater into the hillside, and soaked up the peace of being in her family's place. These lonely, quiet fields dotted with grazing sheep must be the same scene as centuries ago when others breathed and walked and struggled, she'd thought then. She'd wondered whether standing in this place helped her, or should help her, believe that this life is not the end, that there was more.[18]

Now in the little room with Ita, Maura unpacked her paperback Bible, its salmon color faded after nearly ten years of steady use, its pages thick with mementos and notes. The passages she'd read so often in Nicaragua about building the kingdom of God and the Israelites' liberation from slavery were underlined in blue ink. Here in El Salvador, she and Ita would meditate on the Good Shepherd who lays down his life, who does not abandon his sheep when the wolf comes.[19]

It was in September that Maura noticed the skin-and-bones girl come stumbling in front of the church in San Antonio Los Ranchos. She put her hand gently on the girl's thin shoulder. Norella Mejosa Menjí-var* and what remained of her family had been on the run since May or June; she'd lost track of time. Norella and her mother, her twin brother, an older sister, and the sister's three young children were weak with hunger, tormented by mosquitoes, faint with anemia. Norella's family hadn't belonged to any of the people's organizations or the farmworkers' union in their home village of San José Las Flores. They weren't part of a Christian Base Community that talked about throwing off oppression. In their church the priest still celebrated Mass in Latin with his back to the congregation. But it didn't matter; the military treated everyone like guerrillas. Her brother had listened to Archbishop Romero's homilies with a portable radio tuned to a whisper so neighbors wouldn't hear. As the spring of 1980 began, the National Guard burned farmers out of their homes and shot livestock, the family's only source of food and income. Months earlier, before the assassination of Archbishop Romero, the radio-listening brother had disappeared—taken off a bus on the way to San Salvador and never seen again. Two other brothers who worked as farm laborers away from the town began staying where they worked. It had become too dangerous in San José Las Flores. They began collaborating with the guerrillas. The brothers saw it as their only choice. On the day Norella fled, the military came for the family of one of the brothers. The soldiers ordered his wife, his two-year-old daughter, his brothers-in-law, and his parents-in-law to lie face down in the dirt. Then they threw a grenade. Seven people together were burned to ash. Norella only learned about their death from neighbors also on the run. There was no chance to mourn the lost family, no funeral or burial. They had spent the summer wandering in the mountains, sleeping in caves and finding what little food they could. They had no access to their crops, no chance of returning home. Early that morning they had wandered close by Los Ranchos. A man saw their desperation. "You should go to the church. Maybe there you can get help," he told them.

Maura and Ita acted quickly. "There are refugee centers in San Salvador," Maura told Norella and her family. "We'll take you there."

---

* "Menjívar" is a very common name in Chalatenango. The many Menjívars mentioned here are not related.

They planned to leave that day. The capital was a little safer, although enough people showed up dead each day in San Salvador that reporters made it a morning ritual to drive the streets of the poorer neighborhoods, looking for bodies. Still, it was safer than Chalatenango and several church properties had been turned into impromptu refugee centers. San José de la Montaña, the sprawling diocesan seminary, was crowded with people who had fled from their homes. They camped on the once-verdant grounds. More than six thousand displaced people had arrived since the spring. Maura and Ita would take this battered family with them to San Roque, another impromptu refugee center. But first, Maura said, they would stop in Chalatenango to get Norella and her family some decent clothes. What they were wearing was torn to shreds. Maura and Ita hustled the family to a truck the sisters used. "Climb in here; we're going to cover you up," the sisters told the family, drawing a blanket over the back of the vehicle.

The drive to San Salvador from Chalatenango was fraught with risk. It was not unusual to pass twenty military checkpoints along the way, each manned by soldiers who saw every Chalatenango peasant as a guerrilla. But Maura and Ita scheduled their journey for midday. Soldiers were eating or lounging in the shade, back away from the road. They passed checkpoint after checkpoint, soldiers waving them through. As they neared each one, Maura and Ita instructed the family to be perfectly silent and to pray.

After each passage, clear of the death-dealing national guardsmen, the sisters and the family sang. It was a way to keep away the terror. They sang a popular church standard: "Vienen con Alegría, Señor." It is often sung with mariachi trombones and jaunty guitars. Here it was just the voices of Maura, Ita, and Norella and her terrified family—the melody emanating from the vehicle as it progressed down the road, under the watchful vigil of El Salvador's silent volcanoes.

"They come joyfully, Lord. Singing, they come, Lord. Those that walk for life, sowing the seeds of peace and love. They come with joy, Lord, singing."[20]

But Maura and Ita knew they were still in danger. When the family arrived at San Roque refugee center, Maura told them they should use new names. She and Ita did this with each of the families they rescued. The security forces sometimes raided these unofficial centers, coming in with a list of names and dragging people away. Maura named the girl "Aida" and her mother "Rosalina."[21]

Trips like this one constituted a major part of Maura's work for the next three months. Over and over again she and Ita drove that road, smiling at the National Guard checkpoints. It was a little like the work Maura's cousin Linda Kearns had done in the Irish Revolution, a sweet smile getting her through the British checkpoints. But Maura wasn't transporting weapons or guerrillas, just terrified women and children. Bringing refugees out of the conflict zone was just one part of Maura and Ita's work. They also spent their days bringing food, donated by international relief organizations and procured through the archdiocese, to people in villages and more remote encampments in Chalatenango province. Jean and Dorothy sometimes joined them and sometimes helped take refugees from the parish house in Chalatenango back to San Salvador. Maura and Ita went frequently to Los Ranchos to stay with Esperanza Tobar and her husband, Tobías Menjívar. Fr. Sigfredo Salazar had been assigned to the parish a few years earlier. He built up a Christian Base Community and encouraged the lay people to take on leadership in the church. But by the fall of 1980 it was too dangerous for a priest to live there. In July, the security forces had raided the church, knocked the Eucharist to the ground, and defecated and urinated on the altar cloths and priests' robes. Fr. Salazar was now living in the combined parish house in Chalatenango, supervising the seminarians. In his place, Esperanza, Tobías, and other laypeople kept the parish running.[22]

Esperanza managed the storeroom beside the chapel, distributing clothing and food provided by the sisters. When someone was burned out of their home by the National Guard or ORDEN farther up in the hills and came down to Los Ranchos under a guerrilla escort, Esperanza stood in the dark beside the storeroom and tried to offer comfort. Sometimes a local FPL member would let Esperanza know a family was coming from Arcatao or another town farther north near the Honduran border where fighting was particularly fierce. Guerrillas brought their wives and children to Los Ranchos to be ferried to safety. Maura and Ita usually took the people first to the house in Chalatenango, letting them rest and recover before the trip through multiple checkpoints to San Salvador.

In Los Ranchos, there was a telephone that was critical to the women's efforts. Esperanza and the sisters worked out a code. When Maura and Ita got a call from Esperanza saying, "An old woman is sick; bring blankets," it meant someone in danger of death, sometimes a wounded combatant, was waiting for their help. Often people came at midnight to collect beans and corn, cooking oil and rice. They loaded their trucks and drove back into the hills. Some food would go to the guerrillas, some to noncombatants in flight from their homes. Maura and Ita didn't discriminate. It was for human beings in need; that's all that mattered.[23]

The guerrillas were not foreign to the people of Los Ranchos and the other towns. As in Nicaragua, they were sons and daughters. The women and children Maura and Ita ferried to safety were often the wives and children of men who had decided to fight. Everyone made their own personal moral calculation as to whether to join the armed movement or advocate from the political organizations or simply care for the wounded or displaced; but the guerrillas, by and large, were supported by the people. Everyone in Chalatenango was suspect already. As the killing intensified and a long-hoped-for land reform program only led to more dispossession, many people decided they needed to fight for themselves, that waiting for the death squad was not an option. They joined the guerrillas. Others fled to guerrilla encampments in hope of protection, but didn't carry arms or engage in combat. Esperanza and Tobías weren't members of the Popular Revolutionary Bloc or the farmworkers' union or the FPL. They supported the goals of such groups and were happy, grateful when the guerrillas warned them that the army was headed for the village, but their allegiance was only to their conscience as Christians. Esperanza believed that people deserved to live better than they did in El Salvador, facing hunger and constant surveillance.

Whenever she and Ita spent time with Esperanza and Tobías in Los Ranchos, Maura was amazed by the bravery of this couple and others like them, challenged by their commitment to struggling for a better chance. She sat in their tiny house, just as during a hundred home visits in OPEN 3, talking over black beans and fried eggs— it was all the couple ever had. To Esperanza Maura seemed like a mother hen, eager to help, anxious to do whatever she could to protect her friends. As she sat with Esperanza and Tobías one day, turning over more stories of terror and agony, Maura said to her hosts, "Someday, when this is all over I'll take you to my parents' house by the ocean."[24]

But it would be a long time before the fear and danger were over. The guerrillas were planning a massive uprising that they hoped would finish the war. The days of October and November ticked by in expectation and dread, but also in hope for victory. As rumor and news of the offensive spread, noncombatants sympathetic to the guerrillas' cause were deep in discussion about what they would do. The various guerrilla groups had united as a single army, the Farabundo Martí National Liberation Front (FMLN), the previous May, hoping to replicate the successful Nicaraguan revolution that had driven Somoza from power a year earlier. Uprisings in urban neighborhoods, such as OPEN 3, and attacks on military bases in rural areas had pushed the Sandinistas to victory. Would it be possible in El Salvador? Everyone knew the final offensive was coming; the question was only when.[25]

Maura was part of a series of workshops sponsored by the parish in Chalatenango on how to prepare for the war. The classes asked people in the Christian Base Communities to search their conscience: What would they do when this disaster arrived? Closing one's eyes wasn't an option. Christians had to do something, including giving their life if that is what was called for, the priests running the workshops said. Víctor Manuel Méndez was a member of the Christian Base Community in San Antonio Los Ranchos. He'd met Ita and Carla in the spring at a retreat in another part of the county. There Fr. Fabián Amaya, whom Maura and Ita now worked under, had spoken of how a whole society can be separated from God not by personal infractions of morality but by the social structures that keep people in poverty and suffering. It is a liberation theology concept that tracks with Marxism's theory of structural violence. The retreat called El Salvador's poverty, enforced by the oligarchy and the military, a social sin. There Victor and Carla and Ita and the other participants had talked about solidarity, about being connected to the Body of Christ in work for justice. Now there was greater urgency. No one knew when the guerrillas would launch the final offensive. The people needed to be ready, to know what role they'd take.[26]

There were other, more practical classes, too. Sr. Betty Campbell and Peter Hinde, with whom Maura had walked at Carla's funeral, returned in October. In an out-of-the-way place where fleeing families had relocated, Betty, a nurse, led a class on basic medical procedures. Maura paid close attention, carefully practicing how to suture a wound. She was impressed by the studiousness of the young man beside her. They both wanted to be ready to treat whoever needed help, combatant or civilian. Suddenly, the class broke up and everyone scattered. Someone had heard the National Guard was coming. Maura and Betty walked back toward the parish in Chalatenango. On the way they had to pass a house where people they believed were members of ORDEN sat watching on a front porch. Maura tried to control her legs but they were shaking violently and it was difficult to walk.[27]

They made it back to the parish house, and that week a beloved visitor came. Peg Healy, Maura's good friend from OPEN 3, was in El Salvador to gather facts about the repression there. As Maura, Peg, Betty, Peter, and Ita sat in the converted warehouse that night, they smelled gasoline. Had someone poured an accelerant around their house, ready to strike a match and set them on fire? Maura hurried outside with the others, to walk the perimeter of the building. No, it must have only been a leaking car engine. They walked back inside, rattled. It was hard not to be frightened all the time. Just a few days earlier the National Police had surrounded the home of a parish priest in San Salvador and arrested him. His body was found on the outskirts of the city the next day. He'd been shot in the mouth and chest. But with old friends who understood the stakes, Maura and Ita tried to joke. "That's probably how we'll die," they laughed, pointing to the massive sacks of dried beans and rice stored in the rafters and straining the central beam. "We'll be crushed under fifty pounds of rice."[28]

In addition to delivering food and ferrying refugees to safety, Maura and Ita documented the horror they witnessed. They took statements from victims and they filed reports frequently with So-corro Jurídico, the legal aid office established by Archbishop Romero five years earlier. Roberto "Beto" Cuéllar Martínez, the attorney in charge of the office, thought of them almost as colleagues. They were among a handful of the most active documenters of human rights vi-olations, part of a network of concerned nuns and priests and church people around the country who collected specific evidence of the mil-itary repression. Maura and Ita arrived frequently at Socorro Jurídi-co's offices with written testimony, names, and dates to add to the catalog of terror. The goal in writing down the atrocities, in keeping records, finding names, and making sworn statements was to create a record. Someday, these horrors could be prosecuted. For now, they would be tallied and what legal recourse existed, Socorro Jurídico would pursue. Maura and Ita were eager to help, relieved perhaps that they could at least keep a record of the atrocities that burned their eyes and hearts. Cuéllar investigated crimes committed by the left as well. There were kidnappings and the murder of informants. Civilians were killed when guerrillas blew up government buildings or hijacked buses. But there was far, far more military terrorism.[29]

Socorro Jurídico was under constant surveillance by the mili-tary. Its work, carefully stitching together a picture of the repression which could be brought to the United Nations or the Inter-American Commission of Human Rights, made it particularly dangerous to the military. It didn't matter that Socorro Jurídico took no side in the emerging civil war and maintained an assiduous neutrality. The orga-nization's mandate was human rights, not revolution. The office was raided and sacked in the summer, then bombed in September. Cuéllar and other staff received nearly continuous death threats from the mili-tary in 1980. By then, he had stopped living with his family. He didn't want his presence to endanger them. It didn't work. In April, the right discovered where his wife and children were living and arrived at their house with a threat. Death squad members carried three coffins: a regular-size one for Cuéllar's wife, two small ones—for his children.[30]

Cuéllar found it necessary to remind Maura and Ita that Socorro Jurídico was neutral. These nuns had no great love of war, but they wanted to see these Salvadoran people win. They were committed to the possibility of a country where people had basic rights, where farmers owned the land they tilled and workers were paid fairly.

Maura talked about it with Miguel Vásquez, a seminarian who was doing his last year of training in Chaletenango. Being with the Nicaraguan people, organizing and sharing in their suffering and hope, had been a privilege, Maura told Miguel. She'd felt loved there, a part of the people. Now that the Nicaraguans had triumphed, it seemed right to be with people still struggling in El Salvador. They were being crucified. She could be with them now, try to show that God had not abandoned them.[31]

But all this work and the constant threat of violence took its toll on Maura. For the first time in her life, people described her as quiet, reserved. Drawing on the habit her mother had developed as a child in County Antrim, she was careful not to say the wrong thing, not to reveal a fact or impression that might put someone in danger. She'd grown thin, her face drawn. Dark circles appeared below her eyes. Alfredo Rivera Rivera, the teenager who lived with the sisters and seminarians, often noticed Maura walking by herself, her back straight, her stride long. Walking had always cleared her head, brought her back to her childhood strolls on the boardwalk. Now she seemed to be in conversation with God, carefully trying to grow closer to the pain and love she'd wrestled with in her sessions with Sr. Grace. She hoped all these people—the children, women, men being cut down—held the same promise of new life as Christ's crucifixion. She didn't know what each new day would bring, but she was learning to accept the uncertainty. "I am at peace here and searching—trying to learn what the Lord is asking," she told Kay Kelly in an October letter.[32]

On one of their visits to Los Ranchos, Maura and Ita met with a doctor who needed their help. One of the parish catechists, a man who used the name Ramon, had called them to his house to meet Juan Romagoza Arce. Based in San Salvador, Dr. Romagoza had been making trips into the countryside to treat sick and injured people, victims of the military repression and guerrillas wounded in combat. Since he'd begun nearly a year earlier, Dr. Romagoza had been using medical supplies provided by the archdiocese. Now the office that supported him was no longer able to procure the materials.

The military considered contraband anything that could be used to treat the wounded. It was a violation of the Geneva Convention, but denying access to medical treatment fit neatly into the military's campaign to drain the sea and starve out the opposition. To be caught in possession of the basic elements of a medical clinic marked one as a guerrilla sympathizer in the eyes of the armed forces.

Dr. Romagoza gave Maura and Ita a list of the things he needed: anesthesia, strong antibiotics, hydration fluid pouches, and analgesics, powerful pain relievers. They would try, Maura and Ita told him. A week later, the sisters left the medicines with a go-between in one of the villages. For the next three months, Maura and Ita received lists of the supplies Dr. Romagoza needed, then dropped them off with contacts they could trust in Arcatao, San José Las Flores, and San Antonio Los Ranchos. These people passed the items along to the doctor as he worked in clandestine emergency clinics in the mountains. One of his patients was a man who'd been shot at by a gunman in a helicopter. He had a wound in the abdomen and need to get to a real hospital, but it was too dangerous for Dr. Romagoza to take him. Maura and Ita offered. They secreted him past the many checkpoints to a hospital in San Salvador.

Dr. Romagoza had been treating victims of the National Police and army at his medical school clinic since 1977. People came in with tear gas burns and lacerations, bruises and gunshot wounds. By 1979 it was dangerous to even attend classes there because undercover security forces were posted at the gates. In response, Dr. Romagoza wore disguises to work. But many students and medical students were arrested and tortured. Finally, in 1980, the university was forced to suspend classes. Dr. Romagoza treated people who'd fled to the unofficial refugee centers in the capital. They told him their relatives were still in Chalatenango, desperate for help, so at the end of 1979 he began making forays into that region. He didn't know how Maura and Ita got the supplies he needed when, even with all his contacts in the city, friends at hospitals, and private doctors he couldn't achieve this. Maura and Ita did not reveal their source.[33]

The doctor often wondered whether Maura and Ita had tapped into a network of nuns from various religious orders. That might have been the case. During her frequent trips to San Salvador, Maura attended monthly meetings at CONFRES (Confederation of Religious of El Salvador), the national association of priests and nuns. She spent most of these meetings listening, taking in the information the Carmelite or Assumptionist or Divine Providence sisters revealed about their work and the disappearances and torture in the communities they served. The meetings were a rare place where Maura and the sisters of other orders could speak freely. They trusted one another. Maura sat close beside these new sisters, hugged them warmly at the beginning and end of meetings and smiled happily, pleased to be among like-minded people.[34]

She had a similar feeling when a catechist in Chalatenango asked whether he could invite Fr. David Rodríguez to give a presentation at the parish. A diocesan priest from San Vincente province, Fr. Rodríguez had been living under an assumed name and identity since the assassination of Archbishop Romero in March. He traveled the country under the guise of an itinerant fishmonger and led workshops for church groups on Salvadoran history and liberation theology. Long sympathetic to the movement for social and labor rights, he had joined the political wing of the Popular Liberation Front (FPL), the guerrilla organization that controlled parts of Chalatenango, in the late 1970s. He was a leader in the Union de Trabajadores del Campo (UTC), the farmworkers' union, which had strong ties to the Catholic church. For the most part he served as a kind of military chaplain to the guerrillas and people's organizations.

That fall, Fr. Rodríguez traveled to Chalatenango to give a talk in the warehouse where the sisters and refugees lived. Maura and Ita joined catechists and members of the Christian Base Communities for the presentation, eager to learn more about Salvadoran history. It had always been taught in El Salvador from the perspective of the wealthy. Now Rodríguez taught instead from the perspective of the poor farm laborer, examining the social movements embedded in the nation's past. It had begun with the indigenous Nahuatl's resisting the conquistadors in 1522, he explained, and continued through the present moment with these lay religious educators in this room. Maura wanted to learn about La Matanza, the great massacre of 1932, and the long struggles for land, the uprisings and repression, so she could make sense of what was happening today. After the presentation, Fr. Rodríguez stayed to talk with Ita and Maura. He returned a few times that fall because the two sisters were good for a thoughtful conversation. It was a return to Maura's days in Siuna in the 1960s, when Sr. Laura Glynn had pushed the nuns to look critically at their relationship with the Somoza government. With Fr. Rodríguez Maura and Ita could ask the questions they grappled with, and they were never in a rush for simple answers. With them, the priest could hash out complicated moral ideas: What was the Christian duty to support people in their quest for a society that reflected the values Jesus preached? How could one remain Christian in the midst of war? What commitment was God asking of them? Did believing in Jesus as liberator mean accepting violent rebellion?[35]

But the security forces didn't see moral complexity. They saw communists. Maura and Ita's frequent trips to San Salvador, the people who showed up at the convent and were then spirited away, their visits to the military barracks to beg and badger the release of prisoners, their commitment to San Antonio Los Ranchos—these all convinced Colonel Peña Arbaiza at military detachment number 1 across the town square that the sisters were subversives, *comunistas*. After the defiling of the church in San Antonio Los Ranchos in July, Bishop Rivera y Damas wrote to Colonel José Guillermo García, the minister of defense, asking for a meeting between García, Peña Arbaiza, the bishop, and the parish team. His request was never granted. Peña Arbaiza had been complaining steadily to García about the sisters throughout the fall.[36]

First, there was a rumor: Those nuns are keeping guns in the convent. It was whispered by the ORDEN members, by the national guardsmen, by the intelligence police. The rumor itself was a threat.[37]

Then in November, an actual threat appeared on the door of the parish house. It was crudely drawn, a cartoon almost, of a knife stabbed through a head, blood running down its side. Beside it were the words "Everyone who enters this house dies. We know that you are communists. If you don't believe this just try it. We know that the military takes no action against you, but we will execute you." The message was signed by the Mauricio Borgonovo Anti-Communist Brigade.* To be called a communist was the first step before assassination.[38]

Fr. Ephraím López, the pastor at Chalatenango, hastily called a meeting of the parish team, the seminarians, the Assumptionist sisters, and Maura and Ita. They would confine their pastoral work, their visiting and caring for people, to Chalatenango. No longer were they to venture into the remote villages and isolated encampments. But Maura and Ita kept up their work anyway. They weren't going to stop visiting the people in Los Ranchos or San José Las Flores or the people in flight huddled in caves on the mountains. "If we abandon them when they are suffering the cross, how can we speak credibly about the resurrection?" Maura had asked her friend Rose Gorman.[39]

The same day the threat arrived, Maura and Ita drove a woman and her seven children to San Salvador. Her husband and older sons were away from the family, possibly with the guerrillas in a temporary encampment, preparing. The stories Maura heard—and what she saw—again reminded her of John Clarke's stories about the Irish Revolution: the commitment of whole families, sons and fathers hiding in safe houses, bombing government buildings or fleeing into the mountains when the Black and Tans came like the death squads. But it was more vicious and confused here, she wrote to her father. The FPL didn't have as pristine a reputation as the Sandinistas had, she told him. As they drove south toward San Salvador on November 3, Maura admired the sugarcane fields nearly ready for harvest, their feathery flowers like silver silk in the sun. Farmers had brought in their corn and were harvesting the beans and bright green watermelons. She thought of her Uncle Barney, recently dead in Ireland, and what he would have made of the farmland. But many fields in Chalatenango had not been harvested. Farmers were too terrified to venture out in them lest they be shot, like the man Maura and Ita had transported to the hospital for Dr. Romagoza. So many farmers had fled from their homes in the same way as Norella Menjívar's family, driven out by the "drain the sea" policy, that crops were left to rot.

---

* Mauricio Borgonovo was the foreign minister of El Salvador when he was kidnapped and killed in April 1977 by the FPL

The winter would be hungry. Ita feared famine.* The beans, corn, and rice she and Maura hoisted into their rafters and piled into the storehouse in San Antonio Los Ranchos were a response to this.[40]

Back in the United States, the day after the threatening letter arrived, Americans went to the polls. Maura hoped Jimmy Carter would be reelected. As she and Ita waited for news of the election, the US Embassy in San Salvador hosted an election night party at the El Presidente Hotel. It was an awkward affair. The host and the guests backed opposing candidates. Ambassador Robert White and his political staff had been attempting to implement President Jimmy Carter's human rights policy with a military ally that routinely slaughtered civilians. The goal since White arrived in San Salvador less than a year earlier had been to cajole and convince the minister of defense, Colonel García, to rein in his brutal security forces, to stop the death squads that García insisted were not connected to the military. Yet day after day, embassy staff sent cables to Washington detailing the atrocities. Young diplomats jaded by the terror called them not telegrams but grimgrams.

The poolside cocktail party was filled with the top echelon of Salvadoran society: the wealthy land owners and coffee exporters, their fashionable wives, the high command of the Salvadoran officer

---

* The US Embassy also saw potential disaster in the disrupted harvest. But it was worried about threats from the other direction. Protecting the harvest from guerrilla attacks was a major preoccupation at the US Embassy in early October. If the export crops were stolen or damaged, the tiny nation's economy—and with it its government—might collapse. Ambassador White and Colonel Eldon Cummings, head of the US Military Group, agreed a team of special US advisers should be brought in to help the Salvadoran Ministry of Defense protect the harvest from leftists. The advisers would be supervised by Cummings but assigned to work in the Salvadoran ministry of defense. The ministry of defense would be provided with fatigues, boots, grenade launchers, tear gas, and road-clearing equipment. Colonel García desperately wanted helicopters. White suggested to Washington on October 14 that three Salvadoran soldiers begin to be trained as helicopter pilots, but that the provision of helicopters themselves be held off until more progress was made on human rights. [Memos between Department of State, US Embassy in San Salvador, and US Southern Command, "Protecting the Harvest" and "Helicopters for El Salvador," October 8–18, 1980.]

corps. These people disdained White's warnings that human rights needed to improve if the Salvadoran military expected any more US aid. They preferred to deal with the US military advisers assigned to help put down the guerrillas.

Colonel Cummings had begun his career in Laos and Cambodia, then served as military attaché to Pinochet's Chile. He came to El Salvador as a counterinsurgency expert, ready to advocate for his Salvadoran counterparts. The team of advisers he supervised was made up of Cuban Americans who had been part of the failed Bay of Pigs invasion and were eager to prevent any expansion of Castro influence. Cummings shared the Salvadoran military's suspicion that White was "very left wing."

Like Cummings, most of the Salvadorans at the party were pulling for Ronald Reagan. In the Republican candidate they saw a vociferous critic of communism who argued for a muscular foreign policy and took threats from Central America seriously. Reagan wouldn't let El Salvador fall as Nicaragua had. With Reagan in the White House there would be none of this soft talk about human rights, they believed. None of this hesitation and lecturing on international law. With Reagan they could defeat the FMLN, the communists, the socialists, and all their perceived allies in human rights offices, rectories, and church meetings. When news came of the Reagan landslide, the Salvadoran military bosses strutted to the swimming pool and fired their guns in the air. The plantation owners scoffed at White. They cheered, elated, and raised their glasses in jubilant toasts. Finally, they had a real ally in the White House.

As Mark Dion, chargé d'affaires at the embassy, and Carl Gettinger, a young political officer, walked out to their cars, they made their way through what felt like a gauntlet. The wives of the oligarchs jeered, distorting their faces, spitting as they leaned into Dion and Gettinger's path. *"Comunistas!" "Muerte a* White." *"Viva* Reagan!"[41]

Maura, when she learned of Carter's loss, understood what it meant for the poor. She wrote to her friend Mary Manning in Boston, "Death is a constant companion and people here are so brave. The new president won't help. What will happen next is unknown.

The repression is something terrible. Life means nothing. I'm scared at times but these people are such an example."[42]

Maybe it was respect for the brave Salvadorans that drove her to take on increasingly dangerous tasks. In October, Maura and Ita, Dorothy Kazel, and Jean Donovan had met at the coffee shop in the archdiocese's headquarters with Juan Bosco Palacios, a seminarian who until September had been assigned to a village in Chalatenango. After a death squad came looking for Palacios in one of the small villages he served, the archdiocese sent a car for him. Bishop Rivera y Damas didn't want to lose one of his best pastoral workers. Palacios had no choice. He was hustled back to the relative safety of the archdiocesan headquarters in San Salvador. From there he began working with a church-affiliated relief organization that was coordinating the distribution of food and medicine. Palacios moved across San Salvador, stockpiling supplies from friendly pharmacies. One time he bought antibiotics from a pharmaceutical company that was under the impression he represented the right-wing. The medicines went to villages suffering under the "drain the sea" policy and to impromptu groups that included guerrillas and their families and others displaced by violence and simply seeking shelter. Now, Palacios told the four women that he needed to get medical supplies to people on the run. It was a dangerous and demanding mission. Were they willing to deliver the supplies? he asked.

It was the sort of work Maura had felt left out of during the Nicaraguan revolution because she was in the United States. Maura had come to be beside the Salvadorans in their pain, to be with the people struggling for a life of dignity. She'd been pondering all fall what it was that God wanted of her in El Salvador. Maura, Ita, Dorothy, and Jean agreed. They had put their trust in God, the four women told Palacios. It would be less risky for them to deliver the supplies, they explained, They had been trading on their foreignness, their pink faces, and American citizenship since they began working in El Salvador. This would be just another instance of that.

At four a.m. the next morning, Maura, Ita, Dorothy, and Jean were ready. They met at a warehouse, loaded the medical supplies into Jean's van, and drove in the dark out the road to Guazapa, a city halfway between San Salvador and Chalatenango. At the designated mile Jean stopped the car. Palacios's instructions were to drop the bags by the side of the road. Someone would retrieve them; someone else would deliver them to the encampment. They made the drop and drove on for 20 minutes, then according to their instructions, circled back past the site where they'd left the bags. They were gone. The contact had retrieved them. By ten a.m. Maura, Ita, Dorothy, and Jean were back in the capital reporting to Palacios that the mission was successful. Maura was mystified that it could actually work.[43]

While Maura and Ita were doing this dangerous work, the military was plotting against them. In the middle of November, Minister of Defense José Guillermo García called the civilian members of the junta to a meeting at the presidential palace. There he made a half-hour-long presentation meant to prove that the nuns and priests in Chalatenango were collaborating with the guerrillas. A ten-year-old boy had been brought in from Chalatenango to bolster the defense minister's argument. The child wept, overwhelmed and frightened by the drama. To Carlos Federico Paredes, a deputy planning minister, the accusations seemed to miss the point. The guerrillas were the people. Driven by conscience, people the whole country over were doing everything they could to protect themselves from a campaign of extermination. In the deeply hierarchical culture of the Salvadoran military, the minister of defense's making an accusation against individuals was tantamount to an execution order.[44]

Maura, unaware of the machinations of García, was focused on an upcoming trip to Nicaragua. At the end of November she would join Maryknoll sisters from around Central America at a week-long meeting in Managua. Maria Rieckelman, a Maryknoll sister who was a psychiatrist and expert on trauma, would help the four from El Salvador process the terror and violence they'd witnessed all fall. To be with old friends and back in Nicaragua would be a wonderful, Maura wrote to Loran Miller, one of the Capuchin priests she'd been friends with since Siuna. "But I know, at least I think, I must come back here and go on. There is a feeling of quiet peace about this. The Lord is very present here really in His seeming absence."[45]

She went a week early to have time to see as many people as possible. Her first day was spent sitting beside Fr. Martínez in his truck. The two friends crisscrossed Maura's old neighborhoods, visiting friends from the Christian Base Community in Santo Domingo and scores of friends in Ciudad Sandino, the old OPEN 3. Maura had made peace with her feelings for the priest and now it was simply good to be with someone she cared about, a friend with whom she shared a deep understanding. She hugged María Luisa Urbina tight. No one in El Salvador could compete with the closeness, the casual, warm connection she felt to her old neighbor. It had only been four months since she left Nicaragua after the first anniversary of the revolution, but it felt longer.[46]

As the sisters gathered in Managua, the leaders of the Democratic Revolutionary Front (FDR), the broad-based political wing of the Salvadoran opposition, gathered at the Jesuit high school in San Salvador. They had called a press conference, inviting the international and Salvadoran reporters. Socorro Jurídico, housed in the school, had offered its office as a safe location for the political leaders. This group represented an allegiance of trade unions, farmworkers' unions, and white-collar professionals newly united with the guerrilla FMLN—they were the intellectual leaders of the left, the ones the government would have to negotiate with if it wanted to avoid an open civil war. As they spoke, a crowd of plain-clothed, heavily armed men burst into the room and carried them away.

Enrique Álvarez Córdova, FDR's president, was among the men captured. The son of wealthy landowners, he had graduated from Rutgers University after attending prep school in New York's Hudson Valley. His family was firmly part of the tiny oligarchy and he played polo at a country club in San Salvador. After serving briefly as minister of agriculture after the 1979 coup, he resigned in disgust. The coup was cosmetic; in fact, the most extreme military men, including García and National Guard director Carlos Eugenio Vides Casanova, had only gained strength after it. Álvarez joined the left, switching sides, and later became the newly united group's president. The day after the abduction from the Jesuit high school, Álvarez's body along with those of the rest of the FDR leaders were delivered, mutilated, to various places around the city. The murder of the FDR leadership left a vacuum, a hole in the tenuous balancing act Ambassador White was trying to achieve. "Who am I supposed to negotiate with now?" he cursed to his aides.[47]

The murder of the FDR leaders dismayed Maura. So many good people were being cut down. She spent the next few days in the retreat house at Diriamba, outside Managua, that she had so often visited with women's groups and youth retreats from Miralagos and OPEN 3. In those years she'd been laying the groundwork that became the Nicaragua liberation movement. Now she sat beside her sisters, Gerri Brake and Julie Miller, Pat Murray and Bea Zaragosa, as well as sisters from Panama she'd been talking to and praying with for years. She felt safe. A major order of business was the need for more sisters in El Salvador. The four currently in the country wanted more sisters to come and they wanted support for the embattled church in El Salvador to remain a Maryknoll priority.[48]

Maura, Ita, Terry, and Maddie talked with Sr. Maria Rieckelman about the violence they had witnessed, the atmosphere of death that surrounded their work. Maura was glad to get advice, help in thinking through what she'd seen and felt. During a day of reflection with Sr. Maria, the women talked about negative coping mechanisms. They needed to be aware of the tendency to withdraw emotionally, working furiously to avoid contemplating what they were seeing and so fall into denial. It was painful to focus on everything Maura had witnessed, but it felt good, too.[49]

There was also time for fun. The sisters put on a skit, as in the claustrophobic early days in Siuna. One night they danced, letting the music be a release. On the last night of the five-day meeting, the sisters gathered in Diriamba's chapel for a prayer service. Like the services Maura and her friends had taught neighbors to lead in rural villages and city slums across Central America, it was performed without a priest, a group-led prayer with space for individual reflection focused on Bible readings. Maura listened keenly to the familiar words, hoping to understand in a new way how these stories applied to her life now. The sisters took turns reading. The passages, Old and New Testament, focused on the idea of the Good Shepherd:[50]

"The good shepherd is one who lays down his life for his sheep. The hired man is not the shepherd and the sheep do not belong to him. He abandons the sheep and runs away as soon as he sees a wolf coming."[51]

Maura sat beside her friends, some of whom she'd known for close to twenty years, listening to the familiar words, repeating the response: "I am the Good Shepherd. Alleluia."

Another reading told the story of Jesus appearing to a few of the disciples after Easter, while they were fishing. After he grills fish and bread on the shore, Jesus repeatedly asks the apostle Simon Peter whether he loves him. Each time, the confused man says yes, of course. "Then, feed my sheep," Jesus says.[52]

A reading from the book of Ezekiel was explicit about the work of this good shepherd. "I will search for the lost and bring back the strays. I will bind up the injured and strengthen the weak, but the sleek and the strong I will destroy. I will shepherd the flock with justice."[53]

Ita had felt relaxed and embraced at the meeting. She soaked up the affection of the other nuns and spoke about missing Carla, about the drama of the flood. She was trying to make sense of the death of her best friend and trying to accept it. By the end of the five days she seemed stronger and more at peace than she had since August. Now, in this prayer service at the end of the meeting, Ita stood up to read from the homily Archbishop Romero had given on February 10, 1980, six weeks before his assassination:

"Christ invites us not to fear persecution. Believe me, brothers and sisters, anyone committed to the poor must suffer the same fate as the poor. And in El Salvador we know the fate of the poor: To be taken away, to be tortured, to be found dead."

Later, after most of the sisters had gone to bed, Maura and Bea Zaragosa sat up writing letters. Late at night when the house had quieted down and the last visitor had left was often Maura's best time for writing. As a tentative sister superior in Siuna, she saved her writing until the other sisters had turned in, after their evening hangout in the kitchen. In the little house in OPEN 3 after a day of visiting and meetings, sometimes by candlelight, she scribbled a few lines to her parents before bed.

This night, Maura sat on the floor beside the bathroom at the retreat house, capturing the light. She would be able to send letters home safely with Maria Rieckelman, who would be returning to the United States. Maura could write honestly, without fear of Salvadoran spies' reading her mail.

She wrote to Sr. Pat Haggerty, who had been in El Salvador, and now like Maura during the Nicaraguan insurrection, had returned to the United States as things got worse in her chosen country: "The six members of the Frente were killed while we were here in Nicaragua. What a terrible blow. Oh Lord how long? We return tomorrow Pat and go with peace and hope. We feel your prayers and longing for these people that you love. It is so hard to be away at this time. I know Pat, but this offering is for their liberation."[54]

She wrote to her parents as she had thousands of times over the twenty years she'd been away, asking how her father is sleeping and about her mother's rheumatism. She thanked them for their letters. And she included news. "Probably by now you have heard of the death of the six leaders of the Frente, which you might compare to the Sandinistas in Nicaragua or the IRA of Ireland. This is a terrible blow to the organized groups of El Salvador and one doesn't know what will happen next. The Lord will not abandon these poor struggling people. They have so much hope in Him."

She began to close the letter in her usual way, asking her parents to give her love to her sister, brother, their families, a long list of relatives. But then instead of ending the letter, she started up again, almost like the impossibly long good-byes in Ireland when she would hug a cousin or aunt or uncle a dozen times, ending and beginning the conversation as they followed her out the door and down the lane and leaned into the window of the car.

"We are fine and learning so much from these brave but suffering people. So many things that happen here remind me of what you went through Dad in your years of struggle for the liberation of Ireland. The human family will always search and yearn for liberation. Only when the Lord brings us home to heaven will we be truly free. Up Sligo and the hurrah for the Far Downs. I'll call you soon."[55]

At two p.m. in the afternoon of December 2, Dorothy and Jean drove their familiar white van toward the airport. The two friends from La Libertad were picking up Maddie and Terry, who were returning from the meeting in Nicaragua. There had been talk of Maura and Ita's changing their tickets so they could all return together, but that would have required taking time out from the conference to stand in an airline office in Managua. Maura and Ita kept their original tickets and had lunch at the McDonald's in Managua with a bevy of other sisters. After lunch, Maura made one last visit to Ciudad Sandino, to say good-bye to as many friends there as she could. Maura and Ita's flight was due to arrive in San Salvador in the evening. Dorothy and Jean would have to come back for them.[56]

In Chalatenango someone approached the church sacristan in the movie theater not far from the parish house. He showed the sacristan a list: it named everyone on the parish staff. "And tonight," the man said, "this very night, we will begin."[57]

At five p.m. Sr. Maria Rieckelman touched down in San Salvador. She was headed home from Managua to Washington, DC, but it was a cheap ticket and the plane made stops all over Central America. Salvadoran security forces boarded the plane. They needed to see Sr. Maria's passport. They inspected it carefully, conferring with one another, then returned it to her. They seemed to be looking for a North American, but apparently not her.[58]

When Dorothy and Jean returned in the evening, the airport was crowded with international press and sympathizers coming in for the funeral of the FDR leaders.* The customs police were taking bulletproof vests away from reporters, worried that they'd give them to guerrillas. They were always anxious about flights from Sandinista Nicaragua. More so tonight. The whole country had a charged feeling. The military feared the funeral would become the long-awaited uprising. The left feared the funeral would be another occasion for massacre.

National Guard sergeant Luis Colindres Alemán had spent most of September with other Salvadoran officers taking a class at the US

---

* Maura and Ita's friend Fr. Rodríguez was among several priests who concelebrated the funeral Mass.

Military's School of the Americas in Panama. It was called "Defense of Human Rights." In the early evening he told the men he commanded that they had a special job. He ordered them to change into civilian clothes. Then Colindres Alemán went to the San Luis Talpa command post not far from the airport. He wanted to warn the commander there not to be worried if he heard disturbing noises. Colindres Alemán and his men had something they needed to do.[59]

Maura and Ita's flight landed at seven o'clock. They climbed into the van with Dorothy and Jean just as they'd done dozens of times throughout the fall. They drove out the dark airport road. The security forces were waiting.

A Terrible Beauty

We know their dream; enough
To know they dreamed and are dead.
And what if excess of love
Bewildered them till they died?
I write it out in a verse—
MacDonagh and MacBride
And Connolly and Pearse
Now and in time to be,
Wherever green is worn,
Are changed, changed utterly:
A terrible beauty is born.

—W. B. YEATS FROM "EASTER 1916"

On December 5, the United States suspended all aid to El Salvador in response to the murders of Maura, Ita, Dorothy, and Jean. On December 16, after a cursory investigation by the Salvadoran military claimed no evidence of armed forces involvement and after a delegation of high level US State Department officials produced a thin ten-page report that restated facts already published in a hundred newspapers, and found "no conclusive evidence of armed forces involvement," the Carter administration reinstated economic aid to the military dictatorship. One of President Carter's final acts before he left office was the restoration of military aid to El Salvador—and an emergency $5 million on top of that to fight the offensive the FMLN finally launched in January.[1]

Maura's brother and sister flew to El Salvador as soon as they learned of her murder. Judy slept beside Maura's coffin in the chapel of the Assumption Sisters convent in San Salvador. It had been thirty years since they shared a room.[2]

The bodies of the four women were waked at San José de la Montaña, the seminary turned refugee center in San Salvador. A funeral Mass was celebrated in La Libertad for Dorothy Kazel and Jean Donovan and their bodies flown back to the United States. Maura Clarke and Ita Ford's funeral was held in the soaring church of St. John the Baptist in Chalatenango, where they had attended daily Mass. Fr. David Rodríguez, whom Maura and Ita had engaged in deep conversation about the duty of Christians in a time of war, came out of hiding to attend. He stood while the people who loved Maura and Ita processed to receive the Eucharist and sang a song he'd written in their honor. As their bodies were carried to the cemetery he walked boldly beside the bishop, past the National Guard and the army barracks, accompanying these women who had adopted the love and the terror of his country. Following Maryknoll custom, Maura and Ita were buried in the cemetery in Chalatenango, beside Carla Piette whom they had buried just months earlier in a graveyard filled with the people of Chalatenango.[3]

The Salvadoran Civil War raged for twelve years after Maura's death, until the military government and the FMLN signed a peace accord in 1992. Seventy-five thousand Salvadorans, most of them civilians, were killed. The United States supported the Salvadoran military until the end, always searching for a center that had long since ceased to exist, always committed to staving off a leftist victory, always shouting in the wind, cajoling the military to respect human rights even as it provided more and more firepower. Saying he would not be party to a cover-up, at the end of January 1981 Ambassador White disputed the Carter administration's claim—which justified the release of lethal military aid—that El Salvador had taken "positive steps" to solve the churchwomen's murder. He was sidelined by the new administration of President Ronald Reagan, called back to

Washington, and given a desk job. He left the State Department by spring and became a vociferous critic of US policy toward El Salvador. He worked until his death in 2015 to keep his graveside promise: that they wouldn't get away with it this time.[4]

In the end, they didn't. In 1984, five members of the National Guard were tried and convicted in a Salvadoran court for the murders of Maura, Ita, Dorothy, and Jean. It was the first time members of the Salvadoran military were held responsible for a crime, and it was all the more remarkable given that it occurred in the midst of the war. It would take another thirty years to bring to justice the men who directed El Salvador's military and National Guard.

Successive US and Salvadoran investigations reported that Sergeant Colindres Alemán acted on his own, without higher orders. Maura's family, the families of the other women, and the Maryknoll sisters never believed that. In 1993, a United Nations–sponsored truth and reconciliation commission concluded that officers higher in the Salvadoran military had ordered the murders. Julia Keogh and Bill Ford, Ita's brother, spent the twenty years after their sisters' deaths fighting to learn who had ordered their killing. They met with State Department officials and members of Congress. They gave press interviews each time the prospect of more military aid to El Salvador surfaced. They spoke in churches, on campuses, and at rallies, urging Americans to write their Congress members to suspend aid to El Salvador and to launch a serious investigation into the men who ordered the assassinations.[5]

The churchwomen's deaths and President Reagan's fierce commitment to a new domino theory kept Central America in the headlines for a decade. Reagan's foreign policy team made El Salvador a test case, the sliver of land where the cold war would finally be won. Tens of thousands of State Department, CIA, and FBI memos flew back and forth between San Salvador and Washington, DC. At one point the FBI searched its own records to determine whether it had a previous file on Bill Ford; his vocal criticism of US support of El Salvador had won him no fans in the agency.

Human rights organizations took up the churchwomen's cause, wading through blacked-out government documents to find the truth. In 1998, the Lawyers Committee for International Human Rights learned that General José Guillermo García, minister of defense, and General Carlos Eugenio Vides Casanova,* director of the National Guard at the time of the murders, were enjoying a comfortable retirement in Florida. They had relocated, with US government support, toward the end of the war. Also in 1998, four of the five imprisoned guardsmen said they had acted on orders from higher in the chain of command than Sergeant Colindres Alemán.[6]

In 1999, Maura's and Ita's families brought a civil suit against the retired Salvadoran generals under the Torture Victims Prevention Act, hoping for a judicial finding that the two men were responsible for the assassination of their sisters. The suit was unsuccessful. But in 2002, the Center for Justice and Accountability, another human rights organization, won a separate case against García and Vides. This was brought by Juan Romagoza, the doctor Maura and Ita had supplied with medicine in the fall of 1980. He was captured in Chalatenango a week after their murder and tortured for three weeks. As a result of his torture, he no longer has full use of his hands and cannot perform surgery. Dr. Romagoza and two coplaintiffs, also victims of torture, sued García and Vides and won. The judge found the generals responsible for the torture of the doctor and his coplaintiffs by virtue of command responsibility. The Salvadoran military was too strictly organized, the ties of loyalty and deference too strong, to make lone wolves believable.

The Romagoza case set in motion a long series of legal proceedings aimed at deporting García and Gen. Vides from the United States. The generals, both of whom were awarded the US Legion of Merit by President Reagan, argued their removal was unfair because they had acted with the support of US policy makers. In April 2015 and January 2016, respectively, Eugenio Vides Casanova and José Guillermo García were deported to El Salvador. At the airport in El Salvador they were met by protestors holding photos of the disappeared and signs bearing the names of the dead. Dr. Romagoza,

---

* Colonels at the time of the churchwomen killing, they were awarded the rank of general in subsequent years.

who now serves in his nation's ministry of health, was there. It is his hope that the generals will be tried in a Salvadoran courtroom for the crimes they committed and encouraged.[7]

Tutela Legal Dr. María Julia Hernández, a Salvadoran human rights organization that is a successor to Socorro Jurídico, the office Maura and Ita filed reports to, is trying to do that. Tutela Legal wants to open the files of the dark years, peel back a wound that never healed, and account, finally, for what happened when poor people demanded their rights. That is the greatest legacy of Maura, Ita, Dorothy, and Jean: that the perpetrators of years of brutal violence may finally be brought to account.

There are places where crimes are marked and lives lost are remembered. In December 2015, El Salvador's Ministry of Culture declared the place where the bodies of the churchwomen were found as a site of national historic memory. A simple stone cross marks the place their bodies were briefly buried. A chapel stands nearby. The broad, reaching tigüilote tree—grounded in the Salvadoran earth, its branches straining towards heaven—will be protected, the field preserved. The designation signals that the country acknowledges the crime. Reparations, in the form of psychological and economic assistance, will flow to the communities near Santiago Nunualco.[8]

In Ciudad Sandino, Nicaragua, Roberto Somoza's children attend CECIM [Centro de Educación y Capacitación Integral Hna. Maura Clarke (Center for Education and Training Honoring Maura Clarke)]. Maura's spirit is alive at CECIM, the activists dedicated to continuing the work she did, reminding people of their dignity and struggling together for a more just city. CECIM advocates for decent housing, sponsors micro-lending enterprises and women's empowerment classes, and runs literacy programs for adults and out-of-school youth. In addition to being a highly regarded K-12 school, CECIM sponsors art and sewing, baking and dance classes and has painted colorful, uplifting murals in traditional Nicaraguan style around the city. Many of the women on staff were teenagers when Maura worked in OPEN 3 and they take inspiration from her memory. Ciudad Sandino and Managua are filled with people who love Maura Clarke. Her picture adorns the walls in simple, concrete homes; the mention of her name brings a flash of a smile and then a look of sadness on the faces of women grown old, who knew they were loved by this foreigner who sat beside them. Middle-aged men who were once idealistic guerrillas grow sentimental. Those were good years, full of hope. Those sisters formed my conscience, they say, but Maura stood out among them: "When she looked at me, I felt loved."[9]

In Siuna, the public school is named Colegio Maura Clarke. Emperatriz, Brunilda, and Luisa are middle-aged women now. They occupy their whole seat when they sit, not asking permission of anyone, staunch and proud. They are teachers with long careers behind them, whom former students call *maestra* when they see them on the street.[10]

In New York City, students at Cristo Rey New York High School in East Harlem, most of them the children of Latin American immigrants, study the lives of Maura, Ita, Dorothy, and Jean as the spiritual founders of their school. Ita Ford's nephew is the founder and principal. Maryknoll sisters continue to work in human rights, education, health, women's advocacy, and environmental justice in twenty-four countries around the world, including El Salvador. They maintain an Office of Global Concerns in Washington, DC. Each year on December 2, the sisters and the late women's families gather in Ossining to honor Maura and Ita. They are embraced as martyrs, their story turned over and over for lessons on how to carry the love of God into the world.[11]

In County Sligo, Ireland, Maura's name is engraved on the family headstone in the grassy cemetery behind Saint Patrick's well: a daughter of the place, embraced.[12]

Guadalupe Calderón, the teenager in Santa Ana whose commitment Maura admired in her first days in the country, lost twenty-three members of her family in the civil war. Now she runs a public health education and advocacy organization named in honor of the four churchwomen: Fundación para la Salud Natural de la Niñez y la Mujer Maura Ita Dorothy y Jean.[13]

Each year in November, thousands gather outside the gates of Fort Benning in Columbus, Georgia, to protest the School of the Americas/Western Hemisphere Institute for Security Cooperation

(SOA/WHINSEC), which operates on the base. General García and Sergeant Colindres Alemán are graduates, as are thousands of other Latin American military and police implicated in disappearances, torture, massacres, and assassination. The weekend culminates with a solemn vigil during which participants hold aloft small white crosses, each inscribed with the name of one of the many thousand victims of military terrorism linked to the school. The assembled crowd intones the names of the dead, beginning with Maura, Ita, Dorothy, and Jean. It is a litany that lasts many hours. Maryknoll sisters attend each year.[14]

SHARE–El Salvador, a US organization founded during the war, has brought ten thousand Americans to learn about the country. It fosters the memory of Maura, Ita, Dorothy, and Jean in annual pilgrimages to the site of their murder and sponsors community organizations of rural people working together to combat gang violence, lift up young women, advocate for education, and run a farm cooperative and tree nursery, an attempt to preserve agricultural independence in the face of international trade deals that strip Salvadoran farmers of autonomy.[15]

In December 2015, thirty-five years after Maura was killed, my family and I joined one hundred other Americans on a trip to El Salvador organized by SHARE. We visited the place where their bodies were pulled from the ground and the crowded cemetery in Chalatenango. In San Antonio Los Ranchos, the plaza beside the church was festooned with banners of the faces of the four churchwomen and Sr. Carla. Candles burned in a shrine before massive photographs of them. In long, passionate speeches, leaders of the community organizations declaimed their loyalty, their gratitude to these North Americans who had once struggled with their people. Children of the youth group sang. Others read poetry.

And then, late in the dark night, high in the hills of Chalatenango, votive candles were passed through the crowd. We assembled in the street and began to march, holding our candles aloft behind a procession led by people carrying the giant photos of Maura, Ita, Dorothy, Jean, and Carla. This was the road Maura and Ita drove so often, ferrying refugees on their first leg of the journey to San Salvador. We walked through the night, singing, to the place where Carla drowned. As the crowd of hundreds of Los Ranchos residents and another hundred North Americans moved through the night, shouts rose from the crowd: Maura Clarke, *Presente!* Ita Ford, *Presente!* Dorothy Kazel, *Presente!* Jean Donovan, *Presente!* Carla Piette, *Presente!*

Few of the people who lived in San Antonio Los Ranchos in 1980 are there today. The village was abandoned early in the war, its residents forced to flee. Esperanza Tobar left with her children weeks after Maura was killed. Her husband followed shortly after. The repression had become too brutal. Toward the end of the war, Tobar and many others from the village resettled in another part of the country. Likewise, Salvadoran refugees from elsewhere, living in camps in Honduras made forays back into Chalatenango. They resettled San Antonio Los Ranchos to show the Salvadoran military the people had not been defeated. The war of extermination against them, bloody as it was, had failed. They started again in Los Ranchos to build a community of justice. What was this procession now, this spectacle for four women most of the current residents had never known? It was a new religious observance in an old-fashioned guise. Finally I recognized the speeches, the poetry, the procession with talismans of martyrs: it was a patronal feast. A day to honor the patron saints of the village. Instead of the village namesake Saint Anthony, the people of San Antonio Los Ranchos were commemorating their modern patrons: Maura, Ita, Dorothy, Jean, and Carla.

Alfredo Rivera Rivera, the high school student who lived with the sisters in Chalatenango, is now a priest in the same region. He remembers Maura, Ita, and Carla as women who became Salvadoran, who took on the suffering of his country. He uses a particularly Salvadoran idiom to describe their work. "They incarnated themselves in the Salvadoran people," he says. It's an invocation of Christ's becoming human. They became Salvadoran; they suffered with the Salvadoran people.

Researching this book, trying to understand what happened, I often got lost in a tangle of government cables—leads discovered and

dismissed, hours spent parsing the motivations of a handful of operatives and civil servants many now dead. What did this mean? What
was that person selling? Did this man really believe what he wrote in
this memo? Why was there no follow-up to that? Could these names
really be the same, the one appointed to the high-level commission
and the architect of so much killing? Most puzzling was the acknowledgment that many in the US government actually had taken the
churchwomen's death seriously and had sincerely sought answers. But
their horizons were always small. No one lifted their eyes to take in
the full implication of what alliance meant. Was I just creating my
own simple answers, a different sort of black and white, less deadly
than the black and white of the Salvadoran oligarchy, but reductive
nonetheless? Was anyone telling the truth? Another book could be
written on the conflicting theories of the crime, on the efforts to find
the killers, and the efforts to stymy that search. There are so many lies.

When I felt this way I was pulled back to my original inquiry.
How did this woman get here?

What matters in the end is that Maura thought everyone mattered. It remains a radically countercultural belief. Her death was
treated as something different from the festival of killing that engulfed the poor of El Salvador in those years. But in the end, Maura's
death was no different than the death of tens of thousands of others
in El Salvador who yearned to be treated as humans. Maura spent her
life connecting, reaching out, sometimes desperately hoping to find
acknowledgment of herself and her own worth by paying intense attention to people who the world dictated did not matter. In her death
she connected. She became like every other Salvadoran woman—
and she was embraced. She was unwilling to accept that some people
had to suffer, had to be hungry, had to see their children starve, had
to be butchered as holocaust to a rapacious machine of wealth and
power—or an agenda of national security and stability. Her death
scandalized, but for her the scandal was that children of God were
treated so viciously, first by poverty, then by government repression.
Her death was treated as something different, a break from the norm,
something unique that cried out for justice and accounting. But it was
but one of ten thousand that year in that country alone. If everyone

matters, if Angelique Rodríguez Alemán in the slums of Managua and Esperanza Tobar in a terrorized village in El Salvador are worthy of dignity, worthy of their quest to be treated as humans and the social order that made them poor worth pushing off, Maura's death is not unique. García and Peña Arbaiza may have been right. Maura Clarke was subversive. This was her subversion: she had connected.

I puzzled for three years over Maura's death. Was it religious? Was it political? Is there a difference? For Maura it was personal. She had an open heart. Everyone mattered.

Acknowledgments

This book about love and faith was born of the same—out of Julia Keogh's deep love for her slain sister and her unyielding faith in the importance of Maura's story. Without that love and faith, as well as the patient support of the entire Keogh family and their generosity as sources, this project would never have occurred. I am deeply indebted to Julia Keogh and her husband, Peter; to Buddy Keogh; to Deirdre Keogh Anderson, Pamela, Peter, and Scott Eoghan Keogh, who have carried their aunt's memory into a second and third generation; and to their cousin Michael Clarke, who accompanied me to Ireland paving the way for a fruitful and valuable—and fun—reporting trip.

Others in the broad and loyal circle of families and friends affected by the churchwomen's killings were also vital fonts of moral support and practical help, especially Jack Marth, Miriam Ford, the SHARE–El Salvador Foundation, the Center for Justice and Accountability, Patty Blum, Terry Karl, Carlos Mauricio, Julia Leiblich. This book focuses very closely on Maura Clarke. That is not meant to detract from the lives and legacy of Ita Ford, Dorothy Kazel, or Jean Donovan. I set out to understand one of the women but each are worth studying. So many people who worked on the churchwomen case or covered the story or wrote about El Salvador opened doors and shared information and helped me gather shards of fact to build this book. If I fail to mention a name, it is only because so many, many people were kind to me. I'm grateful to all of them. Margaret Groarke, the consummate connector, forwarded me an e-mail that began the process of writing this book. I thank her.

A deft and skilled editor, Katy O'Donnell at Nation Books took what was essentially a very long newspaper article and turned it into a manuscript. Her editing was masterful, her touch light, and her ability to see the book within the tangle of words and attribution truly impressive. It makes me wonder whether she can see through walls. Everyone at Nation Books/Perseus deserves credit for their skill and endless patience as we wrestled a labor of love into printable shape. My agent, Roger Freet, took a chance on a new writer and a challenging book; I'm glad he was right.

Without knowing my younger son was being expertly and lovingly cared for, I couldn't have pursued this project. I thank Ana Ramirez, Carmen Pérez, Diana Guerrero, Amalgamated Nursery School, and Little Leaf Nursery. My mother-in-law, Claire Murphy, woke before dawn every week for more than a year to come to the Bronx and watch her grandson. I am grateful for her care for him and her kindness to me. My mother, Sally Markey, gave yeoman service in childcare and cared for me during the ragged end of this project. In so many ways, I couldn't have written this book without her. My parents, Martin and Sally Markey, introduced me to the churchwomen story and to a Catholicism that loves justice when I was a child. That shaped everything. I thank Patrick Markey and Maureen Markey for making Latin America seem close and all my family for their support and encouragement.

Every time I came home from a day at the Maryknoll Sisters Center in Ossining, interviewing one remarkable Maryknoll sister or the next, I was afloat with admiration and affection. The fact is the story of any one of the tremendous women in that community is as heroic and faith-filled as Maura's. More than once my husband half-joked that he feared I might join up. I'm grateful particularly for Janice McLaughlin, Bernice Kita, Gerri Brake, Maddie Dorsey, and Maria Rieckelman, who made research easy and were generous with their memories and thoughts. All the Maryknoll sisters who shared their stories, warmth, and joy with me—whether in probing and exhaustive hours-long interviews or in lunchtime conversation—made this book possible. I'm grateful for their hospitality, generosity, honesty, and courage. I owe especially warm thanks to Mary Malherek, Gene Lorio, and Peg Dillon, who were good friends to me, opening windows of understanding and continuing their mission of making God's love visible. Peg Healy was generous and kind, offering insight, fantastic records, and a great love of Maura. Ellen Pierce and her staff keep a deep and vast archive and were an unending help in navigating it and finding the best resources from the collective memory of a remarkable organization. I owe a deep debt of gratitude to Judy Noone for the voluminous records she collected soon after the churchwomen's death for her book *Same Fate as the Poor*. Her interviews with so many people who were close to each of the women, several of whom have since died, formed the basis of my research.

PJ Clarke, Martina Kearins, Mary McCarthy, Sandra Carney, Michael Clarke, James Clarke, all the Clarkes, MacSharry's, Corcorans, Annie Murphy in County Sligo, Mary McMullan and Mary MacGowan in County Antrim—all reminded me of why Ireland was so important to Maura. Mrs. Kay Aucoin, who noticed a letter to the editor in the Raleigh, North Carolina, newspaper and passed it on to me through her son, connected me with a source that was the linchpin of understanding how Maura's life began to shift in the 1960s. Jim McCartin at Fordham University's Center on Religion and Culture was endlessly encouraging, helping me talk through concepts and ideas. The Duffy conversations were a lifeline. Angela O'Donnell and the Ann and Francis Curran Center for American Catholic Studies, Michael Lee, Natalia Imperatori, Cristo Rey New York High School and its wonderful religion teachers. Centro Altagracia de Fe y Justicia. Kathryn Kirk Heetderks, who brought her great clarity to genealogical research that helped flesh out the Clarke family history and who has been throughout adulthood a woman whose friendship has nourished me. So has Kristen Zeilinski Nalen's. Jennifer Foray, and Brian Kelly for years of intelligent conversation and for frank faith when I doubted I could do this. My community of friends in the Bronx, Rochamboni, Jo Hirschmann and Elizabeth Wilson, Brian and Sarah Aucoin, Nick Napolitano and Michelle Born, Miriam Neptune, Tessa and Alex Kratz, Heidi and Brian Hynes, Stephanie Woo and Stan Walker, Joe Ryan, Brenna Fitzgerald, Jordan Moss, Colleen Kelly, Jeremy and Maggie Greenfield, and the social action committee at St. John's Visitation Parish, who listened as I talked of nothing but this and probably in much too much detail for the better part of four years, asked clarifying questions, and lived out the values Maura lived. Mary Dailey, who was inspired by the churchwomen and the Salvadoran people as a young woman and who now carries on the long struggle for justice in the United States. And Sarah Townley, Lourdes Rodriguez, Rich Garella, and Bill McGarvey, whose ceaseless support was buoying. Journalist and friend Danielle Mackey helped me understand what the country El Salvador has become and time and time again provided translation of documents, phrases, piece of audio. Rosie Ramsay, for herculean translation and for being great. Maggie Von Voight, Tatiana Valdez, and Erika Murcia; Carlos Corea Lacayo for his desire to connect. The journalists who were imprinted by El Salvador in their youth: Susan Meiselas, Christopher Dickey, June Erlick, and Steven Kinzer. I hope someday to be given the opportunity to be as generous, humane, and wonderful to a younger writer as George Black and Anne Nelson were to me. Cynthia Arnson, who continues to work for justice in Latin America, went far beyond the call of duty to help make this book accurate. A long time ago Tommy Shea and Jack Flynn made me want to be a reporter—and showed me how. Wayne Barrett, Tom Robbins, Jim Dwyer, Annia Ciezadlo, Tracie McMillan, and Robin Shulman shared their contacts and expertise as narrative nonfiction writers and their encouragement as friends. Joe Flood for being a brotherly sounding board as I grappled to understand my own reporting. Maya Kremen, Helaine Olen. Carl Gettinger and family for gracious hospitality. Margot Patterson for insightful early editing. I relied on Fordham University's excellent library for long shelves of volumes on the church and for a quiet and bucolic place to work. It was nice to be back home for this. Ray Schroth, SJ, *America Magazine*, Kaitlin Campbell, the archivists of the Sisters of St. Joseph at Brentwood, Long Island, and the Diocese of Brooklyn and Queens. I followed Maura to Nicaragua and El Salvador, looking to understand her life. I found her alive in the hearts of the fantastic people of Ciudad Sandino, Nicaragua, in particular María Luisa Urbina who opened her door and filled her house with neighbors so that I could understand. I only hope readers will get a sense of the brave hope, the seriousness and realness of the people Maura loved. Listening to Roberto Somoza and Henri Norori analyze and recount *concientización* and the transformation of their barrio, it was easy to understand how Maura gave her heart to Nicaragua. Carmen García and Rafael Valdez and their neighbors and friends in San Pablo Apóstol and Félix Jiménez carry on the hope embodied in their revolution. Angelique Rodríguez Alemán and her fantastic daughter, and Miriam Guerrero. They put Maura back into the history of Nicaragua. I'm grateful to Maura's former students in Siuna who filled a long evening with stories and happy memories and took my arm, introducing me to others. Heysell Ordoñez Fajardo was an indispensable guide and fixer in Siuna. Susan B. Lagos who reached out when I needed a translator and whose dedication to her adopted country, its hopes and promise, is an inspiration. Bernardo Gordillo. Amada Pinéda for speaking to me, and for speaking up. Joe Mulligan, SJ, took care of me in Nicaragua, found me a place to stay, shared his love of the country, translated 16 hours a day, drove, explained, listened, and made every room he went into a little better. Such brave people in El Salvador who opened their door and pulled out a chair and said, of course I'd like to talk about Maura. In particular Juan Bosco Palacios and Alfredo Rivera Rivera who helped me understand the tremendous Salvadoran church of their youth. People who patiently told their story for the millionth time and people who had never before been asked. John Spain, MM whose keen and precise mind is filled with that journalists' oxygen: details. Without Gene Palumbo's encyclopedic knowledge of El Salvador and his bottomless well of goodwill among seemingly endless contacts, my reporting trips to El Salvador would have been farces. Riding beside him in his noisome jeep, our conversation rolling across theology, impunity, the Lindsay administration, writing, ethics, the state of journalism, truth, facts and the glory of the Brooklyn Dodgers was like some sort of journalists' retreat. He made me want to be a better reporter, and a better person. Of course, any errors of fact or interpretation are mine alone. My sons, Owen Markey Murphy and Hugh Kozlowski Markey Murphy, who adopted this story and its meaning and who are beautiful and sweet and big-hearted boys. My greatest gratitude is to my husband, Jarrett Murphy. He counseled and consoled, edited and suggested, puzzled with me and led me out of dark eddies. His unflappable decency and grace keep me afloat. I am so lucky.

And Maura herself. Her clear vision and humble voice spoke powerfully to me three decades after her death through letters and the recollections of friends, informing this project and my life beyond it. I have tried my best to listen.

Eileen Markey
Bronx, New York
June 2016

Notes

INTRODUCTION: FOUR DEAD IN EL SALVADOR

1. *Two of the women*, first-day news reports: After the bodies were exhumed, they were taken to a funeral home in San Salvador. Although an official autopsy was not performed at this time—no doctor would risk angering the regime—a doctor did look at the bodies. The underwear of three of the women was missing and their bodies showed signs of rape. Maura was still wearing her underwear. This information comes from a document Fr. John Spain, MM, filed to the Maryknoll Sisters in January 1981; the findings of an official autopsy, performed January 20, 1981, when Maura was exhumed for a second time also suggests she was not raped. *By orders from:* Commission on the Truth for El Salvador report, "From Madness to Hope: The 12-Year War in El Salvador," 1993, http://www.derechos.org/nizkor/salvador/informes/truth.html, accessed June 20, 2016; *They'd been missing:* interview with Maddie Dorsey, MM, Ossining, NY, February 2013; *In minutes they were hoisted:* interview with Susan Meiselas, December 2014.

2. Violence in El Salvador: interview with Maddie Dorsey, MM, Ossining, NY, January, May, and June 2013.

3. *The ambassador blanched:* UPI, "Bullet-Riddled Bodies of 3 U.S. Nuns and Lay Sister Found in El Salvador," *Washington Star*, December 5, 1980; biographical details of Dorothy, Jean, and Ita: Ana Carrigan, *Salvador Witness, the Life and Calling of Jean Donovan* (New York: Simon and Schuster, 1984); physical description, Susan Meiselas contact sheets, Maryknoll nuns, private collection Susan Meiselas.

4. Charlie Clements, in foreword to *Enrique Álvarez Córdova: Life of a Salvadoran Gentleman and Revolutionary* by John W. Lampieri (Jefferson, NC: McFarland & Company, 2006).

5. Number of people killed, profile of victims: Americas Watch, *Report on Human Rights in El Salvador* (New York: Knopf Publishing Group, 1982); *Ambassador Robert White had been reporting:* Margaret O'Brien Steinfels, "Death & Lies in El Salvador: The Ambassador's Tale," *Commonweal Magazine*, June 14, 2004; *A few days before:* Americas Watch, *Report on Human Rights in El Salvador*; "*They won't get away with it this time*": Vincente Morales, Associated Press, "Three American Nuns, Missionary Found Shot to Death in El Salvador," *Chicago Tribune*, December 5, 1980 (The quote appears in most first-day stories published on the killing); Robert White, "DEATH OF US CITIZENS: DOROTHY

KAZEL, JEAN DONOVAN, ITA FORD, MAURA CLARKE," telegram from US Embassy in San Salvador to State Department Washington, DC, December 5, 1980, SAN SA 08501.

6. Reactions to the bodies' discovery: interview with Fr. Paul Schindler, La Libertad, El Salvador, February 2013; interview with Fr. John Spain, San Salvador, El Salvador, February 2013.

7. Note brought to Fr. López: interview with Ephraím López, San Juan Opico, El Salvador, July 2013;

8. *In the past year, a military intelligence unit:* interview with Alfredo Rivera Rivera, Nueva Concepción, El Salvador, July 2013; *Many, many times Fr. López:* interview with Ephraím López, San Juan Opíco, El Salvador, July 2013; *The commander of the base:* interview with David Helvarg, by phone March 2015.

9. Note taken to bishop, Fr. López's departure: interview with Ephraím López, San Juan Opico, El Salvador, July 2013.

10. Nuns' meeting in Nicaragua: Interview with Gerri Brake, Ossining, NY, February 2013; interview with Maria Rieckelman, MM, Ossining, NY, December 2012; statement from Maryknoll Sisters to US Department of State, February 19, 1982, "Departure of Srs. Maura Clarke and Ita Ford from Managua to San Salvador on Copa Airlines on December 2, 1980."

11. Last night of Nicaragua retreat: program of December 1 prayer service, Maryknoll sisters' meeting in Managua, private collection Peg Healy.

12. *A crowd of sisters accompanied:* statement from Maryknoll Sisters to US Department of State, February 19, 1982, "Departure of Srs. Maura Clarke and Ita Ford from Managua to San Salvador on Copa Airlines on December 2, 1980."

13. Chronology between seven p.m. December 2 and midmorning December 3: Robert White, "MURDER OF THREE AMERICAN NUNS AND ONE LAY MISSIONARY," telegram from San Salvador to State Department, December 5, 1980, SAN SA 08500; interview Fr. John Spain, San Salvador, February 2013; Robert White, "MORE INFORMATION ON MURDER OF FOUR US CITIZENS," telegram from embassy in San Salvador to State Department, December 5, 1980, SAN SA 08455.

14. Looking for missing friends, changed tenor of life in El Salvador, December 3: interview with Fr. Paul Schindler, La Libertad, February 2013.

15. *Paul Schindler got the phone call:* Elizabeth Kochik, "Timeline of Dec. 2–Dec. 4, churchwomen," February 1981, El Salvador Martyrs collection, Maryknoll Sisters Archive (MSA), Maryknoll Mission Archives, Maryknoll, NY; *chi rho ring*, questionnaire and ceremonial for profession, Sisters History collection, MSA, Maryknoll Mission Archives, Maryknoll, NY. Note: For more information about items preserved in the Maryknoll Mission Archives collections, visit http://maryknollmissionarchives.org.

CHAPTER 1: BETWEEN CITY AND SEA

1. Bells, August 15, 1945: Parish files, parish journals, St. Francis de Sales, Box 5, 75th anniversary journal; also, Marie Farragher, *The Miracle of the Bells*, Roman Catholic Diocese of Brooklyn, Diocesan Archives, Brooklyn, NY.

2. Monsignor Reddy: interview with Betty McCann McCarthy, Manhattan, August 2012; Reddy obituary, *New York Times*, January 31, 1981.

3. *Surely many of them wondered:* Chancery, parish files, parish journals, St. Francis de Sales; *Under stained-glass images:* chancery, parish files, St. Francis de Sales; also *A History of the Parish of St. Francis de Sales: Architecture of New Church* (Belle Harbor, NY: St. Francis de Sales, 1939).

4. *Irish immigrants:* Patrick J. McNamara, *A Catholic Cold War: Edmund A. Walsh, S.J., and the Politics of American Anticommunism* (New York: Fordham University Press, 2005).

5. *A narrow stretch of earth:* Lawrence Kaplan and Carol P. Kaplan, *Between Ocean and City: The Transformation of Rockaway, New York* (New York: Columbia University Press, 2003).

6. *A bridge didn't unite:* "History of the Rockaways," *Rockaway Review*, Archives of the Sisters of St. Joseph, Brentwood, NY, December 1948.

7. *Growing up in the Rockaways:* interview with Julia Keogh, Rockaway, NY, July 2012; *Maura's brother, Buddy:* interview with Buddy Clarke, Mount Vernon, NY, August 2012.

8. *In 1947, when Maura was sixteen: Rockaway Review*; Kaplan, *Between Ocean and City*, 18; *Restaurants that were shuttered:* interview with James Clarke, Connecticut, October 2012; *The Rockaways, sometimes called:* interview with Julia Keogh, Rockaway, NY, July 2012.

9. Immigrant time frame: Lawrence J. McCaffrey, *The Irish Catholic Diaspora in America* (Washington, DC: Catholic University of America Press, 1984).

10. Mary Clarke's family: interview with Julia Keogh, Old Brookville, NY, September 2012; interview with Seamus McGowan, Ballymoney, Northern Ireland, November 2014.

11. *On the hilltop at Armoy:* visit to Armoy, County Antrim, Northern Ireland, November 2014; *Once when Mary:* interview with Deirdre Keogh Anderson, April 2016; details of Mary McCloskey's childhood: interview with Julia Keogh, Old Brookville, NY, October 2012.

12. *When World War I created:* interview with Deirdre Keogh Anderson, New York, April 2016; *Mary presented herself carefully:* interview with Mary McMullan, County Antrim, Northern Ireland, November 2014.

13. *In the late 1600s:* Catholics were barred from voting, owning land, or serving on a jury. They couldn't own guns, were barred from residing in several cities, and could be fined or jailed for a year for refusing to act as informers and reveal where Mass was being celebrated or a priest hidden. Gatherings at traditional holy places, such as wells or shrines, were considered riots and groups subject to fines and imprisonment. *Mary McCloskey's experience,* Cromwell Inn story: interview with Buddy Keogh, Mount Vernon, NY, August 2012.

14. *John Clarke:* John Clarke, interview for Judy Noone, 1982, Same Fate as the Poor (SFATP) collection, Maryknoll Sisters Archive (MSA), Maryknoll Mission Archives, Maryknoll, NY.

15. *John's brothers, still at home in County Sligo:* John Clark took pledge for IRB, John Clarke, interview for Judy Noone, 1982, SFATP collection; interview

with Gabriel MacSharry, by phone January 2015; interview with P. J. Clarke, County Sligo, Ireland, November 2014; interview with James Clarke, Connecticut, October 2012.

16. John's guerrilla activity: from John Clarke, interview for Judy Noone, SFATP collection; interview with P. J. Clarke, County Sligo, November 2014; interview, tour with Annie Murphy, County Sligo, November 2014.

17. *But, by 1922:* John Clarke, interview for Judy Noone, SFATP collection; Michael Farry, *Sligo: The Irish Revolution 1912–23* (Dublin: Four Courts Press, 2012).

18. John and Mary's meeting and courtship: interview with Julia Keogh, Old Brookville, NY, November 2012.

19. *Grand Concourse*: Constance Rosenblum, *Boulevard of Dreams: Heady Times, Heartbreak and Hope Along the Grand Concourse in the Bronx* (New York: NYU Press, 2011); *Mary brought her to a photography studio:* photo in private collection, Mary McMullan, County Antrim, Northern Ireland; family history: interviews with Julia Keogh, Old Brookville, NY, 2012–2015.

20. Family history: interview with James Clarke, Connecticut, October 2012; interviews with Julia Keogh, Old Brookville, NY, 2012–2015; origins of Buddy's nickname, move to Rockaway, birth of Julia, interview with James Buddy Clarke, Mount Vernon, NY, August 2012.

21. *On summer Sundays:* interview with Buddy Keogh, Mount Vernon, NY, August, 2012; *In 1930, St. Camillus built:* chancery files, parish files, St. Camillus, Rockaway Park, NY; also parish census 1939, Diocesan Archives, Roman Catholic Diocese of Brooklyn, Brooklyn, NY.

22. *The Catholic Church in New York was growing*: James O'Toole, *The Faithful: A History of Catholics in America* (Cambridge, MA: Harvard University Press, 2008), 126; Monsignor Sharpe, *History of the Diocese of Brooklyn*, 1954, Roman Catholic Diocese of Brooklyn and Queens, Diocesan Archives, Brooklyn, NY; Monsignor Cantley Collection, Diocesan history, folder 17, Roman Catholic Diocese of Brooklyn and Queens, Diocesan Archives, Brooklyn, NY; Ronald H. Bayor, ed, *The New York Irish* (Madison, WI: Johns Hopkins University Press, 1996).

23. Parish-dominated life: O'Toole, *The Faithful*; chancery files, parish files, St. Camillus; parish census 1939, Diocesan Archives, Roman Catholic Diocese of Brooklyn, Brooklyn, NY.

24. Mary as homemaker and mother: interview with James Buddy Clarke, Mount Vernon, NY, August 2012.

25. Mary's generosity: interview with James Clarke, Connecticut, October 2012.

26. *Often Maura's family was evicted:* interview with Julia Keogh, Rockaway, NY, July 2012; addresses: Maura Clarke's academic transcript, St. Francis de Sales school, Belle Harbor, NY, and Stella Maris Academy, Rockaway, NY; summer influx and turnover in Rockaway: Ronald Bayor and Timothy Meagher, eds., *The New York Irish* (Baltimore: Johns Hopkins University Press, 1996), 408.

27. *Francis Cardinal Spellman:* Robert Gannon, *The Cardinal Spellman Story* (Garden City, NY: Doubleday, 1962); *There were Catholic nurses' associations:* O'Toole, *The Faithful,* also Mark S. Massa, SJ, *Catholics and American Culture:*

Fulton Sheen, Dorothy Day, and the Notre Dame Football Team (New York: Crossroad Publishing, 2001).

28. Catholics in American media: Massa, *Catholics and American Culture*, also see Terry Golway, ed., *Catholics in New York: Society, Culture, and Politics, 1808–1946* (New York: Fordham University Press and Museum of the City of New York, 2008).

29. Evenings in the Clarke home: interview with James Buddy Clarke, Mount Vernon, NY, August 2012; interview with James Clarke, Connecticut, October 2012.

30. Connecting to the divine: O'Toole, *The Faithful*, 129.

31. *Most evenings after dinner:* interview with James Clarke, Connecticut, October 2012; Irish and Irish American culture: McCaffrey, *The Irish Catholic Diaspora in America*, 166; *"I'm a rebel":* James Clarke interview. For more on Irish American culture, rooting for underdog, sense of responsibility to communal improvement, attitudes of service, see Maureen Denzell, *Irish America: Coming into Clover* (New York: Anchor, 2002).

32. *On her first day of classes: Brooklyn Tablet*, September 1945, Diocesan Archives, Roman Catholic Diocese of Brooklyn, NY; *At home she pored over* Columba *magazine:* interview with James Clarke, Connecticut, October 2012; *Maura wanted to help people:* interviews with Julia Keogh, Old Brookville, NY, 2012–2015.

33. Sr. Oswald Clarke, 1885–1974: "Sister Mary Oswald: 'Just God's Beggar,'" June 1974, records of the Franciscan Missionaries of Mary, Providence, Rhode Island.

34. Maura's desire to please Miss Mattern: interview with Julia Keogh, Rockaway, NY, 2012, James Clarke, 2012; working toward high school tuition: interview with Sr. St. Philip, Sisters of St. Joseph (CSJ) (the former Kathleen Keily), Floral Park, NY, August 2012, interview with Sr. Grace Andrew, CSJ (the former Lucille Callahan), Brentwood, Long Island, August 2012. For more on modes of femininity, self-reliance, and independence among Irish American women, see Denzell, *Irish America: Coming into Clover.*

35. Maura's adolescence: interviews with Sr. St. Phillip, SSJ; Sr. Grace Andrew, SSJ; Judy Keiley; and Betty McCann McCarthy. "Her generosity is remarkable. She would do anything for anyone," wrote Sr. Maria Regina, SSJ, February 1950, to Maryknoll, in a letter recommending Maura, in Maura Clarke personal file, Maryknoll Mission Archives, Maryknoll, NY; McGuire brothers: Corey Kilgannon, "From a Home Court in Queens to the N.B.A.," *New York Times*, February 5, 2010.

36. *At Maura's basketball games:* interview with Betty McCann McCarthy, Manhattan, July 2012, interview with Sr. St. Phillip, SSJ, Floral Park, NY, August 2012; *Maura and her friend Betty McCann:* interview with McCarthy; *By senior year, Maura was dating Joe Barry:* interview with Julia Keogh, Rockaway, NY, July 2012.

37. Maura and the Clearys: interview with James Clarke, Connecticut, October 2012.

38. Maura's making dinner, Pound Street: interview with James Buddy Clarke, Mount Vernon, NY, August 2012.

39. Social outreach of the Church: David B. Woolner and R. Kurial, eds., *FDR, The Vatican, and the Roman Catholic Church in America, 1933–1945* (New York: Palgrave MacMillan, 2003); O'Toole, *The Faithful*, 146, 158; Golway, *Catholics in New York*.

40. Fr. Curley's recruiting for vocations: interview with James Clarke, Connecticut, October 2012.

41. Letter to Maryknoll: January and May 1950, Maura Clarke personal file, Maryknoll Mission Archives, Maryknoll, NY.

42. Maryknoll's response: Ibid.

43. Trip to Ireland: interview with Julia Keogh, Old Brookville, NY 2012–2015; interviews with Ethne and Mary McCloskey, Belfast, November 2014; interview with Mary McMullan, County Antrim, November 2014; proximity of Slemish: Mary McGowan, Ballymoney, November 2014.

44. Linda Kearns: Proinnsíos Ó Duigneáin, *Linda Kearns: A Revolutionary Irishwoman* (Manorhamilton, N. Ireland: Drumlin Publications, 2002); interview with Martina Kearins, County Sligo, November 2014; Maura's visit to Sligo 1950: interviews with P. J. Clarke, Thomas, Martin, Carol Corcoran, Mary McCarthy, and others, County Sligo, Northern Ireland, November 2014; Seamus Clarke, by phone January 2015; Julia Keogh, multiple interviews, Old Brookville, NY, 2012–2015.

CHAPTER 2: INTO THE SILENCE: NOVITIATE

1. Packing list: Sisters History collection, Maryknoll Sisters Archive (MSA), Maryknoll Mission Archives, Maryknoll, NY; *Wearing a green suit:* interview with Julia Keogh, Old Brookville, NY, July 2012; *Another carload:* private collection, Julia Keogh; *Mary Clarke had told her:* interview with Julia Keogh, Rockaway, NY, July 2012; *A friend of Maura's brother:* Maura letter to her mother, September 1950, private collection Julia Keogh; *All around them:* interview with Dolores Congdon, MM, Maryknoll Mission (MM), Ossining, NY, June 2012.

2. *Fourth floor of the convent*: interview with Dolores Congden, MM, Ossining, NY, June 2012; *She pulled her thick chestnut hair:* Maura letter to her mother, September 1950, private collection Julia Keogh; *But Maura's fancy shoes:* interview with Dolores Congden, MM, Ossining, NY, June 2012; *She felt her confidence wilting:* Maura's two-page autobiography, 1972, Same Fate as the Poor (SFATP) collection, MSA, Maryknoll Mission Archives, Maryknoll, NY.

3. *But she kept these feelings:* interviews with Patricia Haffey, MM; Reina Paz, MM; Eileen Franz, MM, Ossining, NY, 2012; *She was buoyed:* Maura first letter home, 1950, private collection Julia Keogh; Maryknoller helping people: Albert Plé, *Manual for Novice Mistresses* (Newman Press, 1958); *Maura was here because:* interview with Anne Reusch, MM, Ossining, NY, June 2012.

4. Mother Mary Columba: from Penny Lernoux, *Hearts on Fire: The Story of the Maryknoll Sisters* (Maryknoll, NY: Orbis Books, 1993).

5. Ibid.

6. Details of novice life: interview with Eileen Franz, MM, Ossining, NY, 2012; *Their focus:* interview with Peg Kilduff, MM, by phone June 2014; *They would constitute:* Sisters History collection. Mother Mary Joseph Epiphany Lecture, 1952: "Very few of us thought when we entered that our primary duty—the first end of every religious institute—was to sanctify our own souls. We would have considered it a selfish motive and perhaps hesitated. We soon realized of course, that we could only give to others what we had and love alone made it possible for us to pursue even eagerly the virtues so necessary of a missioner."

7. *She joked in a letter:* interview with Sr. Grace Andrew, Sisters of St. Joseph (CSJ), Brentwood, NY, August 2012.

8. Schedule of prayers: Sisters History collection; *Sometimes a fit of giggles:* interview with Anne Reusch, MM, Ossining, NY, June 2012.

9. *"Is there any one of us":* Mother Mary Joseph lecture, Sisters History collection.

10. Maryknollers' experiences abroad: Lernoux, *Hearts on Fire.*

11. Support of McCarthy: ibid.; marketing quote: Lemoux, *Hearts on Fire.*

12. Schedule, work duties: interview Patricia Ring, MM, Ossining, NY, October 2013.

13. Rules of decorum, behavior: rule book, Sisters History collection.

14. Leaf sweeping: Interview with Dolores Congdon, MM, Ossining, NY, June 2012.

15. *In many ways:* Kenneth Briggs, *Double-Crossed: Uncovering the Catholic Church's Betrayal of American Nuns* (New York: Doubleday, 2006); contemplative vs. active nuns: Margaret M. McGuinness: *Called to Serve: A History of Nuns in America* (New York: NYU Press, 2013).

16. *By 1920:* Lernoux, *Hearts on Fire.*

17. Attitude, personality traits of Maryknoll sisters: *Time* magazine, April 1955.

18. Claudette LaVerdiere, MM, *On the Threshold of the Future: Mother Mary Joseph, Founder, Maryknoll Sisters* (Maryknoll, NY: Orbis Books, 2011).

19. Ibid.

20. *While she lectured plainly:* Lectures of Mother Mary Joseph 1950–1955, Sisters History collection.

21. *Subsequent diaries:* Nicaragua diaries, 1950–1954, Nicaragua History collection, MSA, Maryknoll Mission Archives, Maryknoll, NY.

22. *Thinking that she would soon:* interview with Patricia Ring, MM, Ossining, NY, June 2013.

23. *She loved the rolling hills:* Maura letter to mother, September 1950, private collection Julia Keogh; explored caves: William Kehoe letter to Julia Keogh, 2014, private collection Julia Keogh; *They climbed trees, picked apples:* interview with Reina Paz Kalilala, MM, Ossining, NY, June 2012.

24. Song lyrics: Sisters History collection.

25. *Maura wrote every week:* Maura letters from novitiate, 1950–1954, private collection Julia Keogh; cards sent to family: private collection Julia Keogh; *But her parents and siblings:* interview with James Buddy Clarke, Mount Vernon, NY, August 2012.

26. Restricted conversations, desire to connect: interview with Peg Kilduff, by phone 2014.

27. Maura's overextending herself, restricted good-byes: interview with Patricia Ring, MM, Ossining, NY, June 2013; warm spring day: *Farmers' Almanac*, May 7, 1952; *On Wednesday, May 7:* questionnaire and ceremonial, updated 1952: Sisters History collection.

CHAPTER 3: THE BRONX IS MISSION TERRITORY

1. *Maura's first assignment:* interview with Jesse Poynton, MM, Ossining, NY, September 2012; *But as she would quickly learn:* interview with Mary Malherek, MM, Ossining, NY, July 2012.

2. *St. Anthony of Padua:* Home Owner's Loan Corporation, area description 1937; *Joblessness was common:* Bronx diaries, Sisters History collection, Maryknoll Mission Archives, Maryknoll, NY; *To Maura and other sisters:* Bronx diaries, September 1955.

3. *Maura was now:* Church of St. Anthony of Padua parish report, 1946, Sisters History collection.

4. *When Maura arrived:* Church of St. Anthony of Padua parish report, 1946, Sisters History collection, also letters of Columba Tarpey, MM, Sister History collection; setup of parish, semicloistered life: interview with Mary Malherek, MM, Ossining, NY, July 2012.

5. Comparison of parishes: Office of the Bishop, Parish Visitation Files, 1922–1949, Box 2, St. Camillus, Belle Harbor, NY; Canonical Visitation Report, November 14, 1944, Diocesan Archives, Roman Catholic Diocese of Brooklyn, NY; great migration: Bronx African-American History Project, Fordham University, NY.

6. *Cardinal Spellman had recruited:* Mother Mary Joseph correspondence, MSA, Maryknoll Mission Archives, Maryknoll, NY; Puerto Rican emigration to Morrisania: Nelson Denis, *War Against All Puerto Ricans: Revolution and Terror in America's Colony* (New York: Nation Books, 2015)

7. Violence in parish: Bronx diaries, September 1955, other months; wedding gifts stolen: interview with Julia Keogh, Old Brookville, NY, July 2012; St. Anthony relic stolen, Bronx diaries, September 1956; addicts blocking entrance, death of woman: Richard Marie, MM, interviewed September 1982, Same Fate as the Poor (SFATP) collection, Maryknoll Mission Archives, Maryknoll, NY; second grader: interview with Mary Malherek, MM, Ossining, NY, July 2012.

8. Majority trying to get by: Interview with Ed Tucker, alumnus of St. Anthony of Padua, January 2013.

9. *Students stood on their desks:* Richard Marie, MM, interviewed September 1982, SFATP collection; *She was loath to raise her voice:* Marie Russo, MM, et al., interviewed September 1982, SFATP collection; *When she came back:* Richard Marie, MM, interviewed September 1982, SATP collection.

10. Maura's schedule: Bronx diaries, September 1955.

11. Preparations for class, feeling inadequate: Richard Marie, MM, interviewed September 1982, SFATP collection; new phonics method, Marie Russo, MM, et al., interviewed September 1982, SFATP collection.

12. Playing with the children: interview with Gerald Ryan, Bronx, NY, January 2013; helped with mittens and boots: Richard Marie, MM, interviewed September 1982, SFATP collection; painted scenery: Bronx diaries, 1954; made breakfast, interview with. Gerald Ryan, Bronx, NY, January 2013; trip to Rockefeller Center: Marie Russo, MM, et al., interviewed September 1982, SFATP collection.

13. Visiting sisters: Bronx diaries, 1954–1959.

14. *A strong enough parish and faithful parishioners*: interview with Theresa Mangieri, Ossining, NY, December 2012; working with the PTA: Bronx diaries, 1956; *She spoke quietly:* Richard Marie, MM, interviewed September 1982, SFATP collection.

15. *The TV was always on:* Bronx diaries, 1957; piano-playing family: Bronx diaries, 1956.

16. Credit union: Bronx diaries, 1959; sodality: Bronx diaries, 1954; choir: Bronx diaries, 1959; Chantels: Jay Warner, *American Singing Groups: A History from 1940s to Today* (Milwaukee, WI: Hal Leonard, 2006); basketball team dominated, Bronx diaries, 1957; *In the fall of 1954:* Bronx diaries, 1954; racist white parishes: interview with Theresa Mangieri, Ossining, NY, December 2012.

17. Interview with Gerald Ryan, Bronx, NY, January 2013.

18. Visits by Maura's family, jokes: interview with Mary Malherek, MM, Ossining, July 2012; dynamic among sisters at St. Anthony's: Bronx diaries, 1954–1959; Richard Marie, MM, interviewed September 1982, SFATP collection; also Mary Malherek, MM, Ossining, NY, July 2012, and Marie Russo, MM, interviewed September 1982, SFATP collection.

19. *She committed herself:* Marie Russo, MM, et al., interviewed September 1982, SFATP collection; care of habit, poor state of Maura's: Mary Malherek, MM, Ossining, NY, July 2012, also Maura evaluation for second vows, 1955, Maura Clarke personnel file, Maryknoll Mission Archives, Maryknoll, NY.

20. Overcommitment: Richard Marie, MM, interviewed September, 1982, SFATP collection; art class at Fordham, work displayed, Bronx diaries, 1958.

21. Maura letter to friends Nora and Pat Cleary, private collection Julia Keogh.

CHAPTER 4: SIUNA: AWAY IN JUNGLE

1. *Maura packed hurriedly:* Maura letter to family and friends, November 1959, private collection Julia Keogh; departure from Idlewild: from Kay Kelly interview for Judy Noone, June 25, 1982, Same Fate as the Poor (SFATP) collection, Maryknoll Sisters Archive, Maryknoll Mission Archives, Maryknoll, NY.

2. *Somehow she hadn't inherited,* departure: interview with Julia Keogh, Old Brookville, NY, July 2012.

3. First Maryknoll trip to China, liberalization of travel policy: Penny Lernoux, *Hearts on Fire: The Story of the Maryknoll Sisters* (Maryknoll, NY: Orbis Books, 1993), 38.

4. *This is what she'd dreamed about:* Maura application letter to Maryknoll, January 1950, Maura Clarke personnel file, Maryknoll Mission Archives, Maryknoll, NY; *This was the life:* interview with James Clarke, Connecticut, October 2012; *Maura had met:* from Kay Kelly interview for Judy Noone, May 1981, SFATP collection.

5. Flight: Maura letter to family and friends, November 1959, private collection Julia Keogh; *The two sisters stumbled through:* Maura letters to parents December 1959–June 1960, private collection Julia Keogh.

6. *Both the US and the Nicaraguan government:* This is evident both in the reception of the first Maryknoll sisters in 1944 by Anastasio Somoza García and in the later use of the Maryknoll school as an Alliance for Progress project; *Since the establishment:* Message of the President of the United States, 1904, Theodore Roosevelt Papers, Library of Congress Manuscript Division.

7. History of US intervention in Nicaragua, Vanderbilt: Tim Merrill, ed., *Nicaragua: A Country Study: Somoza Years 1936–1974* (Washington, DC: General Printing Office for the Library of Congress, 1993); *Eager to preserve:* https://history.state.gov/milestones/1899–1913/panama-canal, accessed February 19, 2016; *Four years later:* George Black, *Triumph of the People, The Sandinista Revolution in Nicaragua* (London: Zed Books, 1982); James M. McPherson, *Battle Cry of Freedom: The Civil War Era* (New York: Oxford University Press, 1988), 114; William Walker story also described in Black, *Triumphs of the People.*

8. US military interventions, war against Sandino, establishment of National Guard: Black, *Triumph of the People.*

9. Somoza control of economy, government: Merrill, *Nicaragua: A Country Study;* treatment of political dissidents: Joseph Mulligan, *The Nicaraguan Church and the Revolution* (London: Sheed and Ward, 1991).

10. Somoza regime: Merrill, *Nicaragua: A Country Study.*

11. Maryknollers in Nicaragua: Christine Hernández-Baudín, "From 'Supernaturalizing' to Liberation: The Maryknoll Sisters in Nicaragua, 1945–1975," dissertation, St. Luis University, Department of Theology, May 2014.

12. Arrival by plane: Maura letter to family and friends, November 1959, private collection Julia Keogh.

13. *Maura was amazed:* from Kay Kelly interview for Judy Noone, August 8, 1982, SFATP collection; *During the drive:* Maura letter to family and friends, November 1959, private collection Julia Keogh.

14. *It was a bewildering experience:* Maura letter to family and friends, November 1959, private collection Julia Keogh; *The Nicaraguan sisters:* Srs. Marquette Recuerdo de Maura and Inez Cano, SFATP collection.

15. Flight to Siuna: interview with Kay Kelly, SFATP collection; arrival, jaundice, trip into town, people encountered: Maura letters to friends and family, October 26 and November 1959, private collection Julia Keogh.

16. Morning in Siuna: author observations from trip to Siuna, Nicaragua, February 2013; layout of convent: from sketch by Kay Kelly, SFATP collection; quality of classrooms: interview with Guillermo Larrave, Siuna, Nicaragua, February 2013.

17. *Grotto:* Maura letter to her father, October 26, 1959, private collection, Julia Keogh; Capuchins' work: interview with Auggie Seibert, OFM, by phone June 2013.

18. *The division of labor:* Hernández-Baudín, "From 'Supernaturalizing' to Liberation."

19. Late arrival of greeting cards: SFATP collection; Maura correspondence, thoughts, storm in Siuna: Maura letters home, October 26, November 8, and November 19, 1959, from private collection of Julia Keogh.

20. Going-away party: Maura letter home, November 8, 1959, private collection of Julia Keogh, Kay Kelly interview, SFATP collection.

21. Golden Anniversary of the Siuna, Nicaragua Mission, 1994, MMA, MSA Nicaragua History.

22. *That first group of Maryknollers:* "Nicaragua History" and "Siuna, Nicaragua, 1958," Nicaragua History collection.

23. *Siuna was a sorry place:* interview with Esmelia Cruz Gutiérrez, longtime housekeeper to Maryknoll mission, Siuna, Nicaragua, February 2013; mining in Siuna: The first commercial mining began in Siuna in the 1890s, under a Nicaraguan businessman. By 1905 the mine was owned by a Pittsburgh-based consortium. It was attacked and destroyed by Augusto Sandino's anti-imperialist army in 1928. It reopened under the Canadian La Luz Mining Company in 1938. José Luis Rocha, "Siuna: A Hundred Years of Abandonment," *Envio Magazine*, July 2001; unhealthy social life, mission-built community: Hernández-Baudín, "*From 'Supernaturalizing' to Liberation*"; also Maria del Ray, *Prospero Strikes It Rich: The Growth of a Gold Town* (New York: Harper and Row, 1968).

24. *The sisters didn't question:* "50 Years in Nicaragua" and "Siuna, Nicaragua, 1958," Nicaragua History collection; *They believed that:* Hernández-Baudín, *From 'Supernaturalizing' to Liberation*"; *To a certain degree:* interview with Mercedes Steiner, Siuna, Nicaragua, February 2013.

25. Starting of the day at eight a.m.: Maura letter to her parents, November 8, 1959, private collection Julia Keogh; most children barefoot: Kay Kelly memories, SFATP collection; *Maura had perfected*, art classes: interview with Guillermo Larrave, Siuna, Nicaragua, February 2013; request for paints and brushes, November 8, 1959, private collection Julia Keogh.

26. Despite Maura's reliance: interviews with former students Guillermo Larrave, Salvador Padilla Castillo, Brunilda Campos, Emperatriz de los Ángeles Mejía Velásquez, and Luisa Emilia Loza Cruz in Siuna, Nicaragua, February 2013; *Every few steps:* various interviews Kay Kelly, Bea Zaragosa, and Rita Owczarek, SFATP collection.

27. *By 1962, there were 785*: Maura letter to family June 18, 1962, private collection Julia Keogh; *School fees:* "Siuna, Nicaragua, 1958," Nicaragua History collection.

28. Description of activities of school, parish, from "Siuna, Nicaragua, 1958," Nicaragua History collection; gym, social center built by donations: interview with Gustavo Martínez Mendoza, at Siuna airport, Nicaragua, February 2013.

29. Siuna was a one-horse town that felt a little like a gold rush camp out of the Old West; there wasn't much to do and alcohol abuse was a major problem. Memories of monthly movies: interview with Guillermo Larrave, Brunilda Campos, Mercedes Steiner, et al., in Siuna, Nicaragua, February 2013; girls shifting on cue: Kay Kelly, SFATP collection.

30. Health profile of students, interview with Gail Phares (former Sr. William Aurelie), November 2012, Columbus, GA, and by phone, December 2012; *Siuna soil was metallic:* "Siuna, Nicaragua, 1958," Nicaragua History collection; *The sisters lined up:* interview with Mercedes Steiner, Siuna, Nicaragua, February 2013.

31. Food at the mission: Interview with Guillermo Larrave and Salvador Padillo Castillo, Siuna, Nicaragua, February 2013.

32. *Week after week:* interview with Mercedes Steiner, Siuna, Nicaragua, February 2013.

33. Memories of gold leaving Siuna: interview with Guillermo Larrave, Siuna, Nicaragua, February 2013.

34. *The mine abided:* interview with Mercedes Stein, Siuna, Nicaragua, February 2013; also from Sr. Therese Johnson, notes on Maria del Ray, *In and Out of the Andes: Mission Trails from Yucatan to Chile* (New York: Scribner's, 1955), Nicaragua History collection; interview with Rita Owczarek and Bea Zaragosa, SFATP collection.

35. Conflicted attitudes about mine: Hernández-Baudín, *"From 'Supernaturalizing' to Liberation."*

36. Life in Canadian zone, discomfort in being there: interviews, Kay Kelly, Bea Zaragoza, Rita Owczarek, and Ginny Farrell, SFATP collection; Lucy's relationship with Maura: interview with John Plecash Jr., by phone March 2013.

37. Schedule, weekly devotions in church: Siuna diaries, January–September 1959, Nicaragua History collection; Stations of the Cross, physicality of Catholic imagination: James O'Toole, *The Faithful: A History of Catholics in America* (Cambridge, MA: Harvard University Press, 2010); *She wanted to instill:* interview with Brunilda Campos, Emperatriz de los Ángeles Mejía Velásquez, and Luisa Emilia Loza Cruz in Siuna, Nicaragua, February 2013.

38. Service to others and solidarity: interview with Brunilda Campos and Luisa Emilia Loza Cruz, Siuna, Nicaragua, February 2013.

39. Relationship of Maura to Marianistas: interview with Brunilda Campos, Siuna, Nicaragua, February 2013.

40. Need for solitude: interview with Gerri Brake, MM, who knew her years later, Ossining, NY, January 2013.

41. Life in convent in Siuna, cabin fever: interview with Bea Zaragoza, SFATP collection.

42. Emotional impact of JFK candidacy: interview with Julia Keogh, Rockaway, NY, June 2012.

43. Anastasio Somoza Debayle: Philip Berryman, *Religious Roots of Rebellion: Christians in Central American Revolutions* (Maryknoll, NY: Orbis Books, 1984); planned invasion of Bay of Pigs: Anastasio Somoza Debayle and Jack Cox, *Nicaragua Betrayed* (Appleton, WI: Western Islands, 1980).

44. Fr. Brennan at Bay of Pigs launch: Kay Kelly interview, August 1982, SFATP collection.

45. Fidel Castro in popular media, common discussion: interview with Guillermo Larrave, Siuna, Nicaragua, February 2013.

46. *So was Sr. Margaret Therese:* Sr. Margaret Therese letter to headquarters, June 23, 1962; also Maura Clarke personal file, MSA, Maryknoll Mission Archives, Maryknoll, NY.

47. *Maura wrote to her mother:* Maura letter to her mother, June 1962, private collection Julia Keogh.

48. Responsibilities of superior: Judith Noone, *Same Fate as the Poor* (Maryknoll. NY: Orbis Books, 1983); jokes and teasing: Kay Kelly interview, SFATP collection.

49. Maura as superior, work habits: interview with Rita Owczarek and Bea Zaragosa, SFATP collection.

50. Vatican II: Gary MacEoin, *What Happened at Rome? The Council and Its Implications for the Modern World* (New York: Holt, Rinehart and Winston, 1966).

CHAPTER 5: A CHANGING MISSION

1. Somoza visit memories: from interview with Gail Phares, September 2013, and Kay Kelly interview, Same Fate as the Poor (SFATP) collection, Maryknoll Sisters Archive (MSA), Maryknoll Mission Archives, Maryknoll, NY; use of and translation of Te Deum, *Encyclopedia Britannica*, http://www.britannica.com/topic/Te-Deum-laudamus, accessed May 10, 2016.

2. *Eleven-year-old Ramona:* interview with Ramona Arroliga at her home in Managua, Nicaragua, July 2013; Somoza Debayle visit to Siuna, Siuna diaries, Nicaragua History collection, MSA, Maryknoll Mission Archives, Maryknoll, NY.

3. Alliance for Progress speech: President John F. Kennedy, March 13, 1961, *Department of State Bulletin* 44, no. 1136 (April 3, 1961), 471–474; *That handshake:* interview with Guillermo Larrave, Siuna, Nicaragua, February 2013.

4. *It was a response:* Tito Escobar, *Alliance for Progress: Wrong Place, Wrong Time* (Houston, TX: Rice University, Center for the Study of the Presidency and Congress, 2007); *For Maura, Kennedy embodied . . . Many Nicaraguans agreed:* interview, Ramona Arroliga, Managua, Nicaragua, July 2013; *In his inaugural address:* President Kennedy's Inaugural Address, January 20, 1961, John F. Kennedy Presidential Library and Museum, http://www.jfklibrary.org, accessed May 2, 2016.

5. *Under Maura's direction:* interview with Ramona Arroliga, Managua, Nicaragua, July 2013.

6. "Now you are the Body of Christ and each one of you is a part of it": Corinthians 12:27 (New American Bible).

7. Interview with Marta Carmen Davilla Lumby, La Luz, Siuna, Nicaragua, February 2013.

8. *Mother Mary sent a copy:* Penny Lernoux, *Hearts on Fire: The Story of the Maryknoll Sisters* (Maryknoll, NY: Orbis Books, 1993); *The Nun in the World:* Leon Joseph Suenens, *The Nun in the World* (London: Burn & Oates, 1962), 11.

9. Suenens's new metaphor: Suenens, *The Nun in the World,* 14, 17.

10. Interview with Guadalupe Maireno Estrada, Ciudad Sandino, Nicaragua, July 2013.

11. *Maura was deferential:* Kay Kelly interview, SFATP collection; lay catechists: Order of Friars Minor (OFM) magazine *Siuna History*, Middle America collection, MSA, Maryknoll Mission Archives, Maryknoll, NY; *To Guadalupe:* interview with Guadalupe Maireno Estrada, Ciudad Sandino, Nicaragua, July 2013.

12. *Training girls like Guadalupe:* Fr. Smutko article in *Siuna History*, Middle America collection.

13. Maura Clarke, "Women in Development," 1963, Creative Works, MSA, Maryknoll Mission Archives, Maryknoll, NY.

14. Three girls and their attitudes to the sisters: interview with Brunilda Campos, Luisa Emilia Loza Cruz, and Emperatriz de los Ángeles Mejía Velásquez, Siuna, Nicaragua, February 2013.

15. *With Maura as boss:* ibid.; *On Sunday afternoons*, Maura's approach to money, shoeshine boys, charity: Bea Zaragoza, Rita Owczarek, and Kay Kelly, in SFATP collection; *She always answered:* Phyllis O'Toole, MM, e-mail communication with author July 2013.

16. Change in attitudes and Siuna mission: Siuna diaries, Nicaragua History collection, 1964; also Fr. Smutko article in *Siuna History*, Middle America collection.

17. Old mission methods vs. new: interview with Augustin Seibert, OFM, by phone June 2013.

18. *At the end of February:* Maura letters, 1964, SFATP collection.

19. *During her time away:* Maura letters, 1959–1964, SFATP collection; *Judy collected clothing:* interview with Peter Keogh, February 2013.

20. *Betty McCann:* interview with Betty McCann, New York, July 2012.

21. Mary Clarke: interviews with Julia Keogh, Old Brookville, NY, 2012–2015; *The crisis terrified Maura:* Bea Zaragoza and Kay Kelly, SFATP collection; also author interview with Grace Myerjack, Ossining, NY, 2013.

22. While the shifts of Vatican II were substantial, chapter meetings, held every six years, had always grappled with new approaches and innovations. In the 1950s, disparate orders of American nuns began working together in the Sister Formation Conference to improve the standards of education and training of novices. *The Maryknoll sisters were beginning:* Lernoux: *Hearts on Fire.*

23. *The local language decree:* Capuchin records, 1964, *Siuna History*, Middle America collection.

24. Family of God curriculum, Mary Xavier O'Donnell, "Family of God," Creative Works, MSA, Maryknoll Mission Archives, Maryknoll, NY; also Lernoux, *Hearts on Fire.*

25. San Miguelito, Panama: Philip Berryman, *Religious Roots of Rebellion: Christians in Central American Revolutions* (Maryknoll, NY: Orbis Books, 1984).

26. *After immersing themselves:* interviews with Maryknoll sisters who lived in Chile, Guatemala, Mexico, Nicaragua; also Christine Hernández-Baudín, *From 'Supernaturalizing' to Liberation: The Maryknoll Sisters in Nicaragua, 1945–1975,*

dissertation, St. Luis University, Department of Theology, May 2014; Berryman, *Religious Roots of Rebellion*.

27. Implementing Family of God classes: interview with Gail Phares, formerly Sr. William Aurelie, Columbus, GA, November 2012, and by phone January 2013; interviews with Brunilda Campos and Luisa Emilia Loza Cruz, Siuna, Nicaragua, February 2013.

28. Family of God curriculum/teaching methods: interview with Patricia Ring and Jesse Poynton, Ossining, NY, fall 2012.

29. *The sisters spoke clearly:* interview with Ramona Arroliga, Managua, Nicaragua, July 2013; *Brunilda watched:* interview with Brunilda Campos, Siuna, Nicaragua, February 2013.

30. *"The people in the pueblos":* Maura letter to Julia Keogh, SFATP collection.

31. *But in living in Siuna:* "50 Years in Nicaragua" and *Siuna History*, Middle America collection.

32. Abuses in Siuna: José Luis Rocha, "Siuna: A Hundred Years of Abandonment," *ReVista Envio*, no. 239, June 2001; reorientation of mission: Bea Zaragoza and Laura Glynn, interviews, SFATP collection; establishment of Sandinista Front for National Liberation: Berryman, *Religious Roots of Rebellion*.

33. *Maura didn't have answers:* interview with Gail Phares (formerly Sr. William Aurelie), Columbus, GA, November 2012, by phone January 2013; Sr. Laura Glynn interview for Judy Noone, SFATP collection.

34. Reactions to Vatican II, departure of sisters, Lernoux: *Hearts on Fire*.

35. *It was happening in Siuna, too:* interview with Gail Phares (formerly Sr. William Aurelie), Columbus, GA, November 2012, by phone January 2013.

36. *One nun described it as*: interview with Peg Dillon, MM, Ossining, NY, May 2014; *And worse, those who stayed:* Lernoux, *Hearts on Fire*.

37. *That most of the changes were welcome:* multiple sources, including interviews with Patricia Ring, Patricia Murray, Jesse Poynton, Patricia Redmond, Ossining, 2012–2014; Lernoux, *Hearts on Fire*; Bea Zaragoza and Kay Kelly, SFATP collection; *"Pray for us":* Maura letter to parents, October 1967, also *"Religious communities":* Maura letter, August 1967, private collection Julia Keogh.

38. *By 1966 there were sufficient numbers:* interview with Marina Blandón León, Managua, Nicaragua, July 2013.

39. *Since she came to Siuna:* Maura letters, 1965, SFATP collection.

40. Frequent travel: interview with Gustavo Mendoza, Siuna airport, Nicaragua, February 2013; *white handkerchief:* Lois Lorden, MM, Christmas letter 1967, private collection Julia Keogh.

41. *More frequent trips*: interview with members of San Pablo Apóstol Christian Base Community, Managua, Nicaragua, February 2013; studying Vatican II theology: Lois Lorden, Christmas letter 1967; Eucharistic service in Rosita: Maura letter to parents, 1967, SFATP collection.

42. *As a child:* interview with Jenny Sequeira, Managua, Nicaragua, February 2013; *They quickly recruited:* Berryman, *Religious Roots of Rebellion*; typing song lyrics and meeting notes, interview with Gloria Cannillo, Managua, Nicaragua,

February 2013; *The group reflected:* interview with members of San Pablo Apóstol, Managua, Nicaragua, February 2013.

43. *Assenting to this faith:* interview with Jenny Sequeira, Rafael Valdez, and Carmen García, Managua, Nicaragua, February 2013.

44. Tension in parish team and Maura's role: interview with Félix Jiménez, Managua, Nicaragua, July 2013.

45. *Even so, when it came to a central belief:* Kay Kelly, SFATP collection; *It was time:* Contract for Parish Team, April 1968, *Siuna History,* Middle America collection.

46. Maura letter to parents, September 9, 1968, SFATP collection.

47. Earthquake: "Disaster in Siuna," August 1968 news report, *Siuna History,* Middle America collection; *The Clarkes sent enough money* and letter home: Maura letter to parents, September 9, 1968, SFATP collection; payroll: Communications Department, "Report on Siuna (Nicaragua) Dam Break," August 1968, SFATP collection.

48. *At five p.m.:* *Siuna History,* Middle America collection.

CHAPTER 6: INTO MANAGUA

1. Maura's appearance: Kay Kelly, interview, Same Fate as the Poor (SFATP) collection, Maryknoll Sisters Archive (MSA), Maryknoll Mission Archives, Maryknoll, NY; interviews with Julia Keogh, 2012–2015.

2. Delegation: Mission Challenge, 1968 Chapter, Maryknoll Sisters History, MSA, Maryknoll Mission Archives, Maryknoll, NY; *They argued for:* Penny Lernoux, *Hearts on Fire: The Story of the Maryknoll Sisters* (Maryknoll, NY: Orbis Books, 1993).

3. *But the most exciting reading:* Alfred T. Hennelly, ed., *Liberation Theology: A Documentary History* (Maryknoll, NY: Orbis Books, 1990); The resulting papers: Second Generation Conference of Latin American Bishops, *The Church in the Present-day Transformation of Latin America in the Light of the Council: Documents on Justice, Peace and The Poverty of the Church* (Maryknoll, NY: Orbis Books, 1990); interview with Félix Jiménez, Managua, Nicaragua, March and July 2013.

4. *The kids liked her:* interview with Peter Keogh, New York, February 2013 (he was talking about later, but it's an enduring quality); *Maura often came down:* multiple interviews, Julia Keogh, James Clarke, Michael Clarke.

5. *She felt ineffective sometimes:* interview with Gerri Brake, MM, and Bea Zaragoza, MM, SFATP collection; also author interviews with Grace Myerjack, MM, and Peg Dillon, MM, Ossining, NY, 2014; *Whenever Maura was home . . . One day Maura met:* interviews with Julia Keogh, 2012–2015.

6. *Marched in protests*: interviews with Julia Keogh, 2012–2015; *While Cardinal Spellman:* John Cooney, *The American Pope: The Life and Times of Francis Cardinal Spellman* (New York: Times Books, 1984); *On a car ride:* interviews with Julia Keogh, 2012–2015.

7. *She phoned home:* Maura letter to Mary Clarke, February 18, 1970, SFATP collection.

8. *Maura sought her out:* interview with Gerri Brake, MM, Ossining, NY,

January 2013; *During her brief visit to El Salvador:* interview with Patricia Murray, Yonkers, NY, February 2013.

9. Description of house and work in Miralagos, Managua, from Bea Zaragoza letter to Maura Clarke, "A new page in Maryknoll history begins," September 1969, Nicaragua History collection, MSA, Maryknoll Mission Archives, Maryknoll, NY; description of neighborhood, interview with María Hamlin Zúñiga, via Skype January 2014.

10. *Vatican II on priests and nuns:* Austin Flannery, ed., *Vatican Council II: Constitutions, Decrees, Declarations* (Northport, NY: Costello Publishing Company, revised, 1996); voluntary poverty: "Decree on the Adaptation and Renewal of Religious Life" (Perfectae Caritatis), October 1965, item 13.

11. *She was part of a parish team:* Bea Zaragoza, "A new page," Nicaragua History collection; *Hamlin was drawn:* interview with María Hamlin Zúñiga, by Skype January 2014; *Running through all the work:* Maura letters to parents February and March 1970, SFATP collection.

12. *Maura hesitated:* Maura letter to James Buddy Clarke, March 20, 1970, SFATP collection; *But Maura smiled:* interview with Miriam Guerrero, Managua, Nicaragua, February 2013; *The curriculum was the same:* Maura letter to Mary Clarke, March 16, 1970, SFATP collection.

13. Marks in Maura's Bible, private collection, Julia Keogh.

14. Gospel of Luke 4:18 (The New American Bible).

15. *During the day:* Maura letter to James Buddy Clarke, March 20, 1970, SFATP collection; method of discussion in Christian Base Communities: Philip Berryman, *Religious Roots of Rebellion* (Maryknoll, NY: Orbis Books, 1984).

16. *At Miriam's house:* interview with Miriam Guerrero, Managua, Nicaragua, February 2013.

17. Angelique and group: interview with Angelique Rodríguez Alemán, Managua, Nicaragua, February 2013; description of Lake Managua: interview with María Hamlin Zúñiga, by Skype January 2014.

18. *She mentioned it in several letters,* schedule of day: Maura letters to parents, March 16 and 22, 1970, SFATP collection.

19. *In the mornings:* interviews with Peg Dillon, MM, and Gerri Brake, MM, Ossining, NY, February–April 2014.

20. Description of morning, work at Colegio Centro América, Maura letter to James Buddy Clarke, March 20, 1970, SFATP collection.

21. Correspondence with parents: Maura letters to parents, 1970, SFATP collection.

22. Pride in John Clarke: Maura letter to parents, March 22, 1970, SFATP collection.

23. *This Jesus belonged to the people*: interview with members of San Pablo Apóstol, Managua, Nicaragua, February 2013, July 2013, in particular, discussion of Misa Nicaragüense of 1967; *The critique:* Michael Lowy, *The War of Gods: Religion and Politics in Latin America* (New York: Verso Books, 1996), 39.

24. Retreats: interview with Angelique Rodríguez Alemán, Managua, Nicaragua, February 2013.

25. *The practice of social analysis:* Lowy, *The War of Gods*, 33: "The poor themselves become conscious of their condition and organize to struggle as Christians, belonging to a church and inspired by a faith"; *Christina Suoza:* letter from Joseph Mulligan, SJ, 1986, interviews with two Nicaraguans, Maura personal file, El Salvador Martyrs collection, MSA, Maryknoll Mission Archives, Maryknoll, NY.

26. *When Maura was supposed to:* Maura letter to parents, April 28, 1970, SFATP collection; *In the event:* Rita Owczarek, interview, SFATP collection; *She underlined the verse:* 1 John 4:10 (The New American Bible); theological concept of the women finding themselves in Gospel stories, see Luz Beatriz Arellano, in Virginia Fabella, ed., *With Passion and Compassion, Third World Women Doing Theology* (Maryknoll, NY: Orbis Books, 1988), 135–150.

27. *After the talks:* interview with Leila Rodríguez, Managua, Nicaragua, February 2013, photos from Leila and her mother, personal collection Angelique Rodríguez Alemán.

28. *But all these meetings:* Manzar Foroohar, *The Catholic Church and Social Change in Nicaragua* (Albany, NY: SUNY Press, 1989), 75; *Somoza . . . had a name:* interview with Leila Rodríguez, Managua, Nicaragua, February 2013.

29. *Several prominent clergy:* Foroohar, *The Catholic Church*, 70–75; *Opposition to Somoza:* interview with Luz Beatriz Arellano, Managua, Nicaragua, February 2013; Sandinista's position and influence: Berryman, *Religious Roots of Rebellion*; *meanwhile news:* Mónica Baltodano, *Memorias de Lucha Sandinista*, Chronology 1970, http://www.memoriasdelaluchasandinista.org, accessed April 3, 2016; *As the summer of 1970:* Lowry, *War of Gods*, 94; *In Maura's Nicaragua,* ibid., 34: "In order to avoid misunderstanding . . . let us recall first of all that Liberation theology is not a social and political discourse but before anything a religious and spiritual reflection."

30. Fernando Cardenal, *Faith and Joy: Memoirs of a Revolutionary Priest*, ed. Kathy McBride (Maryknoll, NY: Orbis Books, 2015), 4, 7, 10; *Then on the night of September 19:* Baltodano, *Memorias de Lucha Sandinista; Among them were five student leaders,* Cardenal, *Faith and Joy,* 12; sit-in at cathedral: ibid., 14.

31. *She admired their passion:* Maura letter to parents, October 15, 1970, SFATP collection; *They sat in the pews:* Baltodano, *Memorias de Lucha Sandinista*, also Cardenal, *Faith and Joy,* 17.

32. *They reminded her:* Maura letter to parents, October 12, 1970, SFATP collection.

33. Absence of riots: Maura letter to parents, October 15, 1970, SFATP collection.

34. Cardenal, *Faith and Joy,* 16.

35. *But protests continued:* Baltodano, *Memorias de Lucha Sandinista;* Maura joins protest, wishes she still wore habit: Bea Zaragoza, SFATP collection; *Still, she felt a little tentative:* Maura letter to parents October 26, 1970, SFATP collection; for attitude of Sr. Mildred Fritz concerning the Melville incident, see Lernoux, *Hearts on Fire*, 153.

36. *She pushed:* interview with Luz Beatriz Arellano, Managua, Nicaragua, July 2013

37. Ill health in Miralagos: discussion with María Hamlin Zúñiga, by Skype January 2014; *Maura could hear Rita snoring*: Maura letter to her parents, SFATP collection.

38. OPEN 3 was the third such site for displaced people. *Fr. García:* Maura letter to her parents, November 25, 1970, SFATP collection.

39. Need to go home, for enthusiastic assent: Bea Zaragoza and Rita Owczarek, interview SFATP collection; *Maura returned to:* Maura letter to her parents, June 21, 1971, SFATP collection.

40. Mary Clarke letter to Maura, May 18, 1971, private collection Julia Keogh.

41. Nicaraguan bishops' statement about duty of Christians: Foroohar, *The Catholic Church.*

42. *At dawn on August 7:* Danny Kennally and Eric Preston, *Belfast August 1971: A Case to Be Answered,* originally published in London by the Independent Labour Party in 1971; indefinite detention, John McGuffin, *Internment* (Tralee, Ireland: Anvil Books, 1973), chap. 8, both accessed April 5, 2015, through University of Ulster's CAIN web service; also *Conflict and Politics in Northern Ireland: They Were Tortured: Ireland vs United Kingdom,* European Commission of Human Rights, 1976; see also http://www.irishtimes.com/news/crime-and-law/the-torture-centre-northern-ireland-s-hooded-men-1.2296152; *So much tear gas was discharged:* interview with Peter Keogh, husband of Julia, November 2015; People aching: Maura letter to parents, September 12, 1971, SFATP collection.

43. Dinner party, happiness at Fr. Martínez's return: Maura letter to parents, December 12, 1972, SFATP collection. *The other sisters teased:* interview with Peg Healy and Peg Dillon, MM, Ossining, NY, February 2013.

44. Fr. Martínez's party: Maura letter to parents, December, undated 1972, SFATP collection.

45. Christmas Eve: interview with Fernando Cardenal, Managua, Nicaragua, July 2013; interview with San Pablo Apóstol members, Managua, Nicaragua, February 2013.

46. The clock atop the cathedral was still stuck at 12:29 in 2013.

47. Earthquake description: Melba Bantay interview, SFATP collection; Maura Clarke, Kay Kelly, and Melba Bantay, "Tragedy in Managua, Nicaragua, December 23, 1972," private collection Julia Keogh; also Maura letter to family, December 25, 1972, private collection Julia Keogh.

48. Aftermath of earthquake: "Tragedy in Managua, Nicaragua, December 23, 1972"; Maura letters, January 1973, private collection Julia Keogh.

49. Maura letter to Mary Clarke, January 6, 1973, private collection Julia Keogh.

CHAPTER 7: THE CONVENT IS IN THE STREET

1. *Maura thought it looked:* Maura letter to her parents, January 6, 1973, private collection Julia Keogh; quantifying destruction of Managua, Manzar Foroohar, *The Catholic Church and Social Change in Nicaragua* (Albany, NY: SUNY Press, 1989), 87, quoting a Nicaraguan government report; *In the first days:* Maura Clarke, Kay Kelly, and Melba Bantay, "Tragedy in Managua, Nicaragua,

December 23, 1972," private collection Julia Keogh; Anastasio Somoza Debayle named head of National Emergency Committee: Foroohar, *The Catholic Church*, 88.

2. Move to Camp Hope, camp conditions, goals, activities, partnerships: Melba Bantay, "One and a Half Months in Campamento Esperanza," February 1973, Nicaragua History collection, Maryknoll Sisters Archive (MSA), Maryknoll Mission Archives, Maryknoll, NY; grit and dust: Maura letter to her parents, January 6, 1973, private collection Julia Keogh; offer to work in kitchen rebuffed: interview with Peg Dillon, MM, Ossining, NY, February 2013 (this observation was obvious to Peg); *The sisters coordinated:* Clarke, Kelly, Bantay, "Tragedy in Managua"; *All her work knitting together:* interview with Angelique Rodríguez Alemán, Managua, Nicaragua, February 2013; Maura's affinity for children: interview with Carmen García, Managua. February 2013; easy connection to children, Maura's lack of cynicism or guile: discussion with Clarke-Keogh family, numerous interviews in Ciudad Sandino, Nicaragua, February and July 2013, also with Maryknoll sisters, 2012–2015.

3. Desire to form Christian Base Community in camp: Melba Bantay, "One and a Half Months," Nicaragua History collection.

4. *It was horrendous:* Clarke, Kelly, Bantay, "Tragedy in Managua"; *The purpose of church:* interview with Peg Dillon, MM, Ossining, NY, January 3, 2013.

5. Freire's book *Pedagogy of the Oppressed* wasn't published until 1968, but his methods and philosophy were discussed and replicated widely throughout the Latin American church as far back as the mid-1960s, according to sisters and priests who worked in Siuna with Maura. *The third week:* Maura letter to parents, January 1973; *Mertens asked:* Maura two-page autobiography, Same Fate as the Poor (SFATP) collection, MSA, Maryknoll Mission Archives, Maryknoll, NY.

6. *Everything was followed . . . delighted to see the stoic Spaniard:* interview with Peg Dillon, MM, Ossining, NY, March 20, 2013; birthday celebration: Maura letter to parents, January 14, 1973, private collection Julia Keogh.

7. Paulo Freire's books were banned in Nicaragua, so the nuns and staff at the Institute of Human Promotion (IMPRU) made their own materials in the same style, according to former Maryknoll nun Geraldine O'Leary-Macías in *Lighting My Fire: A Memoir* (Bloomington, IN: Trafford Publishing, 2013); Melba's accomplishments while Maura was away, *The community was coming together:* "Requiem for Camp Esperanza, March 30, 1973," Nicaragua History collection; Maura's frame of mind in Camp Hope, moving as a child: Maura letter to parents, March 15, 1973, SFATP collection.

8. Outrage and organizing: Maura letter to James Buddy Clarke, March 18, 1973, SFATP collection.

9. Grit and dust: O'Leary-Macías, *Lighting My Fire*. Description of house, lack of privacy: interview with Peg Dillon, MM, and Peg Healy, New York, January 3, 2013.

10. *Maura tried to keep up:* Maura letter to parents, May 7, 1973, SFATP collection; corruption of Somoza regime: Foroohar, *The Catholic Church*, 88, 90.

11. Lack of services: interview with Peg Dillon, MM, Ossining, NY, March 2013; Men selling metal: O'Leary-Macías, *Lighting My Fire*.

12. Creation of Cruz Grande: interview with Peg Dillon, MM, and Peg Healy, Ossining, New York, February 2013; clanging on railroad metal: interview with Walter López Jirón, Ciudad Sandino, Nicaragua, July 2013.

13. Tension in OPEN 3 over direction of church community: Philip Berryman, *Religious Roots of Rebellion* (Maryknoll, NY: Orbis Books, 1984), 67; Maura and Fr. Martínez trips to Masaya, reestablishment of Christian Base Communities: interview with Angelique Rodríguez Alemán, Managua, Nicaragua, February 2013.

14. Cleaning the house: O'Leary-Macías, *Lighting My Fire*; water conservation: interview with Peg Dillon, MM, and Peg Healy, New York, January 3, 2013; her mother planting flowers: Maura letter to parents, 1973, SFATP collection.

15. Using the kids to help community: interview with group, including Henri Norori and Roberto Somoza, Ciudad Sandino, Nicaragua, February 2013; parents' loosening oversight: interview with Walter López Jirón, Ciudad Sandino, Nicaragua, July 2013.

16. Boys' fascination with nuns: interview with Roberto Somoza and Henri Norori, Ciudad Sandino, Nicaragua, February 2013; asking *porqué* . . . goading of boys to articulate their thoughts: interview with Walter López Jirón, Ciudad Sandino, Nicaragua, July 2013; trek to OPEN 3: interview with San Pablo Apóstol members, Managua, Nicaragua, February 2013; crate houses, Maura's jitteriness and encouragement: Maura letter to parents, June 6, 1973, SFATP collection.

17. *Maura realized:* Maura letter to parents, May 19, 1973, SFATP collection; *In each return letter:* Mary and John Clarke letters to Maura, June 17, July 1 (two letters), July 8 (two letters), private collection Julia Keogh; decision to go to New York: Maura correspondence to Central Governing Board (CGB), July 18, 1973, personal file, MSA, Maryknoll Mission Archives, Maryknoll, NY; Meeting with Sr. Laura John: Laura Glynn obituary, MSA, Maryknoll Mission Archives, Maryknoll, NY, also Maura letter to parents, August 26, 1973, SFATP collection.

18. Being home, return to mission: Maura letter to parents, August 17, 1973, SFATP collection; china teacup, interview with Gerri Brake, MM, Ossining, NY, February 2013.

19. Sr. Estelle had her ways: interview with Patricia Edmiston, MM, July 2015; Maura letter to CGB, July 18, 1973, MSA, Maryknoll Mission Archives, Maryknoll.

20. *By late August:* Maura letter to parents, August 17, 1973, SFATP collection, also interview with María Luisa Urbina, Ciudad Sandino, Nicaragua, February 2013; *community-run classes:* Maura letter to parents, September 6, 1973, SFATP collection; empowering neighborhood women: interview with María Luisa Urbina, Ciudad Sandino, Nicaragua, February 2013; *And Maria Luisa was so solid:* interview with Peg Healy, Ossining, NY, March 2013; *"You must be hungry":* interview with María Luisa Urbina and husband, Julio, Ciudad Sandino, Nicaragua, February 2013.

21. *For Maura it was instinct:* interview with Peg Dillon, MM, Ossining, NY, March 20, 2013, and so many other interviews with Maryknoll sisters.

22. People stopping in and coming together: interview at CECIM (Centro de Educación y Capacitación Integral), Ciudad Sandino, Nicaragua, February 14,

2013; men's discussion: interview with San Pablo Apóstol community, Managua, Nicaragua, February 2013.

23. *Visiting people in their homes:* interview with Peg Dillon, Ossining, New York, February 2013; *One day she got lost:* interview with Denis Sandigo at CECIM, Ciudad Sandino, Nicaragua, February 2013; helping Rosa's family: interview with Peg Dillon, MM, and Peg Healy, Ossining, NY, March 2013; *She was surprised by:* interview with Roberto Somoza, Henri Norori, and Rosa Blandón, Ciudad Sandino, Nicaragua, February 15, 2013.

24. *She slipped off her shoes:* Kay Kelly, 1982, SFATP collection; Peg Healy's arrival: interview with Peg Healy, New York, December 12, 2012; near constant rotation of sisters: interview with Peg Dillon, MM, and Peg Healy, New York, January 3, 2013; *They shared books:* interview with members of San Pablo Apóstol, Managua, Nicaragua, February 2013.

25. Living together in close quarters: interview with Peg Dillon, MM, Ossining, NY, March 20, 2013; name of the town Siuna: Bea Zaragoza, SFATP collection.

26. Feelings for Fr. Martínez: interview with Julia Keogh, New York, April 2016.

27. Friends' concern for Maura: interview with Peg Dillon, MM, Ossining, NY, March 20, 2013; *There was nothing hard about Maura:* interview with Peg Dillon, MM, and Peg Healy, Ossining, NY, March 2013, also interview with Peg Healy, New York, December 12, 2012.

28. Play and Pray and prayer services: interview with Margarita Jamias, MM, Ossining, NY, April 12, 2016.

29. Daily life in OPEN 3 home, October 1974–April 1975, Nicaragua History collection; *But most nights were occupied:* interview with Peg Dillon, MM, and Peg Healy, Ossining, NY, March 2013.

30. Campaign begun for bus service: Maura letter to parents, August 17, 2013, SFATP collection; sisters' supporting and joining march: Maura Otero, interview at CECIM, Ciudad Sandino, Nicaragua, February 2013; *It made it impossible:* interview with Peg Dillon, Ossining, NY, February 9, 2013; *A strong communist element:* Maura letter to parents, August 17, 2013, SFATP collection.

31. Socio-dramas, disrespect for women, drunkenness, high price of food: interview with Walter López Jirón, Ciudad Sandino, Nicaragua, July 2013; purpose of Paolo Freire–style exercises: interview with Peg Dillon, MM, Ossining, NY, February 9, 2016; *It was loving their neighbors:* interview with Roberto Somoza, Henri Norori, and Rosa Blandón, Ciudad Sandino, Nicaragua, February 2013.

32. *On Thursday nights:* Fernando Cardenal, *Faith and Joy: Memoirs of a Revolutionary Priest,* ed. Kathy McBride (Maryknoll, NY: Orbis Books, 2015), 38; national youth retreat: interview with Fernando Cardenal, Managua, Nicaragua, February 2013; *After the earthquake:* ibid.; *In early 1973:* Cardenal, *Faith and Joy,* 43.

33. Fr. Cardenal's Masses and OPEN 3's reputation as a place of subversives: interview with Roberto Somoza, Henri Norori, and Rosa Blandón, Ciudad Sandino, Nicaragua, February 2013; also Cardenal, *Faith and Joy; The day before:* interview with Fernando Cardenal, SJ, Managua, Nicaragua, February 2013;

interview with Roberto Somoza and Henri Norori, Ciudad Sandino, February 2013; also, Pablo Emilio Barretto recounts the cemetery story in *Municipio Ciudad Sandino*, a history of the city, at http:www.anfut.org, a compilation of Nicaraguan popular history [Barretto says the cemetery confrontation occurred in October 1976, but this contrasts with the memories of Roberto Somoza and Henri Norori, who by 1976 had left the barrio to fight with the FSLN; similarly, Peg Healy was not present at the cemetery confrontation. She arrived in OPEN 3 in 1975, for this reason, and because it was recounted by Fernando Cardenal as an *early* incident of Maura's tenacity, I locate it as having occurred in 1974]; Maura's confronting National Guard: interview with Fernando Cardenal, Managua, Nicaragua, February 2013; also from interview with Roberto Somoza, Henri Norori, and Rosa Blandón, Ciudad Sandino, Nicaragua, February 2013.

34. Mother's Day 1974 arrest and bail: interview with Henri Norori and Roberto Somoza, Ciudad Sandino, Nicaragua, February 2013.

35. *Many nights:* interview with María Elena Oliveres, hair salon, Ciudad Sandino, Nicaragua, February 2013; *The nuns were their protectors:* interview with Roberto Somoza, Henri Norori, and Rosa Blandón, Ciudad Sandino, Nicaragua, February 2013, also interview with Walter López Jirón and Humberto Bolaños, Ciudad Sandino, Nicaragua, July 2013.

36. *Plenty of priests and nuns:* Michael Lowy, *The War of Gods: Religion and Politics in Latin America* (New York: Verso Books, 1996), 71–72; Delegates of the Word, collaboration with FSLN, Berryman, *Religious Roots of Rebellion*, 67, 71–73.

37. *Glimpsing Ramon:* interview with Ramón Rodas Martínez, Managua, Nicaragua, July 2013; *Guadalupe:* interview with Guadalupe Maireno Estrada, Ciudad Sandino, Nicaragua, July 2013.

38. *Maura knew it was true:* Maura letter to parents, May 24, 1974, SFATP collection; finding one's place, avoiding extremes: interview with Pat Ring, MM, Ossining, NY, August 2012; taking time out: interview with Gerri Brake, MM, Ossining, NY, January, 2013; *There were years:* Maura letter to parents, May 24, 1974, SFATP collection.

39. *And if that were so:* Interviews with various Maryknoll sisters, 2012–2015; *At monthly talks:* interview with Peg Dillon, MM, Ossining, NY, March 20, 2013.

40. Rape of farm woman: Maura letter to her mother, June 9, 1974, SFATP collection; *Friends told her to flee:* Amada had given birth to nine children, but only four survived beyond the age of two; arrest, interrogation, rape, background: Margaret Randall, *Sandino's Daughters: Testimonies of Nicaraguan Women in Struggle* (New Brunswick, NJ: Rutgers University Press, 1995).

41. *Maura knew it wasn't unusual treatment:* Maura letter to parents, June 9, 1974, SFATP collection; Amada reported her rape: interview with Amada Pineda, Tipitapa, Nicaragua, July 2013. *Kay went to CONFER:* Maura letter to her mother, October 7, 1974, SFATP collection; *It didn't matter:* Bea Zaragoza and Kay Kelly interview with Judy Noone, SFATP collection.

42. *Maura was happy to see:* Some sources note that the Sandinista women's organization was not formed until 1977, but Carmen García says she was at Amada Pineda's trial with AMPRONAC, the women's organization. I've decided to trust

Carmen's memory. Organized vigils and rallies: interview with Carmen García, Managua, Nicaragua, July 2013.

43. *Amada was made to stand:* Bea Zaragoza interview with Judy Noone, SFATP collection; accusations against Amada, sisters' support: interview with Amada Pineda, Tipitapa, Nicaragua, July 2013.

44. *There was something regal in it:* Maura letter to parents, June 9, 1974, SFATP collection; Maura's relationship with Amada: interview with Amada Pineda, Tipitapa, Nicaragua, July 2013.

45. Checks sent by Maura's family: Maura letters to parents, 1973–1976, SFATP collection.

46. Dust: interview with Peg Dillon, MM, Ossining, NY, February 9, 2013; *There were so many people:* interview with Peg Dillon, MM, and Peg Healy, New York, January 3, 2013.

47. John Clarke's visit to OPEN 3: letter from John Clarke to Mary Clarke, December 22, 1973, private collection, Julia Keogh.

48. Christmas raid: William LeoGrande, *In Our Own Backyard: The United States in Central America*, (Chapel Hill, NC: University of North Carolina Press, 2000), 15; Maura listening to radio broadcast: Kay Kelly interview for Judy Noone, SFATP collection. *The regime would be required:* Forooher, *The Catholic Church.*

49. *It felt like liberation:* Kay Kelly interview for Judy Noone, SFATP collection; *But this highly coordinated:* LeoGrande, *In Our Own Backyard*, 15; *Maybe it really would be possible:* interview with Peg Dillon, MM, Ossining, NY, March 20, 2013.

50. Guardsman quote and Somoza's and US responses to raid: LeoGrande, *In Our Own Backyard*, 15, 16; US teaching counterinsurgency techniques: SOA Watch, SOA Graduates 1946–2004, database, http:ww.soawgrads.xls,SOAW.org, accessed June 29, 2016.

51. Misa Campesina: It was sung first in Solentiname, but that is an isolated, tiny community. OPEN 3 was the first truly public celebration of Mejía Godoy's Mass. Its writing and unveiling: interview with Carlos Mejía Godoy, Managua, Nicaragua, February 2013.

52. *"You are the God of the poor":* from the Misa Campesina, translated by Bernardo Gordillo for the author, June 2014.

53. *It was the first time:* interview with Carlos Mejía Godoy, Managua, Nicaragua, February 2013.

54. Disruption of Mass, crowd holding hands: interview with Carlos Mejía Godoy, Managua, Nicaragua, February 2013; *The Frs. Cardenal:* Cardenal, *Faith and Joy*, 38.

55. *In September 1975:* interview with Henri Norori, Ciudad Sandino, Nicaragua, February 2013, also with Walter López Jirón and Humberto Bolaños, Ciudad Sandino, Nicaragua, July 2013.

56. *They knew their altar boys:* interview with Peg Dillon, MM, Ossining, NY, February 9, 2013; These Sandinistas: interview with Humberto Bolaños, Ciudad

Sandino, Nicaragua, July 2013; *In OPEN 3:* interview with Peg Healy, New York, December 12, 2013.

57. Beginning of water fight, tactics for group discussion, worries about spies: interview with Peg Dillon, MM, Ossining, NY, March 20, 2013.

58. *In June 1976:* timeline of the water fight, April–October 1975, Nicaragua History collection; best, most detailed account of the water struggle: Peg Dillon and Peg Healy, "Lucha de Agua," June–October 1976, private collection Peg Healy.

59. Hunger strike at Red Cross: Henri Norori, Ciudad Sandino, Nicaragua, February 2013; Maura thinking of the Irish Revolution: Maura's letters to parents, 1975–1976, SFATP collection.

60. *It seemed to them:* interview with Walter López Jirón, Ciudad Sandino, Nicaragua, July 2013.

61. *It was during the water fight:* interview with Humberto Bolaños, Ciudad Sandino, Nicaragua, July 2013; also with Walter López Jirón, Ciudad Sandino, Nicaragua, July 2013, and Henri Norori and Roberto Somoza, Ciudad Sandino, Nicaragua, February 2013.

62. Humberto's arrest and torture, nun's vigil: interview with Humberto Bolaños, Ciudad Sandino, Nicaragua, July 2013.

63. "The injustice of certain situations cries out for God's attention. Lacking the bare necessities of life, whole nations are under the thumb of others; they cannot act on their own initiative; they cannot exercise personal responsibility; they cannot work toward a higher degree of cultural refinement or a greater participation in social and public life. They are sorely tempted to redress these insults to their human nature by violent means. Everyone knows, however, that revolutionary uprisings—except where there is manifest, longstanding tyranny which would do great damage to fundamental personal rights and dangerous harm to the common good of the country—engender new injustices, introduce new inequities and bring new disasters. The evil situation that exists, and it surely is evil, may not be dealt with in such a way that an even worse situation results." From "Populorum Progressio," Encyclical of Pope Paul VI, March 26, 1967.

64. Teenagers coming to ask for blessing: interview with Peg Dillon, MM, Ossining, NY, March 20, 2013, also drawn from Jean Burke interview for Judy Noone, SFATP collection; Maura's ideas on nonviolence, legitimacy of rebellion—"I believe very much in nonviolence, but also we can never judge anyone who has to resort to violence, as in the case of Nicaragua, because of the institutional injustice and violence present in the country for years and years," quoted in memorial article, *Sign* magazine 60, no. 5 (February 1981).

65. Maura's shouting, lunging, beating hood of truck: interview with Humberto Bolaños, Ciudad Sandino, Nicaragua, July 2013, also with Henri Norori, Roberto Somoza, and Walter López Jirón, Ciudad Sandino, Nicaragua, February 2013 and July 2013; interview with Peg Healy, New York, December 2012, *"This is my convent!":* interview with Patricia Murray, Yonkers, NY, February 2013. Many people remember this story. Some remember it happening at the public Misa

Campesina, others at the end of a protest march, others as occurring outside the sisters' house. I strived to bring my investigation as close as possible to the central participants: in Ciudad Sandino, when people began to tell the story, I asked, "Who was getting arrested that day? Who was in the jeep?" This led me to Humberto Bolaños, who recounted Maura's vigorous intervention and his own torture, Maura's words re-created from his memory.

CHAPTER 8: MISSION TO THE UNITED STATES

1. *A meeting with the youth group was planned for the evening*: timeline of the water fight, April–October 1975, Nicaragua History collection, Maryknoll Sisters Archive (MSA), Maryknoll Mission Archives, Maryknoll, NY; Maura letter to parents, SFATP collection, states the day she'll leave.

2. *Instead of being missionaries:* interview with Jean Fallon, MM, Ossining, NY, June, 2014; a January 1977 note from Sr. Melba Bantay, with whom Maura lived for several years in Managua and OPEN 3, gives an indication of Maura's trepidation about the United States: "May you live the same kind of joy and trust in God our father in this place which seemingly is not a mission place but in reality is one of our missions which is in desperate need of the touch of humanness and authentic community living. Don't let their professionalism and sense of order eclipse your spontaneity," private collection Julia Keogh.

3. Maura's good-bye to Maria Luisa: interview with María Luisa Urbina, Ciudad Sandino, Nicaragua, February 2013, *Maria Luisa's welcome:* interview with Peg Healy and Peg Dillon, MM, Ossining, NY, March 23, 2013; *Miriam would miss:* interview with Miriam Castillo, Ciudad Sandino, Nicaragua, February 2013; *Tearing apart felt like opening a wound:* Maura letter to her father, October 7, 1976, Same Fate as the Poor (SFATP) collection, MSA, Maryknoll Mission Archives, Maryknoll, NY: "I'm relying on God to get me through the goodbyes. It won't be easy as you know. These are such good and wonderful people and I care for them so much."

4. *She'd been looking forward:* Maura letter to Sr. Andre, November 1974, Clarke, Maura (M.M.) personal file, MSA; her feelings for Fr. Martínez: Months later she would speak frankly and without guilt about her feelings for the priest and the confusion they'd caused her. Interview with Jim Hannon, Acton, MA, June 1, 2014; Wanting time to slow down: Clarke, Maura (M.M.) personnel file, Retreat Diary, Retreat Notes, 1976/1977 (13/8), Maryknoll Sisters Archive, Maryknoll Mission Archives, Maryknoll, NY: "Lord I have wanted a retreat of this kind for so long but now after having the fortune of having this time confired [*sic*] I've seemed dumb—somewhat without feeling—I think I do not know how to pray"; *Between prescribed times for prayer:* letter from Jim Stehr, SJ, to the Sisters of Maryknoll, October 27, 1981, SFATP collection.

5. Brahms violin concerto, thoughts about exile: Maura copied down the titles and the names of the performers on the recordings, and mentions the leader of the Sandinistas and the Capuchin report specifically. Clarke, Maura (M.M.) personnel file, Retreat Diary, Retreat Notes, 1976/1977 (13/8).

6. *She would be strengthened:* ibid.

7. *Reading the Bible passage about Jesus:* ibid.: "Then I saw the tortured men who fight for justice today in the place of Christ and I pictured the rulers and the military as the high priests etc.—also I visioned the poor as the tortured Jesus."

8. *It was a trying week:* Ibid.: "You say in Jeremiah, I have brought you back—hope for the future you have a plan of peace and not disaster—this speaks to me—I feel a little bit more hopeful—a little bit rested—tranquil—I am here—you brought me here—It isn't simply my own foolish plan or idea."

9. *In the mid-1970s:* interview with Jean Fallon, MM, Ossining, NY, June 2014.

10. *Official papal teachings on poverty:* "Populorum Progressio," Encyclical Pope Paul VI, March 26, 1967, also interviews with Jean Fallon, MM, June 2014; *She drew up charts:* Margarita Jamias, MM, Ossining, NY, June 2014, also colleague Mary Heidkamp, by phone June 2014 and participant Elaine Hruska, by phone June, 2014.

11. *Maura listening attentively:* Judy Noone interview with Jean Burke, SFATP collection; *She pushed gently:* Elaine Hruska letter to Judy Noone, June 7, 1981, SFATP collection; *The Virginia parish members:* interview with Elaine Hruska, by phone June 2014.

12. *Elaine's comments:* letter from Elaine Hruska to Judy Noone, June 7, 1981 SFATP collection.

13. *At the end of each workshop:* Margarita Jamias, MM, interview for Judy Noone, SFATP collection; This was especially true after June 1978 when Margarita Jamias, who like Maura had served in Nicaragua, replaced Jean Burke (who went to Tanzania); also interview with David Hollenbach, SJ, by phone July 2014. Hollenbach said Maura's presentations were personal, focused particularly on the people she knew and the things she'd seen.

14. *"Does our government know":* interview with Elaine Hruska, by phone June 2014.

15. *Listening to US House debate:* Maura postcard to parents February 1977, SFATP collection; *A month earlier:* Inaugural Address of President Jimmy Carter, January 20, 1977, http://www.jimmycarterlibrary.gov, accessed May 10, 2016.

16. *New York Times* article: Alan Riding, "Bishops in Nicaragua Say Troops Kill Civilians in Fighting Leftists," *New York Times*, March 2, 1977; *The coverage of violence and torture:* Jean Burke, MM, interview with Judy Noone, SFATP collection: "She wanted to be back in Managua, working with Peg and Peg and the people in the barrio, but this was her mission now, educating Americans."

17. *It was always personal:* interview with David Hollenbach, SJ, by phone July 2014.

18. *A letter from Peg Healy:* Peg Healy letter, March 11, continued on March 27, 1977, private collection Julia Keogh; *They brought Lesbia:* notarized declaration of Lesbia's treatment in jail, April 14, 1977, private collection Peg Healy.

19. *"You can imagine":* Peg Healy to Maura, Bea, and Melba, March 11, March 27, 1977, private collection Julia Keogh.

20. *When the baby was born:* interview with Peg Dillon, MM, and Peg Healy, Ossining, NY, March 23, 2013.

21. *In June 1977*: Adam Clymer, "House Bars U.S. Aid to Seven Countries in Rebuff to Carter," *New York Times*, June 24, 1977; *Throughout the United States:* Hector Perla Jr., "Heirs of Sandino: The Nicaraguan Revolution and the U.S.-Nicaraguan Solidarity Movement," *Latin American Perspectives* 36, no. 6 (November 2009): 80–100,

22. *In San Francisco:* interview with Carlos Corea Lacayo, Managua, Nicaragua, July 2013; *A cadre:* Erick Lyle, "Back to the Streets," *San Francisco Bay Guardian* online, February 24. 2011, accessed November 26, 2014; *In 1977:* interview with Roberto Vargas, by phone June 23, 2014; *Earlier in 1977:* interview with Miguel d'Escoto, MM, Managua, Nicaragua, February 2013.

23. *In late July 1977:* notes from Nicaragua Panel by Estelle Coupe, Peg Dillon, and Tom and Chris Amato for 1978 General Assembly, Nicaragua History collection; *They would need to act:* interview with Miguel d'Escoto, MM, Managua, Nicaragua, February 2013.

24. *They agreed that Maura would go into the consulate:* Bea Zaragoza interview with Judy Noone, SFATP collection; d'Escoto's biography, friendship with teenage Maura, plan for consulate takeover: interview with Miguel d'Escoto, Managua, Nicaragua, February 2013; *The consulate staff:* letter from Jim Sinnott, MM, to Maryknoll Sisters, Central Governing Board 1986; memory of consulate takeover: Salvador Martyrs collection, MSA, Maryknoll Mission Archives, Maryknoll, NY; *Echoing her role:* interview with Roberto Vargas, by phone June 2014.

25. Lifted state of siege: LeoGrande, *In Our Own Backyard*.

26. Group of twelve, September attacks: Cardenal, *Faith and Joy*, also George Black, *Triumph of the People: The Sandinista Revolution in Nicaragua* (London: Zed Books, 1982).

27. *Throughout the fall:* Notes from Nicaragua Panel, Nicaragua History collection; *The sisters had taken to carrying baking soda:* interview with Peg Healy and Peg Dillon, MM, Ossining, NY, March 23, 2013.

28. *One soldier began hitting Roberto:* interview with Roberto Somoza and Henri Norori, Ciudad Sandino, Nicaragua, February 15, 2013; *He whacked the nuns:* Notes from Nicaragua Panel, Nicaragua History, also interview with Peg Dillon, MM, Ossining, NY, March, 23, 2013; *"God should consume us, destroy us":* Clarke, Maura (M.M.), personnel file, Retreat Diary, Retreat Notes, 1976/1977 (13/8).

29. Working at Justice and Peace Commission, difficult atmosphere in office: interview with Jim Hannon, Acton, MA, June 1, 2014, also David Hollenbach, SJ, by phone July 2014; Maura feels trapped: Clarke, Maura (M.M.) personnel file, Retreat Diary, Retreat Notes, 1976/1977 (13/8).

30. *She wondered whether she could take it,* Clarke, Maura (M.M.) personnel file, Retreat Diary, Retreat Notes, 1976/1977 (13/8) (This sentiment is so different than what she presented to even her closest friends.); *Sometimes, she even took:* Bea Zaragoza interview with Judy Noone, 1981, SFATP collection.

31. *She dreaded having to say good-bye:* Mary Manning, SSJ, letter from to Judy Noone, May 16, 1981, SFATP collection; relationships with Keogh children: interviews with Deirdre Keogh Anderson, 2012–2015, and Scott Eoghan Keogh, Old Brookville, NY, December 2014.

32. *Fear of leaving her parents:* Carolyn MacDonald, MM, letter to Judy Noone, January 13, 1982, SFATP collection; *"But Kay":* Kay Cussen letter from to Sr. Rose Marie, March 1996, Maura personal file, MSA, Maryknoll Mission Archives, Maryknoll, NY.

33. Work style, division of tasks at workshops: interview with Margarita Jamias, MM, Ossining, NY, June 2014, SFATP collection.

34. *Maura would gently ask:* interview with Elaine Hruska, by phone June 2014. *Her own ideas had shifted:* Jim Hannon letter to Judy Noone, June 7, 1981, SFATP collection: *In Siuna she served tea:* interview with Humberto Bolaños and Walter López Jirón, July 2013, and with Henri Norori and Roberto Somoza, February 2013, all in Ciudad Sandino, Nicaragua. Whether she knew they were avowed members of the FSLN is uncertain. They were young men she'd known for years.

35. Group game with sticks of gum: interviews with Jean Fallon, MM, Ossining, NY, July 2, 2014, also Sr. Margarita Jamias, Ossining, NY, June, 2013.

36. *Maura and Sr. Margarita were in accord:* interview with Margarita Jamias, MM, Ossining, NY, June 2014 and April 2016; *Educating these middle-class Catholics:* interview with Jim Hannon, Boston area, June 1, 2014; preparation for talks, trusting God: Clarke, Maura (M.M.) personnel file, Retreat Diary, Retreat Notes, 1976/1977 (13/8).

37. Friendship with Mary Heidkamp and Jim Lund, insisting they read *Gospel of Solentiname*: interview with Mary Heidkamp, by phone, June 2014; joke about Irish grandmother: interview with Margarita Jamias, MM, Ossining, NY, April 2016.

38. Maura's attitudes to armed conflict: interviews with Margarita Jamias, MM, Ossining, NY, June 2014, and April 2016; also Fr. Charles McCarthy, June 2014; Jim Hannon, June 2014; Jean Burke interview with Judy Noone, SFATP collection; Maura quoted in *Sign* magazine 60, no. 5 (February 1981), also interview between Jean Burke and Ann Narcisso, April 1981, SFATP collection.

39. *Julio's picture*: private collection Julia Keogh; *"It reminded Maura":* Maura letter to Julio, 1977, private collection Peg Dillon.

40. Edgar Taleno's participation in National Palace takeover: described in poem by Mercedes Taleno in Maura's Bible, private collection Julia Keogh; Edgar Taleno as Lesbia's brother: interview with Humberto Bolaños, Ciudad Sandino, Nicaragua, July 2013; also in comprehensive history of Ciudad Sandino at http://www.manfut.org/managua/sandino.html; National Palace takeover: Black, *Triumph of the People*, 125.

41. *Like Jesus' dying:* Maura letter to sisters in Nicaragua, September 25, 1978, private collection Peg Dillon.

42. *Throughout 1978:* Sherri Lipsky, "The Legitimacy of Economic Coercion: The Carter Foreign Aid Policy and Nicaragua," *Loyola of Los Angeles International and Comparative Law Review*, January 1982; preparations for rally: Maura letter to sisters in Nicaragua, September 25, 1978, private collection Peg Dillon.

43. Studying up on International Monetary Fund loans, notes on seminars about economic imperialism: Clarke, Maura (M.M.) personnel file, Retreat Diary 1977 (13/8); rally, crowd, Maura's emotional command of listeners: Jim

Hannon letter to Judy Noone, June 1981, SFATP collection, also interview with Margarita Jamias, MM, Ossining, NY, June 2014.

44. *"We may not see the liberation of Nicaragua:"* interview with Margarita Jamias, MM, Ossining, NY, June 2014; Estelle Coupe, MM, "How does a revolution develop?" Nicaragua History collection.

45. Fast at Riverside Church: interview with Margarita Jamias, MM, Ossining, NY, April 2016; also Dan Driscoll, MM, letter to Maryknoll, MSA, Maryknoll Mission Archives, Maryknoll, NY.

46. Worries about relating, after the war: Maura letter to Maryknoll sisters in Nicaragua, never sent, August 1979, SFATP collection.

CHAPTER 9: INTO THE DARKNESS

1. *As 1980 began:* William LeoGrande, *In Our Own Backyard: The United States in Central America* (Chapel Hill, NC: University of North Carolina Press, 2000); *To Jimmy Carter:* interview with John Spain, MM, San Salvador, February 2013; *And he asked:* interview with Mgr. Urioste, San Salvador, February 2013.

2. Salvadoran economy, militarization: Robert Armstrong and Janet Schenk, *El Salvador: The Face of Revolution* (Boston: South End Press, 1982); *Most peasants lived: José García:* Testimony of Dr. Terry Karl in in *Ford v. Garcia,* 289 F.3d 1283 (11th Cir. 2002).

3. *Archbishop Romero admired:* interview with Mgr. Ricardo Urioste, San Salvador, El Salvador, February 2013.

4. Óscar Romero, letter to President Jimmy Carter, February 1977, quoted in *Voice of the Voiceless: The Four Pastoral Letters and Other Statements,* trans. Michael Walsh (Maryknoll, NY: Orbis, 1985); US aid to El Salvador in late 1970s, Armstrong and Shenk, *El Salvador;* LeoGrande, *In Our Own Backyard;* Armstrong and Shenk, *El Salvador,* app. 3. Interview with Cynthia Aronson, July 2016.

5. *The Democratic president:* Directive 30, February 28, 1978, Jimmy Carter Library, www.jimmycarterlibrary.gov/documents/pddirectives/pd30.pdf, accessed April 23, 2016; *That same policy:* LeoGrande, *In Our Own Backyard;* military aid to El Salvador, 1979–1980, Armstrong and Shenk, *El Salvador,* app. 3; empowering of hardliners: Brian Bosch, *The Salvadoran Officer Corps and the Final Offensive of 1981* (Jefferson, NC: McFarland & Co., 1999); resignation of most civilian members: James Dunkerley, *The Long War: Dictatorship and Revolution in El Salvador* (New York: Verso Books, 1982).

6. Development of political left, popular organizations, armed groups: Dunkerley, *The Long War; One could be a member:* interview with Óscar Chacón, by phone November 2015; *Hanging over:* Thomas Anderson, *Matanza: El Salvador's Communist Revolt of 1932* (Lincoln: University of Nebraska Press, 1971).

7. *White believed keeping El Salvador:* State Department telegram, Robert White, "RESUPPLY OF SALVADORAN ARMED FORCES," January 16, 1981, SAN SA 56388; Avoiding revolution, establishing relationship with Archbishop Romero: Robert White, *Commonweal* magazine, March 22, 2010, also Margaret O'Brien Steinfels, *Commonweal,* October 26, 2001.

8. *She had visited the country:* interview with Carmen García, San Pablo Apóstol, Managua, Nicaragua, February 2013.

9. *El Salvador was breathtakingly poor:* María López Vigil, *Don Lito of El Salvador* (Maryknoll, NY: Orbis Books, 1990); Don Lito, lecture to class at University of Central America, San Salvador, February 2013.

10. *She wrote to Maryknoll sisters:* Maura letter to Nicaragua and El Salvador sisters, Same Fate as the Poor (SFATP collection), Maryknoll Sisters Archive (MSA), Maryknoll Mission Archives, Maryknoll, NY; Two sisters from Chile: Maryknoll sisters in El Salvador letter to Maura, March 20, 1980, SFATP collection.

11. Archbishop's friendship with Fr. Grande, events surrounding death, Clarke, *Oscar Romero; When Grande was killed:* interview with Roberto (Beto) Cuéllar, San Salvador, El Salvador, July 2013.

12. Cases brought to Socorro Jurídico: interview with Beto Cuéllar, San Salvador, El Salvador, July 2013.

13. *In the market:* Robert White, *Commonweal* magazine, March 22, 2010.

14. Archbishop's appeal to soldiers' conscience: quoted in Clarke, *Oscar Romero*.

15. *Nuns who served at the hospital:* interview with Eva Menjívar, San Salvador, El Salvador, February 2013; assassination of archbishop: Carlos Dada, "The Beatification of Óscar Romero," *New Yorker* magazine, May 19, 2015.

16. Archbishop's funeral: interview with Christopher Dickey, who covered the funeral for the *Washington Post*, by phone January 2015, also Christopher Dickey, "40 Killed in San Salvador," Washington Post Foreign Service, March 31, 1980.

17. *Maryknoll cloister:* Claudette LaVerdiere, *On the Threshold of the Future: The Life and Spirituality of Mother Mary Joseph Rogers, Founder of the Maryknoll Sisters* (Maryknoll, NY: Orbis Books, 2011); Peg Healy's suggestion: Bea Zaragoza, interviewed for Judy Noone, SFATP collection.

18. Unless otherwise noted, observations of Maura's thoughts, attitudes, fears, desires for the remainder of the chapter come from interview with Grace Myerjack, MM, Ossining, NY, May 2014.

19. Tutoring in the Catskills: interview with Michael Clarke, New York, September 2013.

20. *Her parents tried to be subtle:* interview with Julia Keogh, Old Brookville, NY, April 2014; confrontation between James Clarke and Maura: interview with Michael Clarke, New York, September 2013.

21. *"If we abandon the people":* interview with Rose Gorman, Ossining, NY, June 2014; see also Rose Gorman, "Speaking Credibly About Resurrection: A Praxis of Nonviolence," paper presented at Catholic Theological Society of America Conference, 2001.

22. *She wrote to her parents:* Maura letter to parents, July 16, 1980, SFATP collection; *But even in grief:* Maura letter to family and friends, July 28, 1980, SFATP collection, MSA, Maryknoll Mission Archives.

23. Anniversary festivities: Maura letter to parents, July 21, 1980, SFATP collection.

24. Poem by Mercedes Taleno Sandoval, remembering her son, found in Maura's Bible, private collection Julia Keogh; *Belief in something new being born*, Maura letter to family and friends, July 28, 1980, SFATP collection: "In the middle of this mystery of pain there is at the same time such a belief in Resurrection, in something new being born."

25. *Sr. Luz Beatriz Arellano had to flee:* Margaret Randall, *Christians in the Nicaraguan Revolution* (Vancouver, BC: New Star Books, 1983); urging Maura to stay in Nicaragua: interview with Luz Beatriz Arellano, Managua, Nicaragua, July 2013.

26. *The people were free:* Maura letter to parents, July 28, 1980, SFATP collection; *"We've won here":* interview with Luz Beatriz, Managua, Nicaragua, July 2013.

27. Interview with Leila Rodríguez, Managua, Nicaragua, February 2013.

CHAPTER 10: IN THE VALLEY OF DEATH

1. Sr. Maddie's use of railroad steel: interview with Maddie Dorsey, MM, Ossining, NY, February 2013; *In OPEN 3:* interview with Walter López Jirón, Ciudad Sandino, Nicaragua, July 2013; targets of death squad: interview with Guadalupe Calderón, San Salvador, El Salvador, February 2013.

2. Banning of public assemblies, fear of attending funeral, Lamatepec, of being seen or overheard, Guadalupe's joint role: interview with Guadalupe Calderón, San Salvador, El Salvador, February 2013.

3. *The Salvadoran elites:* Robert Armstrong and Janet Schenk, *El Salvador: The Face of Revolution* (Boston: South End Press, 1982), 111; Maryknoll sisters in La Libertad: Terry Alexander, MM, SFATP collection.

4. *The next day:* interview with June Erlick, by phone December 2014; interview with John McAward, by phone February 2015.

5. Parish food program: interview with Fr. Paul Schindler, La Libertad, El Salvador, February 2013; Jean Donovan description: Ana Carrigan, *Salvador Witness: The Life and Calling of Jean Donovan* (New York: Simon and Schuster, 1984) and from interview with Peg Healy, March 23, 2013; *The two had traveled:* interview with Tom Cornell, Marlboro, NY, April 2014.

6. *Working under the direction of Fr. Amaya:* interview with Alfredo Rivera Rivera, Nueva Concepción, El Salvador, July 2013; characterization of Chalatenango as most volatile part of country: interview with Beto Cuéllar, San Salvador, El Salvador, July 2013; level of organization in Chalatenango: interview with Juan Bosco Palacios, Santa Tecla, El Salvador, February 2013; *Guerrillas of the Popular Liberation Front:* interview with Eldon Cummings, by phone June 2015; Ita and Carla ferrying people: interview with Maddie Dorsey, MM, Ossining, NY, February 2013, also Judy Noone, *The Same Fate as the Poor* (Maryknoll, NY: Orbis, 1996).

7. *Maura had only just arrived . . . After a few days:* Maura letter to Mary Manning, August 1980, SFATP collection; *She'd stay a few weeks:* Maura letter to Kay Kelly, August 14, 1980, SFATP collection.

8. *It was a way of demonstrating:* Dunkerley, *The Long War*; *Because of the strike:* interview with Guadalupe Calderón, San Salvador, El Salvador, February 2013.

9. Maura's parish work, her protecting the Bibles: interview Maddie Dorsey, MM, Ossining, NY, March 2013; *To Maura it brought back:* Maura letter to Mary McMullan, August 15, 1980, private collection Mary McMullan.

10. United States Bureau of Citizenship and Immigration Services, *El Salvador: The Role of ORDEN in the El Salvadoran Civil War,* October 16, 2000, SLV01001. ZAR, available at: http://www.refworld.org/docid/3dee04524.html [accessed 12 May 2016]; Armstrong and Shenk, *El Salvador,* 77.

11. *At night she sat in the chapel:* Maura letter to Mary Manning, August 11, 1980, SFATP collection; *Colonel Ricardo Peña Arbaiza:* David Helvarg, Pacifica News Service interview with Ita Ford, October, 1980, also interview with David Helvarg, by phone March, 2015.

12. *They might have brought him back:* account of flood: interview with Alfredo Rivera Rivera, Nueva Concepción, El Salvador, July 2013, see also statement of Alfredo Rivera Rivera to Maryknoll sisters in 2000, El Salvador Martyrs collection, MSA, Maryknoll Mission Archives; also account of drowning in Maura letter to parents, September 1980, SFATP collection.

13. María Guadalupe Menjívar's story: interview with María Guadalupe Menjívar, Santa María de Esperanza, El Salvador, February 2013; National Guard and other surveillance of Chalatenango parish: interview with Alfredo Rivera Rivera, Nueva Concepción, El Salvador, July 2013; funeral and burial: interview with Peter Hinde, by phone January 2013.

14. *Carla would be buried:* Maura letter to parents, September 1980, expressing her pride to see Carla buried beside the people she loved.

15. *After the funeral:* interview with Maddie Dorsey, MM, Ossining, NY, March 2013; gathering of Maryknoll sisters at shore and Maura's private thoughts: Maura letter to parents, August 31, 1980, SFATP collection.

16. *Death was everywhere:* Americas Watch, *Report on Human Rights in El Salvador* (New York: Knopf Publishing Group, 1982), 72; see Terry Karl testimony, http://cja.org/downloads/Terry%20Karl.pdf; *Maura was horrified:* Maura letter to Peg Dillon, November 22, 1980, SFATP collection.

17. *In July she had mailed:* "Departure of Srs Maura Clarke and Ita Ford from Managua to San Salvador on Copa Airlines on Dec. 2, 1980," memo from Maryknoll sisters to US Department of State, February 19, 1982, accessed from State Department online reading room, April 22, 2016.

18. Irish souvenir in Maura's room: interview with Julia Keogh, Old Brookville, NY, February 2016; Maura's reflections in Sligo: Maura diary kept in August 1979, private collection Julia Keogh; local beliefs about St. Patrick's Well: interview with Mary McCarthy, Dromard, County Sligo, November 2014.

19. Condition, contents of Maura's Bible: Maura's Bible, private collection Julia Keogh; *Here in El Salvador:* Maura letter to Kay Kelly, October 21, 1980, private collection Kay Kelly, shared with Deirdre Keogh Anderson.

20. All details of Norella's story from interview with Aida Mejosa Menjívar, Mariona, El Salvador, February 2013; *More than six thousand:* interview with Eva Menjívar, San Salvador, February 2013.

21. *The security forces sometimes raided:* "Chronology of Persecution Against the Church," Appendix #2, Statement from the Bishop, Apostolic Administrator, Priests and Women Religious of the Archdiocese of El Salvador, December 5, 1980, accessed from US Department of State public reading room, May 10, 2016; *Maura named the girl "Aida" and her mother "Rosalina":* interview with Aida Mejosa Menjívar, Mariona, El Salvador, February 2013.

22. *Bringing refugees out of the conflict zone:* Carrigan, *Salvador Witness*; *Fr. Sigfredo Salazar had been assigned:* interview with Fr. Sigfredo Salazar, San Sebastian, El Salvador, July 2013; *In July, the security forces:* "Chronology of Death Threats and the Conflict between the Army (under Col. Peña Arbaiza) and the Church in Chalatenango," Lawyers Committee for Human Rights, February 1, 1983, accessed from US Department of State public reading room, May 10, 2016; *In his place:* interview with Esperanza Tobar, Santa María de Esperanza, El Salvador, July 2013.

23. Maura and Ita's work in San Antonio Los Ranchos, communication: interview with Esperanza Tobar and Tobías Menjívar, Santa María de Esperanza, El Salvador, July 2013.

24. Everyone a personal moral calculation: interview with Víctor Manuel Méndez, Santa María de Esperanza, El Salvador, July 2013; *Everyone in Chalatenango was suspect already:* Esperanza's relationship with Maura: interview with Esperanza Tobar and Tobías Menjívar, Santa María de Esperanza, El Salvador, July 2013.

25. *The various guerrilla groups:* Dunkerley, *The Long War*; The Popular Front for Liberation (FPL), Armed Forces of Resistance (FAR), and Peoples' Revolutionary Army (ERP) announced their merger in May 1980 under the umbrella of the Farabundo Martí National Liberation Front (FMLN) named for the leader of the 1932 uprising. However, people continued to refer to the constituent parts of the FMLN by their old names and many still do. *Everyone knew:* interview with Beto Cuéllar, San Salvador, El Salvador, July 2013.

26. *Maura was part of a series:* interview with Víctor Manuel Méndez, Santa María de Esperanza, El Salvador, July 2013.

27. *There were other:* interview with Betty Campbell, by phone January 2013.

28. *Had someone poured:* interview with Peg Healy, Ossining, NY, March 23, 2013; *He'd been shot:* Americas Watch report, "A Year of Reckoning: El Salvador a Decade After the Assassination of Archbishop Romero," 1990, 249; *But with old friends:* interview with Peter Hinde, by phone January 2013.

29. Maura and Ita's work for Socorro Jurídico: interview with Beto Cuéllar, San Salvador, El Salvador, July 2013; *But there was far:* "From Madness to Hope: The 12-Year War in El Salvador, Report on the Commission of Truth for El Salvador," 1993, http://www.derechos.org/nizkor/salvador/informes/truth.html, accessed June 20, 2016.

30. Threats against Socorro Jurídico: interview with Beto Cuéllar, San Salvador, El Salvador, July 2013; threat to Cuéllar's wife and children, Americas Watch, *Human Rights in El Salvador* (New York: Knopf Publishing Group, 1982).

31. *Cuéllar found it necessary,* Maura and Ita political orientation: interview with Beto Cuéllar, San Salvador, El Salvador, July 2013; Maura's feelings about

Nicaragua popular struggle, people: interview with Miguel Vásquez, SJ, San Salvador, El Salvador, July 2013.

32. *But all this work:* interview with Peter Hinde, by phone January 2013; *Maura walking by herself:* interview with Alfredo Rivera Rivera, Nueva Concepción, July 2013; *She hoped all these people:* Maura letter to Kay Kelly, MM, October 1980, SFATP collection.

33. *But many students:* Americas Watch, *Human Rights in El Salvador;* entire story of Maura and Ita's providing medical supplies to Dr. Romagoza, interview with Dr. Juan Romagoza Arce, by Skype June 2015; targeting of medical professionals: testimony of Terry Karl, http://cja.org/downloads/Terry%20Karl.pdf.

34. Maura as a member of CONFRES (Confederation de los Religiosos de El Salvador), shared trust among members: interview with Eva Menjívar, San Salvador, El Salvador, February 2013.

35. Fr. Rodríguez's workshops, conversations with Maura and Ita: interview with David Rodríguez, San Salvador, El Salvador, February 2013.

36. *After the defiling of the church:* Lawyers Committee for Human Rights report, "Chronology of Death Threats and the Conflict between the Army (under Col. Peña Arbaiza and the Church in Chalatenango," February 1, 1983, accessed from US Department of State public reading room, May 10, 2016.

37. *First, there was a rumor:* interview with Alfredo Rivera Rivera, Nueva Concepción, El Salvador, July 2013.

38. *Then in November, an actual threat:* Department of State telegram, "THREATS AGAINST US CITIZEN NUNS WORKING IN CHALATENANGO," December 11, 1980, SAN SA 8676; *To be called a communist:* interview with Fr. Rivera López, Nueva Concepción, El Salvador, July 2013.

39. *Fr. Ephraím López:* interview with Alfredo Rivera Rivera; also Lawyers Committee for Human Rights report, "Chronology of Death Threats."

40. *The stories Maura heard:* Maura letter to parents, November 3, 1980, SFATP collection, *Ita feared famine:* David Helvarg, Pacifica News Service interview with Ita Ford, October 1980.

41. *Maura hoped Jimmy Carter:* Maura letter to parents, November 1980, SFATP collection; election night party: interview with Carl Gettinger, Chevy Chase, MD, January 2015; Cummings's attitude toward White, Cummings career, composition of military advisers: interview with Eldon Cummings, by phone, June 2015.

42. *Death is a constant companion:* Maura letter to Mary Manning, November 1980, SFATP collection.

43. Maura, Ita, Dorothy, and Jean's cooperation with Juan Bosco Palacios: interviews with Juan Bosco Palacios, Santa Tecla, El Salvador, February 2013, July 2013, also by Skype October 2015.

44. *While Maura and Ita:* Lawyers Committee for International Human Rights, "Justice in El Salvador: A Case Study Update," February 1983; John Dinges and Pacifica News Service, "New Account Suggests Killings Were Ordered at Top," *Washington Post,* July 16, 1981; interview with Carlos Federico Paredes, San Salvador, El Salvador, December 2015; *In the deeply hierarchical:*

José Guillermo García-Merino, IJ Removal Proceedings (Feb. 26, 2014), Exh. 11, testimony of Terry Karl.

45. *"But I know, at least I think":* Maura letter to Loran Miller, OFM, November 1980, SFATP collection.

46. Maura in Ciudad Sandino in November 1980, interview with María Luisa Urbina, Ciudad Sandino, Nicaragua, July 2013; visit to Santo Domingo area in November 1980: interview with Angelique Rodríguez Alemán, Managua, Nicaragua, February 2013.

47. Abduction and murder of FDR leaders: LeoGrande, *In Our Own Backyard*, 59; *"Who am I supposed to negotiate with now?":* John Lamperti, *Enrique Álvarez Córdova: Life of a Salvadoran Revolutionary and Gentleman* (Jefferson, NC: McFarland & Company, 2006).

48. Maura's attitudes at November meeting, need for more sisters in El Salvador: Gerri Brake, Ossining, NY, January 2013, SFATP collection.

49. Maura letter to Mary Manning, November 27, 1980, SFATP collection.

50. *One night they danced:* interview with Gerri Brake, Ossining, NY, January 2013; Program for prayer service: December 1, 1980, private collection Peg Healy.

51. Gospel of John 10:12 (New International Version).

52. Gospel of John 21:18–19 (New International Version).

53. Ezekiel 34:16 (New International Version).

54. *"The six members of the Frente":* Maura letter to Patricia Haggerty, December 1, 1980, SFATP collection.

55. *"We are fine":* Maura letter to parents, December 1, 1980, SFATP collection.

56. Tickets and departure: "Departure of Srs. Maura Clarke and Ita Ford from Managua to San Salvador on Copa Airlines on Dec. 2, 1980," memo from Maryknoll sisters to US Department of State, February 19, 1982, accessed from State Department online reading room, April 22, 2016.

57. *In Chalatenango someone:* John Dinges, "El Salvador: Were Murders Planned?" *Los Angeles Times*, July 8, 1981; also interview with Alfredo Rivera Rivera, Nueva Concepción, El Salvador, July 2013; interview with Ephraím López, San Juan Opico, El Salvador, July 2013.

58. Soldiers' boarding Maria Rieckelman's flight in San Salvador: interview with Maria Rieckelman, MM, Ossining, NY, December 2012.

59. *The customs police:* interview with Fr. Greg Chisholm, by phone August 2013; *National Guard sergeant Luis Colindres Alemán:* School of the Americas Watch database of graduates; *In the early evening:* Harold A. Tyler, "The Churchwomen Murders, A Report to the Secretary of State," December 2, 1983, private collection, Julia Keogh; *He wanted to warn the commander:* Commission on the Truth for El Salvador report: "From Madness to Hope."

EPILOGUE: A TERRIBLE BEAUTY

1. News reports; *One of President Carter's final acts:* various news reports.

2. *Maura's brother and sister:* interview with Julia Keogh, Rockaway, NY, July 2012.

3. *The bodies of the four women:* various news reports; attendance by Fr. Rodríguez: interview with David Rodríguez, San Salvador, El Salvador, February 2013; *Following Maryknoll custom:* various news reports.

4. *Saying he would not be party:* Robert White, "Bad Neighbor, The Failure of US Policy in Latin America,," *Commonweal Magazine*, November 14, 2005; also Department of State telegram, Robert White, "INVESTIGATION OF US CHURCHWOMEN," January 20, 1980, SAN SA 00534; Juan de Oris, "Envoy Disputes US on El Salvador Deaths," *New York Times,* January 22, 1981. *He worked until his death:* Margaret O'Brien Steinfels, "Robert E. White 1926–2015 Ambassador to El Salvador, Advocate for Human Rights," *Commonweal*, January 19, 2015.

5. *In 1993, a United Nations–sponsored:* "From Madness to Hope: The 12-Year War in El Salvador, Report on the Commission of Truth for El Salvador," 1993, http://www.derechos.org/nizkor/salvador/informes/truth.html, accessed June 20, 2016; *Julia Keogh and Bill Ford:* interview with Julia Keogh, Old Brookville, NY, August 2012.

6. *Also in 1998:* Larry Rohte, "4 Salvadorans Say They Killed U.S. Nuns on Orders of Military," *New York Times*, April 3, 1998.

7. *In 1999, Maura's and Ita's families:* Center for Justice and Accountability, http://cja.org/what-we-do/litigation/romagoza-arce-v-garcia-and-vides-casanova, also http://cja.org/what-we-do/litigation/romagoza-arce-v-garcia-and-vides-casanova/clients, accessed June 22, 2016; *At the airport in El Salvador:* Linda Cooper and James Hodge, "Former Salvadoran Defense Minister, Tied to Killings of Óscar Romero and Churchwomen, Deported Back to El Salvador," *National Catholic Reporter*, January 13, 2016, http://ncronline.org/news/peace-justice/former-salvadoran-defense-minister-tied-killings-oscar-romero-and-churchwomen, accessed June 22, 2016.

8. *There are places:* Secretary of Culture, Office of Presidency of El Salvador, Internal Resolution No. 008/2015, November 6, 2015.

9. *In Ciudad Sandino:* interview with Roberto Somoza and Rosa Blandón, Ciudad Sandino, Nicaragua, February 2013; *Maura's spirit is alive:* interview with CECIM staff, Ciudad Sandino, Nicaragua, February 2013; *Ciudad Sandino and Managua:* multiple interviews, Managua and Ciudad Sandino, Nicaragua, February and July 2013.

10. *In Siuna:* visit to Siuna, February 2013, interview with alumnae of Colegio Maryknoll, Siuna, Nicaragua, February 2013.

11. *In New York City:* visits to Cristo Rey New York High School, September 2013–2015; *Maryknoll sisters continue:* https://maryknollsisters.org/about-us/our-work/, accessed June 24, 2016.

12. *In County Sligo:* visit to Dromard, County Sligo, Ireland, November 2014.

13. *Guadalupe Calderón:* interview with Guadalupe Calderón, San Salvador, El Salvador, February 2013.

14. Each November: School of the Americas, www.SOAW.org, accessed June 24, 2016; also SOA/WHINSEC; Graduates Database, maintained by School of the Americas Watch; *It is a litany:*, visit to SOA/WHINSEC annual protest, November 2012; *The assembled crowd:* visit to SOA/WHINSEC annual protest, November 2012, also interview with Roy Bourgeois, by phone, May 2016.

15. SHARE-El Salvador, http://www.share-elsalvador.org/about, accessed June 24, 2016; also author trip to El Salvador November 2015, visits to SHARE-sponsored projects.

Index

NATION
BOOKS

The Nation Institute

Founded in 2000, **Nation Books** has become a leading voice in American independent publishing. The imprint's mission is to tell stories that inform and empower just as they inspire or entertain readers. We publish award-winning and bestselling journalists, thought leaders, whistleblowers, and truthtellers, and we are also committed to seeking out a new generation of emerging writers, particularly voices from underrepresented communities and writers from diverse backgrounds. As a publisher with a focused list, we work closely with all our authors to ensure that their books have broad and lasting impact. With each of our books we aim to constructively affect and amplify cultural and political discourse and to engender positive social change.

Nation Books is a project of The Nation Institute, a nonprofit media center established to extend the reach of democratic ideals and strengthen the independent press. The Nation Institute is home to a dynamic range of programs: the award-winning Investigative Fund, which supports groundbreaking investigative journalism; the widely read and syndicated website TomDispatch; journalism fellowships that support and cultivate over twenty-five emerging and high-profile reporters each year; and the Victor S. Navasky Internship Program.

For more information on Nation Books and The Nation Institute, please visit:

www.nationbooks.org
www.nationinstitute.org
www.facebook.com/nationbooks.ny
Twitter: @nationbooks

Photo by Adi Talwar

Eileen Markey is an investigative journalist whose work has appeared in the *New York Times*, *New York Magazine*, *Wall Street Journal*, *Village Voice*, *National Catholic Reporter*, and *America Magazine*. She has worked as a producer for WNYC New York Public Radio and was a contributing editor at City Limits. She has reported from Cambodia, Haiti, and London, and cut her teeth covering crime and corruption in Paterson, New Jersey. A graduate of Fordham University and Columbia University Graduate School of Journalism, she lives in the Bronx with her husband and two sons.